International Techni... [barcode label: MW01679553]

Problem Solving and Troubleshooting in AIX 5L

January 2002

SG24-5496-01

Take Note! Before using this information and the product it supports, be sure to read the general information in "Special notices" on page 439.

Second Edition (January 2002)

This edition applies to IBM @server pSeries and RS/6000 Systems for use with the AIX 5L Operating System Version 5.1 and is based on information available in August, 2001.

Comments may be addressed to:
IBM Corporation, International Technical Support Organization
Dept. JN9B Building 003 Internal Zip 2834
11400 Burnet Road
Austin, Texas 78758-3493

Contents

Figures

Tables

Preface

This redbook covers problem determination and troubleshooting on the IBM @server pSeries and RS/6000 platform. It is intended as a guide to the approach that should be adopted when attempting to resolve a problem on an IBM @server pSeries and RS/6000 system running AIX 5L Version 5.1. It is not intended to replace the comprehensive documentation available for the AIX operating system or the System Installation and Service Guides available for IBM @server pSeries and RS/6000 system hardware. Instead, it should be considered as a useful supplement to guide you through the problem determination process.

A problem can manifest itself in many ways, and very often the root cause of the problem is not obvious. This redbook describes an approach to problem determination that will guide you through the initial steps in problem diagnosis and to narrow down and identify the component or subsystem that is experiencing a problem.

In addition to helping you determine the likely cause of your problem, this redbook describes some of the most common problems that can occur with AIX systems and, where possible, describes the actions you can take to resolve them.

This redbook is a valuable tool for system administrators and other technical support personnel who deal with RS/6000 and AIX problems.

The information in this redbook is not intended to completely cover problem determination on SP systems or systems configured as nodes in an HACMP cluster. This redbook does not cover Itanium™-based systems (IA-64), although many items will be true for both POWER and Itanium-based systems.

The team that wrote this redbook

This redbook was produced by a team of specialists from around the world working at the International Technical Support Organization, Austin Center.

KyeongWon Jeong is a Consulting IT Specialist at the International Technical Support Organization, Austin Center. He writes extensively on AIX and education materials and teaches IBM classes worldwide on all areas of AIX. Before joining the ITSO three years ago, he worked in IBM Global Learning Services in Korea as a Senior Education Specialist and was a class manager of all AIX classes for customers and interns. He has many years of teaching and development experience.

HyunGoo Kim is an Advisory Education Specialist at Global Learning Services in IBM Korea. He has five years of experience of teaching AIX, HACMP, and SP classes to customers and business partners. His area of expertise includes Linux. He has an interest in Clustering Technology.

JaeYong An is an Advisory System Service Representative in IBM Korea ITS Technical Operations. He has six years of experience working on IBM @server pSeries, RS/6000, and AIX. He currently works on AIX-related problem solving for customers, business partners, and IBM internal support. His areas of expertise include IBM @server pSeries, RS/6000, SP systems, AIX dump analysis, and performance problem solving.

John Harrison is an Advisory System Service Representative in IBM United Kingdom. He has worked for IBM for 24 years, for the past ten years as a Field Hardware Specialist on IBM @server pSeries, RS/6000 products, and AIX. He has extensive hardware knowledge on other IBM systems and provides Field Support in the north London area. He is also an instructor for UK IBM @server pSeries and RS/6000 hardware courses and a member of the UK ITS Technical Council.

Tony Abruzzess is an Advisory IT Specialist at the IBM Support Center in Sydney, Australia. He has been serving the IBM AIX customer community in the technical support area for over a decade. He holds a Bachelor of Mathematics from the University of Wollongong and a Graduate Diploma of Finance and Investment from the Securities Institute of Australia. His areas of expertise include SP, AIX, and base related products.

Thanks to the following people for their contributions to this project:

International Technical Support Organization, Austin Center
Wade Wallace

IBM Austin
Jim Shaffer, Anil K, Stephen Haley, Liang (Alan) Jiang, Robert Manning, Darshan Patel, M.G. Akmal, Janis Harris, Roger Bulhof, Andreas Hoetzel, Richard Cutler, Doug Benignus, Beth Morton, Dave Willoughby, Emilia Hezari, Frank Petsche, Grover Davidson

IBM Dallas
John Tesch and Rashid Rahim

IBM UK
Derrick Daines and Michael Pearson

Special notice

This publication is intended to help system administrators and IBM service personnel perform basic problem determination on IBM @server pSeries and RS/6000 systems running AIX 5L Version 5.1. The information in this publication is not intended as the specification of any programming interfaces that are provided by AIX 5L Version 5.1. See the PUBLICATIONS section of the IBM Programming Announcement for AIX 5L Version 5.1, Program Number 5765-C34 for more information about what publications are considered to be product documentation.

IBM trademarks

Comments welcome

Your comments are important to us!

We want our IBM Redbooks to be as helpful as possible. Send us your comments about this or other Redbooks in one of the following ways:

- Use the online **Contact us** review redbook form found at:

  ibm.com/redbooks

- Send your comments in an Internet note to:

  redbook@us.ibm.com

- Mail your comments to the address on page ii.

1

Problem determination introduction

This redbook is intended to help system administrators and other support personnel have a better understanding of problem solving on IBM @server pSeries and RS/6000 systems using AIX 5L Version 5.1. It is not the intention of this book to provide an exhaustive list of all the solutions to all of the possible problems that can be encountered on IBM @server pSeries and RS/6000 systems running AIX. Instead, the book is intended to guide you through the problem determination process and to narrow down and identify the component or subsystem that is experiencing a problem.

This redbook does *not* cover the Itanium™-based systems (IA-64), although many items will be true for both POWER and Itanium-based systems.

The approach detailed in this book will help you to determine the cause of a problem in a component or subsystem that was previously functioning correctly. It is not intended to help you diagnose problems when you are installing and configuring new hardware or software. You should refer to the appropriate documentation supplied with the new component for installation and configuration information.

Note that some of the Web addresses referenced in this redbook are IBM intranet addresses, and are, therefore, not available for general public access. Where possible, Internet sites offering similar information are referenced.

Although the title of this redbook refers specifically to AIX 5L Version 5.1, much of the information supplied applies to other releases of AIX, including Release 4. You may find that some of the commands mentioned may not be present on your system, or may not support the exact syntax given. In this case, refer to the specific documentation supplied with the AIX level you have on the machine in question.

1.1 Problem determination process

For the purposes of this redbook, a problem can be considered as any situation where something that was previously working correctly is now not working as expected.

1.1.1 Defining the problem

The first step in problem resolution is to define the problem. It is important that the person trying to solve the problem understands exactly what the users of the system perceive the problem to be. A clear definition of the problem is useful in two ways. First of all, it can give you a hint as to the cause of the problem. Secondly, it is much easier to demonstrate to the users that the problem has been solved if you know how the problem is seen from their point of view.

Take, for example, the situation where a user is unable to print a document. The problem may be due to the /var file system running out of space. The person solving the problem may fix this and demonstrate that the problem has been fixed by using the **df** command to show that the /var file system is no longer full.

This example can also be used to illustrate another difficulty with problem determination. Problems can be hidden by other problems. When you fix the most visible problem, another one may come to light. The problems that are unearthed during the problem determination process may be related to the one that was initially reported, in other words, multiple problems with the same symptoms. In some cases, you may discover problems that are completely unrelated to the one that was initially reported.

In the example described above, simply increasing the amount of free space in the /var file system may not solve the problem being experienced by the user. The printing problem may turn out to be a cable problem, a problem with the printer, or perhaps a failure of the lpd daemon. This is why understanding the problem from the users perspective is so important. In this example, a better way of proving that the problem has been resolved is to get the user to print their document.

1.1.2 Gathering information from the user

The best way of understanding the problem from the users' perspective is to ask them questions. From their perception of the situation, you can deduce if in fact they have a problem, and the time scale in which they expect it to be resolved. Their expectations may be beyond the scope of the machine or the application it is running.

The following questions should be asked when gathering information from the user during problem determination:

- What is the problem?

  Try to get the user to explain what the problem is and how it affects them. Depending on the situation and the nature of the problem, this question can be supplemented by either of the following two questions:

  - What is the system doing?
  - What is the system *not* doing?

  Once you have determined what the symptoms of the problem are, you should try to establish the history of the problem.

- How did you first notice the problem? Did you do anything different that made you notice the problem?
- When did it happen? Does it always happen at the same time, for example, when the same job or application is run?
- Does the same problem occur elsewhere? Is only one machine experiencing the problem or are multiple machines experiencing the same problem?
- Have any changes been made recently?

  This refers to any type of change made to the system, ranging from adding new hardware or software, to configuration changes to existing software.

- If a change has been made recently, were all of the prerequisites met before the change was made?

Software problems most often occur when changes have been made to the system, and either the prerequisites have not been met, for example, system firmware not at the minimum required level, or instructions have not been followed exactly in order, for example, the person following the instructions second guesses what the instructions are attempting to do and decides they know a quicker route. The second guess then means that, because the person has taken a perceived better route, prerequisites for subsequent steps may not have been met, so the problem develops into the situation you are confronted with.

Other changes, such as the addition of hardware, bring their own problems, such as cables incorrectly assembled, contacts bent, or addressing misconfigured.

The "How did you first notice the problem?" question may not help you directly, but it is very useful in getting the person to talk about the problem. Once they start talking, they invariably tell you things that will enable you to build a picture to help you to decide the starting point for problem resolution.

If the problem occurs on more than one machine, look for similarities and differences between the situations.

1.1.3 Gathering information from the system

The second step in problem determination is gathering information from the system. Some information will already have been obtained from the user during the process of defining the problem.

It is not only the user of the machine that can provide information on a problem. By using various commands, it is possible to determine how the machine is configured, the errors that are being produced, and the state of the operating system.

The use of commands, such as **lsdev**, **lspv**, **lsvg**, **lslpp**, **lsattr**, and others enable you to gather information on how the system is configured. Other commands, such as **errpt**, can give you an indication of any errors being logged by the system.

If the system administrator uses SMIT or the Web-based System Manager to perform administrative tasks, examine the log files of these applications to look for recent configuration changes. The log files are normally contained in the home directory of the root user and are named /smit.log for SMIT and /websm.log for the Web-based System Manager by default.

If you are looking for something specific based on the problem described by the user, then other files are usually viewed or extracted to send to your IBM support function for analysis, such as system dumps or checkstop files.

1.1.4 Resolving the problem

Once you have defined the problem, you should use the flow[illegible] in Figure 1-1 on page 12, Figure 1-2 on page 13, and Figure 1-3 on page [illegible]d the symptom index cross reference chart in Table 1-3 on page 15 to di[illegible]u to the most relevant part of this book to perform basic troublesho[illegible]he suspected device or software component. During the investigat[illegible]ess, you should keep a log of the actions you perform in trying to [illegible]e the cause of the problem, and any actions you perform to correc[illegible]lem.

In some cases, you will encounter a proble[illegible] cannot resolve using the basic troubleshooting techniques describ[illegible]edbook, or the more detailed troubleshooting techniques described [illegible]ete AIX or system hardware documentation. In this situation, you [illegible]rt the problem to IBM. The information you have collected as [illegible]roblem determination process should be supplied to IBM. If possible, you should create a simple test case to replicate the problem. In some cases, a test case may not be possible, for example, if a particular problem appears on a random basis and there is no apparent sequence of actions that trigger the problem.

1.1.5 Obtaining software fixes and hardware microcode updates

Software fixes for AIX and many LPPs and hardware microcode updates are available on the Internet from the following URL:

```
http://techsupport.services.ibm.com/server/fixes
```

For a more customized approach to downloading AIX fixes for AIX 4.3, you can use the AIX application called FixDist instead of the Web. As a Web-alternative application, FixDist provides more discrete downloads and transparently delivers all required images with just one click. It can also keep track of fixes you have already downloaded, so you can download smaller fix packages the next time you need them. FixDist can be downloaded from the Web site mentioned above.

For AIX 5L, the fixes are still obtained from this site but you will need to register as a user. At the time of the writing this redbook, this was free and could be done immediately. FixDist is to be replaced with a service that will dynamically build one .tar file that contains the required filesets and place them on an FTP server. An e-mail is then sent with information on how to get the file and extract the AIX filesets. This service is expected to be integrated with the new tool known as Inventory Scout, which will check what existing fixes are already installed.

Once you have determined the nature of your problem, you should try searching this Web site or using FixDist to see if you are experiencing a known problem for which a fix has already been made available.

Microcode Discovery Service

...ocode Discovery Service gives you two ways to generate a real-time ...arison report, showing subsystems that may need to be updated and ...ine if your IBM @server pSeries or RS/6000 is at the latest microcode ... the later machines, it is the customer's responsibility to obtain and load ... microcode on the system, adapters, and devices.

Serv... ...ent

Service ... an application program that operates on IBM @server pSeries and RS/6... ...uters and monitors them for hardware errors. Service Agent reports de... ...rs, assuming they meet certain criteria for criticality, to IBM for service w... ...omer intervention. Only machines with an IBM Warranty or Maintenan... ...nt can use Service Agent to report errors.

Before using these services, you will need to install Inventory Scout, onto the server you want to survey for microcode information or run Service Agent. Inventory Scout, Microcode Discovery Service, and Service Agent can be obtained from the following URL:

`http://techsupport.services.ibm.com/server/fixes`

1.1.6 Other relevant documentation

Each IBM @server pSeries and RS/6000 machine has a specific set of documentation that should be used in the problem determination process when a hardware problem is suspected. These are an orderable feature for some systems and are not shipped with the machine.

Every IBM @server pSeries and RS/6000 machine has a System Installation and Service Guide, which are supplemented by a number of additional documents, depending on whether the machine is a Micro Channel Bus system or a PCI machine, otherwise known as a Multiple Bus system. Each bus type (Micro Channel and Multiple Bus) has a set of manuals, one covering common diagnostic procedures on machines of that type, and the other describing the adapters, devices, and cables that can be used on systems of that type. In addition, the Multiple Bus systems have a guide detailing the placement rules for PCI adapters.

Most of the hardware documentation can be viewed online at the IBM @server pSeries and RS/6000 Library Internet site. The URL for the site is:

`http://www-1.ibm.com/servers/eserver/pseries/library`

Additionally, hardcopy versions of the manuals can be ordered from your IBM marketing representative. Table 1-1 shows details of the IBM @server pSeries and RS/6000 General Service Documentation. Table 1-2 on page 8 shows the details of the model-specific System Installation and Service Guides.

Table 1-1 pSeries and RS/6000 general service documentation

Document	Form number
IBM RS/6000 Adapters, Device, and Cables Inforamtion for Micro Channel Bus Systems	SA38-0533
RS/6000 Adapters, Devices, and Cable Information for Multiple Bus Systems	SA38-0516
RS/6000 Diagnostics Information for Micro Channel Bus Systems	SA38-0532
RS/6000 and pSeries Diagnostics Informationfor Multiple Bus Systems	SA38-0509

Document	Form number
RS/6000 and pSeries PCI Adapter Placement Reference	SA38-0538
pSeries Customer Support Information	SA38-0584
Site & Hardware Planning Information	SA38-0508

Table 1-2 pSeries and RS/6000 System Guides

pSeries and RS/6000 Model	Form number
7006 Graphics Workstation Service Guide	SA23-2719
7009 Compact Server Service Guide	SA23-2716
7012 300 Series Service Guide	SA38-0545
7012 G Series Service Guide	SA23-2741
IBM RS/6000 7013 500 Series Installation and Service Guide	SA38-0531
7013 J Series Service Guide	SA23-2725
7014 Model S00 Rack 7014 Model S00 Rack Installation and Service Guide	SA38-0550
7014 Series Model T00 and T42 Installation and Service Guide	SA38-0577
7015 Model R00 Rack Installation and Service Guide	SA23-2744
7015 R10/R20/R21 Service Guide	SA23-2708
7015 Model R30, R40, & R50, CPU Enclosure Installation and Service Guide	SA23-2743
7017 S Series Installation and Service Guide	SA38-0548
IBM 7024 E Series Service Guide	SA38-0502
IBM 7025 F Series Service Guide	SA38-0505
IBM RS/6000 7025 F40 Service Guide	SA38-0515
RS/6000 7025 F50 Installation and Service Guide	SA38-0541
7026 CPU Drawer Install and Service Guide	SA38-0535

pSeries and RS/6000 Model	Form number
IBM RS/6000 7043 Service Guide	SA38-0512
7043 260 Service Guide *7043 260 Setup Guide* *7043 260 User's Guide*	SA38-0554 SA38-0555 SA38-0553
RS/6000 44P Series Model 170 Service Guide *44P Series Model 170 Installation Guide* *RS/6000 44P Series Model 170 User's Guide*	SA38-0560 SA38-0561 SA38-0559
RS/6000 44P Series Model 270 Service Guide *RS/6000 44P Series Model 270 Install Guide* *RS/6000 44P Series Model 270 User's Guide*	SA38-0572 SA38-0574 SA38-0573
RS/6000 7046 B50 Service Guide *RS/6000 7046 B50 Setup Guide* *RS/6000 7046 B50 User's Guide*	SA38-0564 SA38-0562 SA38-0563
Enterprise Server H Series CPU Drawer Installation and Service Guide	SA38-0547
Enterprise Server H Series User's Guide	SA38-0546
Enterprise Server Model F80 and pSeries 620 Model 6F1 Installation Guide *Enterprise Server Model F80 and pSeries 620 Model 6F1 Service Guide* *Enterprise Server Model F80 and pSeries 620 Model 6F1 User's Guide*	SA38-0569 SA38-0568 SA38-0567
RS/6000 7026 B80 Installation Guide *Service Guide* *User's Guide*	SA38-0579 SA38-0581 SA38-0580
Enterprise Server Model H80 and pSeries 660 Model 6H1 Installation Guide *Enterprise Server Model H80 and pSeries 660 Model 6H1 Service Guide* *Enterprise Server Model H80 and pSeries 660 Model 6H1 User's Guide*	SA38-0575 SA38-0566 SA38-0565

pSeries and RS/6000 Model	Form number
RS/6000 Enterprise Server Model M80 and eServer pSeries 680 Model 6M1 Service Guide	SA38-0571
RS/6000 Enterprise Server Model M80 and eServer pSeries 680 Mod 6M1 Install Guide	SA38-0576
RS/6000 Enterprise Server Model M80 and eServer pSeries 680 Model 6M1 User's Guide	SA38-0570
RS/6000 Enterprise Server S80 Installation Guide	SA38-0582
Enterprise Server S80, pSeries 680 Model S85 Service Guide	SA38-0558
RS/6000 Enterprise Server S80 User's Guide	SA38-0557
Capacity Upgrade on Demand Installing and Upgrading Processors	SA38-0583

1.2 Troubleshooting starting point

This section contains flowcharts and a table of symptoms of common problems. Based on the problem described by the user, you can either:

- Go directly to the chapter most relevant to your problem. You can use the table of contents at the front of the book or the index at the back of the book to decide which section is most relevant.
- If you have a boot problem, use the boot path flowchart starting in Figure 1-1 on page 12 in this section to decide on a course of action.
- Refer to the symptom index shown in Table 1-3 on page 15 to decide your next action.

1.2.1 Boot path flowchart

The boot path flowchart is designed to assist you in the diagnosis of boot problems. The chart takes you through the stages of the boot process, listing some of the LED or LCD codes that are signposts for either things completing successfully or indicating you have a problem. As you follow the chart, you will eventually come to an exit point. This exit point will direct you to the relevant chapter or section within the book. The section you are referred to will then try to either provide you with suggestions for a solution, or direct you to a publication or Web site that will provide you with additional information to fix the problem. If neither of these solutions provide a solution, contact the organization that provides you with AIX software support.

For later systems with four or more digit LED or LCD panels, the three digit code will be preceded with a 0. For example, 551 would be 0551. Systems may also show eight digit codes and location codes during normal system boot.

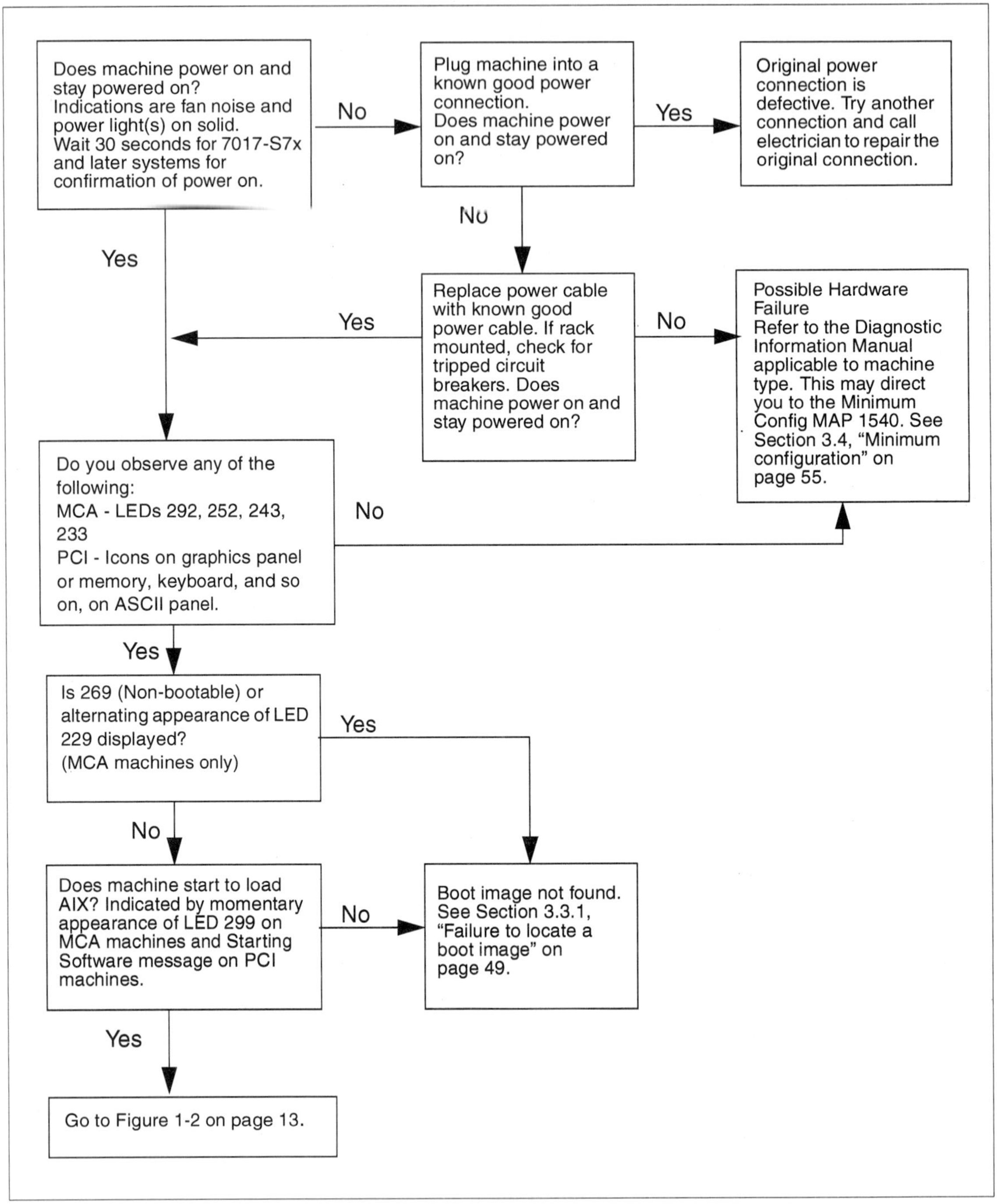

Figure 1-1 Boot path flowchart: part one

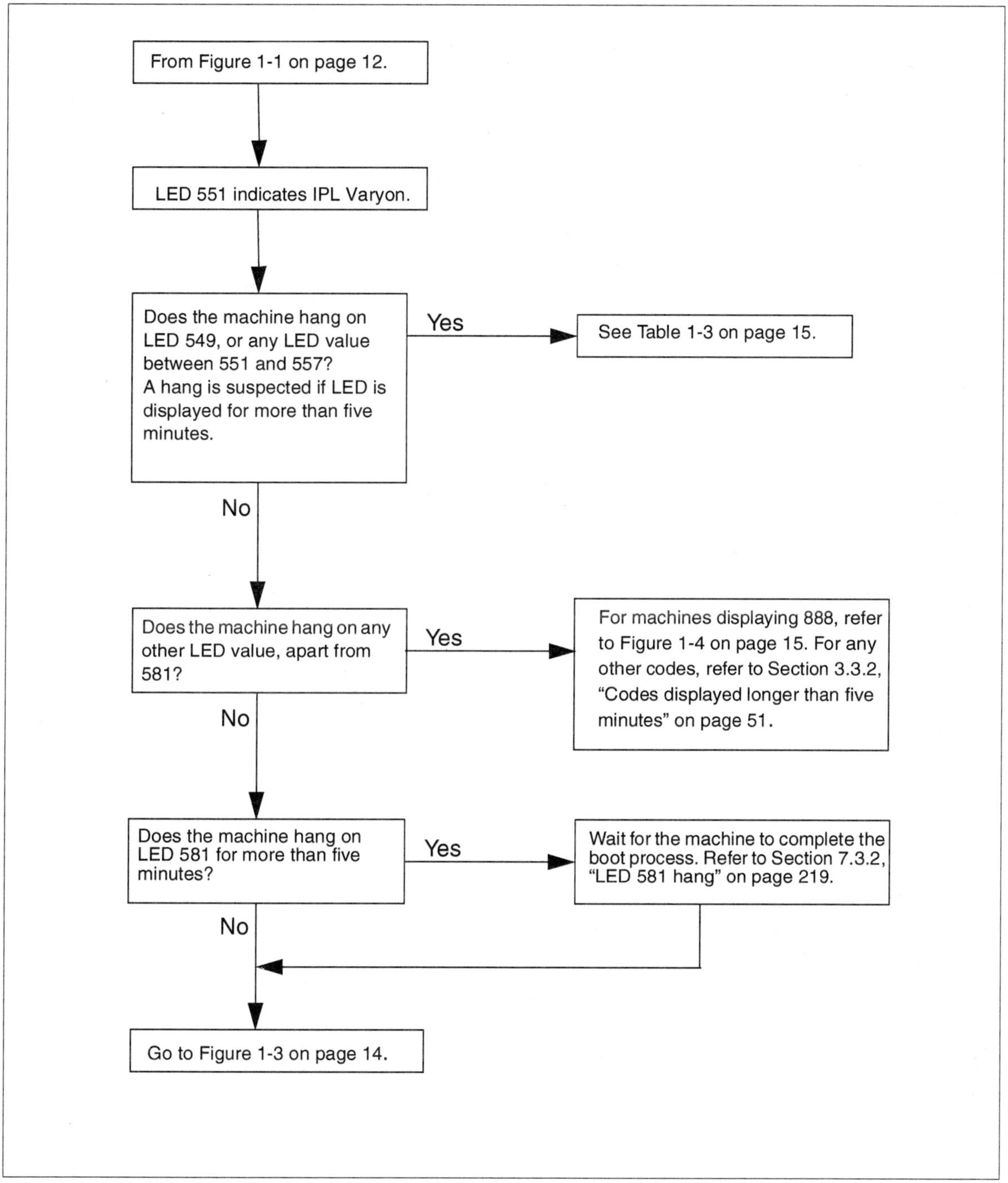

Figure 1-2 Boot path flowchart: Part two

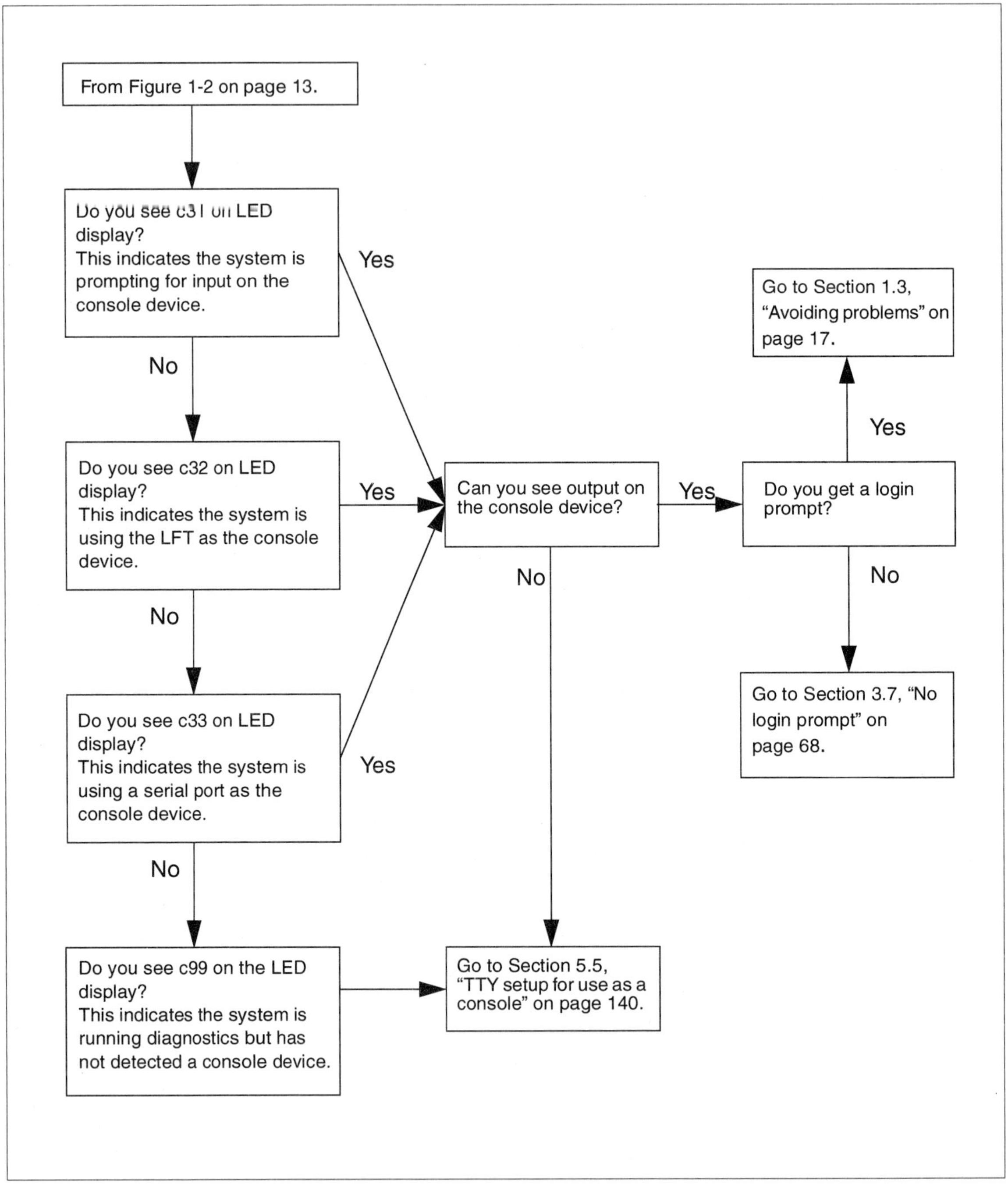

Figure 1-3 Boot path flowchart: part three

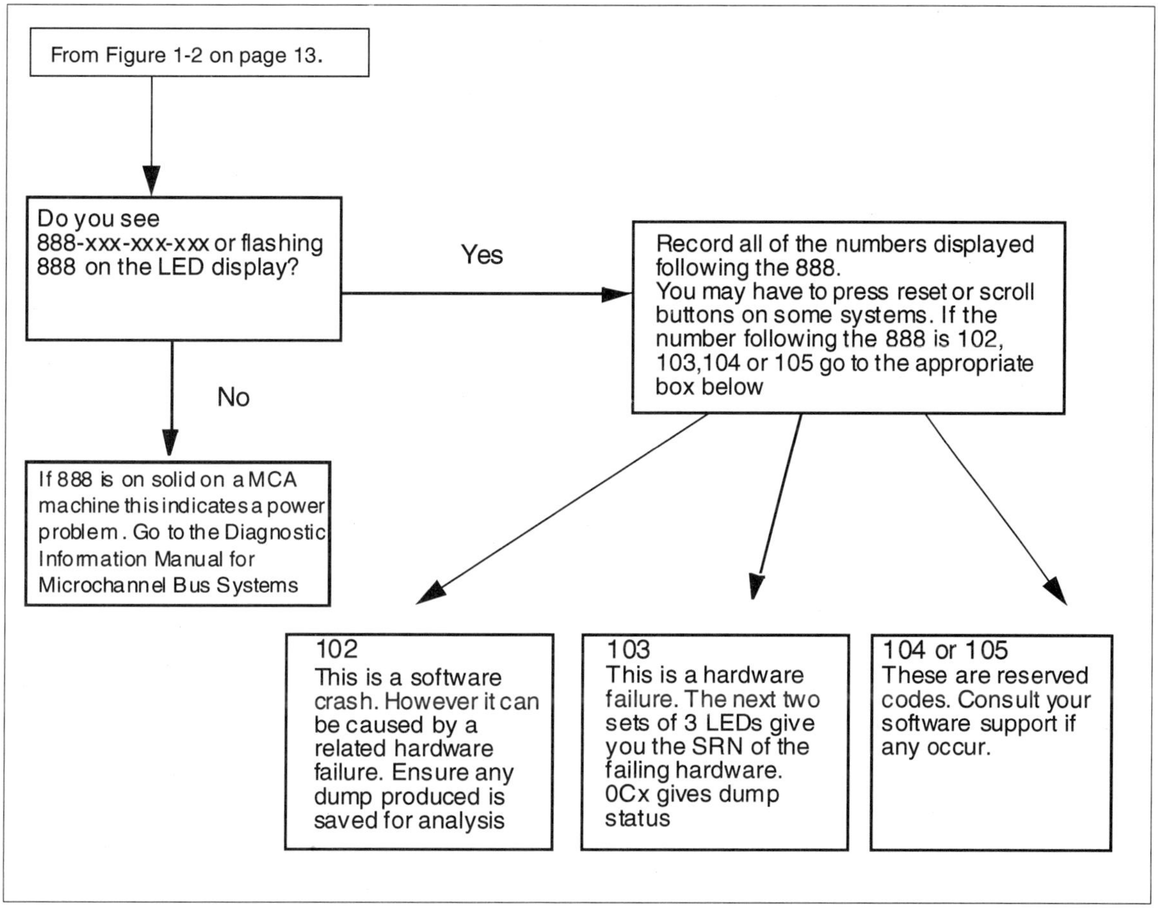

Figure 1-4 Machine displaying 888 in LED or LCD

1.2.2 Symptom index

Use this table as an alternative method for finding the correct section in the book that will help you deal with your problem.

Table 1-3 Symptom cross reference chart

Symptom	Possible cause	Refer to
SCSI devices missing or duplicated	Address conflicts on the bus	"SCSI devices missing or duplicated" on page 147
Checkstops or machine checks in error log	CPU or memory	Section 5.6, "Checkstops and machine checks" on page 141

Symptom	Possible cause	Refer to
LED 553	inittab problem, AIX corruption	Section 3.6.3, "LED 553 halt" on page 64
LED 551, 555, and 557	A corrupted file system, JFS log, or defective disk	Section 3.6.1, "LED 551, 555, or 557 halt" on page 58
LED 552, 554, and 556	A corrupted file system, JFS log bad IPL record, Corrupted Boot LV Defective Disk	Section 3.6.2, "LED 552, 554, or 556 halt" on page 60
LED 549	No system console or console problem with unsaved dump	Section 4.2.1, "LED 549" on page 71
LED 888-102	AIX kernel or kernel extension problem	Chapter 4, "System dumps" on page 69
System hang	AIX system resource	"System hang" on page 113
Tape stuck in drive	Back up not completed, tape or tape drive problem	Section 5.9.4, "4 mm, 8 mm, and DLT tape drives" on page 158
Tape media errors	Defective media or drive needs cleaning	Section 5.9.4, "4 mm, 8 mm, and DLT tape drives" on page 158
TAPE_ERR in error log	Media failure, drive failure, and so on	"Tape error log entries" on page 160
hdisk - pdisk mismatch	Disk from RAID set	Section 5.8.3, "SSA disk does not configure as a hdisk" on page 152
SSA errors in error log	SSA drive or cable	Section 5.8, "Serial Storage Architecture (SSA) disks" on page 150
Cannot log in to specific remote machine	Network problem Remote machine down	Section 7.2.1, "Selective host network problems" on page 197
Cannot log in to any remote machine	Network problem Adapter problem	Section 7.2.2, "No network access" on page 198
LED 581	TCP/IP problem	Section 7.3.2, "LED 581 hang" on page 219
Error log entries	Hardware or software	Section 2.3, "Error log management" on page 22

Symptom	Possible cause	Refer to
Core dump error log entries	Software failure	Section 2.4, "Finding a core dump" on page 34
Machine fails to boot	Hardware or software	Section 1.2.1, "Boot path flowchart" on page 10
Corrupt boot list	Corrupt boot list, erased boot list, or list non-existent device	Section 3.3.1, "Failure to locate a boot image" on page 49
3 Digit LED starting 0c	System dump in progress	Section 4.4.2, "Dump status codes" on page 85

1.3 Avoiding problems

The Reliability, Availability, and Serviceability (RAS) features of AIX are designed to fulfill many functions. As well as helping you determine the cause of a problem once it has actually occurred, such as the diagnostics subsystem, many of the RAS features are designed to provide information on potential problems before they occur. By default, IBM @server pSeries and RS/6000 systems are configured to run periodic automatic diagnostic checks. Any errors or warnings reported by this system will appear in the system error log.

Good system administration is not only fixing problems when they occur, but managing a system in such a way as to minimize the chances of a problem having an impact on the users of the system.

Periodic system maintenance can help reduce the number of problems experienced on a machine. Simple tasks, such as cleaning the tape drive as required, can prevent tape errors. Examining the system error log on a regular basis can help you spot a potential problem when the related error log entries are still warnings rather than errors.

1.3.1 System health check

The following section lists some simple commands that can be run on a regular basis to monitor a system. They will help you to become aware of how the system is operating.

- Use the **errpt** command to look at a summary error log report. Be on the lookout for recent additions to the log. Use the **errpt -a** command to examine any suspicious detailed error log entries.

- Check disk space availability on the system with the **df -k** command. A full file system can cause a number of problems, so it is best to avoid the situation if at all possible. The two solutions to a full file system are to either delete some files to free up space, or use the LVM to add additional resources to the file system. The option you take will depend on the nature of the data in the file system, and whether there is any available space in the volume group.
- Check volume groups for stale partitions with the **lsvg** command. If stale partitions, logical volumes, or physical volumes are reported, try and repair the situation with the **syncvg** command.
- Check system paging space with the **lsps -s** command. A system will not perform very well if it is low on paging space. In extreme circumstances, the system can terminate processes in order to solve the problem. Obviously, it is better that the system administrator ensures that there is enough paging space. You can either increase the size of existing paging space volumes, or add a new paging space volume. Again, the option you take will depend on the available space in the volume groups on the system.
- Check if all expected subsystems are running with the **lssrc -a** command.
- Check the networking by trying to **ping** a well-known address. If you cannot **ping** the address, refer to Chapter 7, "TCP/IP and networking problem solving" on page 195.

2

Error logging

This chapter describes the error logging subsystem on AIX 5L Version 5.1. It shows how you can use various commands to view the error log and interpret the information it contains. AIX 5L provides three enhancements in the area of error logging. You can specify a *duplicate check* that treats identical errors arriving closer than this threshold as duplicates and counts them only once. Second, with the **errpt** command, you can now request an *intermediate format report* that removes seldom needed data from the detailed error report format. A third enhancement, the diagnostic tool, will now put *additional information* into the error log entry.

2.1 Error logging overview

The error logging process begins when an operating system module detects an error. The error-detecting segment of code then sends error information to either the **errsave** kernel service and **errlast** kernel service for pending system crash or the **errlog** subroutine to log an application error, where the information is, in turn, written to the /dev/error special file. The **errlast** preserves the error record in the NVRAM. Therefore, in the event of a system crash, the last logged error is not lost.

This process then adds a time stamp to the collected data. The errdemon daemon constantly checks the /dev/error file for new entries, and when new data is written, the daemon conducts a series of operations.

Before an entry is written to the error log, the errdemon daemon compares the label sent by the kernel or application code to the contents of the *error record template repository*. If the label matches an item in the repository, the daemon collects additional data from other parts of the system.

To create an entry in the error log, the errdemon daemon retrieves the appropriate template from the repository, the resource name of the unit that detected the error, and detailed data. Also, if the error signifies a hardware-related problem and hardware Vital Product Data (VPD) exists, the daemon retrieves the VPD from the Object Data Manager (ODM). When you access the error log, either through SMIT or with the **errpt** command, the error log is formatted according to the error template in the error template repository and presented in either a summary or detailed report. Most entries in the error log are attributable to hardware and software problems, but informational messages can also be logged.

The system administrator can look at the error log to determine what caused a failure, or to periodically check the health of the system when it is running. Service personnel can also examine the log to help them service the machine.

The software components that allow the AIX kernel and commands to log errors to the error log are contained in the fileset bos.rte.serv_aid. This fileset is automatically installed as part of the AIX installation process.

The commands that allow you to view and manipulate the error log, such as the **errpt** and **errclear** commands, are contained in the fileset called bos.sysmgt.serv_aid. This fileset is not automatically installed by earlier releases of AIX Version 4. Use the following command to check whether the package is installed on your system:

```
# lslpp -h bos.sysmgt.serv_aid
```

2.2 Error log file processing

The error log is used by system administrators and IBM service personnel to diagnose system problems as the first tool for problem determination. The error log contains error IDs, time stamp, error type, error class, and resource names associated with each error. Some error log entries also contain detailed data passed by the errlog or errsave routines, such as information about the slot number of the failing card or the name of the file that could not be opened.

Figure 2-1 shows how the error log is processed to allow users to view information about the system errors.

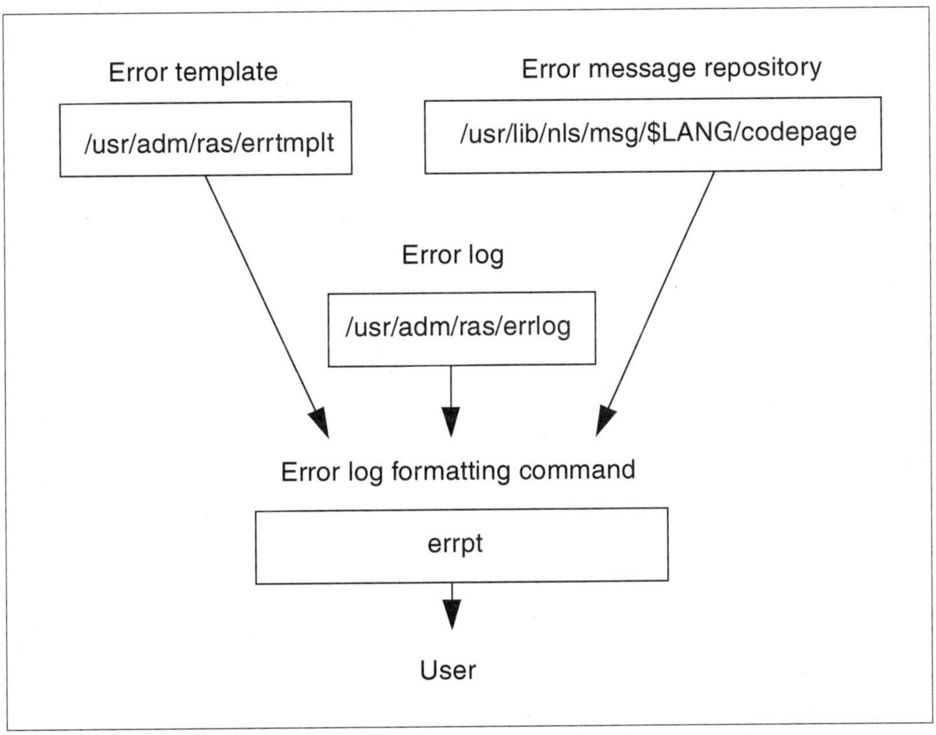

Figure 2-1 Error log file processing

2.2.1 Error templates

The error template contains numbers that correspond to error messages in the codepoint catalogue. These are sometimes referred to as codepoint messages. These error messages are used to communicate possible causes and to recommend actions for an error. They are also used to explain the detailed data that may accompany the error.

The template also is used to indicate whether or not the error should be reportable, loggable, or alertable. If it is not reportable, it will not appear when the **errpt** command is run. If an error is not loggable, it will not be put in the error log. For example, if a developer just wanted concurrent error notification to kick off an action, she or he may not want the error to show up in an error report.

Each template in the template file contains unique information that corresponds to a unique error. The contents of the error template are used to calculate the error ID of the error. The error numbers correspond to error messages indicating causes and recommendations for action.

The templates in the errtmplt file can be viewed by invoking the **errpt** command with the -t flag.

Templates are installed into the errtmplt file using the **errupdate** command. This is carried out automatically as part of the installation process of any filesets that contain new error templates.

2.2.2 Error messages

Error messages are numbered and placed in a separate file, called the codepoint catalogue. Similar to message catalogues, the codepoint catalogue is a translated file that exists in the different language directories. The user's LANG environment variable determines which codepoint catalogue is accessed when the **errinstall**, **errmsg**, or **errpt** commands are run. The error message source is installed in the codepoint catalog using the **errinstall** command. This is carried out automatically as part of the installation process of any filesets that contain new error messages.

The codepoint catalogue can be viewed by using the **errmsg** command with the -w flag. As you make use of **errmsg**, you can add your own messages to the message catalog for the application you made. Beginning with AIX Version 4.3.2, error messages may also come from regular XPG/4, also called NLS, message catalogues.

2.3 Error log management

You can generate an error report from entries in an error log. The **errpt** command allows flags for selecting errors that match specific criteria. By using the default condition, you can display error log entries in the reverse order they occurred and were recorded. In other words, the latest error log entry appears first.

2.3.1 Viewing the error log

There are two main ways of viewing the error log:

- You can use the System Management Interface Tool (SMIT) with a fast path to run the **errpt** command. To use the SMIT fast path, enter:

  ```
  # smit errpt
  ```

  After completing a dialog about the destination of the output and concurrent error reporting, you will see a panel similar to that shown in Example 2-1.

Example 2-1 SMIT Generate an Error Report panel

```
                          Generate an Error Report

Type or select values in entry fields.
Press Enter AFTER making all desired changes.

[TOP]                                                   [Entry Fields]
  CONCURRENT error reporting?                          no
  Type of Report                                       summary              +
  Error CLASSES (default is all)                      []                    +
  Error TYPES   (default is all)                      []                    +
  Error LABELS (default is all)                       []                    +
  Error ID's      (default is all)                    []
  Resource CLASSES (default is all)                   []
  Resource TYPES   (default is all)                   []
  Resource NAMES  (default is all)                    []
  SEQUENCE numbers (default is all)                   []
  STARTING time interval                              []
  ENDING time interval                                []
  Show only Duplicated Errors                         [no]                  +
[MORE...5]

F1=Help              F2=Refresh           F3=Cancel            F4=List
F5=Reset             F6=Command           F7=Edit              F8=Image
F9=Shell             F10=Exit             Enter=Do
```

You can also view the error log from the command line using the **errpt** command. When used from the command line, considerable amounts of output can often be generated, so it is best to control the command by piping the output to either the **more** or **pg** commands, which allow it to be viewed one panel at a time. When invoked with no options, **errpt** will display a summary report, listing one line of information about each error log entry. An example of this is shown in Example 2-2.

Example 2-2 Errpt output

```
# errpt
IDENTIFIER TIMESTAMP  T C RESOURCE_NAME  DESCRIPTION
```

```
35BFC499   0821161601 P H cd0         DISK OPERATION ERROR
0BA49C99   0821161601 T H scsi0       SCSI BUS ERROR
F89FB899   0806150001 P O dumpcheck   The copy directory is too small.
2120313C   0806142301 I H tok0        PROBLEM RESOLVED
75CE5DC5   0806142301 I H tok0        ADAPTER ERROR
FFE305EE   0806142301 P H tok0        WIRE FAULT
2120313C   0806142101 I H tok0        PROBLEM RESOLVED
75CE5DC5   0806142001 I H tok0        ADAPTER ERROR
FFE305EE   0806142001 P H tok0        WIRE FAULT
FFE305EE   0806142001 P H tok0        WIRE FAULT
2120313C   0806141901 I H tok0        PROBLEM RESOLVED
75CE5DC5   0806141801 I H tok0        ADAPTER ERROR
FFE305EE   0806141801 P H tok0        WIRE FAULT
FFE305EE   0806141801 P H tok0        WIRE FAULT
FFE305EE   0806141701 P H tok0        WIRE FAULT
2120313C   0806141701 I H tok0        PROBLEM RESOLVED
499B30CC   0806133601 T H ent1        ETHERNET DOWN
75CE5DC5   0806133501 I H tok0        ADAPTER ERROR
FFE305EE   0806133501 P H tok0        WIRE FAULT
F89FB899   0805150001 P O dumpcheck   The copy directory is too small.
F89FB899   0804150001 P O dumpcheck   The copy directory is too small.
```

In addition to the summary report, the **errpt** command can be used with various flags to generate a customized report detailing the error log entries you are interested in:

- To display information about errors in the error log file in detailed format, enter the following command:

  ```
  # errpt -a
  ```

- In AIX 5L Version 5.1, the **errpt** command now supports an intermediate output format by using the -A flag, in addition to the summary and the details already provided. Only the values for LABEL, Date/Time, Type, Resource Name, Description, and Detail Data are displayed. To display a shortened version of the detailed report produced by the -a flag, enter the following command:

  # errpt -A -j *identifier*

  Where identifier is the eight digit hexadecimal unique error identifier.

  Example 2-3 shows the output of the above command.

Example 2-3 A shortened error report

```
# errpt -A 9DBCFDEE

LABEL:          ERRLOG_ON
Date/Time:      Wed Aug 22 11:03:54 CDT
Type:           TEMP
```

```
Resource Name:   errdemon
Description
ERROR LOGGING TURNED ON
```

- To display a detailed report of all errors logged for a particular error identifier, enter the following command:

  `# errpt -a -j *identifier*`

  Where identifier is the eight digit hexadecimal unique error identifier.

- To clear all entries from the error log, enter the following command:

  `# errclear 0`

- To stop error logging, enter the following command:

  `# /usr/lib/errstop`

- To start error logging, enter the following command:

  `# /usr/lib/errdemon`

- To list the current setting of error log file and buffer size and duplicate information, enter the following command:

  `# /usr/lib/errdemon -l`

If you want to change the buffer size and error log file size, you can use the **errdemon** command. For further detail, refer to the manual page for **errdemon**.

> **Note:** When you remove the errlog file accidently, use the **/usr/lib/errstop** and **/usr/lib/errdemon** commands in sequence to recover the file. **errdemon** creates the errlog file if the file does not exist.

Software service aid configuration information is stored in the /etc/objrepos/SWservAt ODM database. This ODM class is used to store information about the location and size of various log files used by the system. It is also used to hold information about trace hooks available for use by the trace subsystem, described in Chapter 11, "Event tracing" on page 341.

By default, AIX runs a cron job that deletes all hardware error log entries older than 90 days daily at 12 AM and all software and operator message error log entries older than 30 days daily at 11 AM. The cron job simply uses the **errclear** command to delete the old entries. If you are investigating a software problem that has been on a machine for a long time, do not assume that the first instance of the error in the error log was caused the first time the software problem occurred. Previous entries may have been deleted if older than 30 days.

There are some new options introduced in AIX 5L version 5.1. These will reduce your management of same and iterative error log. The first will reduce rapidly logged duplicate error log entries. and the second adds diagnostic output to error log entries.

- Duplicate Removal flag: -D

  The **errdemon** command was enhanced in AIX 5L to support four additional flags. The flags -D and -d specify if duplicate error log entries are to be removed or not. The default is the -D flag, which instructs the command to remove the duplicates.

- Time Range Flag: -t

  With the -t and -m flags, you can control what is considered a duplicate error log entry. A value in the range 1 to 2^{31} - 1 specifies the time in milliseconds within which an error identical to the previous one is considered a duplicate. The default value for this flag is 100 or 0.1 seconds. You should normally not change this time value. If, for example, you make it too large, diagnostics may not consider a condition serious when it really is serious. Diagnostics occasionally depends on an error being logged multiple times within a time period.

- Count Flag: -m

  The -m flag sets a count, after which the next error is no longer considered a duplicate of the previous one. The range for this value is 1 to 2^{31} - 1 with a default of 1000.

The **errpt** command also has a new -D flag, which consolidates duplicate errors. In conjunction with the -a flag, only the number of duplicate errors and the time stamps for the first and last occurrence are reported. This is complemented by a new -P flag, which displays only the duplicate errors logged by the new mechanisms of **errdemon** mentioned previously.

The link between error log and diagnostics is the new function.

When the diagnostic tool runs, it automatically tries to diagnose hardware errors it finds in the error log. Starting with AIX 5L, the information generated by the **diag** command is put back into the error log entry, so that it is easy to make the connection between the error event and, for example, the FRU number required to repair failing hardware. After replacement, we run the **diag** command and go to Task Selection and select the Log Repair Action.

To get the most out of the AIX Error Log and Error Log Analysis in Diagnostics, you must understand the following points:

1. The kernel and device drivers logs errors to the error log, not diagnostics. Diagnostics (Error Log Analysis) analyzes errors that have been logged.

2. In many cases, permanent and temporary hardware errors are logged that are not indicative of a hardware problem. Error Log Analysis should always be run to determine if these errors indicate a hardware problem.
3. Resource Name indicates the resource that detected the error. It does *not* indicated the failing resource. It does indicate the resource that diagnostics and Error Log Analysis should be run on.
4. Failure Causes, Probable Causes, and User Causes are generic recommendations and are not intended to be used to determine what parts to replace. Parts should only be replaced based on diagnostics and Error Log Analysis results.
5. System errors related to the processors, memory, power supplies, fans, and so on, are logged under resource name sysplanar0. Error Log Analysis should be run on sysplanar0 any time there is an error log with a resource name of sysplanar0.
6. Error Log Analysis can be run by running diagnostics in problem determination mode or by running the running the Run Error Log Analysis task. Stand-alone diagnostics do not perform error log analysis.
7. Error Log Analysis will analyze all the errors in the error log associated with a specific resource. For those errors that should be corrected, Error Log Analysis will provide a list of actions or an SRN. For errors that can safely be ignored, Error Log Analysis will indicate that no problems were found.

2.3.2 Reading a summary error log

A summary error log report, obtained by using the **errpt** command with no flags, contains the following information for each error log entry.

Identifier

The error identifier is a 32-bit CRC hexadecimal code that determines which error record template is used to interpret the information contained in the error log entry.

Time stamp

This is the time and date when the error occurred, formatted as MMDDhhmmYY.

Type

The type indicates the severity of the reason for logging the error. There are five different types of errors, along with a sixth type for when the severity cannot be determined:

PEND The loss of availability of a device or component is imminent.

PERF The performance of the device or component has degraded to below an acceptable level.

PERM Condition that could not be recovered from. Error types with this value are usually the most severe errors and are more likely to mean that you have a defective hardware device or software module. Error types other than PERM usually do not indicate a defect, but they are recorded so that they can be analyzed by the diagnostics programs.

TEMP Condition that was recovered from after a number of unsuccessful attempts. This error type is also used to record informational entries, such as data transfer statistics for DASD devices.

UNKN It is not possible to determine the severity of the error.

INFO The error log entry is informational and was not the result of an error.

The summary error log report only displays the first letter of the error type.

Class

This indicates the general source of the error. The classes are as follows:

H This means hardware device failures or media errors. When you receive a hardware error, refer to your system operator guide for information about performing diagnostics on the problem device or other piece of equipment. The diagnostics program tests the device and analyzes the error log entries related to it to determine the state of the device. Refer to Chapter 5, "Hardware problem determination" on page 115 for more information.

S This means software application program failures, system program failures, and kernel problems, such as low paging space.

O This indicates an operator notification error that gets logged when the `errorlogger` command is used.

U This means the source of the error is undetermined.

Resource name

Name of the resource that has detected the error. For software errors, this is the name of a software component or an executable program. For hardware errors, this is the name of a device or system component. It does not indicate that the component is faulty or needs replacement. Instead, it is used to determine the appropriate diagnostic modules to be used to analyze the error.

Description

Gives a description of the logged information.

2.3.3 Reading error logs in detail

To obtain a detailed report of all errors logged by the system, enter the following command:

```
# errpt -a | pg
```

A detailed error log report may contain multiple entries. Each entry contains multiple fields. The exact fields that are displayed depend upon the nature of the error. The following fields are always included in every error entry:

LABEL Predefined name for the event.

ID Numerical identifier for the event.

Date/Time Date and time of the event.

Sequence Number Unique number for the event.

Machine ID Identification number of your system processor unit.

Node ID Mnemonic name of your system.

Class General source of the error. See "Class" on page 28 for a description of the class types.

Type Severity of the error that has occurred. Five types of errors are possible. See "Type" on page 27 for a description of the error log types.

Resource Name Name of the resource that has detected the error. For software errors, this is the name of a software component or an executable program. For hardware errors, this is the name of a device or system component. It does not indicate that the component is faulty or needs replacement. Instead, it is used to determine the appropriate diagnostic modules to be used to analyze the error.

Description Summary of the error.

The following fields may or may not be present, depending on the nature of the error:

Resource Class General class of the resource that detected the failure.

Resource Type Type of the resource that detected the failure.

Location Code Path to the device. There may be up to four fields that refer to drawer, slot, connector, and port, respectively.

VPD
Vital product data. The contents of this field, if any, vary. Error log entries for devices typically return information concerning the device manufacturer, serial number, Engineering Change (EC) levels, and Read Only Storage (ROS) levels.

Probable Causes
List of some of the possible sources of the error.

User Causes
List of possible reasons for errors due to user mistakes. An improperly inserted disk or external devices (such as modems and printers) that are not turned on are examples of user-caused errors.

Install Causes
List of possible reasons for errors due to incorrect installation or configuration procedures. Examples of this type of error include hardware and software mismatches, incorrect installation of cables or cable connections becoming loose, and improperly configured systems.

Failure Causes
List of possible defects in hardware or software.

Note: A failure causes section in a software error log usually indicates a software defect. Logs that list user or install causes or both, but not failure causes, usually indicate that the problem is not a software defect. If you suspect a software defect, or are unable to correct user or install causes, report the problem to your software service department.

Recommended Actions
Description of actions for correcting the failure. For hardware errors, performing problem determination procedures is one of the recommended actions listed. For hardware errors, this will lead to running the diagnostic programs. Refer to Chapter 5, "Hardware problem determination" on page 115 for more information.

Detailed Data
Failure data that is unique for each error log entry, such as device sense data. Depending on the error, this field presents a Device Major/Minor numbers and return code from the program and system error code, as in /usr/include/sys/errno.h. If you are not interested in more data, just send this to the system engineer.

2.3.4 Examples of detailed error reports

The following are sample error report entries that are generated by issuing the `errpt -a` command.

The error log entry in Example 2-4 is taken from a system with a hardware problem. The entry shows that this system has a problem related to the SCSI bus with logical device name scsi0 located in slot number 08.

Example 2-4 A hardware error log sample

```
LABEL:        SCSI_ERR10
ID:           0BA49C99

Date/Time:          Wed Aug 22 11:03:54 CDT
Sequence Number:    50
Machine Id:         000BC6CD4C00
Node Id:            f50right
Class:              H
Type:               TERM
Resource Name:      scsi0
Resource Class:     adapter
Resource Type:      hscsi
Location:           00-08
VPD:
     Device Driver Level.........00
     Diagnostic Level............00
     Displayable Message.........SCSI
     EC Level....................C25928
     FRU Number..................30F8834
     Manufacturer................IBM97F
     Part Number.................59F4566
     Serial Number...............00002849
     ROS Level and ID............24
     Read/Write Register Ptr.....0120

Description
SCSI BUS ERROR

Probable Causes
CABLE
CABLE TERMINATOR
DEVICE
ADAPTER

Failure Causes
CABLE LOOSE OR DEFECTIVE
DEVICE
ADAPTER

    Recommended Actions
    PERFORM PROBLEM DETERMINATION PROCEDURES
    CHECK CABLE AND ITS CONNECTIONS

Detail Data
```

```
SENSE DATA
0000 0000 0000 0000 0000 0000 0000 0000 0000 0000 0000 0000
```

This error is logged by the SCSI device driver in the event of a potentially fatal SCSI bus error including cabling, device adapter, or related hardware. Because these errors are not necessarily catastrophic, operations may or may not continue successfully after the error.

This is a temporary error on the SCSI bus. The system recovered from the error by retrying the operation. However, if these errors are occurring frequently, there is cause for concern. A hardware element may be degrading and more serious problems may occur (complete failure, corrupted data, and so on) unless the problem is corrected.

We recommend the following as a rule of thumb. The following is a general problem determination procedures for SCSI errors:

- Make sure all connectors and terminators are firmly seated.
- Replace any worn or damaged cables, connectors and terminators.
- Make sure there are no extra terminators.
- Check that there is no SCSI address conflict (particularly if a SCSI device has been added to the system or devices have been moved); run **lsdev -C** and look for addresses where xx-yy-zz-ww are identical. If duplicates exist, shutdown and correct the situation immediately.
- Check the microcode level of the SCSI device driver.
- Check the engineering change (EC)-level, ROS-level, part number, and other hardware characteristics of the SCSI adapter (use the **lscfg -v** command). Make sure they are compatible with the AIX system level, SCSI device driver level, and system model. If there are error log entries for devices attached on the SCSI bus indicated by the resource name, run Diagnostic in problem determination mode and take corrective action on the other device. A faulty SCSI device or device driver can cause general SCSI errors. Check other devices connected to the SCSI bus for problems (even if there are no error log entries). If you have recently added a device to the SCSI bus, remove it and see if the SCSI errors go away.

If the problem persists, consider the following actions:

- Run stand-alone diagnostics on the SCSI adapter and all devices on the SCSI bus. Have any problems corrected.
- Contact your hardware service representative.

For more information about hardware diagnostics, refer to Chapter 5, “Hardware problem determination” on page 115.

The example shown in Example 2-5 is an error logged when the software dumped its core image due to software abnormal termination.

Example 2-5 A sample error log of core dump

```
LABEL:          CORE_DUMP
IDENTIFIER:     C60BB505

Date/Time:       Thu Sep  6 16:13:00 CDT
Sequence Number: 46
Machine Id:      000BC6CD4C00
Node Id:         f50right
Class:           S
Type:            PERM
Resource Name:   SYSPROC

Description
SOFTWARE PROGRAM ABNORMALLY TERMINATED

Probable Causes
SOFTWARE PROGRAM

User Causes
USER GENERATED SIGNAL

        Recommended Actions
        CORRECT THEN RETRY

Failure Causes
SOFTWARE PROGRAM

        Recommended Actions
        RERUN THE APPLICATION PROGRAM
        IF PROBLEM PERSISTS THEN DO THE FOLLOWING
        CONTACT APPROPRIATE SERVICE REPRESENTATIVE

Detail Data
SIGNAL NUMBER
          11
USER'S PROCESS ID:
       26238
FILE SYSTEM SERIAL NUMBER
           1
INODE NUMBER
           2
PROGRAM NAME
ftp
ADDITIONAL INFORMATION
read 118
??
```

```
__filbuf 2C0
fgets 134
ftp_fgets 9C
cmdscanne F0
main 57C
__start 8C

Symptom Data
REPORTABLE
1
INTERNAL ERROR
1
SYMPTOM CODE
PIDS/5799J0E00 LVLS/500 PCSS/SPI2 FLDS/ftp SIG/11 FLDS/read VALU/118
FLDS/ftp_fg
ets
```

Another example of software error you meet in the field is a *core dump*. The created core file contains the memory image of the process, and this can be used with the **dbx** command for debugging purposes. The software errors that invoke a core dump include an invalid argument, not enough memory, an invalid user address, or routine not supported. The first thing we need to know is if it was an AIX executable that dumped core. This can be found by looking at the name of the dumped executable, given in the PROGRAM NAME data field. If this program is a user application or a third-party application, it is up to the developer of the application to fix it.

If the core dumping executable is an AIX executable, proceed to debug the problem. Start with the SIGNAL NUMBER in the error log. You can build a debug version of the executable and proceed to debug it with the **dbx** command. To use the **dbx** command, you need to install the bos.adt.debug fileset.

If you have an AIX command that repeatedly terminates and leaves a core dump, you should send the core dump to IBM for further analysis.

The last section of the error log entry produced when an application core dumps normally shows a stack trace of the executable at the time of the failure.

2.4 Finding a core dump

Lots of old core dumps over time can create a problem by filling up file systems. Sometimes you will want to find the core dumps, examine them, and remove them to save space. This is particularly useful if you are administering a multiuser system; you will not know about all the core dumps created because they were most probably created by other users' applications.

To find the core file corresponding to an error log entry, use the **corepath** command located in the /usr/samples/findcore directory. This facility is part of the bos.sysmgt.serv_aid fileset.

When an application core dumps, a core file is placed in the current directory where the program runs. Unfortunately, we are not able to determine the path name of the dump at dump time. The corepath package uses error notification to detect that a core dump has happened. It then finds the core file, if possible, and then logs an operator message with the dump file's path name. This is particularly useful for system administrators who want to look at the dumps, but were not the ones operating the system when the dump occurred.

> **Note:** Currently we only search journaled file systems (JFS). There are a couple of lines to comment out in corepath if you want to search any type of file system. Be aware that this may cause unwanted network traffic and may take hours to find the dump.

The following is a list of commands used to find core dump files:

/usr/samples/findcore/corepath The shell script that finds the dump.

/usr/samples/findcore/getvfsname A binary program used by corepath to get the file system containing the dump.

To run corepath automatically, follow these steps:

1. You must be root to start it.
2. Put the error notification object into ODM. Put the error notification object at the end of this file into a separate file, then run **odmadd <file>** to add the object to the errnotify object class. Note that the file should begin with the line `errnotify:`.

To stop error notification from searching for core dumps, issue the following command:

```
# odmdelete -o errnotify -q 'en_name = corepath

Error notification ODM Object
errnotify:
        en_name = corepath
        en_persistenceflg = 1
        en_label = CORE_DUMP
        en_method = "/usr/samples/findcore/corepath $1 root"
```

AIX 5L Version 5.1 has changed the way it names the core file used for a core dump. In earlier AIX releases, a core file was always named core. If more than one application dumped or the same application dumped more than once, you always lost the earlier core file. Beginning with AIX 5L Version 5.1, each core file can be uniquely named, so no core file will be overwritten with a new one. This feature helps debugging and tracing application failures.

By default, a new core file is named core. To enable the new enhancement, set the CORE_NAMING environment variable to yes. After setting the CORE_NAMING variable, the new core file names are of the format core.pid.ddhhmmss, where pid is Process ID, dd is day of the month, hh is hours, mm is minutes, and ss is seconds.

> **Note:** The expected value of the CORE_NAMING variable is yes. But any value except null has the same meaning as yes. In other words, any value will also work. In case the CORE_NAMING value is unset, the core file name will not be changed.

In AIX 5L Version 5.1, a new feature of gathering core files is announced. This enhancement automates core collection processes and packages them into a single archive. This archive will have all the necessary information to successfully analyze the core on any machine.

The **snapcore** command gathers a core file, program, and libraries used by the program and compresses the information into a pax file. The file can then be downloaded to disk or tape, or transmitted to a remote system. The information gathered with the **snapcore** command allows you to identify and resolve problems with an application.

To collect all the information you might need to debug and analyze the problem, you can use the **snapcore** command, as shown in the following steps:

1. Change to the directory where the core dump file is located:

```
# ls -l
total 43
-rw-r--r--    1 root     staff            72 Aug 22 11:01 .profile
-rw-------    1 root     staff           446 Aug 22 18:01 .sh_history
-rw-r--r--    1 root     system        20987 Aug 24 15:04
core.16928.24200405
```

2. Run the **snapcore** command to collect all needed files:

```
# snapcore -d /tmp/coredir core.16928.24200405
Core file "core.16928.24200405" created by "telnet"
pass1() in progress ....
Calculating space required .
Total space required is 8258 kbytes ..
```

```
Checking for available space ...
Available space is 10292 kbytes
pass1 complete.
pass2() in progress ....
Collecting fileset information .
Collecting error report of CORE_DUMP errors ..
Creating readme file ..
Creating archive file ...
Compressing archive file ....
pass2 completed.
Snapcore completed successfully. Archive created in /tmp/coredir.
```

The **snapcore** command will gather all information and create a new compressed pax archive in the /tmp/coredir directory. If you do not specify a special directory using the -d flag, the archive will be stored in /tmp/snapcore directory. The new archive file will be named as snapcore_<$pid>.pax.Z.

```
# ls -l /tmp/coredir
total 5720
-rw-r--r--   1 root     system      2925093 Aug 24 15:07
snapcore_3580.pax.Z
```

3. To check the content of the pax archive, use the following command:

```
# uncompress -c snapcore_3580.pax.Z | pax
core.16928.24200405
README
lslpp.out
```

If you want to extract the files from the archive, type the following commands:

```
# uncompress -c snapcore_3580.pax.Z | pax -r
# ls -l
total 5872
-rw-r--r--   1 root     system          551 Aug 24 15:23 README
-rw-r--r--   1 root     system        20987 Aug 24 15:23
core.16928.24200405
-rw-r--r--   1 root     system        45593 Aug 24 15:23 lslpp.out
-rw-r--r--   1 root     system      2925093 Aug 24 15:07
snapcore_3580.pax.Z
```

The check_core utility is used by the **snapcore** command to gather all information about the core dump. This is a small C program and is located in the /usr/lib/ras directory.

Change to the directory where the core dump file is located and run the check_core utility against the core dump file. You will receive a list containing the program that caused the core dump and the libraries used by it:

```
# /usr/lib/ras/check_core  core.16928.24200405
/usr/lib/libc.a
/usr/lib/libcrypt.a
```

```
/usr/lib/libbsd.a
/usr/lib/libbind.a
/usr/lib/libi18n.a
/usr/lib/libiconv.a
/usr/lib/libcur.a
/usr/lib/libauthm.a
/usr/lib/libodm.a
/usr/lib/libcfg.a
/usr/lib/nls/loc/en_US
telnet
```

From the information above, we know the name of the program that caused the dump. Also you will know it from the core dump error log. Actually, we run the **telnet** to the other system and run **kill -11 pid_telnet** (where 11 signal means SEGV: Segmentation Violation) command.

3

Boot problems

The aim of this chapter is to guide you through a series of steps that are aimed at diagnosing most problems you will encounter with the boot process. In the first section, we show how the boot process normally works, because in any fault finding, it is always best to first understand how the process should work. This makes the process of determining what is going wrong much easier.

3.1 Types of machines

Certain procedures, particularly those related to the boot process, are implemented in a different way depending on the type of machine. This section describes the two main types of RS/6000 machines, and the terminology used to distinguish between them for the remainder of this redbook.

The RS/6000 family of machines was launched in 1990 and, over the years, has changed to adopt new technology as it becomes available. The first RS/6000 machines were based around the Micro Channel Architecture (MCA) and had a number of features common to each machine in the range, in particular, a three digit LED and a three position key mode switch. Throughout the rest of this redbook, machines of this type are referred to as *MCA machines*.

In recent years, the RS/6000 family has migrated to Peripheral Component Interconnect (PCI) bus technology. Throughout the rest of this redbook, machines of this type are referred to as *PCI machines*. Initial machines of this type (7040 and 7248) did not have the three digit LED or three position key mode switch of the previous MCA machines. Subsequent PCI machines have an LED or LCD display, but none have the three position key mode switch.

3.2 The boot process

The boot sequence, otherwise known as the Initial Program Load (IPL), is, in principle, similar on all computer systems. The basic steps carried out by the hardware are:

Boot Stage One Check the power, CPU, and memory systems.

Boot Stage Two Look for the operating system image.

Boot Stage Three Load and run the operating system image, and configure devices and subsystems.

The IBM @server pSeries and RS/6000 range of machines are no different, so they adhere to the above model, although some machines in the range have a pre-boot state. This pre-boot state is when the service processor (or BUMP) is made accessible in order to alter machine settings and obtain error information. Because of variations in models, such as some machines having service processors, the method by which the boot model is actually achieved varies.

You may find it useful while using this section to refer to the flowchart in Section 1.2.1, “Boot path flowchart” on page 10 to determine at which stage your boot process fails.

3.2.1 Pre-boot state

The Micro Channel Architecture (MCA) machines (7012 G series, 7013 J series, and 7015 R series) and the PCI bus machines (7025-F50, 7026-H50, 7026-H70, and 7043-260 and later machines) have a stage prior to starting the boot process. These machines have a mini processor, often referred to as the Bring Up Multiprocessor (BUMP) or service processor, that can be accessed prior to the start of the boot sequence. Depending on the machine type, the service processor can be used to determine the amount of hardware testing to be performed during the first stage of the boot process and record any errors generated. The service processor can also govern system monitoring while the machine is running AIX.

This rest of this section will explain some of the more often used functions of the service processors.

BUMP program

The Bring Up Multiprocessor (BUMP) function is present within the firmware of the MCA Symmetrical Multiprocessor (SMP) family of machines, consisting of 7012 G series, 7013 J series, and 7015 R series. The program controls the initial stages of the boot process up to the point where the Non-Volatile Random Access Memory (NVRAM) starts looking for a boot image. The program has two stages. The initial stage is where the machine is powered off. The second stage is during a Service mode boot after all CPU and memory testing has been completed.

Standby menu

The standby menu is available only on an ASCII terminal attached to the S1 serial port when the machine is not running AIX but the power is still connected. The LCD control screen will be displaying the word `Standby` at this point and continues to do so while the BUMP program is being accessed. To access this menu, you need to have the key in the Service position and the greater than sign prompt (>) displayed on the console. Type **sbb** and then press the Return key. You will get a menu that displays a number of options. The two most frequently used options are Display Configuration and Set Flags:

Display Configuration This option enables you to view the configuration detected when the last IPL was attempted. If the power has been completely removed from the machine, upon reconnection, this selection will only show the CPU and memory configuration as C for configured but mark other adapter positions as A for absent.

Set Flags This option enables you to set parameters before the machine boots. A full boot of an eight processor machine with 4 GB of memory can take a substantial length of time. The time can be decreased by setting option 6, Fast IPL, to enabled. It is also possible to set this Fast IPL parameter from the AIX command line prior to running the **shutdown** command. When running, the following command will configure the machine so that the next time you shut the machine down the subsequent boot will be the fast one:

```
# mpcfg -cf 11 1
```

This command sets the flag one time only. To enable fast IPL each reboot, you can add this command to /etc/inittab.

To get the machine to boot after altering any of the parameters, exit from the menus out to the > prompt. If you want a Normal mode boot, turn the key to Normal, type **power**, then press the Enter key. If you require a Service mode boot, leave the key in the Service position, type **power**, then press the Enter key. You may need to press the power button on the front of the machine at this time, depending upon how the machine was last powered off.

It is recommended that the BUMP menus relating to system test are only accessed by trained service personnel, since some of the messages that can be displayed are not actually problems and can lead to hours of needless troubleshooting.

PCI service processor access

Machine types 7025-F50, 7026-H50, 7026-H70, and 7043-260 and later have service processors as standard equipment. Certain other PCI models, such as the 7025-F40, can have them as an optional feature. The service processor provides a level of error detection as well as some control over certain settings on the machine. To access the service processor on most of the PCI machines, except for 7017-S70 and some later machines, which will be covered later in this chapter, attach an ASCII terminal to the S1 serial port and press the Enter key when the machine is not running AIX and the power is still connected. With the service processor menu displayed, you will see E075 displayed on the LED panel.

Note: The service processor cannot be accessed from a low function terminal (LFT) display, as the device driver for the graphics adapter card is not loaded at this time.

Once you have exited the service processor menus, you can power on the machine; on later machines, there is an option within the service processor menus.

3.2.2 Boot stage one

This is the portion of the boot sequence where the power supply, CPU, and memory systems are checked. All checks are performed by hardware; no operating system is loaded at this time.

Micro Channel Architecture machines

The Micro Channel Architecture (MCA) range of machines are 7011, 7012, 7013, 7015, 7030, 7009, and 7006. All of these machines have a display on the front of the machine that uses three digits to indicate status of the machine during the boot.

Built-In Self-Test (BIST) LED 100-199

The routines run during this LED sequence include testing of CPU, memory, and the initial bringing up of the power supply. Since it is not possible to test a CPU or any portion of memory while it is in use, it is performed at this time by the On-board Chip Sequencer (OCS). This is a piece of hardware that runs tests on the memory and CPUs, and if it finds a problem, writes an entry in the NVRAM. These tests are usually a quick process, but if the machine is a fully configured eight processor SMP machine, you can expect it to take ten to twenty minutes or more to test all components in the CPU complex.

Stationary LEDs of 185, 111, 112, or 113 indicate that the machine has found a problem that it cannot recover from.

SMP maintenance menu

This menu is displayed on 7012 G series, 7013 J series, and 7015 R series machines after the tests have been run on the CPU and memory, and the adapter cards and the buses have been initialized. This menu will only appear when the flags shown in Table 3-1 have been set on the Set Flags option of the standby menu.

Table 3-1 Flag settings to obtain maintenance menu

Flag	Value
BUMP console present	Enabled
Auto service IPL	Disabled

See “Standby menu” on page 41 for details on how to set these flags.

If the maintenance menu fails to display, and the key is in the Service position, and flags are set as shown above, the most likely cause is that the system ID has been corrupted or lost. This most often happens when both the part containing the master copy of the system ID and the part containing the backup copy are changed together. On the 7013 J series, the master copy is held on the backplane, and on the 7015 R series, the master copy is held on the L2 planar. On both the 7013 and 7015 machines, the backup copy is held on the System Interface Board (SIB). The 7012 G series, being much smaller, has the master copy in the control screen and the backup copy on the system planar.

The maintenance menu will include another view of the configuration giving more detailed information, BUMP error log entries, power off facility, and a boot aid.

PCI bus machines (except 7017 and some later machines)

Boot stage one on 7020, 7024, 7025, 7027, 7043, 7248 and some later machines differs from the 7017 due to firmware differences. These machines also perform the first two stages differently from the MCA bus machines. The difference being that the machines have either a system planar with firmware on it, or they have a service processor with code on it plus the system planar with firmware on it. The firmware on the system planar and service processor can be refreshed when updates become available. The updates are usually to accommodate new hardware releases or cure known problems. Most of the MCA machines have a permanent ROS embedded on the system planar to which no changes can be made. The MCA G, J, and R series machines, however, do use a version of reloadable firmware, but this only controls CPU and memory functions.

The latest firmware is available from:

`http://www.rs6000.ibm.com/support/micro`

When the machine is under the control of the firmware, you will see either a three digit Fxx code or a four digit Exxx or Fxxx code displayed in the LED panel. Later machines have other codes. The codes you see depend on the machine type. The firmware controls the testing and verification of the memory, CPUs, and the initialization of the PCI bus components.

PCI machine icons

After a period of time, the older machines will either display a series of icons depicting keyboard, memory, network, SCSI, and speaker on the graphical screen. As the speaker icon appears, if the machine has a speaker, it will emit a beep. If you are using an ASCI console or graphical screen on newer PCI machines, from IBM @server pSeries 620 (7025 F80), instead of seeing graphical icons, you will see the words keyboard, memory, network, SCSI, and speaker. Throughout the rest of this redbook, this startup screen will be referred to as the *PCI icons screen*.

For example, the IBM @server pSeries 620 (7025 F80) boot sequence starts with OK shown in the screen. Pressing the power on button causes the power LED to flash; 20 seconds later, the fans start and the power LED comes on solid. 9xxx codes appear in the screen, these change to Exxx with location codes appearing on the second LED row. When E1DC appears, the LFT display is turned on. Very soon afterwards, E1F1 appears, and the PCI icons screen appears on the display and the speaker sounds.

Before the speaker icon or word appears, a keyboard response must be received if you want to do anything other than boot the machine in Normal mode.

> **Note:** If you are using an LFT graphics display, you may miss the icons screen while the display is warming up. You must press the required key before the speaker icon or word appears or the machine will start a normal boot and you will have to shutdown and start again.

During this phase of the boot process, additional error codes of eight hexadecimal characters can be displayed on the screen. If the machine has an eight digit LED panel, the codes can also be displayed on it. These codes are generally not fatal but are signalling to you that something requires your attention. The meaning of these codes can be found in the relevant service guide for the machine. System Installation And Service Guides for most IBM @server pSeries and RS/6000 machines can be viewed on the Internet at the IBM @server pSeries library:

`http://www.rs6000.ibm.com/library/`

See Table 1-1 on page 7 and Table 1-2 on page 8 for a full list of current documentation.

7017 Models S70, S7A, S80 and S85 (or P680) and others

Although these machines are PCI-based, they differ substantially in the way that they boot and access service processor menus. The reason for this is that the CPU complex has a large portion of code that is used to run the CPU complex and the Serial Power Control Network (SPCN). This portion of the firmware is unique to this machine and, when it is running, displays eight digit codes in the LED panel. Additionally, when an error code is produced, an orange attention light is illuminated and the first portion of the error code displayed on the screen. There is a possibility of a further eight additional screens of error information being displayed on the control screen. To access these, you need to use the scroll and Enter buttons on the operator screen. These additional fields are quite often used in the process of fault determination and so should be collected any time that an error code is displayed.

Boot process differences

On the S70 and later machines, you can set the speed of the boot process using the control screen buttons. There are three settings for the speed, plus a special condition setting:

F This gives a fast boot path through the CPU memory checks. Basic testing of the CPU complex takes place.

S This is the slow boot option. This fully tests the CPU and the memory and also checks all data paths between each CPU and the memory subsystem. This will take a substantial length of time if you have the maximum 24 processors and 96 GB of memory.

SE This setting should only be used when a part has been replaced and there is a need to get the machine up and running so that firmware code can be loaded to support the EC level of the new part. This setting ignores EC checking during the slow boot process it runs. This setting will probably be used when being directed by IBM support personnel.

V This setting means variable. This enables the machine to decide the speed it will use during the boot process. Normally, the fast option is used. However, anytime the machine has detected an error, either during a previous boot sequence or when the machine has instigated a reboot, for example, after a checkstop has been detected, then a slow boot will be used.

To power on the machine, you need to press and hold the Power button for approximately one second. The machine will not appear to do anything for approximately 30 seconds, then the power LED will start to flash. Once the power supply has fully started, the LED panel will have progress codes made up of eight characters, quite often with one of the characters changing rapidly. This will carry on for a few minutes. You should observe E043 displayed in the LED panel, momentarily followed by E07A accompanied by three beeps from the speaker in the primary I/O drawer. If you wish to enter the service processor menus, press any key on the ASCII terminal after the beeps but within the 10 second window before the E07A code changes on the LED panel. Once the service processor menus have been entered, it is possible to check the service processor error logs, read Vital Product Data (VPD) of components, and perform many other functions.

The service processor is situated in the primary I/O drawer in the rack adjacent to the CPU rack for 7017, and all communication between the service processor and CPU complex is carried out using the JTAG and operator screen cables.

When you exit from the service processor menus, or if you did not enter them, the machine will continue the boot process in a similar way to the other PCI-based machines. However, the time taken to get to a login prompt may be considerable, because it is possible to have a configuration having up to 56 adapters in machines with four I/O drawers configured.

3.2.3 Boot stage two

At this point in the boot process, the CPU and memory have been tested. The machine now starts to look for an operating system image.

MCA machines LEDs 200-299

This LED sequence on all MCA machines is known as the Power-On Self-Test (POST) phase. The LEDs indicate the sequence up to the point where the machine has read a valid boot image and has just handed over the boot process to AIX. At this point, 299 is momentarily displayed on the LED panel on MCA machines.

The POST sequence will only start once it has been established that the hardware present within the machine is capable of running a system, in other words, it has a CPU and some memory. The next step is to look for a boot image. The next series of numbers displayed indicate the adapters and devices it is starting up in the quest to find the boot image. Important numbers to look out for are:

292 Initializing a SCSI adapter. Needed to run the disk containing AIX.

252 Locating the diskette drive or reading from a bootable diskette media.

243 or 233 Booting from a device listed in the NVRAM boot list. Usually hdisk0, a bootable CD-ROM, or a mksysb tape.

Non Volatile Random Access Memory (NVRAM) is the device that holds the boot list, which is the list of the places to look for a boot image.

All PCI machines

On PCI machines, the distinction between stage one and stage two of the boot process is not as clear as it is on MCA machines. The point at which the display attached to the machine first displays the PCI Icon screen, as described in “PCI machine icons” on page 44, nearly matches the start of the 200-299 LED codes of a MCA machine.

Once the icons have disappeared from the screen, the machine then uses the boot list in the NVRAM to look for a boot image. The boot image is then read and AIX is started to be loaded. When the machine finds a valid boot image, it displays the message `Welcome to AIX`, followed by some information detailing the SCSI ID of the device it loaded the boot image from. Unlike the MCA machines, you do not get 299 displayed on the LED panel to confirm that a boot image has been found; instead, you will see LED E105, and eventually see the three digit AIX LED codes you are familiar with displayed. On some machines, the three digit code is actually four digits, but the first digit is always a zero. From this point on, the PCI machines behave in a similar way to the MCA-based machines.

3.2.4 Boot stage three

Boot stage three is common across all platforms and commences at the point when the initial RAM image of AIX is loaded from the boot device. From this point, the /sbin/rc.boot program controls the boot process and all LED codes displayed are generated by AIX. AIX generates codes in the range from 300 to 999 and cxx. Some machine types will place a leading zero to give 0300 to 0999 and 0cxx.

AIX start to login prompt LEDs 300-999

This is generally the longest part of any boot sequence. It is the part where all of the disks are started, tested, and then configured. While this is happening, 570 or 80c will be displayed on the LED panel, interspersed with 538, which indicates that a configuration method is being run. During the whole of the boot sequence, no LED should be displayed for longer than five minutes. However, if you have a large disk configuration or a complex TCP/IP setup, you may see 570, 80c, or 581 displayed for longer than the five minute period. In the case of the 570 and 80c codes, the LED panel is actually alternating between the two numbers very quickly. You may not see them change.

Important LEDs to look out for in this sequence are as follow:

551 This is an indication that all devices in the machine are configured correctly and the machine is ready to varyon the root volume group.

517, 553 Once these two LEDs have been displayed, any problem experienced after this point is more than likely going to be AIX-related as opposed to hardware-related.

581 TCP/IP configuration is taking place. If this number stays on the LED panel for a very long time, you should perhaps look at your TCP/IP settings and routing information once you are able to login to the system. See Section 7.3.2, "LED 581 hang" on page 219 for more information.

c31 This code indicates the system is awaiting input from you on the keyboard. This is usually encountered when booting from a CD-ROM or mksysb tape. This is normally the dialogue to select the system console.

c32, c33 These codes tell you that the boot process is nearly complete. Shortly afterwards, you should see output on the panel from the AIX boot process starting various software subsystems.

3.3 Boot problem determination

Boot problems fall into a number of categories:

- Power on or start up problems
- Failure to find a boot image
- A hang somewhere in the boot process
- Machine gets some or all of the way up and cannot be used or contacted

3.3.1 Failure to locate a boot image

As described earlier in this chapter, the boot list held in the NVRAM stores the list of the locations where the machine will look for a boot image. In some situations, the boot list can be become corrupted, be erased, or list non-existent devices.

Erasure of the boot list is the most usual reason for machines not being able to locate a boot image. Other reasons for the machine not actually finding a boot image are:

- Hardware problem on the boot device or on the SCSI bus to which the boot device is connected. See Section 5.7, "Diagnosis of SCSI problems" on page 142 for more information.
- Devices listed in the boot list are either non-existent or do not contain a valid boot image.

The recovery procedure depends upon the reason for the failure. The first thing to establish is where the boot list tells the machine to look for a boot image. Once you have established what is in the boot list, then you can add to it or correct it as appropriate.

Access boot list on PCI machine

To access the boot list on PCI machines, use the following procedure:

1. Bring the machine up to SMS. (See Section 5.4, "System Management Services (SMS)" on page 139 for details.)
2. Select Multiboot (option 6).
3. Select Boot Devices (option 4).
4. Select Display current settings (option 1).

   If the current settings show a device that you know to be present and in the position that you know it should be, run diagnostics from the CD-ROM against that device. If the diagnostics run clean, the boot image on the disk may be corrupted. To fix this problem, refer to Section 3.5, "Accessing rootvg from bootable media" on page 57. Once you have accessed rootvg, you need to create a new boot image with the **bosboot** command.

   If the current settings show no devices, return to the Select Boot Devices menu. Select Configure first boot device (option 3). You will now see a list of all SCSI devices and network adapters. Choose from the list and enter the number of the device that you want to boot from and press Enter. The panel will now display the current boot list. If you wish to add additional devices, repeat the process.

   Once you have devices listed in the boot list, exit from SMS and continue the boot process.

Access boot list on MCA machine

To access the boot list on MCA machines, perform the following steps:

1. Turn the key to Service and boot from the CD-ROM or diagnostics diskette. See Section 5.3.3, "Stand-alone diagnostics" on page 131 for more details.
2. Select Task Selection from the Diagnostics panel
3. Select the Display or Change Bootlist entry.
4. Use the menus to view and change both the Normal and Service mode boot lists. Be aware when the boot list is viewed from the CD-ROM or diskettes, the hdisk (x) entry may have a comment such as `Not Available Device`. You need not worry about this, as it is a by-product of booting from the CD-ROM. Use the generic entries to construct the boot list to get the machine to boot successfully. It will be possible, once AIX is running, to reconfigure the boot list using AIX logical device resource names.

Note: Take care when deciding if the boot disk is present or not. Do not decide solely by hdisk numbers. hdisk numbering when booting from the CD-ROM is governed by the configuration manager walking the bus. When AIX is running on the machine in question, the numbering is governed by how and when disks were added to the system and the ODM entries available at that time. The disk you want may have a totally different number from the one you are expecting.

3.3.2 Codes displayed longer than five minutes

Trying to decide if a LED code is in a hung state is difficult. The generally accepted convention is that a constant display of five minutes duration or longer is liable to indicate a stalled boot process. To be on the safe side if a code is displayed longer than five minutes, then it is normally better to be absolutely sure there is not a problem before you start to turn the machine off or attempt other remedial actions.

If you are working on a 7017-S70 or later system, then an error condition is indicated by the attention light being permanently illuminated as well as the eight digit code being displayed. However, the attention light may not be turned on when the S70 or later system stops on a code beginning with Exxx, Fxxx, or 0xxx.

There are a number of reasons why a progress LED will hang after AIX has started to load. The most common cause is that a device that is being configured is defective and so the boot process is unable to proceed. At this point, take note of the LED details and then make a Service Request Number (SRN) by adding a 101- to the code. For example, 570 displayed in the LED will give a SRN 101-570. Go to the Diagnostic Information or Service Guide for your machine type either `Micro Channel Systems` or `Multiple Bus Systems`, look up the SRN, and it will give you the Failing Function Code (FFC). This FFC can be used to reference the part number of the part or parts causing the problem.

If the error code is not an AIX system code (300-999 or 0300-0999), the machine is still performing either the BIST or POST phase of the boot. It is easy to decide which phase the machine is in on a MCA machine, because the LED numbering is very specific. On PCI machines, the firmware is less specific and does not differentiate between BIST and POST. Sometimes, if you look at the error description in the service manual, you can make an educated guess about whether the machine is in the BIST or POST phase of the boot process. If the machine is in the BIST part of the boot process, see Section 3.4, “Minimum configuration” on page 55 for information on how to proceed.

Machine hang shortly after power on

The condition here is that the machine is powered on and either almost immediately produces a LED hang condition or the machine is powered on and the LED display cycles through a number of checkpoints but hangs prior to the point that SMS can be accessed or LED codes 252, 243, or 233 are seen on MCA machines. Due to the limited intelligence on the machine at this point, the best method to diagnose the problem is to bring the machine down to minimum configuration. See Section 3.4, "Minimum configuration" on page 55 for details of the minimum configuration process.

Machine attempts to boot

Try and determine whether the machine is trying to find a boot image, often signified by alternating 223 and 229 on an MCA machine. The codes E1F7, E1FB, E105, or E174 may be displayed on PCI CHRP machines. RS/6000 7024-E20, 7024-E30, 7043-140, and 7043-240 may display FCE, FD2, or FDO. If the machine is failing to boot from disk, restart the machine and attempt a boot from a Diagnostic CD-ROM (explained in Section 5.3.3, "Stand-alone diagnostics" on page 131) or an AIX CD-ROM at the same AIX version as loaded on the machine you are working on, or a mksysb image (explained in Section 3.5, "Accessing rootvg from bootable media" on page 57). If the machine can boot to diagnostics, look at the diagnostic list and see if all of the disks that should be present on the system are detected. If the disk that should contain the boot image (logical volume hd5) is not seen, you need to investigate further.

3.3.3 LED code 269 on SMP machines

The 269 Non Bootable message can be displayed both on the ASCII console and the LED panel of the system unit. This message is displayed when the machine cannot find a valid boot image. This situation will often occur after the machine has had work carried out on it that involved splitting the CPU complex from the rest of the machine for a repair or changes to the machine CPUs or memory. This action will cause the boot list held in the NVRAM to be erased.

Recovery

To recover from the 269 message, perform the following actions:

1. Power the machine off.
2. Set the machine into Service mode.
3. Type **sbb** when the > prompt is displayed on the ASCII console.
4. Set the following flags to the values shown:
   - Bump Console present set to `enabled`.
   - Auto service IPL set to `disabled`.

– Fast IPL set to `enabled`.

5. Power on the machine.

   You will see all of the tests being run to the CPU and memory. The adapters will be polled and the corresponding LED number will be displayed on the ASCII panel and on the LCD panel. You should see at least one 292 displayed. This indicates that a SCSI adapter has been initialized. You will eventually be presented by a menu, headed Maintenance Menu (Rev. xx).

6. Select SYSTEM BOOT (option 6).

7. Select BOOT FROM SCSI DEVICE (option 2).

   What you select now depends upon the model of machine. However, what you are attempting to achieve is to get the machine to boot from a particular SCSI device by specifying the SCSI adapter and SCSI ID of the device.

8. Select CHANGE SLOT (option 1). Enter the number of the slot that contains the SCSI adapter that the boot disk is connected to.

9. Select CHANGE SCSI ID (option 2). Enter the address of the device that you know to contain the boot image. If you do not know the address, pick any address. If you do not pick the correct ID the first time, this process will eventually drop you back to the Maintenance menu when 269 is displayed. At this point, you will be able to repeat the process using different values.

10. Select BOOT FROM SELECTED DEVICE (option 5).

    The machine will now attempt to find a boot image on the device you have selected.

    If you get LED 269 again, go to step 12.

    If the machine boots into diagnostic mode, and the source of the diagnostic mode is the AIX system on the boot disk, you can then use the AIX Prompt selection in the diagnostics Task Selection menu to log on as root. Once you have logged on, you can reconstruct the boot list using the following command:

    ```
    # bootlist -m normal hdisk#
    ```

    Where hdisk# is the hdisk number of the disk containing the boot logical volume hd5. This will set the Normal mode boot list. Use the following command to set the Service mode boot list:

    ```
    # bootlist -m service rmt# cd# hdisk#
    ```

11. Turn the key to the Normal position and reboot the machine. This is the end of the procedure.

12. You have arrived at this point because the disk that you have selected either did not contain the boot image hd5 or it did contain an image but this image was corrupted in some way. If you are positive that you picked the disk

containing hd5, return to step 5 and in the selections pick the address of the CD-ROM device and use the Diagnostic CD-ROM or AIX install CD-ROM to boot from. Once the machine has booted successfully, continue to step 13. If you were not sure you picked the correct disk, go to Step 5 and use the address of another disk. Continue this method until you get the machine to boot.

13. If you get the machine to boot from the Diagnostics CD-ROM, test all disks. You can also use the Diagnostics Task Selection to check the boot list. However, since you have used the CD-ROM, you will get a message saying some devices are not available. If you chose to erase the Normal or Service mode boot lists, you will only be able to select the Generic options. These selections cause all devices to be started and the machine searches all of them for a bootable image.

    If you got the machine to boot from an AIX CD-ROM, go to Section 3.5, “Accessing rootvg from bootable media” on page 57. Return to this point once you have a root # prompt. At this point, locate the disk containing hd5 by using the following command:

    ```
    # lspv
    ```

    This displays information detailing the volume group each disk belongs to. For each disk that is part of rootvg, run the following command:

    ```
    # lspv -l hdisk#
    ```

    Where hdiskX is one of the disks in rootvg. Look for hd5 in the output. The disk containing hd5 will be the boot disk.

    Use the following command sequence to set the NVRAM boot list and create a new boot image on the boot disk:

    ```
    # bootlist -m normal hdisk#
    # bosboot -d /dev/hdisk# -a
    # savebase -d /dev/hdisk#
    ```

    The **savebase** command saves the boot customization details to be used on the next boot.

    Reboot the machine after turning the key to the *Normal* position.

3.3.4 LED 549 hang

This LED hang is not listed in the system Common Diagnostic Information books, *RS/6000 Diagnostics Information for Micro Channel Bus Systems*, SA38-0532 or *RS/6000 and pSeries Diagnostics Informationfor Multiple Bus Systems*, SA38-0509. It occurs when the machine has a system dump to be copied off, but because the graphics adapter has not been configured or cannot be configured at this time, it cannot inform you via the panel.

Recovery

Complete the following recovery steps:

1. Power off the machine.
2. Obtain an ASCII terminal or a laptop with a terminal emulator. Set the speed of the screen to 9600 baud, 8 bit, no parity, and 1 stop bit. Set the screen to emulate a vt100 terminal.
3. Connect the ASCII terminal to the S1 serial port on the machine using a RS232 terminal cable.
4. Power on the machine.
5. You will eventually see a message on the screen informing you that a dump is on the paging space. The system is prompting for a device to copy the system dump information.
6. If you have a tape, copy it off and send it to your normal AIX support personnel. If you do not have a tape drive on the machine, you will have to discard this dump by continuing the boot process.
7. When you get the login prompt, use SMIT to configure another dump device on your machine. See Chapter 4, "System dumps" on page 69 for more information.

3.4 Minimum configuration

Removing components from a machine to bring it down to minimum configuration is the best way to diagnose problems when there is not enough intelligence on the machine to enable the diagnostics or firmware to accurately indicate the failing part. The principle behind this method is that every machine has a minimum number of parts that will display a predetermined stable LED code. The code that is displayed is a positive identification that the parts left in the machine are working correctly and have been tested as good by the firmware.

The Installation and Service Guide for each machine will have a specific MAP for this procedure. Every one of the guides assign the same number to the MAP title. The MAP you need to find is MAP1540 (Minimum Configuration MAP). If you are in a situation where you do not have this MAP available, the following directions may be used, but be aware that since you do not have the documentation, you may make incorrect assumptions. If you have the Installation and Service Guide for your machine, it is *essential* that you refer to MAP1540 to ensure you correctly follow the minimum configuration procedure.

Note: Power cables must be removed from the machine prior to any removal or insertion of CPUs, memory, or adapters. Components within the machine are susceptible to static electricity damage, so take electrostatic discharge (ESD) precautions. Failure to observe these rules will result in severe damage to the machine. This procedure should only be attempted by authorized service personnel.

Before proceeding with the minimum configuration procedure, you should check any maintenance contract covering the machine. In many cases, opening of the machine by the customer may void the service contract.

A typical minimum configuration setup consists of:

- Minimum supported number of CPUs. Check that you leave the remaining CPUs in the correct slot that the system expects.
- Minimum amount of memory. Check the memory configuration rules for the machine you are working on. It varies greatly between machine types. In some MCA machines, the minimum configuration for the MAP1540 is just the memory base card or card pair with no SIMMs or DIMMs plugged into them. The 7025-F50 and 7026-H50 minimum is one memory base card with one pair of DIMMs in the first bank position. See MAP1540 for other machine types.
- System planar with no adapters in place except the graphics adapter, assuming the graphics adapter is used for the console screen.
- No cables attached externally except keyboard, mouse, graphics screen, (assuming graphics screen is used for console) or tty terminal cable.
- Base power supply.
- All internal SCSI cables, diskette cables, and DC power cables to internal media, including disks and active backplanes, are disconnected.

When you plug in the power and press the Power button, you should get the check code described in the minimum configuration MAP. If you do not have the service guide for the machine, then the only test that can be applied is whether the code displayed is a different error code to the one you started with.

If you do not get the expected code from the MAP1540, or you get the same code as you started with, you now have to order and change singularly each of the components in the machine at minimum configuration until you get the expected code. If you do not have the MAP1540, your best indication that you may have found the failing part is when the code displayed changes from the one you started with.

If, at minimum configuration, you get the code indicated in MAP1540, one of the components that you removed is defective. Add each component singularly until you reproduce the problem. The last part you added is probably the defective item and should be replaced. Quite often you will find that you will refit all of the original parts and not reproduce the fault again. This can be due to either bad seating of a component or a bad connection.

3.5 Accessing rootvg from bootable media

If you used either an AIX CD-ROM or a mksysb image to boot the system, perform the following actions:

1. Select Start Maintenance Mode for System Recovery (option 3).
2. Select Access a Root Volume group (option 1).
3. Select 0 to Continue.

You will now be presented with a list of volume group information. Look through the list of disks configured and decide, from what you know about the system, which is the root volume group. Enter the selection corresponding to the volume group you wish to select. The next screen will list all of the logical volumes within that volume group. If hd5 is listed, carry on with the next step. However, if hd5 is not listed in the logical volumes of the selected volume group, select option 99 to return to the previous menu and select another listed volume group. If you have correctly chosen rootvg, select Access this Volume group and start a shell (option 1). You are now attempting to find all disks in rootvg and mount them on to the RAM image you have just loaded. Carefully look at the messages produced, as they are your best clue as to the sort of problem you are dealing with.

If you finally get a message indicating that the operation failed, you need to run diagnostics from a CD-ROM to test the disk and also certify it. From the tests of the diagnostics, you can decide if the disk is defective or it has, for some reason, been so badly corrupted that AIX is not capable of being started by any means.

However, if the messages produced indicates that rootvg has been varied on successfully, but the system fails to mount the file systems, refer to the procedure documented in Section 3.6.1, “LED 551, 555, or 557 halt” on page 58 to correct the file systems.

At this stage, it is also possible to access the contents of the Boot alog to see what occurred during the boot process. Use the **smit alog** fast path or:

```
# alog -t boot -o
```

3.6 LED 551, 552, 554, 555, 556, and 557 halts

If the machine stops on any of these LEDs, the first phase of the boot that tests the hardware has completed successfully. It is generally accepted, therefore, that these LED halts are related to problems with AIX. In a small minority of cases, the final resolution will be the replacement of a piece of hardware. To assist in your diagnosis, the following sections contain information that will help you fix the most common causes of the halt.

3.6.1 LED 551, 555, or 557 halt

This section describes the causes for LED 551, 555, or 557 during IPL on a RS/6000. Also outlined is a recovery procedure.

The known causes of an LED 551, 555, or 557 during IPL on an RS/6000 are:

- A corrupted file system
- A corrupted journaled file system (JFS or JFS2) log device
- A failing fsck (file system check) caused by a bad file system helper
- A bad disk in the machine that is a member of the rootvg

To diagnose and fix the problem, boot from bootable media, run **logform** on /dev/hd8, and run **fsck** to fix any file systems that may be corrupted. Follow these steps:

> **Note:** Do not use this procedure if the system is a /usr client, diskless client, or dataless client.

1. Turn the key to the Service position (MCA machines), then power on. On PCI machines, power on and press F5 or 5 when the Icon screen appears. This will start the Service mode boot from CD-ROM or mksysb.
2. Using bootable media at the same version and level as the system, boot the system. The bootable media can be any one of the following:
   - Bootable CD-ROM
   - NON_AUTOINSTALL mksysb
   - Bootable install tape
3. Follow the screen prompts to the following menu:

   ```
   Welcome to Base Operating System
   Installation and Maintenance
   ```

   Choose Start Maintenance Mode for System Recovery (option 3).

The next screen has the maintenance menu.

Choose Access a Root Volume Group (option 1).

The next screen displays a warning that indicates you will not be able to return to the Base OS menu without rebooting.

Choose 0 to continue.

At this stage, the console will display information about all the volume groups on the system. rootvg will usually be the top one in the list. Choose 1 and the console will display the logical volumes contained within the chosen volume group. If it does not appear to be rootvg, take the option to return and choose another volume group. When rootvg has been found, choose Access this volume group and start a shell before mounting the file systems (option 2).

If you get errors indicating that a physical volume is missing from the rootvg, run diagnostics on the physical volumes to find out if you have a bad disk. Do not continue with the rest of the steps in this process.

If you get other errors from the above option, do not continue with the rest of the steps in this process. Correct the problem causing the error. If you need assistance correcting the problem, contact your AIX support personnel.

4. Format the default jfslog for the rootvg JFS file systems with the command:

   ```
   # /usr/sbin/logform /dev/hd8
   ```

   Answer yes when asked if you want to destroy the log.

5. Next, run the following commands to check and repair file systems. The -y option gives the **fsck** command permission to repair file systems when necessary:

   ```
   # fsck -y /dev/hd1
   # fsck -y /dev/hd2
   # fsck -y /dev/hd3
   # fsck -y /dev/hd4
   # fsck -y /dev/hd9var
   ```

   Type **exit**. The file systems will automatically mount after you type exit.

6. If you are running the Andrew File System (AFS), use the following commands to find out whether you have more than one version of the v3fshelper file (otherwise, skip to step 8):

   ```
   # cd /sbin/helpers
   # ls -l v3fshelper*
   ```

   If you have only one version of the v3fshelper file (for example, v3fshelper), proceed to step 8.

7. If there is a version of v3fshelper marked as original (for example, v3fshelper.orig), run the following commands:

```
# copy v3fshelper v3fshelper.afs
# copy v3fshelper.orig v3fshelper
```

8. Determine which disk is the boot disk with the **lslv** command. The boot disk will be shown in the PV1 column of the lslv output.

```
# lslv -m hd5
```

> **Note:** Do not proceed further if the system is a /usr client, diskless client, or dataless client.

9. Recreate the boot image and alter the boot list (hdisk# is the boot disk determined in step 8):

```
# bosboot -a -d /dev/hdisk#
# bootlist -m normal hdisk#
```

10. If you copied the v3fshelper file in step 7, copy AFS file system helper back to v3fshelper:

```
# copy v3fshelper.afs v3fshelper
```

11. With the key in Normal position (MCA machine), run the following command:

```
# shutdown -Fr
```

If you followed all of the preceding steps, and the system still stops at LED 551, 555, or 557 during a reboot in Normal mode, you may want to ask for further system recovery assistance from your AIX support personnel.

For reasons of time, and for the integrity of your AIX operating system, the best alternative at this point may be to reinstall AIX.

3.6.2 LED 552, 554, or 556 halt

This section discusses the known causes of LED 552, 554, and 556, including a procedure for recovery from these errors.

An LED code of 552, 554, or 556 during a standard disk based boot indicates a failure occurred during the varyon of the rootvg volume group.

The known causes of an LED 552, 554, or 556 halt are as follow:

- A corrupted file system
- A corrupted Journaled File System (JFS) log device
- A bad IPL-device record or bad IPL-device magic number (The magic number indicates the device type.)

- A corrupted copy of the Object Data Manager (ODM) database on the boot logical volume
- A hard disk in the inactive state in the root volume group

To diagnose and fix the problem, you will need to boot from bootable media and run the **fsck** command on each file system. If the file system check fails, you may need to perform other steps.

> **Note:** Do not use this procedure if the system is a /usr client, diskless client, or dataless client.

To recover from an LED 552, 554, or 557, complete the following steps:

1. Turn the key to the Service position (MCA machines) then power on. On PCI machines, power on, press F5 or 5 when the Icon screen appears. This will start the Service mode boot from CD-ROM or mksysb.
2. Using bootable media at the same version and level as the system, boot the system. The bootable media can be any one of the following:
   - A bootable CD-ROM
   - mksysb
   - A bootable install tape

   Follow the prompts to the Welcome to Base OS menu.
3. Choose Start Maintenance Mode for System Recovery (option 3). The next screen displays prompts for the Maintenance menu.

   Choose Access a Root Volume Group (option 1).

   At this stage, the console will display information about all the volume groups on the system. rootvg will usually be the top one in the list. Choose 1 and the console will display the logical volumes contained within the chosen volume group. If it does not appear to be rootvg, take the option to return and choose another volume group. When rootvg has been found, choose Access this volume group and start a shell before mounting the file systems (option 2).

   If you get errors from the preceding option, such as missing hard disk messages, do not continue with the rest of this procedure. Correct the problem causing the error. If you need assistance correcting the problem causing the error, contact your AIX support personnel.
4. Run the following commands to check and repair file systems. The -y option gives the **fsck** command permission to repair file systems when necessary.

   ```
   # fsck -y /dev/hd1
   # fsck -y /dev/hd2
   # fsck -y /dev/hd3
   ```

```
# fsck -y /dev/hd4
# fsck -y /dev/hd9var
```

If any of the following conditions occur, proceed accordingly.

If **fsck** indicates that block 8 could not be read, the file system is probably unrecoverable. If **fsck** indicates that block 8 could be read, but one of the following errors is given:

```
fsck: Not an AIX V3 file system.
fsck: Not a recognized file system type.
```

Then go to next step.

If **fsck** indicates that a file system has an unknown log record type, or if **fsck** fails in the logredo process, then go to step 6.

If the file system checks were successful, skip to step 8.

The easiest way to fix an unrecoverable file system is to recreate it. This involves deleting it from the system and restoring it from a backup. Note that hd2 and hd3 can be recreated but hd4 cannot be recreated. If hd4 is unrecoverable, you must reinstall AIX. For assistance with unrecoverable file systems, contact your AIX support personnel.

Do *not* follow the rest of the steps in this procedure.

Attempt to repair the file system with this command:

```
# fsck -p /dev/hd#
```

Replace hd# with the appropriate file system logical volume name.

Now skip to step 7.

5. A corruption of the JFS log logical volume has been detected. Use the **logform** command to reformat it:

   ```
   # /usr/sbin/logform /dev/hd8
   ```

   Answer yes when asked if you want to destroy the log.

6. Repeat step 4 for all file systems that did not successfully complete **fsck** the first time.

   If step 4 fails a second time, the file system is almost always unrecoverable. In most cases, step 4 will be successful. If step 4 is successful, continue to step 8.

7. With the key in the Normal position, run the following commands to reboot the system:

   ```
   # exit
   # sync;sync;sync
   # shutdown -Fr
   ```

As you reboot in Normal mode, notice how many times LED 551 appears. If LED 551 appears twice, **fsck** is probably failing because of a bad fshelper file. If this is the case, and you are running AFS, see step 11.

The majority of instances of LED 552, 554, and 556 will be resolved at this point. If you still have an LED 552, 554, or 556, repeat step 1 through step 3.

8. Run the following commands that remove much of the system's configuration and save it to a backup directory:

```
# mount /dev/hd4 /mnt
# mount /dev/hd2 /usr
# mkdir /mnt/etc/objrepos/bak
# cp /mnt/etc/objrepos/Cu* /mnt/etc/objrepos/bak
# cp /etc/objrepos/Cu* /mnt/etc/objrepos
# /etc/umount all
# exit
```

9. Determine which disk is the boot disk with the **lslv** command. The boot disk will be shown in the PV1 column of the lslv output.

```
# lslv -m hd5
```

10. Save the clean ODM database to the boot logical volume. (# is the number of the fixed disk, determined with the previous command.)

```
# savebase -d /dev/hdisk#
```

If you are running AFS, go to step 11; otherwise, go to step 12.

11. If you are running the Andrew File System (AFS), use the following commands to find out whether you have more than one version of the v3fshelper file:

```
# cd /sbin/helpers
# ls -l v3fshelper*
```

If you have only one version of the v3fshelper file (for example, v3fshelper), proceed to step 12.

If there is a version of v3fshelper marked as original (for example, v3fshelper.orig), run the following commands:

```
# cp v3fshelper v3fshelper.afs
# cp v3fshelper.orig v3fshelper
```

Note: Do not proceed further if the system is a /usr client, diskless client, or dataless client.

Recreate the boot image (hdisk# is the fixed disk determined in step 10):

```
# bosboot -a -d /dev/hdisk#
```

12. If you copied files in the previous step, copy the AFS file system helper back to v3fshelper:

```
# cp v3fshelper.afs v3fshelper
```

Turn the key to Normal position and run the following command:

```
# shutdown -Fr
```

If you followed all of the preceding steps, and the system still stops at an LED 552, 554, or 556 during a reboot in Normal mode, you may want to ask for further system recovery assistance from your AIX support personnel.

For reasons of time, and the for integrity of your AIX operating system, the best alternative at this point may be to reinstall AIX.

3.6.3 LED 553 halt

This section sets out a procedure to recover from an LED 553 and applies to AIX Version 4 and AIX 5L Version 5.1.

An LED 553 occurs during IPL on a RS/6000 if the system cannot read or run the /etc/inittab file.

To recover from an LED 553, check /dev/hd3 and /dev/hd4 for space problems and erase files, if necessary. Check the /etc/inittab file for corruption and fix it, if necessary. If the inittab file was not corrupted, you will need to check the shell profiles, the /bin/bsh file, and some other files:

1. Turn the key to the Service position (MCA machines), then power on. On PCI machines, power on and press F5 or 5 when the Icon screen appears. This will start the Service mode boot from CD-ROM or mksysb.
2. With bootable media of the same version and level as the system, boot the system. The bootable media can be any one of the following:
   - A bootable CD-ROM or DVD
   - mksysb
   - A bootable install tape

   Follow the prompts to the Welcome to Base OS menu.
3. Choose Start Maintenance Mode for System Recovery (option 3). The next screen contains prompts for the Maintenance menu.

- Choose Access a Root Volume Group (option 1). At this stage, the console displays a warning that indicates you will not be able to return to the Base OS menu without rebooting. Choose 0 and press Enter.

- At this stage, the console will display information about all the volume groups on the system. rootvg will usually be the top one in the list. Choose 1 and the console will display the logical volumes contained within the chosen volume group. If it does not appear to be rootvg, take the option to return and choose another volume group. When rootvg has been found, choose Access this volume group and start a shell before mounting file systems (option 2).

  If you get errors from the preceding option, do not continue with the rest of this procedure. Correct the problem causing the error. If you need assistance to correct the problem causing the error, contact your AIX support personnel.

4. Use the **df** command to check for free space in /dev/hd3 and /dev/hd4:

   ```
   # df /dev/hd3
   # df /dev/hd4
   ```

   If **df** shows that either file system is out of space, erase some files from that file system. Three files you may want to erase are /smit.log, /smit.script, and /.sh_history.

5. Check the /etc/inittab file for corruption. It may be empty or missing, or it may have an incorrect entry. For comparison, see the sample inittab file shown in Example 3-1 on page 66. Set your terminal type in preparation for editing the file by setting the TERM environment variable. For example:

   ```
   # TERM=xxx
   # export TERM
   ```

   Where xxx stands for a terminal type, such as lft, ibm3151, or vt100.

   Now, use an editor to create the /etc/inittab file. It may be possible for you to correct a corrupt inittab. If the file is missing, or it is not possible to repair the corruption, it is simpler to create a new file. If your /etc/inittab file was corrupt, and you recreated it, you may not need to perform any of the following steps.

6. Use the following command to check for any modifications or problems with permission:

   ```
   # ls -al /.profile /etc/environment /etc/profile
   ```

   Here is an example output:

   ```
   -rw-r--r--   1 root  system  158 Dec 14 2001 /.profile
   -rw-rw-r--   1 root  system 1389 Oct 26 2001 /etc/environment
   -rw-r--r--   1 root  system 1214 Jan 22 2001 /etc/profile
   ```

7. /etc/profile or .profile may contain a command that is valid only in the Korn shell. Change the command to something that is also valid in the Bourne shell. For example, change the following:

   ```
   export PATH=/bin:/usr/bin/:/etc:/usr/ucb:.
   ```

   to the following:

   ```
   PATH=/bin:/usr/bin/:/etc:/usr/ucb:.
   ```

```
export PATH
```

8. /etc/environment is a special case. The only commands it may contain are simple variable assignments, such as statements of the form var=value. Check this file with an editor to verify the format.
9. Check for missing or moved files with the following command:

```
# ls -al /bin /bin/bsh /bin/sh /lib /u /unix
```

Here is an example output:

```
lrwxrwxrwx 1 root sys       8 Aug 5 2001 /bin -> /usr/bin
-r-xr-xr-x 3 bin  bin 256224 Jun 4 2001 /bin/bsh
-r-xr-xr-x 3 bin  bin 256224 Jun 4 2001 /bin/sh
lrwxrwxrwx 1 root sys       8 Aug 5 2001 /lib -> /usr/lib
lrwxrwxrwx 1 root sys       5 Aug 5 2001 /u -> /home
lrwxrwxrwx 1 root sys      18 Aug 5 2001 /unix -> /usr/lib/boot/unix
```

If any of these files are missing, the problem may be a missing symbolic link. Use the commands from the following list that correspond to the missing links:

```
# ln -s /usr/bin /bin
# ln -s /usr/lib/boot/unix /unix
# ln -s /usr/lib /lib
# ln -s /home /u
```

10. Use the following command to make sure that fsck and rc.boot are not missing or corrupt:

```
# ls -l /etc/fsck /sbin/rc.boot
```

Example output:

```
lrwxrwxrwx 1 root system    14 Aug  5 2001 /etc/fsck -> /usr/sbin/fsck
-rwxrwxr-- 1 root system 33760 Aug 30 2001
```

11. Make sure the /etc/inittab file is for AIX V4 or AIX 5L V5.1. For both versions, the line that begins with brc is:

```
brc::sysinit:/sbin/rc.boot 3 >/dev/console 2>&1
```

See Example 3-1 for a sample of the /etc/inittab file.

Example 3-1 Sample /etc/inittab file

```
init:2:initdefault:
brc::sysinit:/sbin/rc.boot 3 >/dev/console 2>&1 # Phase 3 of system boot
powerfail::powerfail:/etc/rc.powerfail 2>&1 | alog -tboot > /dev/console #
Power Failure Detection
load64bit:2:wait:/etc/methods/cfg64 >/dev/console 2>&1 # Enable 64-bit execs
rc:23456789:wait:/etc/rc 2>&1 | alog -tboot > /dev/console # Multi-User checks
fbcheck:23456789:wait:/usr/sbin/fbcheck 2>&1 | alog -tboot > /dev/console # run
/etc/firstboot
srcmstr:23456789:respawn:/usr/sbin/srcmstr # System Resource Controller
rctcpip:23456789:wait:/etc/rc.tcpip > /dev/console 2>&1 # Start TCP/IP daemons
```

```
rcnfs:23456789:wait:/etc/rc.nfs > /dev/console 2>&1 # Start NFS Daemons
cron:23456789:respawn:/usr/sbin/cron
piobe:2:wait:/usr/lib/lpd/pio/etc/pioinit >/dev/null 2>&1  # pb cleanup
qdaemon:23456789:wait:/usr/bin/startsrc -sqdaemon
writesrv:23456789:wait:/usr/bin/startsrc -swritesrv
uprintfd:23456789:respawn:/usr/sbin/uprintfd
shdaemon:2:off:/usr/sbin/shdaemon >/dev/console 2>&1 # High availability daemon
l2:2:wait:/etc/rc.d/rc 2
l3:3:wait:/etc/rc.d/rc 3
l4:4:wait:/etc/rc.d/rc 4
l5:5:wait:/etc/rc.d/rc 5
l6:6:wait:/etc/rc.d/rc 6
l7:7:wait:/etc/rc.d/rc 7
l8:8:wait:/etc/rc.d/rc 8
l9:9:wait:/etc/rc.d/rc 9
logsymp:2:once:/usr/lib/ras/logsymptom # for system dumps
pmd:2:wait:/usr/bin/pmd > /dev/console 2>&1 # Start PM daemon
itess:23456789:once:/usr/IMNSearch/bin/itess -start search >/dev/null 2>&1
diagd:2:once:/usr/lpp/diagnostics/bin/diagd >/dev/console 2>&1
ctrmc:2:once:/usr/bin/startsrc -s ctrmc > /dev/console 2>&1
```

12. If you have not found any obvious problems, try substituting ksh for bsh with the following commands (the first command saves your bsh before you copy over it):

    ```
    # cp /bin/bsh /bin/bsh.orig
    # cp /bin/ksh /bin/bsh
    ```

    If you can then reboot successfully, you know that one of the profiles was causing problems for bsh. Check the profiles again by running the following:

    ```
    # /bin/bsh.orig /.profile
    # /bin/bsh.orig /etc/profile
    # /bin/bsh.orig /etc/environment
    ```

    If you receive errors with any of these commands, you know there is a command in that profile that bsh cannot handle.

If you followed all of the preceding steps, and the system still stops at an LED 553 during a reboot in Normal mode, you may want to ask for further system recovery assistance from your AIX support personnel.

For reasons of time, and for the integrity of your AIX operating system, the best alternative at this point may be to reinstall AIX.

3.7 No login prompt

If the system boots, and you see output on the console but do not get a login prompt, then there are a number of things that you need to investigate.

If the console is a graphics console, refer to Section 8.6.2, "Login screen does not appear" on page 281.

If the console device is an ASCII terminal, perform the following steps:

1. Try to remotely login to the machine. If you succeed, use the **ps** command to check to see if there is a getty process running against /dev/console. For example:

   ```
   # ps ax | grep console
    10846      0 A     0:00 /usr/sbin/getty /dev/console
   ```

2. If the process is running, ensure that the console output is directed to the serial port the terminal is connected to. This can be done with the **lscons** command. For example:

   ```
   # lscons
   /dev/tty0
   ```

3. Use the **lsdev** command to determine the serial port being used for the console terminal. For example:

   ```
   # lsdev -C -l tty0
   tty0 Available 01-S1-00-00 Asynchronous Terminal
   ```

   Ensure that the terminal is connected to the serial port listed by the **lsdev** command.

   If you cannot login to the machine, then there are two possible problems. The first is that the machine has hung at the end of the boot process, which is why there is no login prompt. The second is that there is no inittab entry to start a getty process on the console. To check the second situation, boot from the AIX CD-ROM and enter the maintenance shell, as described in Section 3.6.3, "LED 553 halt" on page 64. Once you have mounted the file systems, look at the /etc/inittab file. Ensure that there is an entry in the file as follows:

   ```
   cons:0123456789:respawn:/etc/getty /dev/console
   ```

   Once you have done this, try rebooting the machine.

4

System dumps

This chapter describes system dumps and how to handle them.

4.1 Introduction

Your system generates a system dump when a severe error occurs, such as a system halt with an 888 number flashing. It can also be initiated by the system administrator when the system has hung.

The system dump is a copy of the contents of all or part of the physical memory of your system. It is obtained from memory locations used by kernel components. Actually, a system dump is a snapshot of the operating system state at the time of the crash or manually initiated dump.

The **kdb** command is used to examine a system dump. The **crash** command is used to analyze system dump files in AIX Version 4.3 and earlier. In AIX 5L Version 5.1, it has been replaced by the **kdb** command. Using **kdb**, you can examine kernel data structures. These data structures tell what state the system was in when it crashed or became hung. Please refer to Section 4.7, "The kdb command" on page 93 for more information.

4.2 Saving a system dump when system is booting

Since AIX Version 4.1, the default dump device is /dev/hd6, which is also the default paging device. If you have not added a dedicated dump device (for example, /dev/hd7), then on reboot, the system will attempt to copy the dump image from /dev/hd6 to a file (vmcore.X) in a directory in rootvg (the default is /var/adm/ras). This is because the /dev/hd6 device needs to be used as paging space when the AIX system starts. If the copy fails, usually because there is not enough space, it will prompt you to copy off the dump to a tape device or to diskettes.

> **Note:** If you do not copy the dump out of the paging space, it will be overwritten, and the dump will be lost.

The screen shown in Example 4-1 will be displayed on reboot if the default dump device is /dev/hd6 and there was not enough space to copy the dump to a directory.

Example 4-1 Save a system dump screen

```
                    Copy a System Dump to Removable Media

    The system dump is 73862656 bytes and will be copied from /dev/hd6
    to media inserted into the device from the list below.

    Please make sure that you have sufficient blank, formatted
```

```
media before you continue.

Step One:   Insert blank media into the chosen device.
Step Two:   Type the number for that device and press Enter.

        Device Type              Path Name

>>> 1  tape/scsi/8mm             /dev/rmt0
    2  diskette/siofd/fd         /dev/fd0

   88  Help?
   99  Exit -- Warning, the dump will be lost

>>> Choice[1]:
```

The dump file will be copied to tape when you select option 1.

If this step fails for some reason, such as there is no system console, or the system console has been redirected to a file, the system will hang with LED 549.

4.2.1 LED 549

If the system hangs at LED 549 when booting, you need to boot from the install media or mksysb tape. Next, go into maintenance mode and then use the **sysdumpdev** command to either ignore the dump if the copy fails or specify a different location where there is enough space to copy the dump.

If you got a login prompt without seeing the screen shown in Example 4-1 on page 70, the dump was successfully saved to the selected directory or device. You will be able to collect this dump file with the **snap** command. Refer to Section 4.5, “Collecting the dump and related information” on page 89.

4.3 Preparing for the dump

The system needs to be initially configured to capture a dump successfully. This can be done by following steps detailed in this section.

4.3.1 Estimate the size of the dump

First of all, you need to determine how large the dump device for your machine needs to be. This can be done through Web-based System Manager, SMIT, or the command line.

Option 1: Using the Web-based System Manager

Follow the step to get the estimated dump size.

1. In the command prompt, enter the following command:

```
# wsm
```

   The panel shown in Figure 4-1 will be displayed.

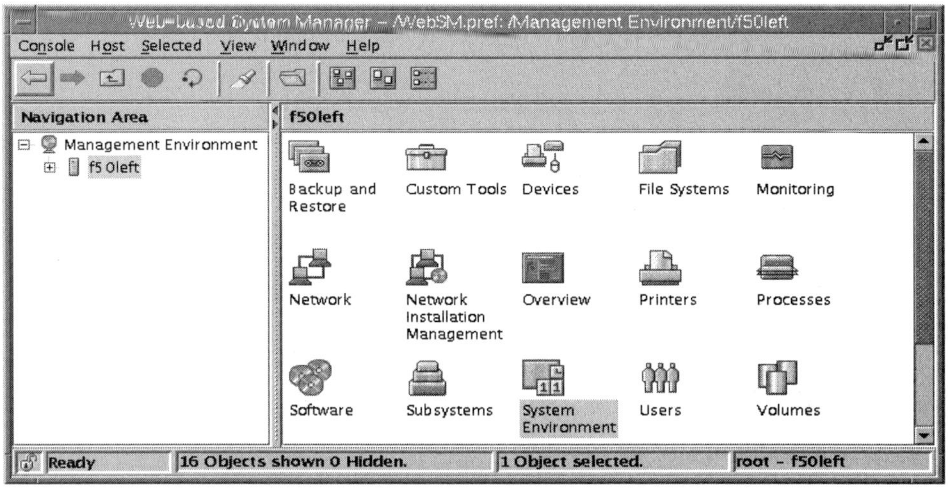

Figure 4-1 Start panel of Web-based System Manager

2. Double-click the System Environment icon in the right frame and then double-click the Settings icon. Then select the Dumps icon in the panel shown in Figure 4-2 on page 73.

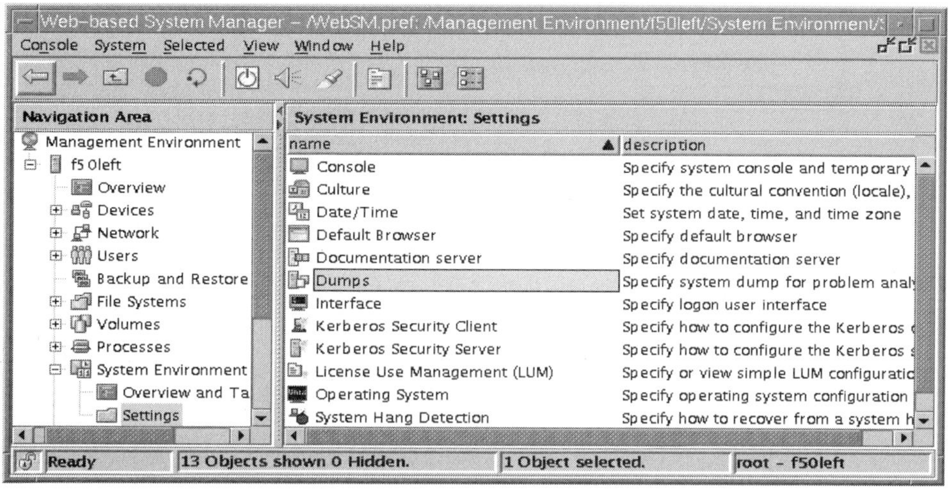

Figure 4-2 System Environment Settings panel

3. The estimated dump size will be displayed, as shown in Figure 4-3.

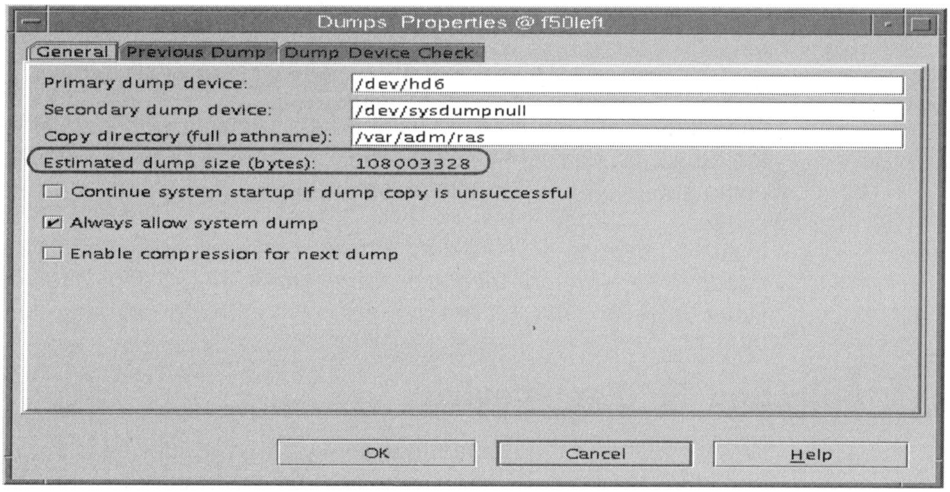

Figure 4-3 Dumps Properties panel

Option 2: Using SMIT

Follow the steps to get the estimated dump size using SMIT:

1. Select the following sequence:

   Problem Determination -> **System Dump** -> **Show Estimated Dump Size**

   or use the SMIT fast path `smitty dump_estimate`.

After selecting this sequence, the estimated dump size will be displayed. You can see the screen shown in Example 4-2.

Example 4-2 SMIT result of estimated dump size

```
                                COMMAND STATUS

Command: OK            stdout: yes           stderr: no

Before command completion, additional instructions may appear below.

0453-041 Estimated dump size in bytes: 106954752



F1=Help                F2=Refresh            F3=Cancel             F6=Command
F8=Image               F9=Shell              F10=Exit              /=Find
n=Find Next
```

Option 3: Using the command line

Run the following command:

```
# sysdumpdev -e
0453-041 Estimated dump size in bytes: 105906176
```

This value can change based on the activity of the system. It is best to run this command when the machine is under its heaviest workload. You should make the dump device slightly larger than the value reported by the **sysdumpdev** command in order to handle a system dump during peak system activity.

In AIX 5L Version 5.1, the dumpcheck facility will notify you if your dump device needs to be larger, or the file system containing the copy directory is too small. Refer to Section 4.3.4, "The dumpcheck command" on page 79.

4.3.2 Selecting the dump device

When you install the operating system, the dump device is automatically configured for you. By default, the primary dump device is /dev/hd6, which is also the default paging logical volume. In AIX 5L Version 5.1, the systems with more than 4 GB of real memory will create a dedicated dump device by default at installation time. The default name of the dump device is lg_dumplv. This dedicated dump device size is determined by the values in Table 4-1 (See Section 4.18.4, "Dedicated dump device (5.1.0)" in *AIX 5L Differences Guide*, SG24-5765 for more information).

Table 4-1 Dedicated dump device size by real memory size

Real memory size	Dedicated dump device size
4 GB to, but not including, 12 GB	1 GB
12 GB to, but not including, 24 GB	2 GB
24 GB to, but not including, 48 GB	3 GB
48 GB and up	4 GB

The secondary dump device is configured by default to be /dev/sysdumpnull. You can also select these dump devices to be disk, tape, or remote.

The secondary dump device is used to back up the primary dump device. If an error occurs during a system dump to the primary dump device, the system attempts to dump to the secondary device (if it is defined).

Bear the following rules in mind when selecting dump devices:

- A mirrored paging space may be used as a dump device.
- Do not use a diskette drive as your dump device.
- The primary paging device hd6 is the only paging device that should be used as the primary dump device. AIX Version 4.2.1 or later supports using any paging device in the root volume group (rootvg) as the secondary dump device.
- The primary dump devices must always be in the root volume group for permanent dump devices. The secondary device may be outside the root volume group unless it is a paging space.

> **Note:** AIX releases prior to Version 4.3.3 do not support dumping to a mirrored logical volume. This is because the dump bypasses the LVM mechanism and writes directly to one copy of the logical volume. In other words, only one of the mirrors will contain the dump; the other mirrors will contain whatever the logical volume had before the dump started. When **crash** tries to read the dump, it uses the normal LVM read mechanism, so it can get data from any of the mirrors, only one of which actually contains tho dump. In other words, **crash** sees good dump data mixed with garbage data and will not read the dump. This limitation is removed with AIX Version 4.3.3, which does support using a mirrored logical volume as the primary dump device.

You can verify and change the primary and secondary dump devices by using the following options.

Option 1: Using Web-based System Manager

The Dumps Properties panel shows you the information about the current dump devices. You can specify the primary and secondary dump devices on this panel. Enter the device you wish and select the OK button (See Figure 4-4).

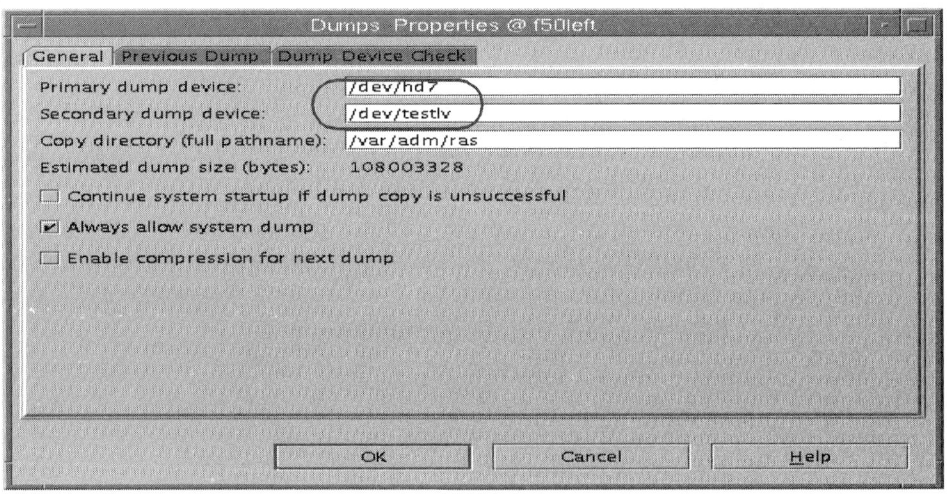

Figure 4-4 Selecting dump device on Web-based System Manager

Option 2: Using SMIT

To view information about the current dump devices, select the following sequence:

Problem Determination -> **System Dump** -> **Show Current Dump Device**

or use the SMIT fast path **smitty dump_show**.

You should get a screen similar to Example 4-3.

Example 4-3 Show Current Dump Device

```
                              COMMAND STATUS

Command: OK            stdout: yes           stderr: no

Before command completion, additional instructions may appear below.

primary               /dev/hd6
secondary             /dev/sysdumpnull
copy directory        /var/adm/ras
forced copy flag      TRUE
always allow dump     FALSE
dump compression      ON


F1=Help               F2=Refresh            F3=Cancel             F6=Command
F8=Image              F9=Shell              F10=Exit              /=Find
n=Find Next
```

To specify the primary or secondary dump device, select the following sequence:

Problem Determination -> **System Dump** -> **Change the Primary Dump Device** or **Change the Secondary Dump Device**

or use the SMIT fast path **smitty dumpchgp** or **smitty dumpchgs**.

Example 4-4 Change Primary Dump Device

```
                         Change Primary Dump Device

Type or select values in entry fields.
Press Enter AFTER making all desired changes.

                                                         [Entry Fields]
* Primary dump device                                  [/dev/hd7]



F1=Help               F2=Refresh            F3=Cancel             F4=List
F5=Reset              F6=Command            F7=Edit               F8=Image
F9=Shell              F10=Exit              Enter=Do
```

Option 3: Using the command line

To view information about the current dump devices, run the following command:

```
# sysdumpdev -l
primary              /dev/hd6
secondary            /dev/sysdumpnull
copy directory       /var/adm/ras
forced copy flag     TRUE
always allow dump    FALSE
```

In this example, the primary dump device is the logical volume hd6, and the secondary dump device is /dev/sysdumpnull, meaning that there is no secondary.

To specify the primary dump device, use the following command:

```
# sysdumpdev -P -p /dev/hd7
primary              /dev/hd7
secondary            /dev/sysdumpnull
copy directory       /var/adm/ras
forced copy flag     TRUE
always allow dump    FALSE
```

To specify the secondary dump device, use the following command:

```
# sysdumpdev -P -s /dev/hd7
primary              /dev/hd6
secondary            /dev/hd7
copy directory       /var/adm/ras
forced copy flag     TRUE
always allow dump    FALSE
```

4.3.3 Create a dump device

If you want to create a standard dump logical volume, perform the following steps:

1. Estimate the size of a dump on the system. Refer to Section 4.3.1, "Estimate the size of the dump" on page 71. Use the command:

   ```
   # sysdumpdev -e
   0453-041 Estimated dump size in bytes: 108003328
   ```

   Remember to make the dump device slightly larger than that reported by the **sysdumpdev** command to handle dumps during peak workloads.

2. Calculate the required number of PPs for the dump device.

   Get the PP size of the volume group by using the **lsvg** command. See Figure 4-5 on page 79 for details.

Example 4-5 Get the PP size

```
# lsvg rootvg
VOLUME GROUP:     rootvg                   VG IDENTIFIER:  0003219400004c00000000e
819d03f76
VG STATE:         active                   PP SIZE:        16 megabyte(s)
VG PERMISSION:    read/write               TOTAL PPs:      1352 (21632 megabytes)
MAX LVs:          256                      FREE PPs:       1091 (17456 megabytes)
LVs:              12                       USED PPs:       261 (4176 megabytes)
OPEN LVs:         10                       QUORUM:         2
TOTAL PVs:        3                        VG DESCRIPTORS: 3
STALE PVs:        0                        STALE PPs:      0
ACTIVE PVs:       3                        AUTO ON:        yes
MAX PPs per PV: 1016                       MAX PVs:        32
LTG size:         128 kilobyte(s)          AUTO SYNC:      no
HOT SPARE:        no
```

Determine the necessary number of PPs by dividing the estimated size of the dump by the PP size. For example:

```
108003328 / 16 megabytes = 6.44 (required number is 7)
```

3. Create a logical volume of the required size, for example:

```
# mklv -y hd7 -t sysdump rootvg 7
hd7
```

4.3.4 The dumpcheck command

In AIX 5L Version 5.1, the **dumpcheck** command is used to check the disk resources used by the system dump. The command logs an error if either the largest dump device is too small to receive the dump or there is insufficient space in the copy directory when the dump is to paging space.

The dumpcheck command syntax

```
/usr/lib/ras/dumpcheck [ [ -l ] [ -p ] [ -t Time ] [ -P ] ] | [ -r ]
```

By default, the **dumpcheck** command is started by a crontab entry each afternoon at 3:00 PM local time. The output of the command will be logged in the system error log. With the -p flag, you can request a dumpcheck at any time and the result is printed to stdout. The output would look similar to the following example:

```
# /usr/lib/ras/dumpcheck -p
There is not enough free space in the file system containing the copy directory
to accommodate the dump.
File system name         /var/adm/ras
Current free space in kb          15936
Current estimated dump size in kb        105472
```

The -l flag logs the command output into the system error log and is the default parameter if no other parameter is specified (See Example 4-6). With the -t flag, you can specify, with a time value in crontab format enclosed in single or double quotation marks, at what time this check will be run by the cron facility.

Example 4-6 The dumpcheck command output in error log

```
LABEL:          DMPCHK_NOSPACE
IDENTIFIER:     F89FB899

Date/Time:       Fri Aug 31 15:00:03 CDT
Sequence Number: 129
Machine Id:      000321944C00
Node Id:         f50left
Class:           0
Type:            PEND
Resource Name:   dumpcheck

Description
The copy directory is too small.

Probable Causes
There is not enough free space in the file system containing the copy directory
to accommodate the dump.

        Recommended Actions
        Increase the size of that file system.

Detail Data
File system name
/var/adm/ras

Current free space in kb
       15936
Current estimated dump size in kb
      105472
```

You can use any of the following interfaces to manage the time and options.

Option 1: Using Web-based System Manager

On the Dumps Properties panel, select the dump device check tab (see Figure 4-5 on page 81). You can change the checking time and select the destination of log output.

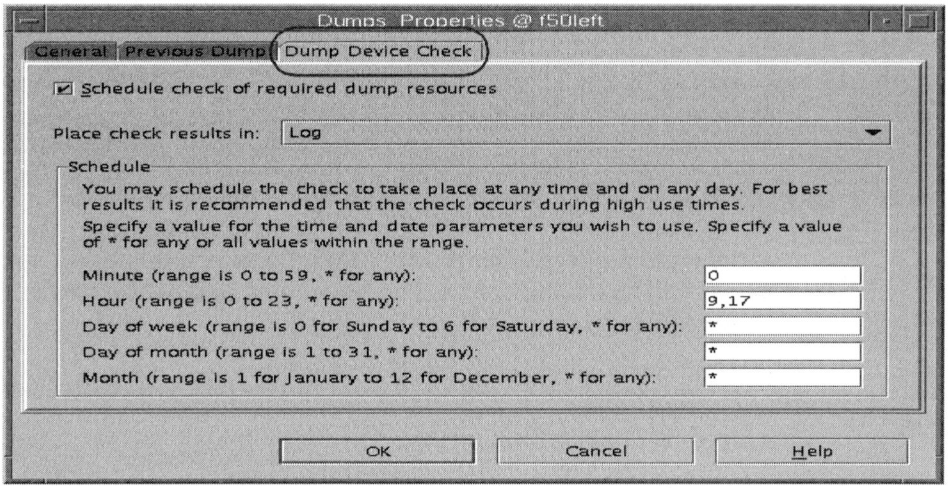

Figure 4-5 Dump Device Check panel

Option 2: Using SMIT

You can also use SMIT to manage the **dumpcheck** command by selecting the following sequence:

Problem Determination -> **System Dump** -> **Check Dump Resources Utility**

or use the SMIT fast path **smitty dump_checkr**.

You should get a screen similar to Example 4-7.

Example 4-7 Check dump resources utility panel

```
                              Check Dump Resources Utility

Type or select values in entry fields.
Press Enter AFTER making all desired changes.

                                                             [Entry Fields]

  Check dump resources                                       yes                  +
  Log or Mail Results                                        log                  +
  cron time parameters                                      [0 15 * * *]



F1=Help             F2=Refresh          F3=Cancel           F4=List
F5=Reset            F6=Command          F7=Edit             F8=Image
F9=Shell            F10=Exit            Enter=Do
```

Option 3: Using the command line

Run the following command:

```
# /usr/lib/ras/dumpcheck -t "0 9,17 * * *"
```

In this example, the **dumpcheck** command will be run at 9:00 AM and 5:00 PM.

4.3.5 Change the size of a dump device

If the system already has a dump device, make sure the estimated dump size can fit into this dump device. The **lslv** command displays the size of the logical volume. See Example 4-8.

Example 4-8 Display dump logical volume size

```
# lslv hd6
LOGICAL VOLUME:     hd6                    VOLUME GROUP:   rootvg
LV IDENTIFIER:      0003219400004c00000000e819d03f76.2 PERMISSION:    read/write
VG STATE:           active/complete        LV STATE:       opened/syncd
TYPE:               paging                 WRITE VERIFY:   off
MAX LPs:            512                    PP SIZE:        16 megabyte(s)
COPIES:             1                      SCHED POLICY:   parallel
LPs:                14                     PPs:            14
STALE PPs:          0                      BB POLICY:      non-relocatable
INTER-POLICY:       minimum                RELOCATABLE:    yes
INTRA-POLICY:       middle                 UPPER BOUND:    32
MOUNT POINT:        N/A                    LABEL:          None
MIRROR WRITE CONSISTENCY: off
EACH LP COPY ON A SEPARATE PV ?: yes
```

Note the values for LPs and PP SIZE. Multiply these two values together to get the size of the dump device in megabytes.

If the dump device is a standard dump logical volume, such as hd7, then the command to use to increase its size is the **extendlv** command. For example:

```
# extendlv hd7 1 hdisk0
```

If it is the primary paging space hd6, then use the **chps** command. For example:

```
# chps -s'1' hd6
```

If the dump device is the paging space, ensure the forced copy flag value, as shown by the **sysdumpdev** command, is set to true and the size of copy directory is enough. The default copy directory is /var/adm/ras. You can check the size of copy directory and modify it by running the following commands:

```
# df -k /var
Filesystem    1024-blocks      Free %Used    Iused %Iused Mounted on
/dev/hd9var         16384     11832   28%      313     8% /var
```

```
# chfs -asize=+100000 /var
Filesystem size changed to 147456
```

4.3.6 Optional setup

This section details other AIX and machine settings that can have an impact on the ability to access a system dump.

- Autorestart

  A useful system attribute is autorestart. If autorestart is true, the system will automatically reboot after a crash. This is useful if the machine is physically distant or often unattended.

  To list these values, use:

  ```
  # lsattr -Dl sys0
  ```

  To set autorestart to true, use SMIT by following the fast path:

  ```
  # smit chgsys
  ```

  Or use the command:

  ```
  # chdev -l sys0 -a autorestart=true
  sys0 changed
  ```

- Always allow system dump

  If this item is set to true, the Reset button or key sequences start a system dump, even when the key mode switch is in the Normal position or when no key mode switch is present. You can change this by using the Web-based System Manager, SMIT, or the **sysdumpdev -K** command.

Option 1: Using Web-based System Manager

Use the settings shown in Figure 4-6 on page 84 to always allow a system dump.

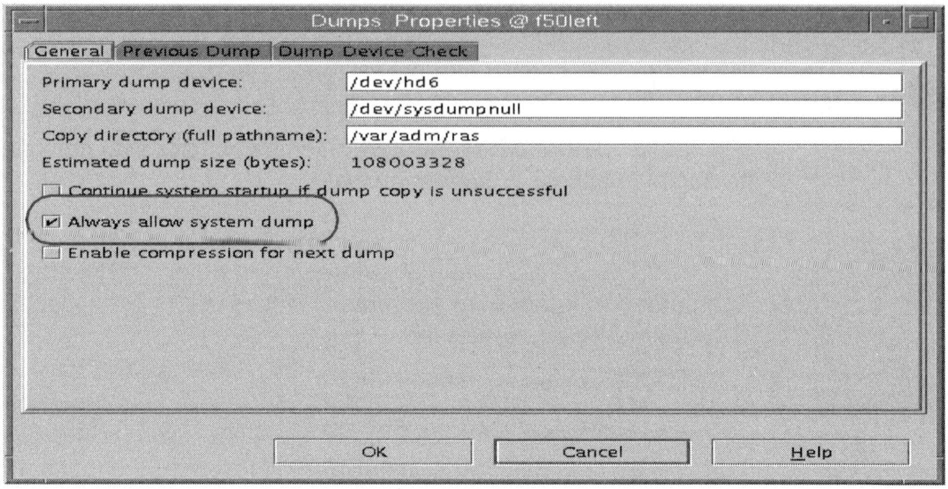

Figure 4-6 Always allow system dump setting

Option 2: Using SMIT

Use the screen shown in Example 4-9 to always allow a system dump.

Example 4-9 The SMIT panel for setting the Always ALLOW System Dump

```
                        Always ALLOW System Dump

Type or select values in entry fields.
Press Enter AFTER making all desired changes.

                                                    [Entry Fields]
  Always ALLOW System Dump                        true                  +



F1=Help              F2=Refresh           F3=Cancel            F4=List
F5=Reset             F6=Command           F7=Edit              F8=Image
F9=Shell             F10=Exit             Enter=Do
```

Option 3: Using the command line

Run the following command to always allow a system dump:

```
# sysdumpdev -K
```

4.4 Checking the dump status

Checking that the system dump is valid and readable before submitting it to IBM for analysis saves time.

4.4.1 Get the last dump information

If you run the **sysdumpdev -L** command, it will display statistical information about the most recent system dump. This includes the date and time of the last dump, number of bytes written, and completion status. See Example 4-10 for an example.

Example 4-10 The sysdumpdev command

```
# sysdumpdev -L
0453-039

Device name:          /dev/mydumplv
Major device number: 10
Minor device number: 12
Size:                 76656640 bytes
Date/Time:            Fri Aug 31 16:51:13 CDT 2001
Dump status:          0
dump completed successfully
```

In this case, the dump was successfully completed.

4.4.2 Dump status codes

Once you see a flashing 888 in the LEDs, the system has crashed. You may see a 0c9 for a short time, indicating a system dump is in progress. When the dump is completed, the dump status code will change to 0c0 if the system was able to dump successfully.

Table 4-2 shows the possible dump status codes along with brief descriptions. Use them to check the status and result of your dump.

Table 4-2 Dump status codes

LED code	sysdumpdev status	Description
0c0	0	Dump successful.
0c1	-4	I/O error during dump.
0c4	-2	Dump device is too small. Partial dump taken.

LED code	sysdumpdev status	Description
0c5	-3	Internal dump error.
0c8	-1	No dump device defined.
0c2	N/A	User-initiated dump in progress. In AIX Version 4.2.1 and above, this code will appear regardless of whether the dump is going to the primary or secondary dump device.
0c6	N/A	User-initiated dump to secondary device in progress. Note that in AIX Version 4.2.1 and above, support dump fails over, so this code is obsolete.
0c7	N/A	Dump waiting for acknowledgment from NFS server.
0c9	N/A	System-initiated dump in progress.
0cc	N/A	Switched to secondary dump device. Indicates dump has performed failover to secondary device. Indicates dump has performed failover to secondary device. Supported on AIX Version 4.2.1 and above.

4.4.3 The sysdumpdev command

The **sysdumpdev** command changes the primary or secondary dump device designation in a system that is running. It can also be used to manage dump devices.

The sysdumpdev command syntax

```
sysdumpdev -P { -p Device | -s Device } [ -q ] [ -i ]
sysdumpdev [ -p Device | -s Device ] [ -q ]
sysdumpdev [ -d Directory | -D Directory | -e | -I | [ -k | -K ] | -l | -L | -p
Device | -q | -r Host: Path | -s Device | -z ]
sysdumpdev [ -c | -C ] [ -i ]
```

Useful flags

-C Turns on compression.

-c Turns off compression.

-d *Directory* Sets the directory to copy the dump into at system boot, but if copy fails, it will not prompt the user at boot time and the dump is lost. The forced copy flag is set to false.

-D *Directory* Same as above, but if copy fails, it will prompt the user during boot to copy the dump to external media. The forced copy flag is set to true.

-z Determines if a new system dump is present and, if yes, writes its size and the name of the dump device to stdout.

4.4.4 Verifying the dump

To check that the dump is readable, start the **kdb** command on the dump file. The **kdb** command needs a kernel file (UNIX) to match the dump file. If you do not specify a kernel file, **kdb** uses the file /usr/lib/boot/unix by default. The **crash** command is used to verify the system dump files in AIX Version 4.3 and earlier.

Example 4-11 Verifying the dump with the kdb command

```
# kdb ./dump ./unix
The specified kernel file is a MP kernel
./dump mapped from @ 70000000 to @ 74920000
Preserving 948322 bytes of symbol table
First symbol __mulh
Component Names:
 1)  dmp_minimal [5 entries]
 2)  proc [257 entries]
:
valid..1 ros....0 holes..0 io.....0 seg....1 wimg...2
Dump analysis on CHRP_SMP_PCI POWER_PC POWER_604 machine with 4 cpu(s)  (32-bit
registers)
Processing symbol table...
.......................done
(0)>
```

If you do not see any message from the **kdb** command about dump routines failing, you probably have a valid dump file. Then, run the stat subcommand at the (0)> prompt. (Example 4-12 has an example.)

Example 4-12 Verifying dump with stat subcommand

```
(0)> stat
SYSTEM_CONFIGURATION:
CHRP_SMP_PCI POWER_PC POWER_604 machine with 4 cpu(s)  (32-bit registers)

SYSTEM STATUS:
sysname... AIX
nodename.. f50left
release... 1
version... 5
machine... 000321944C00
nid....... 0321944C
time of crash: Fri Aug 31 16:51:13 2001
age of system: 1 day, 23 hr., 36 min., 15 sec.
xmalloc debug: disabled
```

```
SYSTEM MESSAGES:

AIX Version 5.1
Starting NODE#000 physical CPU#001 as logical CPU#001... done.
Starting NODE#000 physical CPU#002 as logical CPU#002... done.
Starting NODE#000 physical CPU#003 as logical CPU#003... done.
mga_makegp:  Exit, rc=0
<- end_of_buffer
(0)> more (^C to quit) ?
```

Look at the time of the dump. If these are reasonable for the dump, then perform some initial analysis. Refer to Section 4.7, "The kdb command" on page 93 for more information.

A message stating "corrupted" means the dump is not valid. (See Example 4-13 for an example.)

Example 4-13 Corrupted dump

```
# kdb ./dump ./unix
The specified kernel file is a MP kernel
Preserving 948322 bytes of symbol table
First symbol __mulh
Component Names:
 1)  dmp_minimal [5 entries]
 2)  proc [191 entries]
 3)  thrd [380 entries]
 4)  ldr [1 entries]
Component Dump Table has 577 entries
Kernel not included in this dump.
dump ./dump corrupted
make sure ./unix refers to the running kernel
```

Any other messages displayed when starting the **kdb** command may indicate that certain components of the dump are invalid, but these are generally handled by the **kdb** command. If a required component of the dump image is missing, additional messages will indicate this, and the dump should be considered invalid.

4.5 Collecting the dump and related information

The easiest way to copy a dump and other system information to be used in analyzing the problem is by using the **snap** command. The **snap** command gathers system configuration information and compresses the information into a tar file that can then be downloaded to some other media. The **snap** command automatically creates the /tmp/ibmsupt directory, and several subdirectories are created below this.

4.5.1 The snap command

The **snap** command is a general purpose utility for gathering information about a system.

In general, it is best to run the **snap -a** command when building a snap image for sending to IBM. Also, The -o option is useful for writing the information collected by the **snap** command to removable media, such as a tape. For example:

```
# snap -o /dev/rmt0
```

The **snap** command supports the following information gathering options:

-D	Dump and /unix information
-g	General information
-k	Kernel information
-f	File system information
-S	Security information
-L	LVM information
-l	Product levels for installed compilers
-n	NFS information
-p	Printer information
-s	SNA information
-t	TCP/IP information
-A	TTY (async) information
-b	SSA information
-w	Gathers WLM information

To gather all of the above data, use the -a option.

The **snap** command supports the following output control options:

-c Creates a compressed tar image of /tmp/ibmsupt. It produces snap.pax.Z images in /tmp/ibmsupt.

-o *device* Creates tar image on device.

-d *directory* Uses directory for **snap** operations, it replaces the /tmp/ibmsupt directory.

-r Removes all directories created by snap under /tmp/ibmsupt. Please make sure cleaning up the previous **snap** output. The **snap** command appends information to some **snap** output files.

The **snap** command in AIX 5L Version 5.1 uses the **pax** command instead of the **tar** command to create the snap file. This is necessary to manage the ever increasing sizes of the dump files, as file sizes larger than 2 GB are only supported by the **pax** command. Refer to Section 2.18, "The pax command enhancements" in *AIX 5L Differences Guide*, SG24-5765.

4.6 Initiating a system dump

Normally, a system dump will occur automatically when the system crashes. When a system has hung, the system administrator can force a dump to determine the cause of the hang.

If you see the LED code 0c9, then a system dump is in progress. When the dump is successfully completed, this code will change to 0c0. Please refer to Section 4.4.2, "Dump status codes" on page 85 for other dump related LED codes. If you press the Reset button, the LED code will cycle through a set of codes, which will be something like 888-102-700-0c0-888.

If the kernel debugger (KDB) is enabled, a c20 will appear in the LEDs, and an ASCII terminal connected to the s1 or s2 serial port will show an KDB screen. Typing **quit dump** will initiate a dump. Use the Low-Level Debugger (LLDB) instead of the KDB in AIX Version 4.3 and earlier.

The LED codes are:

888 This value flashes to indicate a system crash.

102 This value indicates an unexpected system halt.

nnn This value is the cause of the system halt (reason code).

0cx This value indicates the dump status.

4.6.1 LED reason codes

The reason code is the second value after 888 appears. Also, this code can be found using the stat subcommand in **kdb**. The reason codes are:

000
Unexpected system interrupt (hardware related)

2xx
Machine check

A machine check can occur due to hardware problems, for example, bad memory, or because of a software reference to a non-existent address.

3xx
Data storage interrupt

A page fault always begins as a DSI, which is handled in the exception processing of the VMM. However, if a page fault cannot be resolved, or if a page fault occurs when interrupts are disabled, the DSI will cause a system crash. The page fault may not be resolved if, for example, an attempt is made to read or write a pointer that has been freed, in other words, the segment register value is no longer valid, and the address is no longer mapped.

400
Instruction access exception

Instruction Access Interrupt. This is similar to a DSI, but occurs when fetching instructions, not data.

5xx
External interrupt

Interrupt arriving from an external device.

700
Program interrupt

Usually caused by a trap instruction that can be a result of failing an assert, or hitting a panic within kernel or kernel extension code.

800
Floating point unavailable

An attempt is made to execute a floating point instruction but the floating point available bit in the Machine Status Register (MSR) is disabled.

4.6.2 How to force a dump

You only force a dump on a machine that is completely hung. If the machine can be accessed at the console or remotely and commands can be run, then the machine is not hung. There are several ways of initiating a dump. You can choose one of these methods depending on the status of your machine.

Forcing a dump on MCA systems

To force a dump:

1. Turn the key mode switch to the Service position.
2. Press the Reset button once.
3. The system will start a dump and the LED panel will display LED 0c2.

Forcing a dump on PCI systems

There are a few different methods of forcing system dumps on PCI machines. The following information details briefly how to accomplish this for the different systems:

- Set the system option Always Allow System Dump to true using the **smit** command. Refer to Section 4.3.6, "Optional setup" on page 83, or run the **sysdumpdev -K** command.
- 6015/6050/6070/7020/7248 All Models

  Press the Ctrl-Alt-Numpad 1 key sequence.
- 7017-Sxx
  a. Select Function 22 on the operator panel and press Enter. The response A1003022 displays on the operator panel.
  b. Select Function 22 again and press Enter. The response D1823080 displays on the operator panel. This indicates the dump request has been accepted by AIX, and the process continues, displaying four-character progress messages.

  Please refer to the *7017 S Series Installation and Service Guide*, SA38-0548 for more information.
- 7024-E Series

  Press and hold the Power button for longer than two seconds.

  The power LED will blink quickly to indicated that the dump has been started.

  Please refer to the *IBM 7024 E Series Service Guide*, SA38-0502, as shown in Table 1-2 on page 8.
- 7025-F30 (old)

  Press and hold the Power button, located on the front of the system, for approximately three to five seconds. A system dump is in progress when you see the disk activity light flash rapidly.
- 7025-F40/50 (old)

  Press and hold Reset button until the dump completion code is displayed. Alternatively, press the soft-power button for about five seconds or until 0c2 is displayed.

- Other PCI-based machines

  Press the Reset button.

> **Note:** You can start a system dump by Ctrl-Alt-Numpad 1 key sequence only on the native console keyboard.

4.7 The kdb command

This section allows you to recognize some common problems using the **kdb** command, and to make a basic determination as to what caused the problem.

4.7.1 Uses of kdb

The **kdb** command can be used on a running system. Invoking **kdb** with no parameters essentially allows you to view the memory and state of the currently running system by examining /dev/mem. In this case, root permissions are required.

The **kdb** can also be used on a system dump. It is the primary tool used to analyze a dump resulting from a system failure. Invoking **kdb** with a parameter specifying a dump file allows you to examine a dump file for problem analysis.

Using **kdb**, you can examine:

- Addresses and symbols
- Kernel stack traceback
- Kernel extensions
- The process table
- The thread table
- The file table
- The inode table

In addition to the items listed above, you can use **kdb** to look at anything else contained in the kernel memory.

4.7.2 What is the kernel?

The kernel is the program that controls and protects system resources. It runs in Privileged mode. It operates directly with the hardware. The major functions of the kernel are:

- Creation and deletion of processes/threads
- CPU scheduling
- Memory management
- Device management
- Provides synchronization and communication tools for processes

If the kernel has an error, the machine will crash. A user program will only create a core dump and halt.

The **kdb** command is used to debug these kernel problems.

4.7.3 Examining a system dump with the kdb command

The **kdb** command needs a kernel /unix file to match the dump file under analysis.

The **kdb** command uses the kernel file to interpret symbols and allows for symbolic translation and presentation. If the kernel file does not match the dump, you will get an error message when you start **kdb**. (See Example 4-14.)

If the dump file is compressed, it must be uncompressed before running **kdb**.

Example 4-14 The compressed dump

```
# kdb ./dump ./unix
The specified kernel file is a MP kernel
./dump mapped from @ 70000000 to @ 709757ff
Preserving 948322 bytes of symbol table
First symbol __mulh
The dump appears to be compressed.
It needs to be uncompressed before running kdb
```

> **Note:** If you run the **kdb** command on a 32 bit machine, it only handled the crash problem from the 32-bit kernel. If you have a system dump from the 64 bit kernel, you must run the **kdb** command in 64 bit kernel mode.

4.7.4 Basic kdb subcommands

Once you initiate the **kdb** command, the prompt character is the current cpu and greater than sign (0)>. For a list of the available subcommands, type the h character. To exit, type e. You can run any shell command from within the **kdb** command by preceding it with an exclamation mark (!). Refer to the *AIX 5L Version 5.1 Kernel Extensions and Device Support Programming Concepts* or visit the following Web site:

http://publibn.boulder.ibm.com/doc_link/en_US/a_doc_lib/aixprggd/kernextc/kernextctfrm.htm

- stat

  Shows the system status and messages.
- p (alias: proc) [*/slot/symb/eaddr]

  Displays the process table.
- u (alias: user) [-?][slot/symb/eaddr]

  Displays u_area.
- th (alias: thread) [*/slot/symb/eaddr/-w ?]

  Displays the thread table.
- mst [slot] [[-a] symb/eaddr]

  Displays the mstsave area for the specified thread.
- f (alias: stack) [+x/-x][th {slot/eaddr}]

  Displays all stack frames for specified thread.
- h (alias: ?) [topic]

  Lists all subcommands.

  Provides information about subcommands of **kdb**.
- errpt

  Displays error log messages.

stat subcommand

The stat subcommand gives plenty of useful information about a dump, such as the dump code, the panic string, time of the crash, version and release of the operating system, name of the machine that crashed, and how long the machine had been running since the last crash or power off of the system. Example 4-15 shows an example of this subcommand.

Example 4-15 The stat subcommand

```
(0)> stat
SYSTEM_CONFIGURATION:
CHRP_SMP_PCI POWER_PC POWER_604 machine with 1 cpu(s)  (32-bit registers)

SYSTEM STATUS:
sysname... AIX
nodename.. aix51
release... 1
version... 5
machine... 004232044C00
```

```
nid....... 4232044C
time of crash: Wed Jul 11 07:39:56 2001
age of system: 27 min., 36 sec.
xmalloc debug: disabled

CRASH INFORMATION:
CPU 0 CSA 00891EB0 at time of crash, error code for LEDs: 30000000
pvthread+000100 STACK:
[01AC0644]ethchandd:ech_to+000188 (2FAE0000 [??])
[01AC0550]ethchandd:ech_to+000094 (??)
[000D7180]watchdog+0000C4 ()
[0001B880]sys_timer+0004E8 (??)
[0001BD00]clock+000134 (??)
[0001CE04]i_softmod+000264 ()
[00057A5C]flih_603_patch+0000CC (??, ??)
[000579A0]flih_603_patch+000010 (??, ??)
____ Exception (2FF3B400) ____
iar   : 00026BCC  msr   : 00009032  cr    : 22002080  lr    : 00026BF0
ctr   : 00026B54  xer   : 00000000  mq    : 00000000
r0  : 00000000  r1  : 2FF3B328  r2  : 0052B810  r3  : 00000000  r4  : 01945000
r5  : 00000004  r6  : 01945800  r7  : 00000001  r8  : 00000000  r9  : 00000000
r10 : 00000000  r11 : 00000000  r12 : 00000000  r13 : DEADBEEF  r14 : DEADBEEF
r15 : DEADBEEF  r16 : DEADBEEF  r17 : DEADBEEF  r18 : DEADBEEF  r19 : DEADBEEF
r20 : DEADBEEF  r21 : DEADBEEF  r22 : DEADBEEF  r23 : DEADBEEF  r24 : DEADBEEF
r25 : DEADBEEF  r26 : DEADBEEF  r27 : 01945984  r28 : 00180170  r29 : 000034E0
r30 : 0015C48C  r31 : 01945000
s0  : 00000000  s1  : 00004010  s2  : 00004C13  s3  : 00004411  s4  : 007FFFFF
s5  : 007FFFFF  s6  : 007FFFFF  s7  : 007FFFFF  s8  : 007FFFFF  s9  : 007FFFFF
s10 : 007FFFFF  s11 : 007FFFFF  s12 : 007FFFFF  s13 : 007FFFFF  s14 : 00001004
s15 : 007FFFFF
prev      00000000 kjmpbuf   00000000 stackfix  00000000 intpri    0B
curid     00000204 sralloc   F1EF0000 ioalloc   00000000 backt     00
flags     00 tid       00000000 excp_type 00000000
fpscr     00000000 fpeu            00 fpinfo          00 fpscrx    00000000
o_iar     00000000 o_toc     00000000 o_arg1    00000000
```

The stat subcommand should always be the first command run when examining a system crash.

f subcommand

The f subcommand gives you a kernel stack traceback.

This subcommand gives you information on what was happening in the kernel when the crash occurred. The f subcommand gives you a history of function calls and what interrupt processing was going on in the system. If the crash occurred while interrupt processing was going on, this is the command to use. This command traces the linked list of mstsave areas (Figure 4-7). The mstsave areas basically contain a history of what interrupt processing was going on in the system.

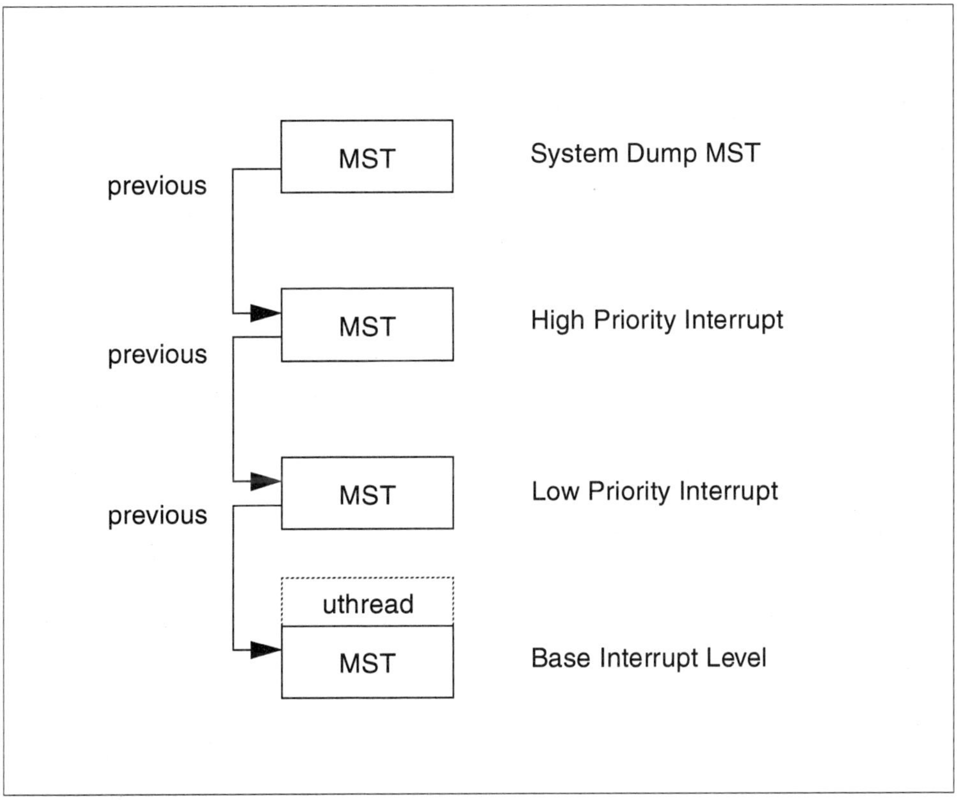

Figure 4-7 Machine state save area

The machine state save area, or MST, contains a saved image of the machine's process context. The process context includes the general purpose and floating point registers, the special purpose registers, and other information necessary to restart a thread when it is dispatched. Example 4-16 on page 98 has an example of a stack trace back.

Example 4-16 stack trace back

```
(0)> f
pvthread+000100 STACK:
[01AC0644]ethchandd:ech_to+000188 (2FAE0000 [??])
[01AC0550]ethchandd:ech_to+000094 (??)
[000D7180]watchdog+0000C4 ()
[0001B880]sys_timer+0004E8 (??)
[0001BD00]clock+000134 (??)
[0001CF04]i_softmod+000264 ()
[00057A5C]flih_603_patch+0000CC (??, ??)
[000579A0]flih_603_patch+000010 (??, ??)
____ Exception (2FF3B400) ____
[00026BCC]waitproc+000078 ()
```

In this example, there are two levels of stack traceback.

When looking at a stack traceback, realize that the first thing on the stack was the most recently running function, which was called by the function below it, which was called by the function below it, and so on. So, in the case of the middle stack traceback in our example, we see that sys_timer called watchdog, which called ech_to in ethchandd module and an exception occurred in ech_to. You would have to look at the code for this to try to find out the cause of this exception. Anyway, you can be sure that the ethchandd did something wrong.

Make sure the failing module is at the latest version. Problems are frequently resolved in later versions of software. You can use the lke subcommand in **kdb** and the **`lslpp -w`** command to find the fileset that contains the specific module. Refer to "Finding addresses in kernel extensions" on page 101 for more information. You can get the latest fileset information from the Internet at:

`http://techsupport.service.ibm.com/server/support`

Use the lke subcommand with an argument of the address listed in the stack trace back. The address is displayed in brackets after the name of the module. Example 4-17 has an example of list loaded extensions.

Example 4-17 List loaded extensions

```
(0)> lke 01AC0644
     ADDRESS     FILE FILESIZE    FLAGS MODULE NAME

  1 0567DC00 01ABFB00 00008A7C 00000262 ethchandd32/usr/lib/drivers/ethchandd
le_flags....... TEXT DATAINTEXT DATA DATAEXISTS
le_next........ 058FE580 le_fp.......... 00000000
le_filename.... 0567DC58 le_file........ 01ABFB00
le_filesize.... 00008A7C le_data........ 01AC3D20
le_tid......... 00000000 le_datasize.... 0000485C
le_usecount.... 00000001 le_loadcount... 00000001
```

```
le_ndepend..... 00000001 le_maxdepend... 00000001
le_ule......... 00000000 le_deferred.... 00000000
le_exports..... 00000000 le_de......... 6E6C732F
le_searchlist.. 00000000 le_dlusecount.. 00000000
le_dlindex..... 00000000 le_lex......... 00000000
le_fh.......... 00000000 le_depend.... @ 0567DC54
TOC@........... 01AC84AC
                              <PROCESS TRACE BACKS>
                .ech_rearp 01ABFC00          .ethchan_icmp_output 01ABFFCC
        .ethchan_icmp_input 01AC0290              .ech_switch_adap 01AC0364
                  .ech_to 01AC04BC                .ethchan_trace 01AC0694
                .init_ccs 01AC0784                .ethchan_close 01AC0A14
            .ethchan_open 01AC0B98               .ethchan_output 01AC0E70
(0)> more (^C to quit) ?
```

One of the fields listed by the lke subcommand is the Name of the module. You can then use the **lslpp -w** command to determine the fileset that contains the module. For example:

```
# lslpp -w /usr/lib/drivers/ethchandd
  File                                      Fileset                      Type
  ----------------------------------------------------------------------------
  /usr/lib/drivers/ethchandd
                           devices.common.IBM.ethernet.rte               File
```

proc subcommand

The proc subcommand displays entries in the process table. The process table is made up of entries of type struct proc, one per active process. Entries in the process table are pinned so that they are always resident in physical memory. The process table contains information needed when the process has been swapped out in order to get it running again at some point in the future. Example 4-18 shows the displayed process table.

Example 4-18 Display process table

```
(0)> p
              SLOT NAME     STATE    PID  PPID  PGRP   UID  ADSPACE  CL #THS

pvproc+000400    2*wait     ACTIVE 00204 00000 00000 00000 00004C13   0 0001

NAME....... wait
STATE...... stat  :07  .... xstat :0000
FLAGS...... flag  :00000303 LOAD NOSWAP FIXPRI KPROC
........... flag2 :00000002 WAITPROC
........... atomic :00000000
LINKS...... child      :00000000
........... siblings   :E2000200 <pvproc+000200>
........... uidinfo    :0019A588
```

```
........... ganchor    :00000000
THREAD..... threadlist :EA000100 <pvthread+000100>
DISPATCH... synch      :FFFFFFFF
WLM........ class/wlm  :00/0000
IDENTIFIER. uid        :00000000  ........... suid        :00000000
........... pid        :00000204  ........... ppid        :00000000
........... sid        :00000000  ........... pgrp        :00000000
MISC....... lock      @ E20004EC 00000000
........... lock_d    @ E2000554 00000000
...... parent_lock    @ E2000550 00000000
(0)> more (^C to quit) ?
```

th subcommand

The thread table contains per-thread information that can be used by other threads in a process. There is one structure allocated per active thread. Entries that are in use are pinned to avoid page faults in kernel critical sections. Example 4-19 shows the displayed thread table.

Example 4-19 Display thread table

```
(0)> th
                 SLOT NAME      STATE    TID PRI   RQ CPUID  CL WCHAN

pvthread+000100    2*wait      RUN    000205 OFF    0 00000   0

NAME................ wait
FLAGS............... KTHREAD
...............state :00000002   ...............wtype :00000000
...............flags :00001000   ..............flags2 :00000000
DATA.........pvprocp :E2000400 <pvproc+000400>
LINKS.....prevthread :EA000100 <pvthread+000100>
..........nextthread :EA000100 <pvthread+000100>
DISPATCH.......synch :FFFFFFFF
SCHEDULER...affinity :00000000   .................pri :000000FF
.............boosted :00000000   ...............wchan :00000000
IDENTIFIER.......tid :00000205
MISC..........tsleep :FFFFFFFF
CHECKPOINT......vtid :00000000   .............chkfile :00000000
LOCK........ lock_d @ EA000108 00000000
PROCFS......procfsvn :00000000
THREAD.......threadp :01946C00   ................size :00000148

FLAGS............... KTHREAD FUNNELLED
(0)> more (^C to quit) ?
```

Looking for the error log

You can examine the last few error log entries from the dump using the errpt subcommand. For example:

```
(0)> errpt
ERRORS NOT READ BY ERRDEMON (ORDERED CHRONOLOGICALLY):

Error Record:
erec_flags .............         0
erec_len ...............        44
erec_timestamp ......... 3B4C491C
erec_rec_len ...........        24
erec_dupcount ..........         0
erec_duptime1 ..........         0
erec_duptime2 ..........         0
erec_rec.error_id ....... 9D035E4D
erec_rec.resource_name .. SYSVMM
40000000 00004C13 2FF22FF8 FFFFFFFA
```

Finding addresses in kernel extensions

The lke subcommand can indicate what kernel extension an address belongs to. Take, for example, the address 0x019e6C00. This is a kernel address, since it starts 0x01, which indicates it is in segment 0, the kernel segment. To find the kernel module that contains the code at this address, use the lke subcommand. Example 4-20 shows the displayed kernel extension

Example 4-20 Display kernel extension

```
(0)> lke 019E6C00
     ADDRESS     FILE FILESIZE    FLAGS MODULE NAME

  1 05566580 019E6C00 000317E8 00000272 pse32/usr/lib/drivers/pse/pse
le_flags....... TEXT KERNELEX DATAINTEXT DATA DATAEXISTS
le_next........ 05566600 le_fp.......... 00000000
le_filename.... 055665D8 le_file........ 019E6C00
le_filesize.... 000317E8 le_data........ 01A152C0
le_tid......... 00000000 le_datasize.... 00003128
le_usecount.... 0000000C le_loadcount... 00000001
le_ndepend..... 00000001 le_maxdepend... 00000001
le_ule......... 00000000 le_deferred.... 00000000
le_exports..... 055B8000 le_de.......... F00C4530
le_searchlist.. 00000000 le_dlusecount.. 00000000
le_dlindex..... 00000000 le_lex......... 00000000
le_fh.......... 00000000 le_depend.... @ 055665D4
TOC@........... 01A175CC
                              <PROCESS TRACE BACKS>
               .start_pse_kdb 019E6D00           .strmod_print_term 019E6E1C
          .strdev_print_term 019E6E84                 .strmod_print 019E6EEC
                .strdev_print 019E6F50              .medthresh_init 019E6FB4
```

```
          .lowthresh_init 019E7028              .strthresh_init 019E709C
                .str_term 019E7110                    .str_init 019E7368
(0)> more (^C to quit) ?
```

In this case, we can see that the code at address 0x019e6C00 is in module /usr/lib/drivers/pse/pse.

The lke subcommand is only helpful for modules that are already loaded into the kernel.

VMM error log

When the Dump Status code indicates a DSI or an ISI, you need to look at the VMM errorlog entry. This is done using the vmlog subcommand. For example:

```
(0)> vmlog
Most recent VMM errorlog entry
Error ID                =  DSI_PROC
Exception DSISR/ISISR   =  40000000
Exception srval         =  00004C13
Exception virt addr     =  2FF22FF8
Exception value         =  FFFFFFFA
```

In this example, the exception value is `FFFFFFFA`, which means the system crashed by the page fault. The various exception values and meanings are shown below:

0000000E This return code indicates an EFAULT. It comes from errno.h (14) and is returned if you attempt to access an invalid address. See /usr/include/sys/errno.h file.

FFFFFFFA This return code indicates you tried to access an invalid page that is not in memory. This is usually the result of a page fault. This will be returned if you try to access something that is paged out while interrupts are disabled.

00000005 This is a hardware problem. An I/O error occurred when you tried to either page in or page out, or you tried to access a memory mapped file and could not do it. Check the error log for disk or SCSI errors.

00000086 This return code indicates a protection exception. This means that you tried to store to a location that is protected. This is usually caused by low kernel memory.

0000001C This return code indicates no paging space. This means that the system has exhausted its paging space.

4.7.5 Examining a system dump with the crash command

The **crash** command is used to analyze system dump files in AIX Version 4.3 and earlier. The **crash** command also needs a kernel /unix file to match the dump file under analysis. For example:

```
itsosrv1:/dumptest> crash dumpfile unix
>
```

If no kernel file is specified, the default is /unix. For example:

```
itsosrv1:/dumptest> crash dumpfile
Using /unix as the default namelist file.
>
```

The **crash** command uses the kernel file to interpret symbols and allows for symbolic translation and presentation. If the kernel file does not match the dump, you will get an error message when you start the **crash** command.

Basic crash subcommands

Once you initiate the **crash** command, the prompt character is the greater than sign (>). For a list of the available subcommands, type the ? character. To exit, type q. You can run any shell command from within the **crash** command by preceding it with an exclamation mark (!).

Please refer to the online documentation of *AIX Version 4.3 Kernel Extensions and Device Support Programming Concepts* for more information of the crash utility and all **crash** subcommands.

- stat

  Shows dump statistics.

- proc [-] [-r] [processTableEntry]

  Displays the process table (proc.h). Alias p and ps.

- user [ProcessTableEntry]

  Displays user structure of named process (user.h). Alias u.

- thread [-] [-r] [-p] [threadTableEntry]

  Displays the thread table (thread.h).

- mst [addr]

  Displays the mstsave portion of uthread structure (uthread.h, mstsave.h).

- ds [addr]

  Finds the data symbol closest to the given address.

- knlist [symbol]

  Displays address of symbol name given. Opposite of the ds subcommand.
- trace [-k][-m][-r][ThreadTableEntry]

  Displays kernel stack trace. Alias t.
- le

  Displays loader entries.
- nm [symbol]

  Displays symbol value and type as found in the /unix file.
- od [symbol name or addr] [count] [format]

  Dumps count number of data words starting at symbol name or addr in the format specified by format.
- ? or help[]

  Lists all subcommands.

  Provides information about crash subcommands.
- fs [thread slotNumber]

  Dumps the kernel stack frames for the specified thread.
- dlock [tid] | -p [processor_num]

  Displays deadlock information about all types of locks: simple, complex, and lockl.
- errpt [count]

  Displays error log messages. The errpt subcommand always prints all messages that have not yet been read by the errdemon. Count specifies the number of messages to print.
- ppd

  Display per processor data area, useful for multiprocessor systems. Shows all data that varies for each processor, such as Current Save Area (CSA).

stat subcommand

The stat subcommand gives plenty of useful information about a dump, such as the dump code, the panic string, time of the crash, version and release of the operating system, name of the machine that crashed, and how long the machine had been running since the last crash or power off of the system. For example:

```
> stat
        sysname: AIX
        nodename: kmdvs
        release: 3
```

```
version: 4
machine: 000939434C00
time of crash: Mon May  3 17:49:46 KORST 1999
age of system: 2 day, 4 hr., 28 min.
xmalloc debug: disabled
dump code: 700
csa: 0x384eb0
exception struct:
        0x00000000 0x00000000 0x00000000 0x00000000 0x00000000
panic: HACMP for AIX dms timeout - ha
```

The stat subcommand should always be the first command run when examining a system crash.

trace -m subcommand

The trace -m subcommand gives you a kernel stack traceback.

This is typically the second command you will run when examining a system dump.

This subcommand gives you information on what was happening in the kernel when the crash occurred. The trace -m subcommand gives you a history of function calls and what interrupt processing was going on in the system. If the crash occurred while interrupt processing was going on, this is the command to use. This command traces the linked list of mstsave areas. For example:

```
> trace -m
Skipping first MST

MST STACK TRACE:
0x002baeb0 (excpt=00000000:00000000:00000000:00000000:00000000) (intpri=3)
        IAR:      .[atmle_dd:atmle_ready_ind]+d8 (01b05cb0): tweqi   r5,0x0
        LR:       .[atmle_dd:atmle_ready_ind]+34 (01b05c0c)
        002ba940: .[atmle_dd:atmle_receive_ether_data]+1ec (01b0c35c)
        002ba9a0: .[atm_demux:atm_dmx_receive]+204 (01adc0e8)
        002baa00: .[atmdd:atm_deqhandler]+1254 (01ac7e6c)
        002babc0: .[atmdd:atm_HandleCardRsp]+1a4 (01aba084)
        002baca0: .[atmdd:atm_handler]+48 (01aba350)
        002bad40: .[atmdd:atm_intr]+ac (01ac4a04)
        002bad90: .i_poll_soft+9c (0001ef84)
        002badf0: .i_softmod+c8 (0001e964)
        002bae70: flih_603_patch+c0 (0000bb9c)

0x2ff3b400 (excpt=00000000:00000000:00000000:00000000:00000000)(intpri=11)
        IAR:      .waitproc+c0 (0000edb0):     lwz   r3,0x6c(r28)
        LR:       .waitproc+d4 (0000edc4)
        2ff3b388: .procentry+14 (00045414)
        2ff3b3c8: .low+0 (00000000)
```

In this example, there are two levels of stack traceback. The first level shows the Instruction Address Register (IAR), pointing to a trap instruction, `tweqi r5, 0x0`. IAR has an address that caused the crash. Link Register (LR) called the fatal function or where last call returns to.

This trap instruction is what you will see when you get a crash of type Program Interrupt, or Dump Status = 700. This was probably the result of assert or panic. We can also see that the interrupt priority is 3 (intpri=3). In this case, we can see that interrupt processing was occurring when the crash happened because the interrupt priority was less than 11 or 0xB. The base interrupt priority is indicated by 0xB or 11. This is the level at which a normal process runs.

When looking at a stack traceback, realize that the first thing on the stack was the most recently running function, which was called by the function below it, which was called by the function below it, and so on. So, in the case of the middle stack traceback in our example, we see that i_softmod called i_poll_soft, which called some functions in the atmdd and atm_demux modules, which called atmle_receive_ether_data, which called atmle_ready_ind, and an assert was hit in atmle_ready_ind. You would have to look at the code for this to try to find out the cause of the assert action. Anyway, you can be sure that the atmle_dd module did something wrong.

Use the le subcommand with an argument of the address listed in the IAR of the topmost MST area. The address is displayed in brackets after the name of the module. For example:

```
> le 01b05cb0
LoadList entry at 0x04db7780
  Module start:0x00000000_01b016e0  Module filesize:0x00000000_00030fbc
  Module *end:0x00000000_01b3269c
  *data:0x00000000_0125ef40  data length:0x00000000_0000375c
  Use-count:0x000c  load_count:0x0001  *file:0x00000000
  flags:0x00000272 TEXT KERNELEX DATAINTEXT DATA DATAEXISTS
  *exp:0x04e0e000  *lex:0x00000000  *deferred:0x00000000  *expsize:0x69626f64
  Name: /usr/lib/drivers/atmle_dd
  ndepend:0x0001  maxdepend:0x0001
  *depend[00]:0x04db7580
  le_next:  04db7380
```

One of the fields listed by the le subcommand is the Name of the module. You can then use the **`lslpp -w`** command to determine the fileset that contains the module. For example:

```
itsosrv1:/> lslpp -w /usr/lib/drivers/atmle_dd
  File                                        Fileset               Type
----------------------------------------------------------------------------
  /usr/lib/drivers/atmle_dd                   bos.atm.atmle         File
```

This command is available in AIX Version 4.2 or later.

Look at the following line:

```
002ba940: .[atmle_dd:atmle_receive_ether_data]+1ec (01b0c35c)
```

You can see (in the first column) the address of the entry on the stack (not really important). The last column contains the return address of the code (01b0c35c). This address corresponds to the function shown, atmle_receive_ether_data, which is contained in the module atmle_dd. The square brackets around the [module:function] pair indicate that this is a kernel extension. In addition, the instruction at this return address is at offset 1ec from the beginning of the module atmle_dd.

The last of the stack tracebacks indicates that the user level process (intpri=b) and the running process is *wait.* If you run the user subcommand, you will see that the running process is wait. However, wait did not cause the problem here; the problem was caused by a program running at interrupt level, and looking at the MST stack traceback, as we have shown, is the only way to see the real problem.

When a Data Storage Interrupt (DSI) with dump code 300 occurs, the exception structure is filled in as follows:

```
0x2ff3b400 (excpt=DAR:DSISR:SRV:DAR2:DSIRR) (intpri=?)
```

The exception structure shows various machine registers and the interrupt level. The registers shown in the exception structure are defined as follows:

DAR Data Address Register

DSISR Data Storage Interrupt Status Register

SRV Segment Register Value

DAR2 Secondary Data Address Register

DSIRR Data Storage Interrupt Reason Register

The interrupt priority of the running context is shown in the (intpri=?) field at the end of the line. The intpri value ranges from 0xb (INTBASE) to 0x0 (INTMAX).

The exception structure is not used for code 700 dumps.

proc subcommand

The proc subcommand displays entries in the process table. The process table is made up of entries of type struct proc, one per active process. Entries in the process table are pinned so that they are always resident in physical memory. The process table contains information needed when the process has been swapped out in order to get it running again at some point in the future. For example:

```
> proc - 0
SLT ST    PID   PPID   PGRP   UID  EUID  TCNT  NAME
  0 a       0      0      0     0     0     1  swapper
        FLAGS: swapped_in no_swap fixed_pri kproc

Links:  *child:0xe3000170  *siblings:0x00000000  *uidl:0xe3001fa0
    *ganchor:0x00000000  *pgrpl:0x00000000  *ttyl:0x00000000
Dispatch Fields:  pevent:0x00000000  *synch:0xffffffff
    lock:0x00000000  lock_d:0x01390000
Thread Fields:  *threadlist:0xe6000000  threadcount:1
    active:1  suspended:0  local:0   terminating:0
Scheduler Fields:   fixed pri: 16  repage:0x00000000  scount:0  sched_pri:0
    *sched_next:0x00000000  *sched_back:0x00000000 cpticks:0
    msgcnt:0    majfltsec:0
Misc:  adspace:0x0001e00f  kstackseg:0x00000000  xstat:0x0000
    *p_ipc:0x00000000  *p_dblist:0x00000000  *p_dbnext:0x00000000
Signal Information:
    pending:hi 0x00000000,lo 0x00000000
    sigcatch:hi 0x00000000,lo 0x00000000 sigignore:hi 0xffffffff,lo 0xfff7ffff
Statistics:  size:0x00000000(pages)  audit:0x00000000
    accounting page frames:0   page space blocks:0

    pctcpu:0    minflt:1802    majflt:7
```

The fields in the first few lines of the output are as follows:

SLT This is the process slot number, and simply indicates the process's position in the process table. You use this number to tell the **crash** command which specific process block or u-block to display. Note that the slot numbers are in decimal.

ST This is a 1-character field indicating the status of the process, and may be a=active, i=idle, t=stopped, or z=zombie.

PID This is the actual process ID by which the process is known to the system. The process slot number is used to generate the process ID.

PPID Parent process ID.

PGRP Process group ID.

UID User ID.

EUID Effective user ID.

TCNT Thread count.

NAME Program name.

FLAGS Status flags.

thread subcommand

The thread table contains per-thread information that can be used by other threads in a process. There is one structure allocated per active thread. Entries that are in use are pinned to avoid page faults in kernel critical sections. For example:

```
> thread - 0
SLT ST    TID      PID    CPUID  POLICY PRI CPU    EVENT  PROCNAME
  0 s       3        0  unbound    FIFO  10  78            swapper
        t_flags:  wakeonsig kthread

Links:  *procp:0xe3000000  *uthreadp:0x2ff3b400  *userp:0x2ff3b6e0
    *prevthread:0xe6000000  *nextthread:0xe6000000,  *stackp:0x00000000
    *wchan1(real):0x00000000  *wchan2(VMM):0x00000000 *swchan:0x00000000
    wchan1sid:0x00000000  wchan1offset:0x00000000
    pevent:0x00000000  wevent:0x00000001  *slist:0x00000000
Dispatch Fields:  *prior:0xe6000000  *next:0xe6000000
    polevel:0x0000000a  ticks:0x0139  *synch:0xffffffff  result:0x00000000
    *eventlst:0x00000000  *wchan(hashed):0x00000000  suspend:0x0001
    thread waiting for:  event(s)
Scheduler Fields:  cpuid:0xffffffff  scpuid:0xffffffff  pri: 16  policy:FIFO
    affinity:0x0003  cpu:0x0078    lpri:  0  wpri:127    time:0x00
sav_pri:0x10
Misc:  lockcount:0x00000000  ulock:0x00000000  *graphics:0x00000000
    dispct:0x000000e4  fpuct:0x00000001  boosted:0x0000
    userdata:0x00000000
Signal Information:  cursig:0x00  *scp:0x00000000
    pending:hi 0x00000000,lo 0x00000000  sigmask:hi 0x00000000,lo 0x00000000
```

The fields in the output of the thread subcommand are as follows:

SLT Slot number.

ST Status. This may be i=idle, r=running, s=sleeping, w=swapped out, t=stopped, or z=zombie.

TID Thread ID.

PID	Process ID of the associated process. There may be multiple threads per process, but only one process per thread.
CPUID	CPU ID of the CPU running the thread. On a uniprocessor system, this will always be 0.
POLICY	This is the scheduling policy used for the thread and may have the values FIFIO, RR, or other.
PRI	Dispatch priority. This is not the nice value.
CPU	CPU utilization. This value is used for scheduling.
PROCNAME	The name of the process for this thread.
EVENTS	This is the wait channel if not zero.
FLAGS	Status flags.

Display memory with od

You can display and examine memory areas from the dump using the od subcommand. The syntax of the subcommand is as follows:

```
od [symbol name] [count] [format]
```

Formats are ascii, octal, decimal, hex, byte, character, instruction, long octal, and long decimal. For example:

```
> od vmker 15
000bde48: 00002001 00006003 00000000 00008004
000bde58: 00200000 00000012 0000000d 00000200
000bde68: 00080000 00000017 00078c93 00066320
000bde78: 00000ab2 00020000 00002870

> od 0xbde48 15 a
000bde48: 00002001 00006003 00000000 00008004  |.. ...`.........|
000bde58: 00200000 00000012 0000000d 00000200  |. ..............|
000bde68: 00080000 00000017 00078c93 00066320  |..............c |
000bde78: 00000ab2 00020000 00002870           |..........(p|
```

Looking for the error log

You can examine the last few error log entries from the dump using the errpt subcommand. For example:

```
> errpt
ERRORS NOT READ BY ERRDEMON (MOST RECENT LAST):
Sun Apr  6 01:01:11 1997 : DSI_PROC data storage interrupt : processor
Resource Name: SYSVMM
42000000 007fffff 80000000 fffffffa
>
```

Finding addresses in kernel extensions

The le subcommand can indicate what kernel extension an address belongs to. Take, for example, the address 0x0123cc5c. This is a kernel address, since it starts 0x01, which indicates it is in segment 0, the kernel segment. To find the kernel module that contains the code at this address, use the le subcommand. For example:

```
> le 0123cc5c
LoadList entry at 0x04db7780
  Module start:0x00000000_012316e0  Module filesize:0x00000000_00030fbc
  Module *end:0x00000000_0126269c
  *data:0x00000000_0125ef40  data length:0x00000000_0000375c
  Use-count:0x000c  load_count:0x0001  *file:0x00000000
  flags:0x00000272 TEXT KERNELEX DATAINTEXT DATA DATAEXISTS
  *exp:0x04e0e000  *lex:0x00000000  *deferred:0x00000000  *expsize:0x69626f64
  Name: /usr/lib/drivers/pse/pse
  ndepend:0x0001  maxdepend:0x0001
  *depend[00]:0x04db7580
  le_next:  04db7380
```

In this case, we can see that the code at address 0x0123cc5c is in module /usr/lib/drivers/pse/pse.

The le subcommand is only helpful for modules that are already loaded into the kernel.

VMM error log

When the Dump Status code indicates a DSI or an ISI, you need to look at the VMM error log. This is done using the od subcommand and looking at the vmmerrlog structure. See Table 4-3. For example:

```
> od vmmerrlog 9 a
000c95b0: 9d035e4d 53595356 4d4d2000 00000000  |..^MSYSVMM .....|
000c95c0: 00000000 0a000000 00000000 0000000b  |................|
000c95d0: 00000086                             |....|
```

Table 4-3 vmmerrlog structure components

Offset	Meaning
0x14	The Data Storage Interrupt Status Register (DSISR)
0x1C	Faulting address
0x20	VMM return code

In this example, the VMM return code 0x86 means PROTECTION EXCEPTION.

Handling crash output

Some crash subcommands generate many more lines than can fit on one screen. Also, crash does not pause its output after each full screen. You will want to have some way of seeing scrolled-off data.

In the past, the **script** or **tee** commands were used for this. For example:

```
# tee -a outf | crash /tmp/dump /unix | tee -a outf
```

There is now a new way to obtain a log file by using the set logfile subcommand. For example:

```
> set logfile crash.log
```

Once this has been entered, **crash** starts logging all input and output to the specified file. The set variable subcommand is available in AIX Version 4.1.5, Version 4.2.1, Version 4.3, and above.

In addition to the log file support, command pipeline support was added to **crash**, allowing you to pipe long output to other commands, such as **more**, **pg**, and **grep**. For example:

```
> le 0123cc5c | grep Name
  Name: /usr/lib/drivers/pse/pse
```

4.7.6 Types of crashes

Common problems requiring the dump analysis include the following:

Kernel panic or trap

This is usually the cause of a system crash with the LED sequence 888-102-700-0cx.

In AIX, kernel panics manifest themselves as traps. The panic() routine in the kernel puts its message into a buffer, writes it to the debug tty using the kernel debug program, and calls brkpoint(). If the kernel debugger is loaded, and an ASCII terminal is connected on a serial port, this will start the debugger; otherwise, it will cause a dump. If a panic or assert occurs, you must examine the source code to understand the condition that caused the panic or assert.

Addressing exception or data storage interrupt

This type of crash is accompanied by the LED sequence 888-102-300-0cx.

The 300 in the LED sequence indicates an addressing exception (a Data Storage Interrupt or DSI). This is usually caused by a bad address being accessed, or page fault occurring when interrupts are disabled. When you get this type of crash, check the VMM return code. Refer to "VMM error log" on page 102 for more information.

System hang

A dump can be forced when the system locks up to determine the cause of the hang.

A system hang is a total system lockup. A dump forced by turning the key to the Service position and pressing the Reset button can be examined to see what locks are being held by whom. Refer to Section 4.6.2, "How to force a dump" on page 91 for more information.

4.7.7 Data required by IBM support

In any type of system crash (Trap or DSI), the following data is required by IBM support to perform problem determination.

Ideally, the output of the **snap** command, collected as follows:

```
/usr/bin/snap -a -o /dev/rmt#
```

This collects the system dump, /unix, and other required information and puts it onto a tape drive.

In the event that a dump cannot be sent, the following minimum information is a mandatory requirement for IBM support to analyze the problem:

- The system status and messages, obtained by using the stat subcommand at the **kdb** or **crash** prompt. For example:

  ```
  (0)> stat
  ```

- If you are using the **crash** command, obtained a kernel stack trace by using the trace -m subcommand. For example:

  ```
  # crash <dump> <unix>
  > trace -m
  ```

  This is usually sufficient unless the crash occurred in a kernel extension or device driver.

- The error log from the dump, obtained by using the errpt subcommand at the **kdb** or **crash** prompt. For example:

  ```
  (0)> errpt
  ```

5

Hardware problem determination

This chapter guides you through the process of running diagnostics. There are various modes of running diagnostics, each with some limitations. This chapter will help you decide which mode is best for you. The process of running diagnostics enables you to confirm whether or not the problem you are experiencing is hardware related.

5.1 General advice

Where possible, run diagnostics concurrently in Problem Determination mode while AIX is running. This will analyze the error log and show any problems found. Check the date of the problem, as it may show up an unrelated event. If it is not possible to test the suspect device concurrently, or there is a doubt about the integrity of the AIX system, then run stand-alone diagnostics from CD-ROM, NIM, or diskette to the suspected device using the correct additional parts requested, such as wrap plugs or test media. If you run diagnostics and get a `No Trouble Found` report, you will probably be more successful in resolving the problem by concentrating on investigating software issues.

It is important that you use the exact replacement parts requested by the diagnostic system. The diagnostics system specifies each required part by part number. The use of a similar, but incorrect, part can cause the diagnostics system to report a failure when none exists, or to report `No Trouble Found`, when in fact there is a problem.

5.1.1 Diagnostic tips

To get the most out of the online and stand-alone diagnostics, you must understand the following points:

1. Error log analysis (ELA) is a major part of the diagnostic strategy.
2. Stand-alone diagnostics does NOT perform error log analysis except for Power-On-Self-Test (POST) Errors that occurred while booting stand-alone diagnostics and checkstops that just occurred.
3. Online diagnostics will perform error log analysis only when the Problem Determination selection is selected from the DIAGNOSTIC MODE SELECTION menu or when the Run Error Log Analysis task is selected.
4. Stand-alone diagnostics should only be used when you are unable to run the online diagnostics.
5. If a part is replaced as a result of error log analysis, a log repair action must be done to prevent the problem from being reported again. A repair action can be logged by using the Log Repair Action task or by running Advanced Diagnostics in System Verification mode.
6. Except for the floating-point tests and the system exerciser, all processor and memory testing are done by POST. Errors that prevent the system from booting are reported by 8-digit error codes on later PCI machines. Errors that do not prevent the system from booting are logged and are reported when the memory, processor, or sysplanar diagnostics are run. Although memory and processor are not fully tested by Standalone and online diagnostics, they are

monitored for correct operation by various checkers. If one of these checks occurs, it is logged in the AIX error log.

7. Some systems support a fast and slow boot. Additional POSTs are run in slow boot. Normally, the system should be booted in slow mode, if you suspect a problem in the base system or if you have no idea where the problem may be.
8. Sysplanar diagnostics not only test the system planar functions, they test and monitor other major system components, such as power supplies and fans. Always run sysplanar diagnostics in problem determination mode to ensure that there is not a system problem.

5.1.2 Device location notation

You will see, both in this chapter and other chapters, output from various commands showing the location of devices or adapters in the system. This section explains the notation used to describe device location. The location is shown either as an AIX Location Code or a Physical Location Code.

> **Note:** These Location Codes are case sensitive. For example, 4a is not the same as 4A.

AIX Location Codes

The format of the output from the **lsdev** command normally consists of four fields, as shown below:

```
<logical_name> <status> <location> <description>
```

The first field is the logical name of the device or adapter. This is the name normally used as input to other commands that display or alter the configuration of the device. The second field shows the status of the device. Normally, this is either `Available` or `Defined`. The third field is the device location information. The fourth field is a description of the device.

The format of the device location field is as follows:

- For non-SCSI devices/drives

  AB-CD-EF-GH

  - The AB value identifies a bus type, or PCI parent bus, as assigned by the firmware.
  - The CD value identifies the adapter number, adapter's devfunc number or physical location. The devfunc number is defined as the PCI device number times 8, plus the function number.
  - The EF value identifies a connector.

- The GH value identifies a port, address, device, or FRU.

- For SCSI devices/drives

  AB-CD-EF-G,H

The following example is the output from the command **lsdev -Cc disk** run on an MCA machine. The command has produced a list of all the SCSI disks:

```
hdisk0 Available 00-08-00-0,0 670 MB SCSI Disk Drive
hdisk1 Available 00-08-00-1,0 2.0 GB SCSI Disk Drive
```

The device location is the third field on each line. In this example, the format of the location code is as follows:

- The first pair of zeros denotes a system unit.
- 08 is the slot number on the I/O Planar on bus 0.
- The third pair of digits on some adapters would indicate the port or connector number. For example, some SCSI adapters have an external connector and an internal edge connector.
- In this case, 1,0 is the SCSI address of the disk but could be the address of a controller followed by the child device address number.

The format for PCI adapters shown below is slightly different. The first two pairs of numbers are read together and they correspond to a particular PCI bus and slot. You will, however, need to refer to the system documentation for your machine type to correlate this to a particular slot number in the machine, since most PCI-based machines have more than one PCI bus. The last two pairs of numbers have the same function as the MCA example above. For example:

```
hdisk0 Available 30-68-00-8,0  16 Bit SCSI Disk Drive
```

Physical Location Codes

Physical Location Codes indicate the physical position of the slot, adapter, or device. The Service Guide and, usually, the User Guide will show the AIX Location Code (logical) to Physical Location Code relationship. Diagnostics will normally display the Physical Location Code (if available) instead of the AIX Location Code.

Below is some of the output of the **lscfg -vp** command run on an IBM @server pSeries 620 (7025 F80):

```
scsi2            27-08            Wide/Ultra-2 SCSI I/O Controller

      DUAL CHANNEL PCI TO ULTRA2 SCSI ADAPTER:
        Part Number.................03N3606
        EC Level....................D72901
        Manufacture ID..............A16592
```

```
Serial Number...............1427
Device Specific.(YL)........P1-I8/Z1
```

The 27-08 is the AIX Location Code (positions AB-CD). The device specific (YL) shows (in this example) the Physical Location Code P1-I8/Z1. The P1 denotes Planar 1, I8 denotes PCI slot 8, and Z1 is the first channel (SCSI bus) of the Dual Channel Adapter card.

Other examples of physical location codes displayed by AIX are:

P1-C1 Processor card in slot 1 of planar 1

U1-P1-M2.12 Memory DIMM 12 in system planar slot 2

U0.2-P2-I1 PCI adapter in secondary I/O drawer, slot 1

5.2 Problem diagnosis

The best method of initial diagnosis of a problem is to run Diagnostics in Problem Determination mode to let the system analyze the error log and test any suspect devices. See Section 5.3.1, “Concurrent mode” on page 125.

Diagnosis of hardware problems depends upon observation, error information collection, and the results of running diagnostics. Generally, the first indication of a problem is an entry in the error log. The first entry for a problem can be many days or even weeks old before you notice a problem. Sometimes, there may be multiple similar entries showing a degradation in device performance before a failure. In other cases, there may only be a single error log entry.

There are several ways of accessing the error log. You can use SMIT, the command line, or use the Display Hardware Error Report task, which provides options to display both the summary and detail hardware error logs. Refer to Section 2.2, “Error log file processing” on page 21 for more information.

Observation of a how a problem manifests itself will quite often give you an indication as to what may be the cause.

One of the more powerful tools to help you resolve a fault is the Diagnostics system, available through AIX when loaded on the machine and on a separate CD-ROM or diskette. Additionally, a set of utilities are included in the diagnostics in the Task Selection or Service Aid section. Included in this section are aids to help further diagnose SCSI, LAN, and disk subsystem faults.

5.2.1 Making sense of the error log

To get the most out of the AIX Error Log, you must understand the following points:

1. The kernel and device drivers log errors to the error log, not diagnostics. Diagnostics (Error Log Analysis) analyzes errors that have been logged.
2. In many cases, permanent and temporary hardware errors are logged that are not indicative of a hardware problem. Error Log Analysis should always be run to determine if these errors indicate a hardware problem.
3. Resource Name indicates the resource that detected the error. It does NOT indicated the failing resource. It does indicate the resource that diagnostics and Error Log Analysis should be run on.
4. Failure Causes, Probable Causes, and User Causes are generic recommendations and are not intended to be used to determine what parts to replace. Parts should only be replaced based on diagnostics and Error Log Analysis results.

> **Note:** Sysplanar0 errors are *detected* by Sysplanar0, not necessarily *caused* by Sysplanar0, although the error log may list it as a probable cause. Run the Error Log Analysis task or Diagnostics in Problem Determination mode to find the true cause.

5. System errors related to the processors, memory, power supplies, fans, and so on, are logged under resource name sysplanar0. Error Log Analysis should be run on sysplanar0 any time there is an error log with a resource name of sysplanar0.
6. Error Log Analysis can be run by running diagnostics in problem determination mode or by running the running the Run Error Log Analysis task. Stand-alone diagnostics do not perform error log analysis.
7. Error Log Analysis will analyze all the errors in the error log associated with a specific resource. For those errors that should be corrected, Error Log Analysis will provide a list of actions or an SRN. For errors that can safely be ignored, Error Log Analysis will indicate that no problems were found.

For information on how to access the error log, refer to Section 2.2, “Error log file processing” on page 21.

The error log can contain many hundreds of entries, so it is always best to start with the summary format. This format will give you a chronological list of events, starting with the latest event at the top of the screen. The following is an example of the summary output of the **errpt** command:

```
IDENTIFIER TIMESTAMP  T C RESOURCE_NAME  DESCRIPTION
```

```
C60BB505   0511122901 P S SYSPROC        SOFTWARE PROGRAM ABNORMALLY TERMINATED
C60BB505   0511122901 P S SYSPROC        SOFTWARE PROGRAM ABNORMALLY TERMINATED
C60BB505   0511122901 P S SYSPROC        SOFTWARE PROGRAM ABNORMALLY TERMINATED
74533D1A   0510182901 U H SYSIOS         LOSS OF ELECTRICAL POWER
9DBCFDEE   0511083901 T O errdemon       ERROR LOGGING TURNED ON
192AC071   0510182501 T O errdemon       ERROR LOGGING TURNED OFF
0734DA1D   0503110401 P H fd0            DISKETTE MEDIA ERROR
C60BB505   0422105301 P S SYSPROC        SOFTWARE PROGRAM ABNORMALLY TERMINATED
C60BB505   0422105301 P S SYSPROC        SOFTWARE PROGRAM ABNORMALLY TERMINATED
C60BB505   0422105301 P S SYSPROC        SOFTWARE PROGRAM ABNORMALLY TERMINATED
3573A829   0422105001 U S CMDCRASH       SYSTEM DUMP
AD331440   0422104501 U S SYSDUMP        SYSTEM DUMP
AE26DD07   0422083001 P S SYSSPECFS      DRIVER RETURNED WITH INTERRUPTS
DISABLED
9DBCFDEE   0422104701 T O errdemon       ERROR LOGGING TURNED ON
```

Look through the first couple of screens to see the sort of errors being produced and the frequency. Also check whether the errors fall into an obvious sequence, for example, a disk error followed by a SCSI error. Look at the time stamps of the errors for any pattern, for example, if they occur at or near the same time each day. For tape drive entries, look back over several weeks. Media errors on the same day of the week may indicate a particular tape is failing. The time stamp format is MMDDHHMMYY. So, the first error in the example output above occurred on May 11th, 2001 at 12:29. The column marked C denotes the class of error. Class types are H for hardware, S for software, and O for operator message. See “Class” on page 28 for a full description of the class entries. Once you have decided which of the errors interest you the most, expand the error log into the detail or intermediate format. Example 5-1 shows a complete detailed error log entry.

Example 5-1 Example of a detailed error log entry

```
LABEL: DISK_ERR4
IDENTIFIER:1581762B

Date/Time:        Thu Apr 29 08:08:04
Sequence Number:  604
Machine Id:       00018367A400
Node Id:          test1
Class:            H
Type:             TEMP
Resource Name:    hdisk0
Resource Class:   disk
Resource Type:    2000mb
Location:         00-08-00-0,0
VPD:
        Manufacturer................IBMRISC
        Machine Type and Model......0664M1H
        Part Number.................86F0101
```

```
        ROS Level and ID...........5 5A
        Serial Number..............00438487
        EC Level...................895186
        FRU Number.................86F0118
        Device Specific.(Z0).......000002029F00001E
        Device Specific.(Z1).......75G3644
        Device Specific.(Z2).......0983
Device Specific.(Z3)........95333
        Device Specific.(Z4).......0002
        Device Specific.(Z5).......22
        Device Specific.(Z6).......895180

Description
DISK OPERATION ERROR

Probable Causes
MEDIA
DASD DEVICE

User Causes
MEDIA DEFECTIVE

   Recommended Actions
   FOR REMOVABLE MEDIA, CHANGE MEDIA AND RETRY
   PERFORM PROBLEM DETERMINATION PROCEDURES

Failure Causes
MEDIA
DISK DRIVE

   Recommended Actions
   FOR REMOVABLE MEDIA, CHANGE MEDIA AND RETRY
   PERFORM PROBLEM DETERMINATION PROCEDURES

Detail Data
SENSE DATA
0600 0000 0800 10F3 0100 0000 0000 0000 0102 0000 7000 0100 0000 0018 0000 0000
1500 0180 0001 0000 01A6 0000 000E 02FF 0000 0000 0000 0000 0000 0000 0A06 0000
0000 0000 100E 0801 0000 0032 4000 1800 0000 0000 1106 0100 0000 0000 0F0E 8080
0000 0001 0000 0001 0000 0000 2020 2020 2020 2020 2020 4C31 2020 2020 2020 2020
2020 2020 2020 3539 4833 3438 3120 2020 2020 4533 0000 0028 0002 7600
```

The Error Log Analysis program within Diagnostics, Task Selection, will decode the sense data and give a possible cause and Action Plan. For an older version of AIX, this can also be run remotely by IBM support personnel, who will cut and paste the sense data into the following IBM intranet Web interface URL:

http://starbase5.austin.ibm.com/cgi-bin/hardware/dsense/dsense_form.sh

The next area of the error log entry to look at is the area starting at the resource name and finishing at the end of the VPD section.The information given here will help you to identify the type of device that has detected the problem, its size, and, more importantly on a complex system, its location. Additionally, the VPD will often give you the part number and FRU number to enable you to arrange for a replacement part to be ordered if diagnostics determine the part is failing.

Note: Do not replace any parts solely due to errors in the error log.

The VPD can also indicate the microcode level of the device at the time the error occurred.

Most diagnostic routines, except when running diagnostics from CD-ROM or via network boot, use the sense data in the error log when run in Problem Determination mode. This use of the error log data by the diagnostics is the main way of deciding what is the cause of any hardware errors logged in the AIX error log. To run the diagnostics in this way, the date set on the machine must be within seven days of the error log time stamp on machines running AIX Version 4.3.1 and above (using Diagnostic Run Time options within Task Selection under AIX Version 4.3.1 and above allows you to set a value of 1 to 60 days). Machines running AIX Version 4.3.0 and below must have the date set within 24 hours of the time stamp for the error log analysis diagnostic to give correct results.

5.2.2 Physical inspection

The most obvious thing to look for when starting a diagnosis is physical damage, such as impact damage. Is anything obviously broken or does anything look incorrect to you? Look at cables going into the machine: Are any of them showing damage? Is the cable securely fixed to the adapter and to the device that is at the other end? Most installations end up with a tangle of cables either at the rear of the machine or under the floor. Try and look to see if there is any additional cabling nearby or intertwined with the cables of the machine you are looking at that might be a source of electrical interference. Power cables carrying heavy current are a prime source of electrical noise.

Look at the cabling of devices attached to the machine, especially their routing, the tightness of the fixing of cabling, damage to cabling, and the proximity of heavy current carrying power cables. The positioning of adapters and devices can also influence problems.

If the machine you are working on is a PCI Bus machine, check the adapter positions in the machine against the recommended positions shown in the *RS/6000 and pSeries PCI Adapter Placement Reference*, SA38-0538. The latest copy of this publication can be found at the following URL:

http://www.ibm.com/servers/eserver/pseries/library/

This guide will show whether the PCI card and slot within the system are compatible. Details of voltage (3.3 or 5V), bus width (32 or 64bit), bus speed (33, 50 or 66 MHz), hot-pluggable or not, customer or service representative installable, maximum cards per system/bus, and restrictions causing performance problems are listed. Note that some restrictions are rules that must not be broken and others are just performance related guidelines. The placement of the adapters should also be checked against a search by your IBM marketing support representative to ensure that you have the most recent information. This especially applies to high-bandwidth adapters, such as SP Switch, SSA RAID, and ATM. While you are looking at the adapter placement, make sure that the adapters are securely clamped to the chassis and are as deep into the card slot as possible. The correct seating of adapters is most important, especially in the case of J and R series SMP machines. An improperly seated adapter will, sometimes, not have a problem itself but will cause another adapter elsewhere on the bus to cause strange or intermittent problems.

5.3 Running diagnostics

Diagnostics on hardware can be run in four different ways. The first way of running the diagnostics is in concurrent mode, that is, the system is up and running with users on and all processes running and all volume groups being used. The second way is Service mode; this is when you have the machine with AIX running but with the minimum of processes started and only rootvg varied on. The third way is stand-alone diagnostics from a CD-ROM, diskette or tape. The diskette and tape options have been discontinued on later machines. The CD-ROM-based diagnostics are a completely isolated version of AIX and so any diagnostics run are totally independent of the AIX setup on the machine being tested. The fourth way is to network boot a diagnostic image from another machine using NIM. This is required on the later machines that do not have the optional CD-ROM drive.This is also independent of the AIX setup on the machine being tested but is dependent on the diagnostic image being correct on the other machine. Device drivers and software fixes may be at different levels.

Which of these methods you use depends upon the circumstances, such as:

- Are you able to test the device? Is the device in use?
- Do you need to decide if the problem is related to hardware or AIX? Stand-alone diagnostics from a CD-ROM or diskette are independent of the machine operating system. Advanced diagnostics run using the diagnostic CD-ROM at a level that supports your machine and completing successfully should be taken as proof of probably no hardware problem. Running diagnostics from a hard disk or network boot rely on the device support being

correctly installed and at the right level for the device being tested. This may sometimes give incorrect results.

> **Note:** If you are going to boot from a CD-ROM on a machine that is in any configuration that has two or more SCSI adapters sharing the same SCSI bus, check that no SCSI adapters on the shared bus are set at address 7. If you boot from bootable media, the bootable media will automatically assign address 7 to all SCSI adapters in the machine being booted and will cause severe problems on any other machines sharing the same SCSI bus that have address 7 IDs set on their adapters. This is often used in HACMP environments.

The method by which you run diagnostics varies between machine type. The next sections describe how to run the diagnostic modes on all machine types.

There are two RS/6000 models that do not have the capability to run AIX-based diagnostics. These machines are 7020-40P and 7248-43P. To run diagnostics on these models, you must have the SMS diskette for the machine.

5.3.1 Concurrent mode

Concurrent mode diagnostics are run while AIX is running on the machine and, potentially, with users on. To run diagnostics concurrently, you must have root authority (or the customer can create a user login with the required authority) and use one of the methods listed below:

1. To run diagnostics on a specific device, use the following command:

   ```
   # diag -d [resource name]
   ```

   This command will enable you to test a specific device directly without the need to pass through a number of menus. The diagnostic process run is the Advanced Diagnostic process.
2. To go directly to the main diagnostics menu, use the **diag** command.
3. Using SMIT, take the following menu route:
   - Problem Determination
   - Hardware Diagnostics
   - Current shell

Methods 2 and 3 will get you to the entry screen of the diagnostics menu. If you press Enter to continue from the entry screen, you will be presented with a menu, shown in Example 5-2 on page 126.

Example 5-2 FUNCTION SELECTION menu

```
                        FUNCTION SELECTION                             801002


Move cursor to selection, then press Enter.

  Diagnostic Routines
    This selection will test the machine hardware. Wrap plugs and
    other advanced functions will not be used.
  Advanced Diagnostics Routines
    This selection will test the machine hardware. Wrap plugs and
    other advanced functions will be used.
  Task Selection(Diagnostics, Advanced Diagnostics, Service Aids, etc.)
    This selection will list the tasks supported by these procedures.
    Once a task is selected, a resource menu may be presented showing
    all resources supported by the task.
  Resource Selection
    This selection will list the resources in the system that are supported
    by these procedures. Once a resource is selected, a task menu will
    be presented showing all tasks that can be run on the resource(s).

F1=Help                F10=Exit                F3=Previous Menu
```

The menu options shown in Example 5-2 are explained in the following paragraphs:

Diagnostic Routines This set of routines is primarily aimed at the operator of the machine. When the diagnostics are run using this option, there will be no prompts to unplug devices or cables, and no wrap plugs are used. Therefore, the testing done by this method is not as comprehensive as the testing performed under Advanced Diagnostics. In some cases, it can produce a `No Trouble Found` result when there is an actual problem.

Advanced Diagnostics This set of routines will run diagnostic tests that will ask you to remove cables, plug and unplug wrap plugs, and use various other items. As a result, the tests run are as detailed as possible. Generally, if you get a **`No Trouble Found`** result using Advanced Diagnostics, you can be reasonably certain the devices tested have no hardware defects at the time of testing.

Task Selection This section is sometimes referred to as Service Aids. There are many useful tools within this section. The use of this option is discussed in Section 5.3.5, “Task selection or service aids” on page 137.

After you have selected the level of diagnostics you wish to run, you will then be presented with a menu that asks you to decide to use either the Problem Determination method or the System Verification method.

Problem Determination This selection will make the diagnostic routine search the AIX error log for any errors posted in the previous seven days against the device you are testing. It will then use the sense data from any error log entry for the device being tested in conjunction with the results of the diagnostic testing of the device to produce a Service Request Number (SRN). This method must be used to determine the cause of any hardware errors logged in the AIX error log. If you are performing diagnostics more than seven days since the machine check occurred, then you will need to set the system date and time to within seven days of the machine check time stamp. The seven day period is required when using AIX Version 4.3.1 and later. If you are using AIX Version 4.3.0 or below, then the system date and time must be within 24 hours of the checkstop entry. See Section 5.2.1, “Making sense of the error log” on page 120 for more information. Be aware that there may be more than one error posted within this time so the results may be for an error unrelated to the problem you are investigating. Check the date and time of the error to ensure you are looking at the correct one.

System Verification Use this selection if you have just replaced a part or performed a repair action. System verification runs a diagnostic to the device but does not refer to the AIX error log, so it reflects the machines condition at the time of running the test. If a repair action has taken place, you will be asked by the system if the problem has been resolved. Answering yes will place an entry in the error log with the description REPAIR ACTION. This will stop Problem Determination from analyzing this problem again. The error Label in the error log detail is FRU REPLACED, which can be misleading as there may not have been a FRU Replacement, but just a reseat, adjustment, or load of latest firmware. You can also use system verification when you just want to run a straight test to a device or whole machine.

Concurrent mode provides a way to run online diagnostics on the system resources while AIX is up and running and users are logged on.

Since the system is running in normal operation, some resources cannot be tested in concurrent mode. The following list shows which resources cannot be fully tested, although the error log analysis in PD Mode may highlight a problem:

- SCSI adapters used by disks connected to paging devices
- The disk drives used for paging
- Memory
- Processor

Depending on the status of the device being tested, here are four possible test scenarios in concurrent mode:

- Minimal testing is used when the device being tested is under the control of another process.
- Partial testing occurs when testing is performed on an adapter or device that has some processes controlling part of it. For example, testing unconfigured ports on an 8-port RS232 adapter.
- Full testing requires the device be unassigned and unused by any other process. Achieving this condition may require commands to be run prior to the commencement of the diagnostic testing.
- When tests are run to the CPU or memory, the diagnostics refer to an entry in the NVRAM that records any CPU or memory errors generated during initial testing at system power on time. By analyzing these entries, the diagnostics produce any relevant SRNs.

CE Login can be used to run concurrent diagnostics, too. CE login enables a user to perform operating system commands that are required to service the system without being logged in as a root user. CE login must have a role of Run Diagnostics and a primary group of systems. This enables the user to:

- Run the diagnostics, including the service aids, such as hot plug tasks, certify, format, and so forth.
- Run all the operating system commands run by system group users.
- Configure and unconfigure devices that are not busy.

In addition, CE login can have the shutdown group enabled in order to allow:

- Use of the Update System Microcode service aid
- Use of shutdown and reboot operations

To use CE login, you need to create a unique user name and configure these characteristics for that name. Refer to the Users and Groups section of the *AIX 5L Version 5.1 System Management Guide: Operating System and Devices*, which can be found at:

`http://publibn.boulder.ibm.com/cgi-bin/ds_form?lang=en_US&viewset=AIX`

After this is set up, you will need to set up a password to log in with these capabilities. The recommended CE login user name is qserv.

5.3.2 Online diagnostics in service mode

This mode enables you to run tests to the devices that would ordinarily be busy if you ran diagnostics with the machine up in Normal mode boot, for example, the network adapter ent0. However, you still will not be able to test any SCSI device that is attached to disks containing paging space or rootvg. Online diagnostics from disk are started when you boot up the machine in Service mode boot. The method that you employ to get a Service mode boot depends upon the type of machine.

MCA machines

To start a Service mode boot, power off the machine, then:

1. Set the key mode switch of the machine to the Service position.
2. Power on the machine without a CD-ROM, tape, or diskette in the machine.

After a period of time, you will see the Diagnostics Entry screen appear on the console. Press Enter and you will then get to the screen giving you the choice of diagnostics to run.

PCI machines

This section applies to machines of model type 7017, 7024, 7025, 7026, 7043, 7044 and later. It does not apply to PCI machine types 7020 or 7248.

To start a Service mode boot, power off the machine, then:

1. Turn on the machine power.
2. After a short period of time you will see the Icons screen. The Icons screen is described in “PCI machine icons” on page 44. At this point, press F6 if using a graphics console, or 6 if using an ASCII terminal or a graphics console on later machines. If you are using the graphics console, sometimes the display device will have power saving enabled, and so will take time to warm up and display images. This can lead you to miss the Icon screen being displayed. In this situation, observe the power LED on the display device, and when it changes from orange to green, simply press the F6 or 6 key.

Once the keyboard input has been processed, the machine will display a Software Starting screen. This can then be followed by more information indicating the SCSI ID of the boot device being used. Once diagnostics have been loaded, you will have the Diagnostic Entry screen displayed.

In addition to using the F6 or 6 key, most newer systems provide a method to boot the system in service mode from the service processor menus. Boot Mode menu allows users to set the system to automatically start a specific function on the next system start. This setting applies to the next boot only and is reset to the default state of being disabled following a successful boot attempt.

The boot mode menu is as follows:

```
BOOT MODE MENU
1. Boot to SMS Menu: Currently Disabled
2. Service Mode Boot from Saved List: Currently Disabled
3. Service Mode Boot from Default List: Currently Disabled
4. Boot to Open Firmware Prompt: Currently Disabled
98. Return to Previous Menu
1>
```

Enabling the Boot to SMS Menu option causes the system to automatically stop at the System Management Services menu during the boot process. Enabling this option is equivalent to pressing 1 on the attached ASCII terminal (or F1 on a graphics terminal) while the system initialization indicators display on screen.

Enabling the Service Mode Boot from Saved list option causes the system to perform a service mode boot using the service mode boot list saved in NVRAM. If the system boots AIX from the disk drive and AIX diagnostics are loaded on the disk drive, AIX boots in service mode to the diagnostics menu. Using this option to boot the system is the preferred way to run online diagnostics.

Enabling the Service Mode Boot from Default List option is similar to Service Mode Boot from Saved List, except the system boots using the default boot list that is stored in the system firmware. This is normally used to try to boot diagnostics from the CD-ROM drive. Using this option to boot the system is the preferred way to run stand-alone diagnostics.

Enabling the Boot to Open Firmware Prompt option causes the system to automatically enter open firmware prompt (also called the OK prompt). This option should only be used by service personnel to obtain additional debug information.

For additional information, see the relevant Service Guide.

5.3.3 Stand-alone diagnostics

Stand-alone diagnostics run from CD-ROMs or diskettes are a good way of proving if the problem is a hardware fault or an AIX problem. The CD-ROM or diskettes load a totally independent version of AIX onto the machine as a RAM image. If you get a `No Trouble Found` result using while advanced diagnostics using all of the test equipment asked for during the diagnostic, the probability of there being a hardware problem is extremely small. In such cases, the underlying cause of the problem is most often software related.

> **Note:** If you are going to boot from a CD-ROM on a machine that has two or more SCSI adapters sharing the same SCSI bus, check that no SCSI adapters on the shared bus are set at address 7. If you boot from bootable media, the bootable media will automatically assign address 7 to all SCSI adapters in the machine being booted, and so will cause severe problems on any other machines sharing the same SCSI bus that have address 7 IDs set on their adapters.

MCA machines

This section describes how to boot from a CD-ROM on MCA machines and from diskette for the early level of MCA machines.

Boot from CD-ROM

To boot from CD-ROM, complete the following steps:

1. Power off the machine.
2. Turn the key mode switch to the Service position.
3. Power on the machine, then place the Diagnostic CD-ROM in the drive.

   For the machine to boot from the Diagnostic CD-ROM, there must be an entry in the boot list that includes the CD-ROM. Using the code on the CD-ROM, the machine will boot, eventually pausing when displaying c31 in the LED panel. The code c31 is an indication to you that you need to select a system console. After selecting a console at the prompt, you will get the Diagnostic Entry screen followed by subsequent screens. One of these subsequent screens will prompt you to enter the terminal type. Make sure you know the type before you proceed, because a wrong entry could result in you having to restart the whole process again. If in doubt, try using vt100.

Boot from diskettes

The booting of a machine from diskette will only be possible on uniprocessor MCA machines. It is also a more complex method to use than the Diagnostic CD-ROM.

The machine types that support booting Diagnostic diskettes are:

- 7011 Models 220 - 250
- 7012 Models 320 - 390
- 7013 Models 520 - 59H

To boot a machine from diskette, the procedure is as follows:

1. Power off the machine.
2. Place diskette 1A or 1B into the disk drive and then power on the machine. The difference between diskette 1A and diskette 1B is the minimum size of memory required to run the diagnostics. If your machine is running with more than 8 MB of memory, either diskette will work satisfactorily.
3. The diskette is being read when 252 is displayed on the LED. When diskette 1 has been read and processed, c07 will be flashing on the LED. Insert diskette 2. The LED will then display c09 as it reads the diskette.
4. When c07 displays with diskette 2 in the drive, select diskette 3A, 3B, or 3C. The number 3 diskettes each correspond to different sorts of graphics cards. Select the diskette that corresponds to the graphics cards in your machine and place it in the drive. This is then followed by diskette 4 after c07 is displayed when diskette 3 is in the drive. However, if you only have an ASCII terminal and no graphics card, you can skip diskette 3 and place diskette 4 in the drive.
5. When diskette 4 has finished processing, the LED will display c31. This means the machine is prompting for input on the console. Make your console selection as prompted on the screen. If you are using a vt100 emulator on a PC, you may have no text displayed on the screen. This is due to the boot process resetting the serial port. If the emulator is connected to serial port one, then type a `1` and then press Enter. The c31 should then disappear, and you should then get the Diagnostics screen displayed. If this does not work, then try typing `2` then Enter. You will then be able to test the system unit. Should you wish to test any other devices, such as disks, you will need to load the corresponding diskette associated with the device. In the case of disks, this will be diskette 5.

PCI bus machines

This section applies to machines of model type 7017, 7024, 7025, 7026, 7043, 7044, and later. It does not apply to PCI machine types 7020 or 7248.

On later machines you have the option of starting the Service mode boot from the Service Processor menus. See the relevant Service Guide for details.

To start a CD boot:

1. Power off the machine.
2. Turn on machine power.
3. Place the CD-ROM into the drive.
4. After a short period of time, you will see the Icons screen. At this point, press F5 if you are using a graphics console, or 5 if you are using an ASCII terminal or graphics console on a later machine. If you are using the graphics console, sometimes the display screen will have power saving enabled, and so take time to warm up before anything can be seen on the screen. This can lead you to miss the Icon screen being displayed. In this situation, observe the power LED on the display device, and when it changes from orange to green, then press the F5 or 5 key.

After doing the above, you will get various screens displayed, one of which will indicate the SCSI address of the device that the machine is booting from. Following this screen, you will then have the Diagnostic Entry screen displayed.

If your system contains ISA adapters, you will not be able to automatically test them. You will have to configure the adapters to the system using the ISA Configuration menu found in the Service Aids or Task Selection.

The ISA Configuration Service Aids will display all the ISA adapters supported by the diagnostics that you are running. Diagnostic support for ISA adapters not shown in the list may be supported from a supplemental diskette supplied with the adapter.

Configuring ISA adapters from diagnostics

As mentioned above, when booting diagnostics from CD-ROM, you can only test the ISA adapters in your system after they have been configured. The configuration is only for diagnostic purposes and will not affect the adapters' configuration within AIX.

The following procedure explains how to configure an adapter using diagnostics. For the purpose of the explanation, we have used an 8-port adapter as an example.

1. Before you boot into diagnostics, note the ISA adapter parameters that are set for the adapter(s) you wish to test. These will either be the parameters you entered to install the card or parameters you have set on the card if the card has not yet been configured by AIX. For example, the only parameter we had to record was the Bus I/O Address.
2. Boot into diagnostics from the CD-ROM, as explained above.

3. Select Service Aids or Task Selection. The item that you select is dependent upon the level of diagnostics you are using. Since AIX Version 4.3.2, Service Aids were under the Task Selection option.
4. Select ISA Device Configuration Service Aid. This will provide you with a menu similar to the one shown in Example 5-3.

Example 5-3 ISA device configuration screen

```
                ISA DEVICE CONFIGURATION SERVICE AID

    Move cursor to the selection, then press Enter.

    Add an ISA Adapter
    Remove an ISA Adapter
    List all Defined ISA Adapters
    List all Supported ISA Adapters



    F3=Cancel                F10=Exit
```

5. From the menu, select Add an ISA Adapter.
6. Choose the desired adapter.
7. Enter the parameters, as requested, as shown in Example 5-4. For our 8-port card, we only had to enter the Bus I/O Address.

Example 5-4 ISA adapter attribute screen

```
                    ISA ADAPTER ATTRIBUTE SELECTION

    Press 'List' to select additional values. If a
    range is indicated below the description, then enter a
    value within the range. Press 'Commit' when finished.


    Bus I/O Address                                [0x104]
    Bus Memory Address                             [0xd0000]
    ISA Interrupt Level                            [   ]



    F1=Help      F2=Refresh     F3=Cancel     F4=List
    F5=Reset     F7=Commit      F10=Exit
```

8. After selecting Commit, a message similar to the following will appear:

```
Adding ISA Adapter 'IBM 8-Port Async, EIA-232 (ISA)'
Please Standby
```

If the addition was successful, you should also see a message similar to:

```
ISA Adapter device 'sa2'
Configuration complete
```

9. Return to the main Diagnostics menu.

You should now be able to test the ISA adapter in addition to other devices in your system.

5.3.4 Stand-alone diagnostics from NIM server

A client system connected to a network with a Network Installation Management (NIM) server is capable of booting stand-alone diagnostics from the NIM server if the client system is registered on the NIM server, and the boot settings on both the NIM server and the client system are correct.

> **Note:** The boot image on the NIM server must be at the right AIX level and have the required device drivers to support the system, adapters and devices of the client system. Unpredictable results and missing devices or adapters will occur if the levels are not correct.

For further information, see *RS/6000 and pSeries Diagnostics Information for Multiple Bus Systems*, SA38-0509.

Client configuration

To run stand-alone diagnostics on a client system from the NIM server, do the following:

1. Remove all removable media (tape or CD-ROM disc).
2. Stop all programs, including the AIX operating system (get help if needed).
3. Turn off the system unit power.
4. Turn on the system unit power.
5. When the keyboard indicator displays (the word `keyboard` on an ASCII terminal or the Keyboard icon on a graphical display), press the number 1 key (in case of F80) on the keyboard to display the SMS menu.
6. Enter any requested passwords.
7. Select Utilities.
8. Depending on the console type, select RIPL or Remote Initial Program Load Setup.
9. Depending on the console type, select Set Address or IP Parameters.

10.Enter the client address, server address, gateway address (if applicable), and subnet mask into the Remote Initial Program Load (RIPL). If there is no gateway between the NIM server and the client, set the gateway address to 0.0.0.0. To determine if there is a gateway, either ask the system network administrator or compare the first three octets of the NIM server address and the client address. If they are the same (for example, if the NIM server address is 9.3.126.16 and the client address is 9.3.126.42, the first three octets (9.3.126) are the same), then set the gateway address in the RIPL field to 0.0.0.0.

Note: RIPL is located under the Utility menu in System Management Services (SMS) and should be referred to for information on setting these parameters.

11.If the NIM server is set up to allow the pinging of the client system, use the ping option in the RIPL utility to verify that the client system can ping the NIM server. Under the `ping` utility, choose the network adapter that provides the attachment to the NIM server to do the ping operation. If the ping comes back with an OK prompt, the client is prepared to boot from the NIM server. If ping returns with a FAILED prompt, the client does not proceed with the boot.

Note: If the ping fails, refer to Boot Problems/Concerns in the service guide for the appropriate system unit. Then follow the steps for network boot problems.

Network boot

Use the following procedure to temporarily change the system bootlist so that the network adapter attached to the NIM server network is first in the bootlist:

1. Exit to the SMS Main screen.
2. Depending on the console type, select Multiboot or Select Boot Devices.
3. Depending on the console type, select Boot Sequence or Select Boot Devices.
4. Record the current bootlist settings. (You will have to set the bootlist back to the original settings after running diagnostics from the NIM server.)
5. Change the bootlist so the network adapter attached to the NIM server is first in the bootlist.
6. Exit completely from SMS. The system should start loading packets while doing a bootp from the network.Follow the instructions on the screen to select the system console. If Diagnostics Operating Instructions Version x.x.x is displays, stand-alone diagnostics has loaded successfully.

If the AIX login prompt displays, stand-alone diagnostics did not load. Check the following items:

- The bootlist on the client might be incorrect.
- The Cstate on the NIM server might be incorrect.
- There might be network problems preventing you from connecting to the NIM server.

Verify the settings and the status of the network. If you continue to have problems, refer to Boot Problems/Concerns in the service guide for the system unit. Then follow the steps for network boot problems.

After running diagnostics, reboot the system and use SMS to change the bootlist sequence back to the original settings.

5.3.5 Task selection or service aids

This section is known by two names *service aids* or *task selection*, depending upon the level of diagnostics you are using. Task selection is the name used since AIX Version 4.3.2; however, in AIX Version 4.1.4, the same menu is known as service aids. This portion of the diagnostic package is equally as useful in the diagnosis of faults as the diagnostic routines themselves. The next few sections will cover a selection of the service aids available, but not all of them.

System exerciser

This service aid is useful for exercising selected resources to verify basic functionality.

Hot plug task

This task is used to work with hot pluggable PCI cards and SCSI disks. See the appropriate service or user guide for your machine to see if cards or disks are hot pluggable and the procedures to use.

Local area network analyzer

This service aid is useful in the diagnosis of network problems. It enables you to type in IP addresses of both a source machine and a target machine. When activated, it will tell you if it managed to connect to the target machine. If it failed, it will try and give you a reason why it could not reach the destination host. The result of this can sometimes help in furthering fault diagnosis.

Microcode download

Using this service aid makes manipulation of microcode much easier than doing it from the command line. As a result, you are less liable to make a mistake.

The microcode download facility is also available when using the Diagnostic CD-ROM. This enables the downloading of microcode to devices that are not capable of being updated when AIX is running.

Use the method listed in the instructions accompanying the new microcode.

SCSI bus analyzer

This is probably one of the most useful service aids. It enables you to issue a SCSI inquiry command to any device on any SCSI bus connected to the machine. The results that are returned give you a good idea of the problem. The results returned are:

- The exerciser transmitted a SCSI Inquiry command and did not receive any response back. Ensure that the address is valid, then try this option again.
- The exerciser transmitted a SCSI Inquiry command and received a valid response back without any errors being detected.
- A check condition was returned from the device.

To run this service aid:

1. From the Task Selection menu, select SCSI Bus Analyzer.
2. At the next screen, select the adapter that has the device that you wish to test attached to it.
3. Use the Tab key to increment the SCSI ID field to the number you want to test.
4. Press F7 to confirm your selection.
5. Press Enter to commence the test.

If the device is working correctly, the response saying so should be returned almost instantly. If there is a problem, it should return an answer after a few seconds. Sometimes, a device that has a severe check condition will hang the service aid. If this is the case, you need to Ctrl-C out of the service aid. Refer to Section 5.7, “Diagnosis of SCSI problems” on page 142 if you get this condition,

Disk maintenance

The disk to disk copy will only work with SCSI disks that pass diagnostics and ideally have minimal errors when the certify process is run. If the error rate is too high when disk-to-disk copy is being run, the program will fail. You will find it useful if the customer situation is such that they have no backup and the disk is unstable but running. Disk-to-disk copy differs from an AIX-based migrate operation because it does not alter the source disk when finished as the **migratepv** command does. Disk-to-disk copy is best run from CD-ROM diagnostics, which requires you to have the exclusive use of the machine while the disk copying takes place. Also, the disk to be copied to must *not* be smaller than the source disk or more than 10 percent larger in size than the source disk. The copied disk will have the same PVID as the original, so the defective disk must be removed from the machine before starting AIX.

SSA service aids

This service aid can be used to help diagnose SSA subsystem problems. It is also used to physically identify and control SSA disks in the tower or drawer. This function greatly speeds the locating of specific disks, especially in very large installations.

> **Note:** This service aid is only present when SSA devices are configured on the machine.

5.4 System Management Services (SMS)

System Management Services (SMS) is the diagnostic and configuration portion of the firmware. It is used on all PCI-based machines. The method of starting SMS varies between machines and is explained below. In the 7020 and 7248 machine types, SMS is very important, because it is the only way of diagnostically testing the machine due to the fact that AIX diagnostics are not supported. On these two machines, SMS is loaded from the SMS diskette.

5.4.1 Firmware-based SMS

SMS on machine types 7017, 7024, 7025, 7026, 7043, and later is contained within the firmware and can be accessed during system boot. SMS on these machines can be accessed by pressing F1 (graphics console on old machines) or 1 (ASCII terminal or graphics console on later machines) when the PCI Icons screen is displayed on the console during the boot sequence.

You will then be shown a menu enabling you, among other things, to change the boot list or update system firmware on some machines.

5.4.2 Diskette-based SMS

As previously mentioned in this chapter, there are two types of machines on which it is not possible to run any form of AIX diagnostics. These machines are 7020-40P and 7248-43P.

The only method by which hardware tests can be run is by using the SMS diskette that was shipped with the machine.

Note: The 7248 43P SMS microcode is for the 7248 machine only. Do not attempt to load it onto any 7043 43P machine. This will irreparably corrupt the firmware and permanently damage the machine.

5.4.3 Using SMS on 7020 and 7248

To start SMS, do the following:

1. Power off the machine.
2. Place the SMS diskette in to the diskette drive.
3. Power on the machine.
4. When the icons appear on the screen, press F1 anytime after the second icon but before the last.

You should now have a menu that gives you four options. Select the option marked Test the Computer. You can now run the test to the component you wish to test. Be aware that the level of code on the machine is designed to test IBM components only and so any other non-IBM devices may give incorrect results.

Additionally, within SMS, you can change the boot list, manage configuration changes, and load or refresh machine microcode.

5.5 TTY setup for use as a console

The tty console is primarily used when booting from a CD-ROM, diskettes, or mksysb. At this point, output is displayed on the screen using spaces and characters. Therefore, any terminal will work, provided the following settings are used:

- 9600 baud
- 8 bit
- 1 stop bit
- No parity
- Xon/Xoff

Once AIX is running or the Diagnostics screens are in use, screen addressability is used and a definite screen type must be configured.

The supported screen types are as follows

- IBM models 3101, 3151, 3161, 3162, 3163, 3164, ibmpc, and lft

- vs100
- vt100, vt320, vt330, and vt340
- wyse30, wyse50, wyse60, wyse100, and wyse350
- sun

If your terminal type is not listed, you can use an emulator, such as Hyperterm or Netterm, often supplied with Windows family operating systems. Set the emulation mode to vt100 and use the communication settings shown above.

You will also need to ensure the cable has the correct interface and presents the signals on the correct pins. A crossover or interposer may be required.

5.6 Checkstops and machine checks

Most machine checkstops and machine checks are caused by problems in the CPU complex. The most common symptom seen when a checkstop occurs is that the machine will be up and running quite satisfactorily, then, all of a sudden, the machine halts unexpectedly and undertakes a reboot. The reason for a checkstop rebooting the machine is that, if the processor logic detects a problem within the processor or memory, the only way that it can do any problem determination itself is to shut the machine down. On the way down, the processor writes the error data from the problem to the NVRAM. Once the machine has shutdown completely, it will reboot and then the processor and memory can be fully tested. If there is a problem at this stage, a LED code will be displayed. If no problem is found, the error information from the NVRAM is transferred to the error log during the boot process.

5.6.1 How to use the data

The method of processing the checkstop or machine check data depends on the technology of the machine and the AIX version and fix level.

MCA machines will have an error log entry indicating a checkstop. At the end of the error log entry, you will see the full path name of the checkstop file. Error log analysis or diagnostics run in Problem Determination mode will analyze this file and provide an action plan. On earlier levels of AIX, these files required a special program to decode the cause of the problem. This could either be run on the machine or the file could be sent to your software support with a copy of the detailed error report and a full VPD listing. Software support could then provide you with an action plan.

The CHRP machines models, 7017-S70, 7017-S7A, 7025-F50, 7026-H50, 7026-H70, 7043-150, 7043-260, and later, transfer the machine check details to the error log. It is then possible to run advanced diagnostics in problem determination mode to get the cause of the machine check. See Section 5.2.1, "Making sense of the error log" on page 120 for time stamp parameters. This is possible because as you select problem determination mode, the diagnostics then read the error log entry for the machine check, take the sense data from the entry, and perform an analysis of it. This will then produce an SRN and a list of failing FRUs.

On the later machines, the system can automatically and dynamically deallocate CPUs that are found to be failing via the in-built service processor.

5.7 Diagnosis of SCSI problems

Diagnosis of problems within the SCSI subsystem requires you, in most cases, to have the machine to yourself so that you can perform tests that require having the power removed from the machine.

There are several distinct variants of SCSI devices and adapters, each having different properties. The two main distinctions are:

Single-ended SCSI Over the years, this implementation of SCSI has progressed from SCSI 1 to SCSI 2 then onto SCSI 2 Fast and Wide and various levels of Ultra SCSI. Each of them is different in speed and bus width. Interchanging of devices between the bus types can have an effect on bus performance. Differential SCSI devices and terminators should not be attached to a single-ended SCSI bus, because they will not work and will cause unpredictable results and may damage devices or the adapter.

Differential SCSI This is another implementation of the SCSI bus. The speeds and bus widths are the same as the corresponding single-ended implementation, but the permitted cable lengths are between 18 to 25 meters, which is much longer than single-ended SCSI. Because of the technology used to achieve a greater bus length, no differential device should be attached to a single-ended SCSI bus; likewise, single-ended devices should not be attached on a differential SCSI bus (with one exception; see "Low-voltage differential/single-ended (LVD/SE)" on page 144.

It should be noted, however, that some differential SCSI adapters may also have a single-ended SCSI bus on them, so they can run single-ended devices on this bus and differential devices on a separate bus. It should also be noted that differential adapters have a set of terminator resistors on the adapter. These will be removed when the adapter is used in a shared SCSI bus environment, and if you remove an adapter from such a system, you should remember to replace the resistors or use a terminator on a pigtail Y cable.

Later implementations of SCSI include Low Voltage Differential (LVD) and High Voltage Differential (HVD). These adapters may also have multiple SCSI busses on the same card, but it is not possible to mix LVD and HVD devices on the same bus. Serious hardware damage can occur if this happens.

SCSI bus length guidelines

Single-ended

The maximum supported cable length depends on what type of devices are attached (SCSI-1, SCSI-2, and so on). Device types are classified as follows:

- SCSI-1: Maximum transfer rate of 5 MB/sec (one byte transfers)
- SCSI-2 Fast: Maximum transfer rate of 10 MB/sec (one byte transfers)
- SCSI-2 Fast Wide: Maximum transfer rate of 20 MB/sec (two byte transfers)
- Ultra SCSI: Maximum transfer rate of 20 MB/sec (one byte transfers)
- Ultra SCSI Wide: Maximum transfer rate of 40 MB/sec (two byte transfers)

The maximum supported cable length for configurations without any SCSI-2 fast or UltraSCSI devices is six meters (approximately 20 feet).

The maximum supported cable length for configurations that include SCSI-2 fast, but not ultra-SCSI, is three meters (approximately 10 feet).

The maximum supported cable length for configurations of four or less Ultra SCSI devices is three meters (approximately 10 feet); for configurations larger than four Ultra SCSI devices, it is 1.5 meters (approximately five feet).

High-voltage differential (HVD)

The maximum supported cable length for high-voltage differential is 25 meters (approximately 80 feet).

Low-voltage differential/single-ended (LVD/SE)

If a single-ended device is attached to a low-voltage differential adapter the entire bus will operate as a single-ended bus, with the same cable length limitations. To operate in low-voltage differential mode, all devices on the bus must be low-voltage differential, including the terminator. High-voltage differential devices are not supported on a low-voltage differential bus and will prevent any devices on the bus from working and may damage the devices or adapter.

The maximum allowed cable length for point-to-point low-voltage differential SCSI bus configurations is 25 meters (approximately 80 feet). The maximum cable length for multi-drop low-voltage differential connections is 12 meters (approximately 40 feet).

Most IBM devices, cards, and cables will be marked with the kind of SCSI they can connect to. If there are no markings ensure that you are using compatible items. See Figure 5-1 on page 145 for labelling examples

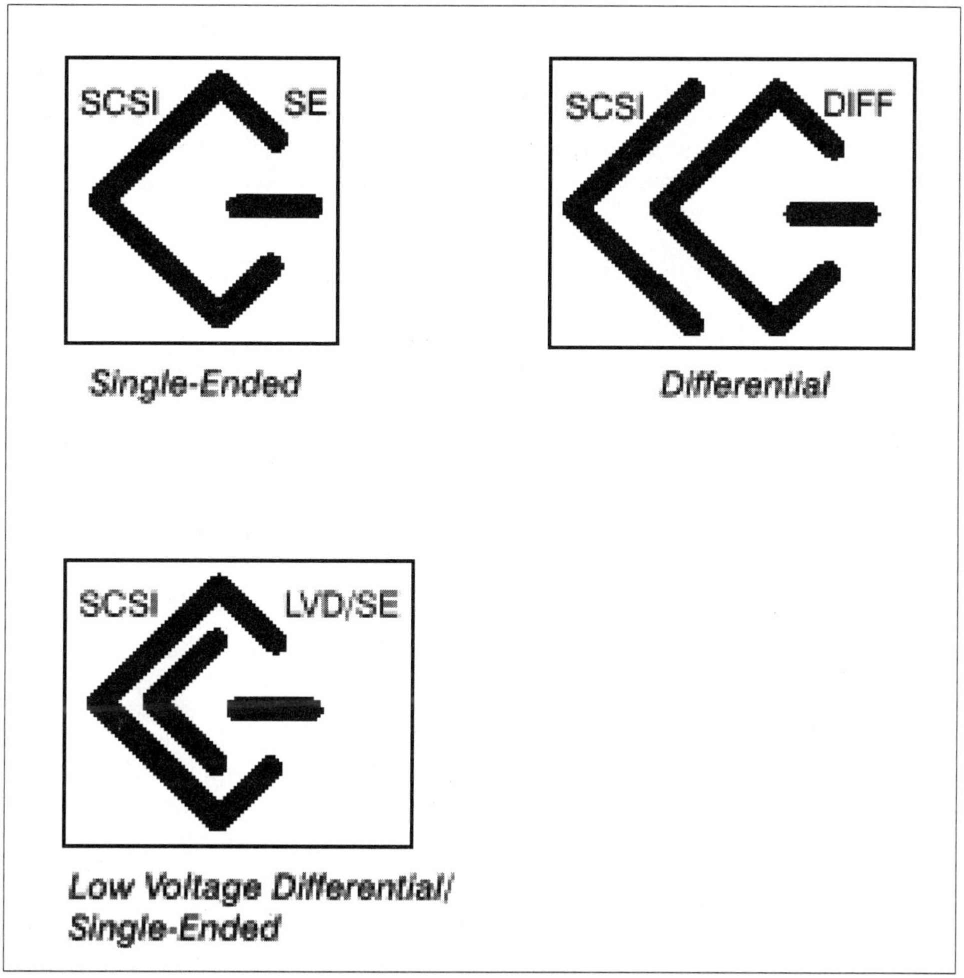

Figure 5-1 Example of SCSI labelling

SCSI problems can be caused by either a device, cables, or a terminator. You can sometimes end up diagnosing a SCSI problem when the original call was, for example, a disk drive. There are a number of ways to diagnose the various faults, some of which are listed in the following sections.

5.7.1 Basic SCSI checks

Check the cabling thoroughly for the security of the cables connected to the devices; also, cross reference the cables used with the diagrams in the publications *RS/6000 Adapters, Devices, and Cable Information for Multiple Bus Systems*, SA38-0516, and *IBM RS/6000 Adapters, Device, and Cables*

Inforamtion for Micro Channel Bus Systems, SA38-0533. In each of these publications, you will find wiring diagrams for many different device scenarios. Each diagram will give you the feature code and part number of all components in the diagram; cross check with your setup, paying particular attention to the termination of the bus. In addition, make sure that all devices are compatible and that you do not have a mixture of differential and single-ended cables or terminators. Also, check the documentation for your particular devices and adapters.

Next, run the following command:

```
# lsdev -Cs scsi
```

You should then get similar output to what is shown below:

```
rmt0   Available 11-08-00-0,0  SCSI 8mm Tape Drive
cd0    Available 11-08-00-1,0  16 Bit SCSI Multimedia CD-ROM Drive
hdisk0 Available 11-08-00-2,0  16 Bit LVD SCSI Disk Drive
hdisk1 Available 11-08-00-4,0  16 Bit LVD SCSI Disk Drive
hdisk2 Available 27-08-00-8,0  16 Bit LVD SCSI Disk Drive
hdisk3 Available 27-08-00-9,0  16 Bit LVD SCSI Disk Drive
hdisk4 Available 27-09-00-8,0  16 Bit LVD SCSI Disk Drive
hdisk5 Available 27-09-00-9,0  16 Bit LVD SCSI Disk Drive
ses0   Available 27-08-00-15,0 SCSI Enclosure Services Device
ses1   Available 27-09-00-15,0 SCSI Enclosure Services Device
```

The output you get should show all of the SCSI devices listed in the as ODM both available and defined. Are all of the devices you would expect to see shown as available? If not, check that the device has the power turned on, check the cabling for bent pins, improper termination, such as additional terminators on the bus, or missing terminators. SCSI requires one terminator at each end of the bus. There is usually one on the adapter and one on the last device. Some SCSI devices have jumpers or switches on the device to provide termination with that device. Another jumper can provide Term Power. For IBM systems, Term Power is usually provided by the adapter and should be set to off at the device. If you find that you are having difficulty finding the problem, then, if possible, start with one device on the bus and keep adding devices until the fault occurs. However, *never* hot plug onto a live SCSI bus; it has been known to seriously corrupt rootvg or customer data. The exception to this, of course, are hot plug SCSI disks available in machine types 7017, 7025, 7026, and later. The problem may also be with one of the devices added previously, but the cumulative effect of adding the last device has caused the symptom to show. Poor connections or bad/additional terminations often cause this difficult to diagnose condition, which may only give problems intermittently, such as during heavy workloads or only when data backups are running.

If you cannot get the SCSI bus to work even with just one device on the bus, then before replacing the adapter, refer to *RS/6000 and pSeries Diagnostics Informationfor Multiple Bus Systems*, SA38-0509, or *RS/6000 Diagnostics Information for Micro Channel Bus Systems*, SA38-0532. These two documents contain procedures for testing the adapters PTC thermal cutout and a test for correct bus termination on some adapters.

SCSI devices missing or duplicated

Quite often, when you add devices or change the layout of a SCSI bus, you will get one of the following scenarios:

- SCSI device missing. The most common cause of this is that you set the SCSI ID or address to the same as another device. This can easily be done accidently if the device has the push button address switch on the rear of the device. The only effective way to sort this situation out is to physically recheck the address of each device connected to the bus. If the backplane is providing the SCSI address, ensure the device is addressed as 0 (check for jumpers and switches). Remember that active SCSI backplanes on machines will often have SCSI IDs 14 or 15 assigned to them. Also, check to see that terminators are in the correct place, especially if there is an OEM device on the bus. Some OEM devices are sent out with a default setting of termination enabled. A device after a terminator may not be seen. Check to see that all cables are seated squarely and firmly in their sockets. A misplaced cable or terminator can also cause an incorrect SCSI ID to be reported. SCSI address probing is accomplished by the adapter monitoring data lines for a response during bus initialization. The responses received are used to determine the addresses used. For example, a response received on line 0 equates to address 0, a response on line 5 equates to address 5, and so on. Therefore, anything that can result in the signal being misrouted or misinterpreted can give address misreporting.
- Multiple instances of a device. For example, **`lsdev -Cc tape`** reports back rmt1, rmt2, and rmt3 through to rmt7. The cause of this is that one of the tape drives has the same SCSI ID as the SCSI adapter, generally 7. Again, this can be done during installation of the device or by accident. If no device duplicating the address of the SCSI adapter is found, see the previous bullet for instructions on how to check SCSI cabling.
- The SCSI bus service aid, available from diagnostics, is most useful for the diagnosis of missing SCSI devices. It will give you an indication as to the state of the device at a specific SCSI address. The three possible replies are:
  - The exerciser transmitted a SCSI Inquiry command and did not receive any response back. Ensure that the address is valid, then try this option again.

This message will be produced when there is no device using the SCSI ID, or the device using the ID is powered off for some reason, for example, the power cable not being plugged in or there is a power problem on the device itself.

- The exerciser transmitted a SCSI Inquiry command and received a valid response back without any errors being detected.

  This response indicates that the device at the polled ID is capable of responding to some instructions from the adapter and therefore is connected to the SCSI bus. If the device you tested is not being seen correctly or not working as expected, run diagnostics to see if it finds a problem.

- A check condition was returned from the device.

  If a check condition is returned by the device, it will usually fail diagnostics as well and should be replaced. Should the failing device be a disk, and, due to the lack of a good backup, you are desperate to save the data, then in a small number of cases, this may be possible by changing the electronics. The success of this will depend on what is causing the check condition. If the electronics change is successful, it is strongly advised that you immediately take a backup of the data followed by the complete replacement of the disk assembly. Should all efforts be unsuccessful in saving the data, professional assistance should be sought from a reputable data recovery service.

SCSI RAID

Problem determination procedures in a SCSI RAID environment are different than in a non-RAID environment. The configuration of the RAID array is done at the adapter level, not at the AIX level, and it is the adapter that controls the RAID environment. AIX will just see the RAID level 5 array as one large hdisk. If you have a SCSI RAID adapter, follow the reference guide for your adapter. Procedures may change between different kinds of adapter and different RAID levels so ensure you follow the correct procedure for your specific environment.

- *Ultra SCSI PCI RAID Adapter Reference Guide*, SC23-4302
- *PCI 4-Channel Ultra3 SCSI RAID Adapter Reference Guide*, SA23-1239

Identifying and recovering from drive failures.

If a drive attached to the Ultra SCSI PCI RAID Adapter fails, procedures are provided by the PCI SCSI Disk Array Manager (PDAM) for removing and replacing the failed drive. Instructions on how to recover the data from the failed drive (in redundant environment) or restoring the data from the drive (on non-redundant environments), and information describing the various RAID levels and how drive failures are handled by each of the levels are included in the appropriate reference guide. The Ultra SCSI PCI RAID Adapter handles drive failures differently, depending on the RAID level involved.

> **Note:** After following the procedures in the reference guides, you may need to return to the procedures that sent you there to complete your recovery.

To access PDAM, use the SMIT fast path **`smit disk_array`**.

Drive status

There are five possible values that may be displayed for the status of a disk array and seven possible values that may be displayed for the status of a physical drive.

- Disk Array States

  The state of a disk array is uniquely determined by the states of the physical drives that make up the disk array. Depending on the number of failed physical drives, replacement of a failed drive with a good drive may change the state of the disk array from Dead to Degraded or Optimal after a data rebuild. When a failed physical drive is replaced in a Degraded disk array, the data is rebuilt onto the replaced drive before the disk array state transitions to the Optimal.

  Optimal The disk array is in good functional state.

  Degraded One of the physical drives that is part of a disk array is in the failed state.

  Dead For a non-redundant disk array, this state indicates that one or more physical drives are in the failed state. For a redundant disk array, this state indicates that two or more physical drives are in the failed state. A Dead disk array is not accessible.

  Compressing This is a special state for RAID level 5E disk arrays only.

  Decompressing This is a special state for RAID level 5E disk arrays only.

- Physical Disk States

  Online The drive is part of a disk array and is in good functional state.

  Spare The drive is connected to the adapter, but not configured into a disk array. This drive is available for the creation of a disk array.

Failed

The drive was failed by the Ultra SCSI PCI RAID Adapter or by the user and must be replaced. A drive goes to failed state when one of the following conditions occur:

- Drive does not respond to selection.
- Drive failed to spin-up.
- Fail in inquiry or read capacity.
- Fail to read or write reserve area.
- Drive fails to respond to SCSI commands.
- Inquiry, capacity, serial number and SCSI ID do not match configuration data stored on the adapter NVRAM.
- User failed the drive using PDAM.

Reconstruct

The drive is undergoing a data reconstruction operation.

Warning

The drive has set its Predictive failure Analysis (PFA) indication. Although the drive may remain functional, this is an indiction that a serious failure of the drive is imminent. The severity of this status depends to some extent on the RAID level of the disk array. The Warning drive should be replaced as soon as possible.

Hot Spare

The drive automatically replaces an equivalent Failed drive in a redundant disk array.

Non Existent

A drive location is marked as non existent if no disk was detected at that channel/SCSI ID.

5.8 Serial Storage Architecture (SSA) disks

This disk subsystem is capable of being externally connected to one or more systems. Certain models of IBM @server pSeries and RS/6000 can also be configured with internal SSA disks. SSA devices are connected through two or more SSA links to an SSA adapter, which is located in the system used. The devices, SSA links, and SSA adapters are configured in loops. Each loop provides a data path that starts at one connector of the SSA adapter and passes through a link (SSA cable) to the devices. The loop continues through the devices, then returns through another link to a second connector on the SSA adapter. Each adapter is capable of supporting two loops. Each loop can have between one and 48 devices. A loop can have as many as eight SSA adapters connected in up to eight systems, but this is dependent on the type of SSA adapter being used and how they are configured. Again, depending on adapters, disk subsystem, and cables in use, the aggregate loop speed per adapter can either be 80 MB/sec or 160 MB/sec. As you can see, the number of possible combinations is almost endless and changes at each product announcement. Therefore, the SSA configuration rules detailed below cover basic considerations.

5.8.1 General SSA setup rules

The following rules must be followed when connecting a 7133 subsystem:

- Each SSA loop must be connected to a valid pair of connectors on the SSA adapter card.

  A1 and A2 form one loop, and B1 and B2 form another loop.
- Only one pair of connectors of a SSA adapter can be connected in a particular SSA loop.

  A1 or A2, with B1 or B2, cannot be in the same SSA loop.
- A maximum of 48 disks can be connected in a SSA loop.
- A maximum of three dummy disk drive modules can be connected next to each other.
- A maximum of two adapters can be in the same host per SSA loop.
- Cabling joining SSA nodes should not exceed 25 meters.
- There is no addressing setup for any SSA device, as every device is manufactured with a unique address.
- There is no termination, because all connections should form a loop.

The maximum number of adapters per SSA loop at the time of this writing is shown in Table 5-1.

Table 5-1 SSA adapter information

Feature Code	Description	Identifier	Maximum number per loop
6214	MCA Adapter	4-D	2
6216	MCA Enhanced SSA 4 port adapter	4-G	8
6217	MCA SSA RAID adapter	4-I	1
6218	PCI SSA RAID adapter	4-J	1

Feature Code	Description	Identifier	Maximum number per loop
6219	MCA Enhanced RAID adapter	4-M	Between 1 and 8 per loop depending on microcode level, and whether RAID and Fast Write Cache are used
6215	PCI Enhanced RAID Adapter	4-N	
6225	PCI Advanced Serial RAID adapter	4-P	
6230	PCI Advanced Serial RAID+ adapter	4-P	as above

For the most comprehensive and up to date information on SSA adapters, refer to the following URL:

`http://www.storage.ibm.com/hardsoft/products/ssa/`

The user guides for each SSA adapter are available on this Web site. They contain information on the valid adapter combinations allowed on the same loop.

5.8.2 SSA devices

SSA subsystem components use microcode to control their functionality. When dealing with any SSA problem, you should ensure that the microcode level and any drivers on all devices in the loop are at the latest published level. The latest code can be obtained from the following URL:

`http://www.storage.ibm.com/hardsoft/products/ssa/`

5.8.3 SSA disk does not configure as a hdisk

If you configure an SSA disk into a system, and it only shows as a pdisk with no corresponding hdisk, the most probable cause is that the disk was originally part of a RAID array set up on another machine. If disks are removed from a RAID array for any reason to be incorporated into any other system as a normal disk, the following procedure must be used:

1. Type **smitty ssaraid** (the fast path to SSA RAID SMIT panels).
2. Select Change Show use of an SSA Physical disk. The disk must be returned to general use as an AIX system disk.
3. If the disk is to be removed from the system, use the relevant AIX commands. Do not remove the pdisk until you have removed the disk from the system using the SSA service aids.

Obviously, if you are presented with this situation, and the disk with the problem was not a member of a RAID set on this machine, your only option to return this disk to normal use is to do a low-level format using the SSA service aid. This can take some time if the disk is 9 GB or larger. This can only be done if the disk is connected to a RAID capable adapter.

SSA RAID

The SSA subsystem is capable of being operated by some adapters as either single system disks or as RAID LUNs. Provided that all has been set up correctly, then the RAID implementation works well. If you have any doubts as to how the RAID is set up, refer to the *SSA Adapters: User's Guide and Maintenance Information*, SA33-3272 or the *Advanced SerialRAID Adapters User's Guide and Maintenance Information*, SA33-3285 (for the 4-P feature code 6225 and 6230).

If you propose to do any actions involving an SSA RAID array, then use the relevant procedure listed. This will ensure that the integrity of the RAID set is maintained at all times.

To see the relationship between physical and logical disks, use the ssa translation command **ssaxlate -l hdisk4**, which may return `pdisk0 pdisk1 pdisk3 pdisk4`. This shows that this a RAID array containing four physical disks, pdisk0,1, 3, and 4.

If you use the command **ssaxlate -l pdisk0**, the reply from the system will be `hdisk4`, which does not show that it is an array logical disk.

Changing SSA disks

SSA disk changing activity is hot swappable. While preparing to remove an SSA disk, do *not* **rmdev** the pdisk prior to physically removing the disk from the enclosure. You will need the pdisk to do the following steps:

1. Remove the pdisk only when all steps are completed.
2. Use the SSA Service aid to power the disk off prior to removal. This is done by using the set Service mode and identify facility. This will put the disks on either side of the one you want to remove into string mode and power off the disk to be removed.
3. When the replacement disk or blanking module is inserted, you use the same service aid to reset Service mode. This will start up the new disk and take the other disks out of string mode.
4. At this point, you can now **rmdev** the pdisk allocated to the disk you removed. The disk change procedures will tell you to run the **cfgmgr -l ssar** command.

Note: The **cfgmgr** command should *not* be executed on any system that is in an HACMP cluster. To do so can seriously damage the configuration of the machine, possibly resulting in the crashing of the complete cluster.

If the disk to be changed is a defective RAID disk and was in use by the system, then you need to follow the procedures in *SSA Adapters: Users Guide and Maintenance Information*, SA33-3272 or the *Advanced SerialRAID Adapters User's Guide and Maintenance Information*, SA33-3285 (for the 4-P feature code 6225 and 6230). Read these procedures carefully, because some of the earlier editions of this book indicate that you have finished the procedure when, in fact, you need to perform other steps to return the array to a protected state. Below is a list of the important steps that need to be completed before you can be sure that the array will function correctly.

Steps involved in the replacement of a RAID SSA disks are:

1. Addition of the replacement disk to the system using the **cfgmgr** command or the **mkdev** command on HACMP systems.
2. Make the disk an array candidate or hot spare using the SMIT fast path **smit ssaraid**.

If the disk was removed from a RAID array, leaving it in an exposed or degraded state, you now need to add the disk to the array using SMIT. While the array is being rebuilt, error messages will be seen each hour in the error log. These will cease when the array is completely rebuilt.

Note: Microcode and device driver levels on SSA disks, enclosures and adapters need to be kept at compatible levels. If any component has been replaced, ensure all other parts of the loop, including other systems, are still compatible.

For further information on SSA RAID disk replacement, see "SSA RAID disk replacement" on page 191.

5.9 Peripheral devices

Peripheral devices can cover a multitude of equipment that can be directly connected to IBM @server pSeries and RS/6000 system units. The more obvious of these are disk drives, tape drives, tape libraries, and CD-ROM juke boxes. Most of these devices are usually connected using an SCSI bus of some description. Any problem shown by a peripheral device could be ultimately caused by the SCSI bus. Therefore, always include SCSI bus checking in any problem determination on a peripheral device that is connected to a SCSI bus. (See Section 5.7, “Diagnosis of SCSI problems” on page 142 for more details.)

5.9.1 Disk drawers or towers

Most disk drawers and towers contain one or more power supplies and cooling fans. The power supply can sometimes be fuse protected, so the fuse should be checked prior to replacement of the power supply.

> **Note:** Refer to the documentation supplied with the equipment prior to performing any service actions. Always use the manufacturers recommended replacement parts.

Most disk enclosures have fans to keep the internal components cool. The power supplies will often use internal logic to check for fan rotation speed before they allow power to stay up. Therefore, check that no debris has blocked the fan from rotating or is decreasing the speed at which the fan rotates.

The inside of a drawer or tower of disks can contain from one to sixteen disks or more. The disks can be accessed individually or grouped together into RAID sets. If the disks are RAID or controlled by a logic card, then problem determination should only be carried out using the supplied documentation, so data integrity is protected.

External disk enclosures containing no logic can be treated as just a straight SCSI bus and diagnosed accordingly. This means that diagnostics should be run from either Service mode boot or from a CD-ROM. If the diagnostics fail, all connections on the data bus within the enclosure should be checked for tightness and bent or deformed connections prior to changing components. Some enclosures can provide bus termination, so always check to see that the enclosure is supplying bus termination only at the end of the bus and without any other external terminator being used. Two terminators on the same end of the bus will cause unpredictable results.

For more information about SSA disk drawers and towers, see Section 5.8, “Serial Storage Architecture (SSA) disks” on page 150.

5.9.2 External tapes and tape libraries

Tape drives and libraries range from a QIC tape drive capable of saving 150 MB, to tape silos containing tens of thousands of 1/2 inch tape cartridges. Physical connections to the IBM @server pSeries and RS/6000 can range from SCSI to ESCON.

Due to the diversity of sizes and methods of connection, this redbook will only cover QIC, 4 mm, 8 mm, and DLT devices, and their desktop libraries. The larger drives require specific training to enable repairs to be carried out. The tape silos can also be dangerous to enter, as the robots are under automatic control and can move without warning.

There are, however, a number of things that can cause problems on tape drives that will apply to all drives and libraries regardless of size or complexity.

5.9.3 General tape troubleshooting

Tape drives are very expensive and often are the reason a customer cannot read or write a tape. Problems are usually caused by one or more of the following:

- Bad blocksize. The customer attempts to read at one blocksize when the tape is written at another. Or the blocksize the customer is attempting to write at is preceded by a 0 (ZERO); 0512 is not the same as 512. The zero is recognized by the system as octal and some applications do not support octal values. The **tcopy** command can be used to determine the blocksize of a tape. Invoking the **tcopy** command with the name of the tape drive as the only argument will cause it to attempt to read the tape in the drive and display information about the blocksize and tape files. For example:

  ```
  # tcopy /dev/rmt0
  tcopy: Tape File: 1; Records 1 to 7537; Size 512.
  tcopy: File: 1; End of File after 7537 Records, 3858944 Bytes.
  tcopy: Tape File: 2; Records 1 to 2900; Size 512.
  tcopy: File: 2; End of File after 2900 Records, 1484800 Bytes.
  tcopy: Tape File: 3; Record 1; Size 512.
  tcopy: File: 3; End of File after 1 Records, 512 Bytes.
  tcopy: Tape File: 4; Records 1 to 514048; Size 1024.
  tcopy: File: 4; End of File after 514048 Records, 526385152 Bytes.
  ```

  This may take a considerable amount of time to run, since it will attempt to read the tape at many different blocksizes until it succeeds.

- Device buffering turned off, causing the drive to write every block of data as it is received. Normal operation is to buffer the data, allowing the drive to stream the data to the tape as a continuous operation. Device buffering being turned off will create a sort of shoe shining effect that will greatly accelerate

head wear on the drive, and slow down the operation.
Check this parameter using the **smit tape** command.

- Writing a tape with one command then attempting to read the tape with a non-compatible command, such as writing the tape with a **tar** command and attempting to read the tape with a **restore** command.

  Rather than attempting to read the tape directly with various backup commands, it can be quicker to determine the format of the tape by reading a small portion of the start of the tape using the **dd** command, then using the **file** command to attempt to determine the format of the archive. For example:

  ```
  # dd if=/dev/rmt0 of=/tmp/tape.data bs=512 count=4
  4 + 0 records in.
  4 + 0 records out.
  # file /tmp/tape.data
  /tmp/tape.data: tar archive
  ```

  When attempting to read tapes written on other systems, the data format may be incompatible depending on the options used to write the tape. The **cpio** command is particularly prone to this problem. The GNU version of the **cpio** command, available at many sites on the Internet, can very often read the non-standard format archives.

- Poor quality media or worn out media being used. Clean the drive and retest the customer operation with a new IBM data cartridge recommended for the drive.
- Misunderstanding of the meaning of the LEDs on the tape drive.
- Not cleaning the tape drive, using cleaning cartridges that are used up, or not following the recommended cleaning frequency or cleaning instructions.

  Check that you are using the correct cleaning cartridge. The part numbers of the IBM cleaning tapes are given in Section 5.9.4, “4 mm, 8 mm, and DLT tape drives” on page 158, and Section 5.9.5, “QIC tape drives” on page 159.

- Not cleaning the tape drive after an I/O error prior to retrying the failing operation.
- Improper SCSI bus termination. See Section 5.7, “Diagnosis of SCSI problems” on page 142 for further information.
- Conflict of tape drive’s SCSI address with another device on the bus.
- Another device causing noise on the bus.
- Environment not suitable for tape drive operation, for example, the area around the machine has deposits of dirt or abrasive dust. Ideally, the operating temperature of the drive and the tapes should also be the same. Using tapes that are much colder than the drive itself will promote

condensation on the tape surface that will accelerate dirt depositing on the read/write head.

- Software level of the system does not support the tape drive. When adding a new type of tape drive, you may need to add PTFs to the system to fully support the new device.
- Device microcode not at the latest level, even on new devices or replacement parts direct from stock. Check the following IBM @server pSeries and RS/6000 microcode download Web site for the latest levels of microcode:

  `http://www.rs6000.ibm.com/support/micro`

- Trying to read or write a data density not supported on the drive. Check the documentation supplied with the drive. For example, trying use a 2.3 GB 8 mm tape drive to read a tape written on a 5 GB 8 mm drive.
- Inconsistencies in the backup script. Use a new data tape and **tar** a large portion of data onto the tape. If this copies without error, use the **tar -tvf** command to read the tape back. /var is often a sufficiently large enough mount point to use to test the drive.
- Incorrect positioning of tape labels. The use of sticky labels anywhere on the tape cartridge except on the proscribed indentations will cause the tape to position itself incorrectly within the tape path resulting in excessive errors. The use of labels on the metal reference surfaces of QIC and 3570 tapes will cause errors while reading or writing to the tape and may result in possible damage to the drive itself. In some cases, the tape drive will fail to eject a tape cartridge due to incorrect positioning of labels on the tape cartridge or multiple labels stuck on top of one another. To correct this problem, the tape device will have to be disassembled to remove the tape cartridge. This should only be attempted by trained service personnel.

5.9.4 4 mm, 8 mm, and DLT tape drives

These families of drives are the most common of the drives used on IBM @server pSeries and RS/6000 machines. Their capacities range from 2 GB uncompressed to as much as 80 GB using data compression. For example:

- Removal of stuck tapes can sometimes be effected by resetting the drive. These devices can be reset by either pressing the Eject button for 20 seconds or by using the following command:

  ```
  # diag -c -d /dev/rmt(x)
  ```

  If the above fails, then, when possible, power off the drive or, if it is an internal device in a system, power off the system.

- Media errors can occur if the customer has not been cleaning the drive regularly or has been using an incorrect cleaning tape. Take an IBM cleaning tape and clean the drive three times in succession. Be sure to mark off the three uses on the label of the cleaning tape.

At the time of this writing, the cleaning tapes are:

- 4 mm Tape Drives Cleaning Cartridge P/N 21F8763. Maximum use is fifty cleanings.
- 8 mm 2.3 GB, 5 GB, and 7 GB Tape Drives Cleaning Cartridge P/N 16G8467 (do not use this cleaning cartridge on the 20 GB 8 mm drive). Twelve cleanings on 2.3 GB drive and 22 cleanings on 5 GB and 7 GB drives.
- 8 mm 20 GB tape drives. These will request a cleaning tape each time a 5 GB or 7 GB data tape is read. Writing to tapes, other than 20 GB capacity, is not possible with this drive. Use Cleaning Cartridge P/N 59H2898 (only use this cleaning cartridge on the 20 GB 8 mm drive). The minimum number of cleanings per tape is 18. Cleaning tape usage depends on the reason the tape drive is being cleaned, whether due to normal usage or after a 5 GB or 7 GB tape has been read.
- DLT Cleaning Cartridge P/N 59H3092. Twenty cleanings per tape.

If you want to return a tape drive to the default configuration, the quickest way is normally to **rmdev** the device, then run the **cfgmgr** command to add it to the system again.

> **Note:** Ensure you are not in an HACMP environment before running **cfgmgr**.

5.9.5 QIC tape drives

The Quarter Inch Cartridge (QIC) drive comes in many capacities, from 150 MB to 13 GB. All cartridges are dimensionally the same, but the densities are not universally interchangeable. When conducting diagnostics, make sure that you are using the correct part number test tape as asked for in the dialog panel. If you use the wrong test tape, you will get an incorrect test result.

Cleaning cartridges for the QIC drives are:

- 1/4 inch Tape Drives Cleaning Cartridge P/N 16G8572 (except 7207-122/315); 50 cleanings
- 1/4 inch 7207-122/315 Tape Drive Cleaning Cartridge P/N 59H4366 (use only for 7207-122/315); 50 cleanings

When checking the settings for these drives, make sure that the retension setting is enabled. This setting is sometimes changed to save the 5 to 10 minutes taken to retension a tape when it is inserted into the drive. If the setting is changed, then for the first couple of times, the tape will perform correctly, but as the tension decreases, loop back errors will occur.

Tape error log entries

The error log entries for tapes can be useful in deciding if one particular tape cartridge is causing the problem, or if it is the tape drive itself. The type of error logged, plus whether the tape operation completed or not, will give an indication of where the problem may lie.

The following is an abbreviated list of the possible tape errors and their meanings:

TAPE_ERR1 This is likely to be a media failure. The process using the tape drive normally terminates on encountering this error.

TAPE_ERR2 This is normally a drive failure, but can be caused by a media failure. The process using the tape drive normally terminates on encountering this error.

TAPE_ERR3 This is likely to indicate that the tape media is starting to fail. The process using the tape drive will not normally terminate on encountering this error.

TAPE_ERR4 Unknown cause, requires further analysis. The process using the tape drive normally terminates on encountering this error.

TAPE_ERR5 Unknown cause, requires further analysis. The process using the tape drive normally terminates on encountering this error.

TAPE_ERR6 The 5 GB, 7 GB, and 20 GB 8 mm tape drives log this error when the drive exceeds the preset limit of tape motion hours since the drive was last cleaned. The process using the tape drive does not normally terminate on encountering this error.

Note: The 20 GB 8 mm tape drive will also set the cleaning indicator LED and log TAPE_ERR6 on most media errors.

Tape libraries

Tape libraries are tape drives with a controller card that controls and operates an auto tape feeder mechanism of some description. The tape load and feed mechanism is controlled by a software product called Atape. This product includes the **tapeutil** command, which provides a command line interface that can be used to move the tapes within the library.

If you are experiencing tape movement problems during backup or restores, you may get a better idea of what is happening if you use **tapeutil** commands and watch the library at the same time. This diagnostic procedure cannot be used with the model 7337 or model 7332 tape libraries, because the auto feed mechanism is hidden from view.

Tape movement problems can often be eliminated by performing a calibration of the library using the control panel of the device. This will require the service documentation for the tape library device, since the method used varies between machine types. Additionally, for persistent problems where hardware has been eliminated as the cause of the problem, or all of the hardware components have been changed, install the latest version of the Atape product. This product can be downloaded from the Storage Systems Web site at:

`ftp://index.storsys.ibm.com/devdrvr/AIX/`

When installing or upgrading the Atape product, examine the README files carefully because the installation process requires certain conditions to be met prior to installation.

If the Atape product is removed from the system, you will need to reload any device drivers supplied with the tape drive if you wish to use them instead of Atape. If this is not done, the drivers will not work, even though the **lslpp** command shows them as correctly installed.

5.9.6 CD-ROM jukeboxes

These machines are usually connected to the system using a SCSI Differential Fast Wide bus. Most devices require special training to set them up, so the only problem determination you can do is regarding the SCSI bus. See Section 5.7, "Diagnosis of SCSI problems" on page 142 for more details.

6

LVM and JFS

This chapter explains the basic concepts of the LVM and JFS systems and how to repair some of the more common problems that can occur.

6.1 Logical Volume Manager (LVM)

The set of operating system commands, library subroutines, and other tools that allow you to establish and control logical volume storage is called the Logical Volume Manager (LVM). The LVM controls disk resources by mapping data between a more simple and flexible logical view of storage space and the actual physical disks. The LVM does this by using a layer of device driver code that runs above traditional disk device drivers.

The Logical Volume Manager (LVM) consists of two main components.

- The first is the library of LVM subroutines. These subroutines define volume groups and maintain the logical and physical volumes of volume groups. They are used by the system management commands to perform system management tasks for the logical and physical volumes of a system. The programming interface for the library of LVM subroutines is available to anyone who wishes to provide alternatives or to expand the function of the system management commands for logical volumes.
- The other main component of LVM is the logical volume device driver. The logical volume device driver is a pseudo-device driver that processes all logical I/O. It exists as a layer between the file system and the disk device drivers. The logical volume device driver converts a logical address to a physical address, handles mirroring and bad-block relocation, and then sends the I/O request to the specific disk device driver. Interfaces to the logical volume device driver are provided by the open, close, read, write, and ioctl subroutines.

The LVM consists of:

- High-level commands
- Intermediate commands
- Library commands
- LVM device driver
- Disk device driver
- SCSI device driver
- Actual disk

6.1.1 High-level commands

The LVM high level commands are the commands that provide the user interface to the LVM. The commands are used by users from the command line or shell scripts and are called from the LVM screens in SMIT.

The high-level commands are a mixture of shell scripts and binaries and provide a high degree of error checking on input arguments. Most of the LVM commands reside in /usr/sbin. There are exceptions, such as the library commands that reside in /usr/lib/liblvm.a, /usr/lib/libsm.a, and /etc/cfgvg.

The high-level commands are:

chlv, **chpv**, **chvg**, **cplv**, **exporting**, **extendlv**, **extendvg**, **importvg**, **lslv**, **lsvg**, **lsvgfs**, **migratepv**, **mklv**, **mkvg**, **reducevg**, **reorgvg**, **rmlv**, **rmlvcopy**, **syncvg**, **synclvodm**, **varyonvg**, **redefinevg**, **replacepv**, **recreatepv**, and **migratelp**.

6.1.2 Intermediate commands

The intermediate commands are called by the high-level commands. These commands have been designed to only be called from the high-level LVM commands, so little or no error checking is performed on the input arguments. This is because the arguments have been generated by the high-level commands that would terminate before calling the intermediate commands, if they were invoked with erroneous input.

Sometimes, it is necessary to use an intermediate command during the problem determination process. Care should be taken to invoke the command with the correct arguments.

The intermediate commands are:

getlvcb, **getlvname**, **getlvodm**, **getvgname**, **lvgenmajor**, **lvgenminor**, **lvrelmajor**, **lvrelminor**, **putlvcb**, **putlvodm**, **lchangelv**, **lcreatelv**, **ldeletelv**, **lextendlv**, **lquerylv**, **lreducelv**, **lresynclv**, **lchangepv**, **ldeletepv**, **linstallpv**, **lquerypv**, **lresyncpv**, **lcreatevg**, **lqueryvg**, **lqueryvgs**, **lvaryonvg**, **lvaryoffvg**, **lresynclp**, and **lmigratepp**.

6.1.3 Library calls

The LVM library calls are part of the LVM Applications Programmer Interface (API) that lets programmers access the LVM layer directly through the library layer provided by /usr/lib/liblvm.a. It is unusual for this API to be used because of the complexity of issues within LVM. Users mostly rely on shell scripts that call the high-level commands. The API library functions begin with lvm_ and are documented within the AIX documentation. These library calls are only used in situations where the user is writing C code and does not want to access the high-level commands from within a C program, or they require a faster response from LVM than they can achieve with the high-level commands. Writing an LVM specific program using the API certainly does give a performance improvement to some applications. Note that the LVM library API is not a thread-safe library. Thus, threaded user programs that reference the LVM API may not work correctly.

In AIX 5L, the libraries implementing query functions of the logical volume manager (LVM) functions (liblvm.a) are now thread-safe. Because LVM commands must be able to run even when the system is booting or being installed, the LVM library cannot rely on the availability of the pthread support library. Therefore, the internal architecture of the liblvm.a library ensures that the library is thread safe.

The following libraries are now thread safe:

- lvm_querylv
- lvm_querypv
- lvm_queryvg
- lvm_queryvgs

6.1.4 LVM device driver

The LVM device driver comes in two portions: the pinned portion (/usr/lib/drivers/hd_pin_bot) and the non-pinned portion (/usr/lib/drivers/hd_pin). The non-pinned portion is called hd_pin for backwards compatibility with AIX Version 3, where the driver was just called hd_pin and the entire driver was pinned into memory (not pageable). With AIX Version 4, the driver's true non-pageable portion is in hd_pin_bot, and the hd_pin is now pageable. The LVM device driver is called directly by the JFS file system and the LVM library routines. When a request is received by the LVM device driver, it calls the disk device driver.

6.1.5 Disk device driver

There are various disk device drivers in AIX. The most common disk device drivers are the ones for SCSI device drivers, /usr/lib/drivers/scdisk and /usr/lib/drivers/scdiskpin. The second most common disk device driver is probably the one for the 7133 SSA dasd device. This is contained in the binaries /usr/lib/drivers/ssadisk and /usr/lib/drivers/ssadiskpin. In both devices, *pin* is that which is pinned into memory and cannot be paged out of memory. When a request from the LVM device driver is received by the disk device driver, the request is packaged and then transferred down to the SCSI device driver.

6.1.6 SCSI device driver

There are several SCSI device drivers for AIX and they have the common name string of SCSI residing as part of their name. The most common of them is the original SCSI-1 device driver, /usr/lib/drivers/hscsidd. The SCSI device driver takes a command for a SCSI device, such as tape or disk, and processes it to be sent to the SCSI device connected onto the SCSI bus. The SCSI device is device neutral; it does not know or care which device sent it a command or even what that command is. It treats all requests the same and puts them into the same type of SCSI command packaging required by all SCSI devices.

6.2 LVM system data

The different pieces of data required by the LVM system to operate correctly are stored in a number of places.

6.2.1 LVM data on disk control blocks

VGDA It is the most important data structure of LVM. It contains the complete PV and LV allocation information of the entire volume group.

VGSA It is only used when mirroring has been configured. It tracks the state of the mirrored copies, which means whether the copies are synchronized or stale.

LVCB It resides in the first 512 bytes of each logical volume. If raw devices are used (for example, many databases use raw logical volumes), then care should be taken so that the LVCB is not destroyed.

6.2.2 LVM data in the operating system

ODM This contains information regarding the LVM. Items such as Physical Volumes, Volume Groups, and Logical Volumes have device configuration entries in the Customized ODM.

AIX system files /etc/vg/vgVGID, /dev/hdiskX, /dev/VGname, /dev/LVname, and /etc/filesystems.

6.2.3 Physical volumes

Each disk is assigned a Physical Volume Identifier (PVID) when it is first assigned to a volume group. The PVID is a combination of the serial number of the machine creating the volume group and the time and date of the operation. The PVID is stored on the disk itself and is also stored in the ODM of a machine when a volume group is created or imported.

You should not use the **dd** command to copy the contents of one physical volume to another, since the PVID will also be copied; this will result in two disks having the same PVID, which can confuse the system.

6.2.4 Volume groups

Each volume group has a Volume Group Descriptor Area (VGDA). There are multiple copes of the VGDA in a volume group. A copy of the VGDA is stored on each disk in the volume group. The VGDA stores information about the volume group, such as the logical volumes in the volume group and the disks in the volume group.

The VGDA is parsed by the **importvg** command when importing a volume group into a system. It is also used by the **varyonvg** command in the quorum voting process to decide if a volume group should be varied on.

For a single disk volume group, there are two VGDAs on the disk. When a second disk is added to make a two disk volume group, the original disk retains two VGDAs and the new disk gets one VGDA.

Adding a third disk results in the extra VGDA from the first disk moving to the third disk for a quorum of three with each disk having one vote. Adding each additional disk adds one new VGDA per disk.

A volume group with quorum checking enabled (the default) must have at least 51 percent of the VGDAs in the volume group available before it can be varied on. Once varied on, if the number of VGDAs falls below 51 percent, the volume group will automatically be varied off.

In contrast, a volume group with quorum checking disabled must have 100 percent of the VGDAs available before it can be varied on. Once varied on, only one VGDA needs to remain available to keep the volume group online.

A volume group also has a Volume Group Identifier (VGID), a soft serial number for the volume group similar to the PVID for disks.

Each disk in a volume group also has a Volume Group Status Area (VGSA), a 127 byte structure used to track mirroring information for up to the maximum 1016 physical partitions on the disk.

Since AIX Version 4.3, AIX supports the Big Volume Group. It overcomes the limitation of 32 PVs. This type of Volume Group must be created by using the **mkvg -B** command. AIX introduced the scale factor -t option to increase the maximum number of partitions on a disk (1016 PPS on one PV).

6.2.5 Logical volumes

Each logical volume has a Logical Volume Control Block (LVCB), that is stored in the first 512 bytes of the logical volume. The LVCB holds important details about the logical volume, including its creation time, mirroring information, and mount point, if it contains a journaled file system (JFS).

Each logical volume has a Logical Volume Identifier (LVID) that is used to represent the logical volume to the LVM libraries and low-level commands. The LVID is made up of VGID.*num*, where num is the order in which it was created in the volume group.

If you create the file system on the logical volume, AIX has file system data on the disk control block following the LVCB. These data are super block, inode, indirect block, and allocation map.

6.2.6 Object Data Manager (ODM)

The Object Data Manger (ODM) is used by the LVM to store information about the volume groups, physical volumes, and logical volumes on the system. The information held in the ODM is placed there when the volume group is imported or when each object in the volume group is created.

There exists an ODM object known as the vg-lock. Whenever an LVM modification command is started, the LVM command will lock the vg-lock for the volume group being modified. If, for some reason, the lock is inadvertently left behind, the volume group can be unlocked by running the **varyonvg -b** command, which can be run on a volume group that is already varied on.

6.3 LVM problem determination

By far, the most common LVM-related problems have to do with disk failures. Depending on the extent of the failure, you may be able to recover the situation with little or no data loss.

Depending on the exact nature of the problem you are experiencing, a recovery attempt that fails may leave the system in worse condition than before. In some situations, the only way of recovery is to restore from a backup.

6.3.1 Data integrity

AIX has a lot of functions to keep data integrity between disks or within disk. AIX provides mirroring and bad block relocation and quorum checking.

Bad block relocation

When a problem occurs with a disk drive, sometimes data relocation takes place. There are three types of data relocation:

- Internal to the disk
- Hardware relocation ordered by LVM
- Software relocation

Relocation typically occurs when the system fails to perform a read or write due to physical problems with the disk platter. In some cases, the data I/O request completes but with warnings. Depending on the type of recovered error, the LVM may be wary of the success of the next request to that physical location, so it orders a relocation to be on the safe side.

The lowest logical layer of relocation is the one that is internal to the disk. These types of relocations are typically private to the disk and there is no notification to the user that a relocation occurred.

The next level up in terms of relocation complexity is a hardware relocation called for by the LVM device driver. This type of relocation will instruct the disk to relocate the data on one physical partition to another (reserved) portion of the disk. The disk takes the data in physical location A and copies it to a reserved portion of the disk, location B. However, after this is complete, the LVM device driver will continue to reference physical location A, with the understanding that the disk itself will handle the true I/O to the real location B.

The top layer of data relocation is the *soft* relocation, handled by the LVM device driver. In this case, the LVM device driver maintains a bad block directory, and whenever it receives a request to access a logical location A, the LVM device driver will look up the bad block table and translate it to actually send the request to the disk drive at physical location B.

Ability to detect stale mirror copies and correct

The Volume Group Status Area (VGSA) tracks the status of 1016 physical partitions per disk per volume group. During a read or write, if the LVM device driver detects that there was a failure in fulfilling a request, the VGSA will note the physical partition(s) that failed and mark that partition(s) *stale*. When a partition is marked stale, this is logged by AIX error logging and the LVM device driver will know not to send further partition data requests to that stale partition. This saves wasted time in sending I/O requests to a partition that most likely will not respond. And when this physical problem is corrected, the VGSA will tell the mirror synchronization code which partitions need to be updated to have the mirrors contain the same data. If the disks are mirrored and there is a fault in the disks, LVM detect the staleness. The stale PPs are tracked in VGSA. Stale partitions quantities are checked using the **lsvg -l <vgname>** command. No further writes are sent to the stale PP, to save write time. When the problems are solved, stale portions can be updated from other mirrors by using **varyonvg**. AIX provides another command to synchronize the mirror. Use the **syncvg** command if you suspect that one or more mirror copies has become stale. (Actually, this command is called by **varyonvg**.) The command can be used to re-synchronize an individual logical volume, a physical disk, or an entire volume group. For example:

- `# syncvg -l lv02`

  Will synchronize the mirror copies of the logical volume lv02.

- `# syncvg -v myvg`

  Will synchronize all of the logical volumes in the volume group myvg.

6.3.2 Re-synchronizing the ODM

Problems with the LVM tend to occur when a physical disk problem causes the ODM data to become out of sync with the VGDA, VGSA, and LVCB information stored on disk.

ODM corruption can also occur if an LVM operation terminates abnormally (**kill -9**) and leaves the ODM in an inconsistent state. Improper use of low-level commands and system crashes cause problems. This may also happen, for example, if the file system on which the ODM resides (normally /) becomes full during the process of importing a volume group.

If you suspect the ODM entries for a particular volume group have been corrupted, a simple way to re-synchronize the entries is to vary off and export the volume group from the system, then import and vary on to refresh the ODM. This process can only be performed for non-rootvg volume groups.

Here is an example:

```
# varyoffvg data_vg
# exportvg data_vg
# importvg -y data_vg hdisk#
```

For the rootvg volume group, you can try using the **redefinevg** command, which examines every disk in the system to determine which volume group it belongs to and then updates the ODM. For example:

```
# redefinevg rootvg -d hdisk1
```

If you suspect the LVM information stored on disk has become corrupted, use the **synclvodm** command to synchronize and rebuild the LVCB, the device configuration database, and the VGDAs on the physical volumes. For example:

```
# synclvodm -v myvg
```

6.3.3 Collecting data

If your LVM problem cannot be traced to a faulty disk or corrupted ODM data, you need to collect information to determine the cause of the problem.

Problem determination involves a information gathering process of forming deeper and deeper hypotheses. For LVM, this generally means starting with the high level commands and working down deeper towards the contents of the ODM and the low level LVM structures: the VGDAs, VGSAs, and LVCBs. Once again, it is important to understand the problem before the attempt to fix it is made. Some people just use **synclvodm**, **exportvg**, and **importvg** to solve a problem, making the common assumption that the ODM must be corrupt and allowing the scripts to sort out the damage. Of course, this is sometimes possible, but when you are dealing with VGDA corruption, these tactics can make things worse.

Gathering ODM data

Use the following script to find LVM data in ODM. Name it as you want. Run it with one argument, such as LV_NAME. or PV_NAME.

```
#!/usr/bin/ksh
for class in CuAt CuDv CuDep CuDvDr PdAt PdDv
do
odmget $class | grep -ip $1
done
```

Gathering LVM data in the disk control block

Use the following commands to collect data in disk control area like VGDA or LVCB:

```
Checking free file system space: df
 The high-level commands: lspv, lslv, lsvg
 Checking fileset levels: lslpp
 Checking device availability: lsdev, lsattr
The low-level commands: getlvcb, lqueryvg, lquerypv, lquerylv
 Examining raw physical volumes, VGDAs, and logical volumes: dd
 Examining in-kernel memory structures: crash, kdb
```

Korn shell script debug

Since many of the high-level LVM commands are shell scripts, you can alter the scripts to add the -x option, which causes the commands executed by the script to be displayed on standard out. The first line in an executable shell script is normally similar to:

```
#!/bin/ksh
```

Edit the command you are having a problem with, and add -x to the end of the first line, as follows:

```
#!/bin/ksh -x
```

Now invoke the script with the correct arguments to recreate the problem. Redirect the standard output and standard error to a file to generate a log trace of the command. For example:

```
# synclvodm rich > /tmp/synclvodm.log 2>&1
```

The output in the log file will contain a record of each command executed by the script, along with the arguments used. A small portion of the output is shown below:

```
+
PATH=/usr/bin:/etc:/usr/sbin:/usr/ucb:/usr/bin/X11:/sbin:/usr/bin:/etc:/usr/sb
in:/usr/ucb:/usr/bin/X11:/sbin:/usr/sbin/perf/pmr:.:/usr/samples/kernel:/usr/lo
cal/bin
+ EXIT_CODE=1
+ + basename /usr/sbin/synclvodm
PROG=synclvodm
+ + odmget -q attribute=TCB_STATE and deflt=tcb_enabled PdAt
TCB_ON=
+ trap cleanup 0 1 2 15
+ getopt vPDL:FckR rich
+ set -- -- rich
```

You can use this log file to determine the exact point where the high-level command is failing. For further information, refer to the redbook *AIX Logical Volume Manager from A to Z: Troubleshooting and Commands*, SG24-5433.

Before starting the recovery, make a copy of files that can be restored in case something goes wrong. A good example would be something like the ODM database files that reside in /etc/objrepos; sometimes the recovery procedures involves deleting information from that database, and once deleted, if you are unsure of their form, you cannot recreate some of the structures or values.

6.3.4 Problems with importvg

If you experience problems with the **importvg** command when importing a volume group into a system, you should check that the volume group you are importing is supported by the level of AIX running on the system.

Various new features have been added to the LVM system at different levels of AIX, such as support for large volume groups. A number of these features required a change to the format of the VGDA stored on the disk, and will not be understood by previous levels of AIX.

Check that all of the disks in the volume group you are trying to import are marked as Available to AIX and have valid PVIDs stored in the ODM. This can be checked using the **lspv** command. If any disks do not have a PVID displayed, use the **chdev** command to resolve the problem.

For example, the PVID for hdisk5 is not shown by the **lspv** command for some reason:

```
# lspv
hdisk0          00000000003bedca    rootvg
hdisk1          00000000da5aaa02    rootvg
hdisk2          00000108b4dff0f9    nimvg
hdisk3          00000259b2faeefe    nimvg
hdisk4          00000108b4d688c5    none
hdisk5          none                none
```

This may be resolved by running the **chdev** command as follows:

```
# chdev -l hdisk5 -a pv=yes
```

This will read the PVID from the disk and place it in the ODM if the disk is accessible. It will only write a new PVID if there truly is no PVID on the disk (it also sometimes put a new PVID on OEM (like EMC) drives). Alternatively, you can use the **rmdev** command to remove the disk, for example:

```
# rmdev -l hdisk5 -d
```

Run the **cfgmgr** command to configure the disk. If the disk is accessible, it will be configured in the system with the correct PVID, and therefore, the **importvg** command should work.

A command for importing Volume Group: recreatevg

The **recreatevg** command is used when you have a disk to disk copy to perform, but you want to create a unique volume and not an exact mirror. A direct **dd** copy would create a problem, because all the information, such as VGDAs and LVs, in one disk is copied to the other. Duplicate volume group, logical volume, and file system mount points are prevented by using the **recreatevg** command. The command options allow you to specify a logical volume name (a prefix label to uniquely define the Volume Group). Automatic name generation is the default (vg00). You can use this command as a tool for importing VGs from other systems and avoid creating conflicting names of logical volumes or file systems that already exist. Therefore, you can recreate the Volume Group that already exists on a specified set of disks. But if you already remove VGDA by using **reducevg**, the command will not work.

```
# lspv
hdisk0          000bc6cdc3e0502a                    rootvg
hdisk1          000bc6cdf35adc98                    rootvg
hdisk2          000bc6cd722de8b9                    data_vg
hdisk3          000bc6cdf35ad901                    data_vg
hdisk4          000bc6cddea6dd02                    Newvg
# lsvg -l Newvg
Newvg:
LV NAME             TYPE       LPs    PPs    PVs  LV STATE      MOUNT POINT
newlv               jfs        30     30     1    closed/syncd /testfs1
# exportvg Newvg
# lspv
hdisk0          000bc6cdc3e0502a                    rootvg
hdisk1          000bc6cdf35adc98                    rootvg
hdisk2          000bc6cd722de8b9                    data_vg
hdisk3          000bc6cdf35ad901                    data_vg
hdisk4          000bc6cddea6dd02                    None
# recreatevg hdisk4
vg00
# lspv
hdisk0          000bc6cdc3e0502a                    rootvg
hdisk1          000bc6cdf35adc98                    rootvg
hdisk2          000bc6cd722de8b9                    data_vg
hdisk3          000bc6cdf35ad901                    data_vg
hdisk4          000bc6cddeb229e2 vg00
# lsvg -l vg00
vg00:
LV NAME             TYPE       LPs    PPs    PVs  LV STATE      MOUNT POINT
fsnewlv             jfs        30     30     1    closed/syncd /fs/testfs1
```

6.4 JFS problems

As with the LVM, most JFS problems can be traced to problems with the underlying physical disk.

As with volume groups, various JFS features have been added at different levels of AIX, which preclude those file systems being mounted if the volume group is imported on an earlier version of AIX. Such features include large file enabled file systems and file systems with non-default allocation group size.

For the purpose of gathering information about file system and file system usage, use the following commands.

- **dumpfs**: Displays the super block, inodemap, and disk map information.
- **fuser**: Identifies processes using a file or file structure. The **fuser** command lists the process numbers of local processes that use the local or remote files specified by the File parameter. For block special devices, the command lists the processes that use any file on that device. This command is a good tool for finding open files that use specific file systems.
- **df**: Displays file system usage, including superblock, inode, disk map, deleted files still opened by a process and data block.
- **du**: Displays disk usage, including only data block.
- **fsdb**: A low level debugging tool for a file system. This is a very powerful tool that can alter file systems metadata. Incorrect usage can lead to file system corruption and loss of data.

6.4.1 Mounting file systems

Mounting makes file systems, files, directories, devices, and special files available for use at a particular location. It is the only way a file system is made accessible. The **mount** command instructs the operating system to attach a file system at a specified directory.

You can mount a file or directory if you have access to the file or directory being mounted and write permission for the mount point. Members of the system group can also perform device mounts (in which devices or file systems are mounted over directories) and the mounts described in the /etc/filesystems file. A user operating with root user authority can mount a file system arbitrarily by naming both the device and the directory on the command line. The /etc/filesystems file is used to define mounts to be automatic at system initialization.

Problems can occur when mounting a file system if it was not previously unmounted correctly, as can happen if a system experiences a kernel crash. The status of the file system structure may be inconsistent and require repair actions before being mounted.

6.4.2 File system recovery

In the AIX system, the **fsck** command is used to check file system consistency. It can also be used to interactively perform repairs the file system.

File system inconsistencies can stem from the following:

- Stopping the system with file systems mounted.
- Physical disk deterioration or damage. This procedure should be used before mounting any file system.

The **fsck** command checks for the following inconsistencies:

- Blocks or fragments allocated to multiple files.
- i-nodes containing block or fragment numbers that overlap.
- i-nodes containing block or fragment numbers out of range.
- Discrepancies between the number of directory references to a file and the link count of the file.
- Illegally allocated blocks or fragments.
- i-nodes containing block or fragment numbers that are marked free in the disk map.
- i-nodes containing corrupt block or fragment numbers.
- A fragment that is not the last disk address in an i-node. This check does not apply to compressed file systems.
- Files larger than 32 KB containing a fragment. This check does not apply to compressed file systems.
- Size checks:
  - Incorrect number of blocks.
  - Directory size not a multiple of 512 bytes.
  - These checks do not apply to compressed file systems.
- Directory checks:
  - Directory entry containing an i-node number marked free in the i-node map.
  - i-node number out of range.
  - Dot (.) link missing or not pointing to itself.

  - Dot dot (..) link missing or not pointing to the parent directory.
  - Files that are not referenced or directories that are not reachable.
- Inconsistent disk map.
- Inconsistent i-node map.

The **fsck** command does not make changes to a mounted file system. You should unmount the file system before invoking **fsck**.

If the / (root) or /usr file systems require consistency checking, you should only invoke **fsck** on them from the maintenance shell obtained after performing a Service mode boot of the system from bootable media. Through this route, you can access the root volume group and start a shell before mounting file systems. This will then allow you to perform the **fsck** operation on the / (root) and /usr file systems, since at this point they are not mounted.

Orphaned files and directories (those that cannot be reached) are, if you allow it, reconnected by placing them in the lost+found subdirectory in the root directory of the file system. The name assigned is the i-node number. If you do not allow the **fsck** command to reattach an orphaned file, it requests permission to destroy the file.

You can invoke the **fsck** command with the -y parameter, which instructs the command to take whatever actions it deems necessary to repair the file system. Only use this option on severely damaged file systems.

When a superblock is accidentally corrupted, use the secondary block as a source. The system has a copy of the super block for recovery. This secondary block is located at 32 block. For example:

```
# dd count=1 bs=31k skip=31 seek=1 if=/dev/lv00 of=/dev/lv00
1+0 records in.
1+0 records out.
```

6.4.3 JFS log problems

The jfslog device used with JFS can become overloaded in some situations. This can occur when a large amount of JFS I/O is taking place on file systems that share the same log device.

This problem can be avoided by creating an individual jfslog device for each file system that has a high amount of file system structure changes.

The size of the jfslog device should be in proportion to the amount of JFS file system data it is being used to log. A general rule of thumb is to use one PP of jfslog space for every 512 PPs of JFS space. This rule holds true regardless of the PP size.

To create a new jfslog device for an existing file system, use the following procedure:

1. Create a logical volume to be used for the jfslog device. The logical volume must exist in the same volume group as the file system that will use it. The name of the logical volume does not matter, although you may wish to indicate that it is a jfslog device. For example:

   ```
   # mklv rootvg loglv01 1
   ```

2. Format the logical volume for use as a jfslog device:

   ```
   # logform /dev/loglv01
   ```

   The command will warn you that the action will destroy all data on the logical volume. Enter y to continue.

3. Unmount the file system that will use the new jfslog device.

4. Edit the /etc/filesystems entry for the file system that will use the new jfslog device. Change the log= stanza to reference the new jfslog device. For example:

   ```
   /export:
           dev             = /dev/lv00
           vfs             = jfs
           log             = /dev/loglv01
           mount           = true
           options         = rw
           account         = false
   ```

   Note: This step leaves the LVCB pointer to the old jfslog. If you export/import the Volume Group, the file system will not mount. You need to run **chfs**.

5. Mount the file system that will use the new jfslog device. For example:

   ```
   # mount /export
   ```

6. Check that the file system is now using the new jfslog device by examining the output of the command. For example:

   ```
   # mount | grep /export
            /dev/lv00        /export          jfs     Jul 01 17:06
   rw,log=/dev/loglv01
   ```

If the jfslog device for a file system becomes corrupted, you may have to reformat the jfslog device. To do this, use the following procedure:

1. Unmount any file systems using the jfslog device.
2. Format the jfslog device. For example:

   ```
   # logform /dev/loglv01
   ```

   The command will warn you that the action will destroy all data on the logical volume. Enter y to continue.
3. Mount the file systems that uses the jfslog device.

If the jfslog used by the / (root), /usr, /tmp, and /var file systems, normally called /dev/hd8, becomes corrupted, you will need to perform the **logform** operation from the maintenance shell obtained by booting the machine in Service mode from installable media.

If you need to increase the size of an existing jfslog device, use the following procedure:

1. Unmount any file systems using the jfslog device.
2. Increase the size of the logical volume used for the jfslog. For example:

   ```
   # extendlv loglv01 1
   ```
3. Format the jfslog device. For example:

   ```
   # logform /dev/loglv01
   ```

   The command will warn you that the action will destroy all data on the logical volume. Enter y to continue.
4. Mount the file systems that use the jfslog device.

As described previously, if you need to change the size of the jfslog used by the / (root), /usr, /tmp, and /var file systems, normally called /dev/hd8, you will need to perform the **logform** operation from the maintenance shell obtained by booting the machine in Service mode from installable media.

6.4.4 Enhanced Journaled File System (JFS2)

The Journaled File System 2 (JFS2) is an enhanced and updated version of the JFS on AIX Version 4.3 and previous releases. The journaled file system JFS and JFS2 are native to the AIX operating system. The file system links the file and directory data to the structure used by storage and retrieval mechanisms. Both JFS (the default) and JFS2 are available on POWER systems. Only JFS2 is supported on Itanium™-based systems. AIX 5L enhanced file system functions from the availability point of view.

- Dynamic disk inode allocation

JFS2 dynamically allocates space for disk inodes as required, freeing the space when it is no longer required. This support avoids the traditional approach of reserving a fixed amount of space for disk inodes at file system creation time, thus eliminating the need for customers to estimate the maximum number of files and directories that a file system will contain.

Files in the enhanced journaled file system (JFS2) are represented internally as index nodes (i-nodes). JFS2 i-nodes exist in a static form on the disk and they contain access information for the files as well as pointers to the real disk addresses of the file's data blocks. The i-nodes are allocated dynamically by JFS2.

Each disk i-node in JFS2 is a 512 byte structure. The index of a particular i-node allocation map of the file system produces the unique number (i-number) by which the operating system identifies the i-node Variable Number of I-nodes for Enhanced Journaled File System JFS2 allocates i-nodes as needed. Therefore, the number of i-nodes available is limited by the size of the file system itself.

- On-line file system free space defragmentation

JFS2 supports the defragmentation of free space in a mounted and actively accessed file system. Once a file system's free space has become fragmented, defragmenting the file system allows JFS2 to provide more I/O-efficient disk allocations and to avoid some out of space conditions.

- In-line log

A new type of log can be created for JFS2 type file systems. An inline log is a feature specific to JFS2 file systems that allows you to create the log within the same data logical volume.

With an inline log, each JFS2 file system can have its own log device without having to share this device. For a scenario with multiples of hot swap disk devices and large number of file systems, this feature can be used to improve RAS if a system loses a single disk that contains the log device for multiple file systems.The default inline log size is 0.4 percent of the LV size.

6.5 Disk replacement management

AIX, like all the other operating systems, can be vexing when you have to change a disk. It is not advisable to change a faulty disk, restore the data, and just walk away without doing suitable procedures.

There are many reasons for the replacement of a disk:

- The disk is too small.
- The disk is too slow.
- The disk produces many DISK_ERR4 logs.

With AIX, you have the ability to prepare the system for the change by using the LVM facilities. You can perform the disk replacement and then use the LVM to restore the system. This process manipulates not only the data on the disk itself but also the way of keeping the Object Data Manager (ODM) intact.

The ODM is a database that holds device configuration data (in detail) and AIX system configuration, such as network configurations. The function of the ODM is to store the information between reboots and also to provide rapid access to system data. Since this database holds so much vital information regarding the configuration of a machine, any changes made to the machine, such as the changing of a defective disk, need to be done in such a way as to preserve the integrity of the database.

The procedures in the following sections provide a number of methods of using AIX commands to remove a disk and its associated ODM entries to enable its replacement. and the procedures incorporate the replacement disk back into the system to the point where data, if any, needs to be restored.

6.5.1 Disk replacement procedure

In case one of your disks has failed, you first run diagnostics on the failed disk drive. The disk you are dealing with is probably in an unstable condition or is liable to become totally defective at anytime before the replacement procedure successfully completes. Therefore, you should attempt to back up the data in advance. We will now show you the disk replacement procedures step by step. The following sections cover a number of methods for changing disks; however, we cannot cover all the possibilities.

Situation 1: Mirrored disk

This section describes how to replace a failing hard drive in a mirrored configuration. Mirroring is used to increase the data availability, but you should always have a backup ready just in case something goes wrong. In a non-mirrored configuration, if a hard drive dies, your only solution is to use the backup. In a mirrored configuration, this failure should be transparent to users, and you should be able to replace the disk without loosing any data. Based on your version of AIX, this procedure can be quite simple, such as with AIX Version 4.3.3 and the **replacepv** command, or more complex, such as with a sequence of commands in earlier versions of AIX.

Assume that we have a system with one physical volume (hdiskx) that is part of a volume group (data_vg) and contains mirrored copies of logical volumes (lv_xx) as well as parts of un-mirrored logical volumes (lv_yy). Follow these steps to replace the drive:

1. Remove all copies from disk:

```
# rmlvcopy lv_xx 1 hdiskx
```

2. Remove any (un-mirrored) logical volumes that used partitions from the failed disk:

```
# rmlv -f lv_yy
```

3. Remove the disk from the volume group:

```
# reducevg data_vg hdiskx
```

4. Remove the disk from ODM:

```
# rmdev -l hdiskx -d
```

   If the disk to be changed is SCSI and not in the hot wwap bay, then power off the system. Remove/replace the disk. Then power on the system.

5. Connect the new disk to the system and reboot. If the disk to be changed is SSA, then go to the SSA Service Aids. Use the Set Service Mode and Identify utility to power down the disk. After replacement, use the utility to power up the disk. Once this is complete, the pdisk can be removed using the **rmdev -l pdiskX -d** command. If the disk replaced was SSA or in a hot swap bay, then use **cfgmgr -vl <parent_adapter>** to add the disk to the system.

6. Add the new disk to the volume group:

```
# extendvg data_vg hdiskx
```

7. Create new copies and synchronize the copies:

```
# mklvcopy lv_xx 2 hdiskx
# syncvg -v data_vg
```

8. Recreate any un-mirrored logical volumes and restore the data from backup.

Using the **replacepv** command is a much simpler option. The original definition of the failed disk is left, and the physical volume itself is replaced. In this example, hdisk2 is a source disk and hdisk4 is a spare disk:

```
# lspv
hdisk0          000bc6cdc3e0502a                    rootvg
hdisk1          000bc6cdf35adc98                    rootvg
hdisk2          000bc6cd722de8b9                    data_vg
hdisk3          000bc6cdf35ad901                    data_vg
hdisk4          000bc6cdf35bd62c                    None
# lslv -m lv_xx
lv_xx:/testfs1
LP    PP1  PV1                PP2  PV2              PP3  PV3
```

```
0001  0110 hdisk2          0110 hdisk3
0002  0111 hdisk2          0111 hdisk3
0003  0112 hdisk2          0112 hdisk3
0004  0113 hdisk2          0113 hdisk3
0005  0114 hdisk2          0114 hdisk3
0006  0115 hdisk2          0115 hdisk3
0007  0116 hdisk2          0116 hdisk3
...
# replacepv hdisk2 hdisk4
0516-014 linstallpv: The physical volume appears to belong to another
        volume group.
000bc6cd00004c00
0516-631 extendvg: Warning, all data belonging to physical
        volume hdisk4 will be destroyed.
extendvg: Do you wish to continue? y(es) n(o)? y
0516-1232 replacepv:
        NOTE: If this program is terminated before the completion due to
        a system crash or ctrl-C, and you want to continue afterwards
        execute the following command
        replacepv -R /tmp/replacepv3540
# lspv
hdisk0          000bc6cdc3e0502a                    rootvg
hdisk1          000bc6cdf35adc98                    rootvg
hdisk2          000bc6cd722de8b9                    None
hdisk3          000bc6cdf35ad901                    data_vg
hdisk4          000bc6cdf35bd62c                    data_vg
# lspv -l hdisk4
hdisk4:
LV NAME               LPs   PPs   DISTRIBUTION          MOUNT POINT
lv_xx                 20    20    00..20..00..00..00    /testfs1
loglv00               1     1     00..01..00..00..00    N/A
```

As a result, the hdisk2 will be none and the hdisk4 contains data_vg.

Note: In the process of replacing a disk, the **reducevg** command updates VGDA and ODM data. The **rmdev** command only updates ODM data. If you skip one of two commands, there will be an inconsistency between VGDA and ODM.

Situation 2: Non-mirrored disk

A second situation is the case of a non-mirrored disk that needs to be replaced. The steps in this section cover two main procedures, depending on the accessibility of the disk.

First, if the replaced disk is accessible and you can run **migratepv** or **replacepv**, the following steps will help you do the job:

1. Connect the new disk to the system; you must have spare disks.
2. List all the disks using the **lsdev** command:

   ```
   # lsdev -C -c disk
   ```
3. Make the disk available using the **chdev** command:

   ```
   # chdev -l hdisky -a pv=yes
   ```
4. Add a new disk to the volume group:

   ```
   # extendvg data_vg hdisky
   ```
5. Migrate the old disk to the new disk:

   ```
   # migratepv hdiskx hdisky
   ```

   or

   ```
   # replacepv hdiskx hdisky
   ```

   (If hdiskx has the LV of rootvg. Refer to the note below.)
6. Remove the old disk from the Volume Group:

   ```
   # reducevg data_vg hdiskx
   ```
7. Remove the old disk from ODM:

   ```
   # rmdev -l hdiskx -d
   ```

> **Note:** If the disk contains hd5, the following extra procedure is required. We recommend using the **migratepv** command instead of the **replacepv** command in case of rootvg.
>
> ```
> # migratepv -l hd5 hdiskx hdisky
> # bosboot -ad/dev/hdisky
> ```
>
> This updates boot logical volume in hdisky. In addition to creating a boot image, the **bosboot** command always saves device configuration data for the disk. It does not update the list of boot devices in the NVRAM; therefore, you need to run bootlist:
>
> ```
> # chpv -c /dev/hdiskx (to clear boot record on hdiskx) or # mkboot -d
> /dev/hdiskx -c
> # bootlist -m normal hdisky
> ```

A second scenario is when your disk is *totally* inaccessible. In that case, follow these steps (you must have a backup of data):

1. List all LVs and file systems on the falling disk that you need to identify:

   ```
   # lspv -l hdiskx
   ```

2. Unmount all file systems on the failing disk:

```
# umount /dev/lv_xx
```

(If the file system is not inaccessible due to device busy, check it using the **fuser** command.)

3. Remove all file systems from the failing disk:

```
# rmfs /fs_name
```

4. Remove all LVs from the failing disk:

```
# rmlv lv_xx
```

5. Remove the disk from the Volume Group:

```
# reducevg data_vg hdiskx
```

6. Remove the disk from ODM:

```
# rmdev -dl hdiskx
```

7. Add a new disk to a volume group:

```
# extendvg data_vg hdisky
```

8. Recreate all LVs on new disk:

```
# smit mklv
```

9. Recreate all file systems on a new disk:

```
# smit crfs
```

10. Restore the file systems from backup:

```
# restore -rqvf /dev/rmt0
```

If you would prefer not to reboot the system after reformatting the disk drive, you must configure the disk and create the device entry by entering **cfgmgr** or **mkdev -l hdiskx**. If you want to only check the SSA disks, use the **cfgmgr -l ssar** command (the -l option means that the **cfgmgr** command only configures the named device and its children.)

> **Note:** If the failing disk is in an active state (Using **lspv hdiskx**, you can see the PV state), you cannot remove any copies or logical volumes from the failing disk. In this case, the only way to bring the disk into a *removed* or *missing* state is to reboot your system.

Situation 3: Volume Group lost

This section covers situations where a volume group is lost, whether it is a non-rootvg or rootvg failure.

In case of total non-rootvg failure

This situation applies to a total failure of a non-rootvg volume group. Follow these steps:

1. Export the Volume Group from the system:

   ```
   # exportvg data_vg
   ```

2. Check /etc/filesystems. Verify that there are no references to the LV of data_vg.
3. Remove the bad disk from ODM and the system:

   ```
   # rmdev -l hdiskx -d
   ```

4. If needed, shut down the system to replace the disks. Connect new disks and reboot.
5. Use the Volume Group backup, if available (savevg):

   ```
   # restvg -f /dev/rmt0 hdiskx
   ```

   If you have more than one disk, you must specify these disks after hdiskx.
6. If you have no savevg backup available, remake the Volume Group:

   ```
   # smit mkvg
   ```

7. Recreate the LV and FS:

   ```
   # smit mklv
   # smit crfs
   ```

8. Restore the file system data from the backup:

   ```
   # restore -rqvf/dev/rmt0
   ```

In case of a total rootvg failure

This situation might come up when your rootvg is composed of many disks and failed one of the key Operating System LV or FS (for instance, /dev/hd4, /dev/hd2). You need to have the latest mksysb backup. Follow these steps:

1. Shut down the system and replace the bad disks.
2. Boot in maintenance mode.
3. Restore from a mksysb image (the procedure depends on the machine model; see below).
4. Import each Volume Group into a new ODM, if needed. (If your mksysb tape does not include an user defined Volume Group, you have to import the user volume group after restoring the mksysb):

   ```
   # importvg -y data_vg hdiskx
   ```

Doing a restore of a mksysb (image backup of rootvg) requires a bootable mksysb tape or an AIX install CD-ROM and a non-bootable mksysb.

- For MCA machines

  Booting from a mksysb tape or AIX install CD-ROM requires the machine to perform a Service mode boot. Complete the following steps:

  a. Power off the machine.
  b. Turn the key to Service.
  c. Power on the machine.
  d. Immediately place the bootable media in the CD-ROM or tape drive.
  e. Answer any screen prompts.
  f. When the Installation Screen appears, select Start Maintenance Mode for System Recovery (option 3).
  g. Select Install from a System Backup (option 4).

- For PCI machines

  To start a Service mode boot:

  a. Power off the machine.
  b. Turn on the machine power.
  c. Place the bootable media in the CD-ROM or tape drive.
  d. After a short period of time, you will see the Icons screen. At this point, press F5 if you are using a graphics console, or 5 if you are using an ASCII console or a graphics terminal on later machine types. If you are using the graphics console, they will sometimes have power saving on them and will take time to restart. This can lead you to miss the symbols being displayed. In this situation, observe the power LED on the display monitor, and when it changes from orange to green, press the F5 key.

     After doing the above, you will get various screens displayed, one of which will give you the SCSI address of the device that it is booting from.
  e. Answer all of the screen prompts.
  f. When the Installation and Screen appears, select Start Maintenance Mode for System Recovery (option 3).
  g. Select Install from a System Backup (option 4)

Using a LVM hot spare disk

A hot spare disk is a disk or group of disks that replaces a failing disk. The LVM marks a physical volume missing due to write failures. It then starts the migration of data to the hot spare disk. In AIX 5L Version 5.1, the **chpv** and the **chvg** commands are enhanced with a new -h flag that allows you to designate disks as hot spare disks in a volume group and to specify a policy to be used in the case of failing disks. These commands are not replacements for the sparing support available with SSA disks; they complement it. You can also use them with SSA disks when you add one to your volume group. These new options have an effect only if the volume group has mirrored logical volumes.There is a new -s flag for the **chvg** command that is used to specify synchronization characteristics.

- Hot Spare disk requirements
  - Spares are allocated and used by Volume Group.
  - Logical Volumes must be mirrored.
  - All logical partitions on hot spare disks must be unallocated.
  - Hot spare disks must have at least equal capacity to the smallest disk already in the Volume Group.

We will now show an example of a hot spare disk configuration.

The following command defines hdisk1 as a hot spare disk:

```
# chpv -hy hdisk1
```

Using n instead of y would remove the hot spare disk marker.The following command sets an automatic migration policy, which uses the smallest hot spare that is large enough to replace the failing disk, and automatically tries to synchronize stale partitions:

```
# chvg -hy -sy testvg
# lspv hdisk4
PHYSICAL VOLUME:    hdisk4                    VOLUME GROUP:     data_vg
PV IDENTIFIER:      000bc6cdf35bd62c VG IDENTIFIER
000bc6cd00004c00000000e8d
a599952
PV STATE:           active
STALE PARTITIONS:   0                         ALLOCATABLE:      no
PP SIZE:            16 megabyte(s)            LOGICAL VOLUMES:  0
TOTAL PPs:          542 (8672 megabytes)      VG DESCRIPTORS:   1
FREE PPs:           542 (8672 megabytes)      HOT SPARE:        yes
USED PPs:           0 (0 megabytes)
FREE DISTRIBUTION:  109..108..108..108..109
USED DISTRIBUTION:  00..00..00..00..00
# lsvg -p data_vg
data_vg:
PV_NAME             PV STATE            TOTAL PPs    FREE PPs    FREE DISTRIBUTION
hdisk2              active              542          521 109..87..108..108..1
09
hdisk3              active              542          521 109..87..108..108..1
09
hdisk4              active/hotspare     542          542 109..108..108..108..
109
```

You can see that the HOT SPARE flag is set to yes in the above output. After setting this up, Volume Group Status Area (VGSA) write failures and Mirror Write Consistency (MWC) write failures will mark a physical volume missing and start the migration of data to the hot spare disk.

Disk-to-disk copy

This method can only be employed to copy SCSI disks. The disk to be copied to (target disk) must *not* have a smaller capacity than the disk to be copied from (source disk) or *more* than a 10 percent larger capacity than the source disk.

Complete the following steps:

1. Power the machine off.
2. Connect the target disk to a SCSI bus using a free SCSI ID.
3. Boot the machine using a Diagnostic CD-ROM. Refer to Section 5.3.3, "Stand-alone diagnostics" on page 131 for instructions.
4. At the Diagnostics screen, select the Task Selection menu option or the Service Aids option, if using an AIX Diagnostics CD-ROM older than Version 4.1.5.
5. Select Disk Maintenance.
6. Select Disk to Disk copy.
7. Enter the addresses of the target and source disks. Care should be taken not to get the addresses confused. A mistake at this point will damage data irreparably.
8. Start the copying.
9. When the copy has completed, power off the machine and immediately remove the defective disk from the machine. Both the disks carry the same PVID, which would cause problems if you started AIX with both disks left in the machine. Since both disks carry the same PVID, you might also forget which is the defective disk.

> **Note:** This procedure will only be completed successfully if the defective disk passes diagnostics with minimal errors. If the error rate is too high, the service aid will be terminated.
>
> This process is not suitable for use on 7020 model 40P and 7248 model 43P machines, because these machines are not capable of loading AIX diagnostics.

SSA RAID disk replacement

Here we discuss replacing SSA RAID disks.

Replacing used hot spare drives

Consider this scenario:

An SSA RAID hdisk is configured to use a hot spare disk. The disk has failed, the hot spare has been transferred into the array, and the SSA RAID manager (SSA adapter normally) is logging A SRN of 49500. At this point, do the following:

1. Identifying the disk
   a. Enter the SSA RAID manager SMIT screens with **smit saraid**.
   b. List/Identify SSA Physical disks.
   c. Identify the rejected array disks.
   d. Choose the appropriate RAID manager.
   e. Press PF4 to list the rejected disks.
   f. Select the rejected disk with PF7 (make a note of its name).
   g. Press Enter to set the disk to Identify mode (check light flashes).
2. Remove the disk
   a. Run **# rmdev -l pdiskX -d**.
   b. Physically remove the disk from the subsystem or system, if 7025, using the appropriate service guide.
3. Replace the disk
   a. Fit the new disk in the original position using the appropriate service guide.
   b. Configure the disk using the commands:

```
# cfgmgr -l ssar
# lsdev -Cc pdisk (to make sure pdisk has been configured)
```

4. Reconfigure the disk as a hot spare disk.
   a. Enter the SSA RAID manager SMIT screens with **smit ssaraid**.
   b. Change/show Use of an SSA Physical Disk.
   c. Move down the list of physical disks and stop on the line for pdiskX.
   d. Change the use of the physical disk to a hot spare disk.

Replacing a rejected disk

Consider this scenario:

An SSA RAID hdisk is not configured to use a hot spare disk. The disk has failed and is in a rejected state.

At this point, do the following:

1. Identifying the disk.
   a. Enter the SSA RAID manager SMIT screens with **smit ssaraid**.
   b. List/Identify SSA Physical disks.
   c. Identify the rejected array disks.
   d. Choose the appropriate RAID manager.
   e. Press PF4 to list the rejected disks.
   f. Select the rejected disk with PF7 (make a note of its name).
   g. Press Enter to set the disk to Identify mode (check light flashes).
2. Remove the disk.
   a. Run # **rmdev -l pdiskX -d**.
   b. Physically remove the disk from the subsystem or system, if 7025, using the appropriate service guide.
3. Replace the disk.
   a. Fit the new disk in the original position using the appropriate service guide.
   b. Configure the disk using the commands:

      ```
      # cfgmgr -l ssar
      # lsdev -Cc pdisk
      ```

      Make sure the pdisk has been configured with the same number as before.
4. Configure the disk and add the disk to the array.
   a. Enter the SSA RAID manager SMIT screens with **smit ssaraid**.
   b. Change/show Use of an SSA Physical Disk.
   c. Move down the list of physical disks and stop on the line for pdiskX.
   d. Change the use of the physical disk to an array candidate disk.
   e. Change member disks in an SSA RAID Array in the main RAID menu.
   f. Add a disk to an SSA RAID Array.
   g. Press PF4 to list the Array Candidate Disks.
   h. Choose pdiskX and press PF7 to select.

Replacing an active disk in a SSA RAID ARRAY

Consider this scenario:

An SSA RAID manager (SSA adapter normally) is NOT logging errors, but a pdisk within a SSA RAID hdisk is logging temporary disk errors (SSA_DISK_ERR2, SSA_DISK_ERR3 or DISK_ERR4). At this point, do the following:

1. Identifying the disk.
   a. From the error report, determine which pdisk is faulty.
   b. Identify which hdisk this pdisk is a member of with the **`ssaxlate -l pdiskX`** command.
   c. Enter the SSA RAID manager SMIT screens with **`smit ssaraid`**.
   d. List/identify the SSA Physical Disks.
   e. Identify disks in an SSA RAID Array.
   f. Choose the hdisk from the list that was identified with the **`ssaxlate`** command.
   g. Select the pdisk identified from the error log entry and press PF7.
   h. Press Enter to set the disk to Identify mode (check light flashes).
2. Removing the disk from the array.
   a. Change the member disks in an SSA RAID Array in the main menu.
   b. Remove a disk from an SSA RAID Array.
   c. Choose the hdisk from the list that was identified with the **`ssaxlate`** command.
   d. Choose pdiskX and press PF7 to select.
3. Removing the disk.
   a. Run # **`rmdev -l pdiskX -d`**.
   b. Physically remove the disk from the subsystem or system, if 702*, using the appropriate service guide.
4. Replacing the disk.
   a. Fit the new disk in the original position using the appropriate service guide.
   b. Configure the new disk using the # **`cfgmgr -l ssar`** command.
   c. Run # **`lsdev -Cc pdisk`** (to make sure the pdisk has been configured correctly).
5. Configure the disk and add the disk to the array.
   a. Enter the SSA RAID manager screens with # **`smit ssaraid`**.

b. Change/show the use of an SSA Physical Disk.
c. Move down the list of physical disks and stop on the line for pdiskX.
d. Change the use of the physical disk to an array candidate disk.
e. Press PF3 until the SSA RAID Array menu is displayed.
f. Change member disks in an SSA RAID Array.
g. Add a disk to an SSA RAID Array.
h. Choose the Array hdisk from the list.
i. Press PF4 to list the array candidate disks.
j. Choose pdiskX and press PF7 to select.
k. Press Enter (this adds the disk to the array and the array will start to rebuild)

Note: To check the status and the amount the array has rebuilt, use the SSA RAID Array menu item Change/Show Attributes of an SSA RAID Array.

7

TCP/IP and networking problem solving

This chapter deals with network problem source identification and resolution on different types of networks. The following problem determination assumes that the underlying network has been wired in accordance with the applicable networking standards.

7.1 General network problem isolation

Prior to beginning any network debugging, a series of questions need to be asked in order to isolate the problem:

- Is the problem with your own machine?
  - The physical network?
  - The network device?
  - Routing tables?
- Is the problem with the target host?
- Is the problem with name resolution?
- Is the problem with a router (external equipment)?

7.2 Problem isolation steps for TCP/IP network problems

The problems listed here are the most commonly encountered. Sometimes, it is very difficult to discover exactly where the problem lies – within your machine or outside of it.

To determine the problem, you must use status tools and commands and a process of elimination. If none of the following steps lead to resolution of the problem, you will need to open a PMR, gather the required test case documentation, and send the problem in for analysis.

As seen in Figure 7-1, if you are unable to connect to any host, or if you have a general network problem, go to Section 7.2.2, "No network access" on page 198.

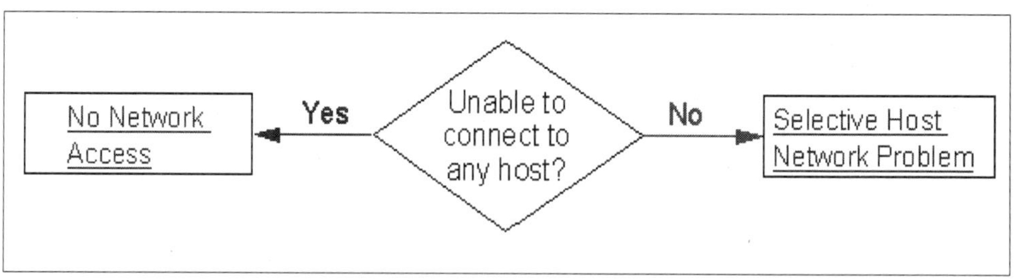

Figure 7-1 TCP/IP network connection

If the problem is only with specific hosts, go to Section 7.2.1, "Selective host network problems" on page 197.

7.2.1 Selective host network problems

As seen in Figure 7-2, if networking is generally working, but you are unable to access a particular host, try to **ping** by IP address and host name. Refer to Section 7.2.2, “No network access” on page 198 if necessary.

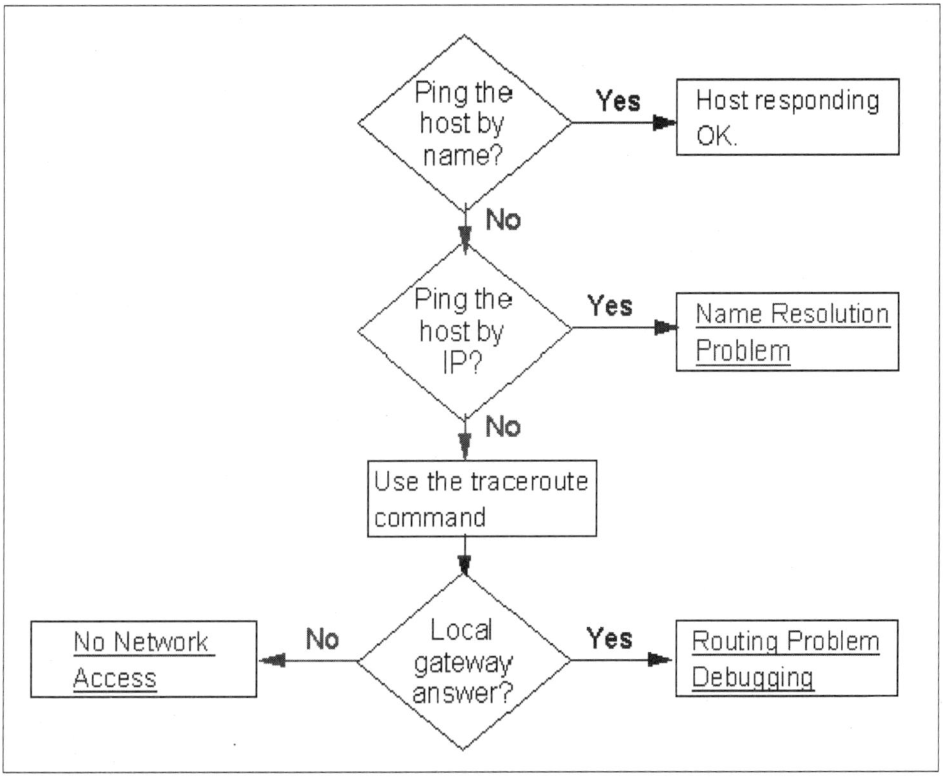

Figure 7-2 Selective host

If this is a name resolution problem, refer to Section 7.2.3, “Name resolution problems” on page 200 to verify the correct setup.

Try the **traceroute** command to see the attempted route to the host:

```
# traceroute <hostname>
```

The **traceroute** output shows each gateway that the packet traverses on its way to finding the target host. If possible, examine the routing tables of the last machine shown in the **traceroute** output to check if a route exists to the destination from that host. The last machine shown is where the routing is going astray.

Perhaps the host is just down, in which case you will not be able to ping it.

traceroute uses the UDP protocol and **ping** uses the ICMP protocol, so both should be tried; they may have different results.

- Did you receive any answer from the local gateway?

  If the answer is yes, you probably have a routing or a remote host problem. Check Section 7.2.4, "Routing problem debugging" on page 202 for help. The **traceroute** output will be similar to Example 7-1.

Example 7-1 traceroute showing routing problem

```
Tracing route to 206.183.54.220
over a maximum of 30 hops:
1     1 ms     *        1 ms  itso240.itsc.austin.ibm.com [9.3.240.1]
2     2 ms     1 ms     1 ms  9.111.195.1
3     2 ms     1 ms     2 ms  bb6r-def.austin.ibm.com [9.3.63.253]
4     *        *        *     Request timed out.
5     *        *        *     Request timed out.
```

If the answer is no, you might have a local network problem or local machine problem. Check Section 7.2.2, "No network access" on page 198 for help. The **traceroute** output will be similar to Example 7-2.

Example 7-2 traceroute showing no network access

```
Tracing route to 206.183.54.220
     over a maximum of 30 hops:
       1   *        *        *     Request timed out.
       2   *        *        *     Request timed out.
```

7.2.2 No network access

When you have the `No Network Access` message, you might have a problem in your local machine, such as the wrong configuration or a defective adapter, some local network interface problem, or some defective external network equipment.

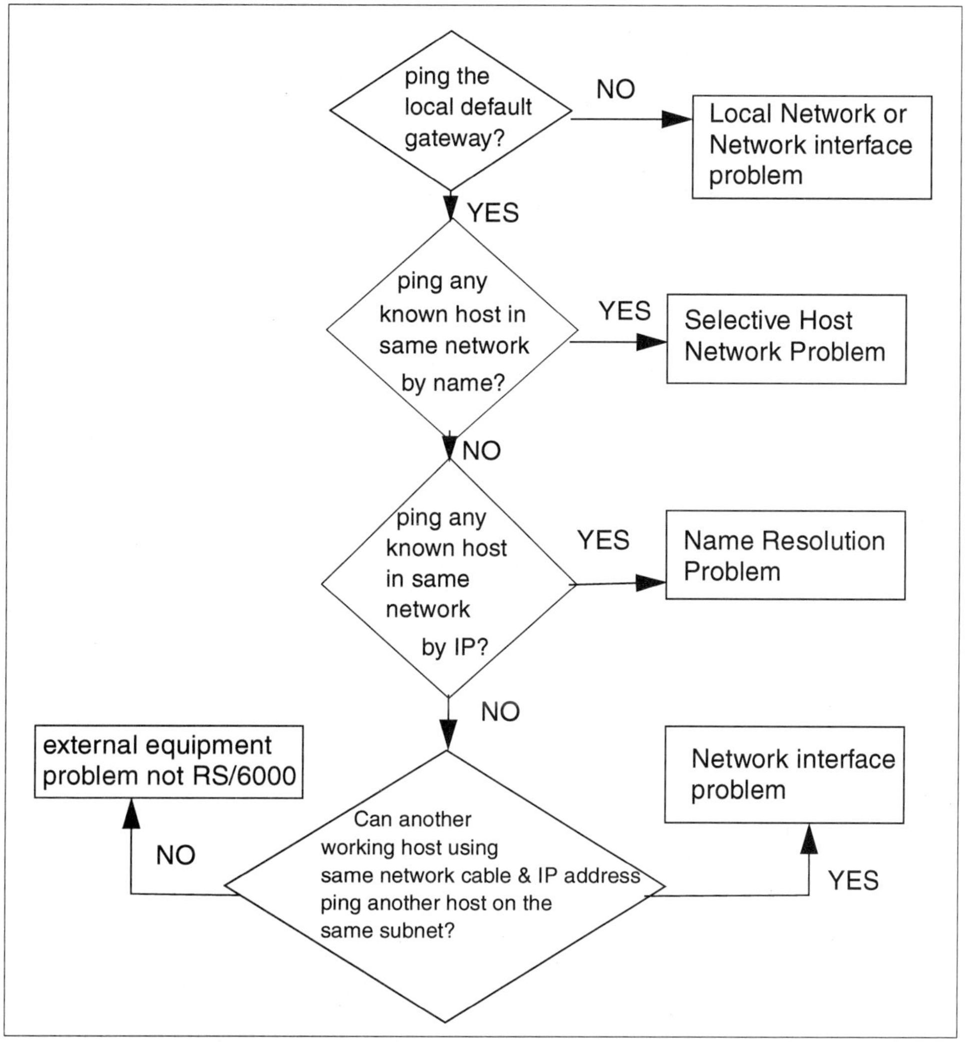

Figure 7-3 No network access

As seen in Figure 7-3, you should execute the following steps to determine where the problem is:

- Can you **ping** the default gateway?

If the answer is yes, check to see if you can reach machines in the same network as your machine.

If the answer is no, you might have a local network problem or a problem in your machine. Check Section 7.2.7, “Network interface problems” on page 207 for help.

- Can you **ping** the host by name?

If the answer is yes, you are having problems reaching the remote host only. Check Section 7.2.1, “Selective host network problems” on page 197 for help.

If the answer is no, try to **ping** the machine by IP address.

- Can you **ping** the host by IP address?

If the answer is yes, you probably have a Name Resolution problem. Refer to the Section 7.2.3, “Name resolution problems” on page 200 for help.

If the answer is no, can another working host using the same network cable and IP address **ping** another host on the same subnet?

If the answer is yes, you might have a local host problem, such as the wrong configuration or bad adapters. Check the Section 7.2.7, “Network interface problems” on page 207 for help. If the answer is no, troubleshoot the external equipment, such as the switch, router, cable, or hub.

7.2.3 Name resolution problems

Resolver routines on hosts running TCP/IP attempt to resolve names, using the following sources in the order listed:

- Domain name server (named)
- Network Information Service (NIS)
- Local /etc/hosts file

When NIS+ is installed, the lookup preferences are set using the irs.conf file.

The order can be changed in the /etc/netsvc.conf file or by using the NSORDER environment variable; check these for your particular name resolution ordering.

Client host

If you cannot get a host name resolved, and you are using flat name resolution (using the /etc/hosts file), verify that the host name and correct Internet Protocol (IP) address information is in the /etc/hosts file.

If you cannot get a host name resolved, and you are using a name server:

- Verify that you have a resolv.conf file specifying the domain name and Internet address of a name server.

- Verify that the local name server is up by issuing the **ping** command with the IP address of the name server (found in the local resolv.conf file).
- If the local name server is up, verify that the named daemon on your local name server is active by issuing the **lssrc -s named** command on the name server.
- If you are running the syslogd, check for logged messages. The output for these messages is defined in the /etc/syslog.conf file.

If these steps do not identify the problem, check the name server host.

Name server host

If you cannot get a host name resolved:

- Verify that the named daemon is active by issuing the following command:

  ```
  # lssrc -s named
  ```

- Verify that the address of the target host exists and is correct in the name server database. Send a SIGINT signal to the named daemon to dump the database and cache to the file /var/tmp/named_dump.db. Verify that the address you are trying to resolve is there and is correct.

  Add or correct name-to-address resolution information in the named hosts data file for the master name server of the domain. Then issue the following SRC command to reread the data files:

  ```
  # refresh -s named
  ```

- Verify that the name resolution requests are being processed. To do this, enter the named daemon from the command line and specify a debugging level. Valid debug levels are 1 through 9. The higher the level, the more information the debug mechanism logs. Use the command:

  ```
  # startsrc -s named -a "-d DebugLevel"
  ```

- Check for configuration problems in the named data files.

> **Note:** A common error is the incorrect use of the . (period) and the @ (at sign) in the DOMAIN data files.

If external users cannot reach your domains, make sure that all your non-master name servers (slave, hint) have equal time-to-live (TTL) information in the DOMAIN data files.

If external resolvers query your servers constantly, make sure your servers are distributing DOMAIN data files with reasonable TTL values. If the TTL is zero or another small value, the data you transfer times out very quickly. Set the minimum value in your start of authority (SOA) records to a week or more to solve this problem.

If the /etc/resolv.conf file exists but has no entries, remove the file. Then retry the name resolution with **ping**.

If the local name server is up, check with the network administrator and verify that the named daemon on your local name server is active with the **lssrc -s named** command (if using an AIX name server). Also check that the target host is correctly identified in the name server configuration database.

If you are using NIS, go to Section 7.5, "NIS and NIS+ troubleshooting" on page 236.

You can tell if you are using Network Information Services (NIS) by using the **ps -ef** command and looking for the ypserv and ypbind processes. Use the **ypwhich** command to display the name of the NIS server being used.

If you are resolving some or all host names locally, check the /etc/hosts file for the correct target host name and IP address.

Name resolution is working if you can translate host names to addresses and addresses to host names.

7.2.4 Routing problem debugging

If you are not able to **ping** by host name or IP address, you may have a routing problem.

First, check the routing tables as follows:

- Use the **netstat -rn** command to show the content of your local routing table using IP addresses.
- Check the netmask displayed and ensure that it is correct (ask the network administrator what it should be if you are unsure).
- If there is a default route, attempt to **ping** it.
- If you have more than one network interface, attempt to determine if any interfaces are working.

If you cannot **ping** your default route, either it is down, or your local network connection may be down. Attempt to **ping** all of the other gateways listed in the routing table to see if any portion of your network is functioning:

```
# netstat -rn
Routing tables
Destination      Gateway           Flags   Refs     Use  If   PMTU  Exp  Groups

Route Tree for Protocol Family 2 (Internet):
default          9.185.112.254     UG         1    1656  tr0     -    -
9.185.112/23     9.185.113.7       U         26    4642  tr0     -    -
127/8            127.0.0.1         U          5     424  lo0     -    -
192.168.1/24     192.168.1.10      U          0       0  en0     -    -

Route Tree for Protocol Family 24 (Internet v6):
::1              ::1               UH         0       0  lo0 16896  -
```

Note: Make sure the host you want to communicate with has a routing table entry to your machine.

If you cannot **ping** any host or router interface from among those listed in the routing table, try to **ping** your local loopback interface (lo0) with the following command:

```
$ ping localhost
```

If the **ping** is successful, you have either an adapter or network hardware problem or a routing problem. Continue in this section for routing problem determination or go to Section 7.2.7, "Network interface problems" on page 207.

If the **ping** is not successful, you need to:

- Ensure that the inetd process is active using the **lssrc -g tcpip** command. If inetd is not active, issue the **startsrc -s inetd** or **startsrc -g tcpip** commands.
- Check the state of the loopback interface (lo0) with the **netstat -i** command. If you see `lo0*` in the output, check the /etc/hosts file for an uncommented local loopback entry as follows:

  ```
  127.0.0.1 loopback localhost # loopback (lo0) name/address
  ```

  An asterisk (*) after the interface name in the output from the **netstat** command indicates that the interface is down. Use the following command to start the lo0 interface:

  ```
  # ifconfig lo0 inet 127.0.0.1 up
  ```

7.2.5 Dynamic or static routing

If you are using dynamic routing, verify that the gateway is listed and correct in the kernel routing tables by issuing the **netstat -r** command.

If the gateway host is using the Routing Information Protocol (RIP) with the routed daemon, make sure that a static route to the target host is set up in the /etc/gateways file.

> **Note:** You need to do this only if the routing daemon cannot identify the route to a distant host through queries to other gateways.

If the gateway host is using the RIP with the gated daemon, make sure that a static route to the target host is set up in the gated.conf file.

If you are using dynamic routing with the routed daemon:

- If routed cannot identify the route through queries, for example, if the target host is not running the RIP, check the /etc/gateways file to verify that a route to the target host is defined.
- Make sure that gateways responsible for forwarding packets to the host are up and running the RIP. Otherwise, you will need to define a static route.
- Run the routed daemon using the debug option to log such information as bad packets received. Invoke the daemon from the command line using the following command:

  ```
  # startsrc -s routed -a "-d"
  ```

- Run the routed daemon using the -t flag, which causes all packets sent or received to be written to standard output. When routed is run in this mode, it remains under the control of the terminal that started it. Therefore, an interrupt from the controlling terminal kills the daemon.

If you are using dynamic routing with the gated daemon:

- Verify that the /etc/gated.conf file is configured correctly and that you are running the correct protocols.
- Make sure the gateway on the source network is using the same protocol as the gateway on the destination network.
- Make sure that the machine with which you are trying to communicate has a route back to your host machine.
- Verify that the gateway names in the gated.conf file correspond to the gateway names listed in the /etc/networks file.

If you are using the rip or hello protocols, and routes to the destination cannot be identified through routing queries, check the gated.conf file to verify that a route to the target host is defined. Set static routes under the following conditions:

- The destination host is not running the same protocol as the source host, so they cannot exchange routing information.
- The host must be reached by a distant gateway (a gateway that is on a different autonomous system than the source host). The RIP can be used only among hosts on the same autonomous system.

If you are not using dynamic routing, you are probably using default static routing, which may have some direct routes set up, but all other routes are directed to a gateway machine that handles forwarding of the data. In this case, you can manually add and delete routes. If there are routes in the routing table that look obviously wrong, delete them with the **route** command:

```
route delete <target network> <route address>
```

Routes can be added the same way:

```
route add net <target network> <route address>
```

For example, to add a default route:

```
# route add default 129.35.128.1
```

To delete a network route:

```
# route delete net 9.3.199 9.3.189.45
```

7.2.6 SRC problems

If changes to the /etc/inetd.conf file do not take effect, update the inetd daemon by issuing the **refresh -s inetd** command or the **kill -1 InetdPID** command.

If the **startsrc -s [subsystem name]** returns the following error message:

```
0513-00  The System Resource Controller is not active.
```

The System Resource Controller subsystem has not been activated. Issue the **srcmstr &** command to start SRC, then reissue the **startsrc** command. Also, try starting the daemon from the command line without SRC support.

If the **refresh -s** *[subsystem name]* or **lssrc -ls** *[subsystem name]* returns the following error message:

```
[subsystem name] does not support this option.
```

The subsystem does not support the SRC option issued. Check the subsystem documentation to verify options the subsystem supports. If the following message is displayed:

```
SRC was not found, continuing without SRC support.
```

a daemon was invoked directly from the command line instead of using the **startsrc** command. This is not a problem. However, **src** commands, such as **stopsrc** and **refresh**, will not manipulate a subsystem that is invoked directly.

If the inetd daemon is up and running correctly and the appropriate service seems to be correct but you still cannot connect, try running the inetd daemon processes through a debugger.

- Stop the inetd daemon temporarily:

  ```
  # stopsrc -s inetd
  ```

  The **stopsrc** command stops subsystems like the inetd daemon.

- Edit the syslog.conf file to add a debugging line at the bottom. For example:

  ```
  # vi /etc/syslog.conf
  ```

  Add the line "*.debug /tmp/tonya" at the bottom of the file and exit.

  The file that you specify must exist (/tmp/tonya in this example). You can use the touch command to make your file exists.

- Refresh the file:

  If you are using src, enter:

  ```
  # refresh -s syslogd
  ```

  If you are not using src, kill the syslogd daemon:

  ```
  # kill -1 `ps -e | grep /etc/syslogd | cut -c1-7`
  ```

- Start the inetd daemon backup with debugging enabled:

  ```
  # startsrc -s inetd -a "-d"
  ```

  The -d flag enables debugging.

- Try to make a connection to log errors in the /tmp/tonya debugging file. For example:

  ```
  tn power
  Trying...
  connected to power
  login:>
  Connection closed
  ```

- See if anything shows up as a problem in the debugging file. For example:

  ```
  # tail -f /tmp/tonya
  ```

7.2.7 Network interface problems

Network interfaces are configured automatically during the first system startup after the adapter card is installed. However, there are certain values that must be set in order for TCP/IP to start. These include the host name and Internet address and can be set using the Web-based System Manager, or the SMIT fast path **smit mktcpip**.

General interface debugging

This section applies to all TCP/IP interface types and should be checked prior to using the following interface specific sections.

If host name resolution does not work and you cannot **ping** any address in the routing table, the interface itself may be the culprit. The first step should be to check the installed adapter types and states using the **lsdev -Cc adapter** and **lsdev -Cc if** commands.

> **Note:** Check **errpt** for adapter and interface errors.

If all adapters and interfaces you are using are listed and available, use the **netstat -i** command and check the output for Ierrs (input errors), Oerrs (output errors), and Coll (collisions).

Also check the Ipkts and Opkts (input and output packets) to see if there has been any successful network traffic since the last reboot. For example:

```
# netstat -in
Name Mtu   Network     Address              Ipkts Ierrs    Opkts Oerrs  Coll
lo0  16896 link#1                            2107     0     2109     0     0
lo0  16896 127         127.0.0.1             2107     0     2109     0     0
lo0  16896 ::1                               2107     0     2109     0     0
en0* 1500  link#2      2.60.8c.2e.e1.c9         0     0        9     0     0
en0* 1500  192.168.1   192.168.1.10             0     0        9     0     0
tr0  1492  link#3      10.0.5a.a8.70.67   1102168     0    84137   406     0
tr0  1492  9.185.112   9.185.113.7        1102168     0    84137   406     0
at0  9180  link#4      8.0.5a.75.20.f6       2788     0     2661     0     0
at0  9180  192.168.84  192.15.15.2           2788     0     2661     0     0
```

Check that all listed interfaces have unique network addresses, and if these are correct, use the **ifconfig** command to check the state of any interface that has an asterisk next to the interface name. In the preceding example, the **ifconfig en0** command would show en0 in a down state.

Verify the interface state with the **ifconfig** *<interface>* command, and if it is shown as down, detach it, bring it up, and verify its status again, as shown in the following terminal session example:

```
# ifconfig en0
en0:
flags=e080862<BROADCAST,NOTRAILERS,RUNNING,SIMPLEX,MULTICAST,GROUPRT,64BIT>
        inet 192.168.1.10 netmask 0xffffff00 broadcast 192.168.1.255
# ifconfig en0 detach
# ifconfig en0 inet 192.168.1.10 up
# ifconfig en0
en0:
flags=e080863<UP,BROADCAST,NOTRAILERS,RUNNING,SIMPLEX,MULTICAST,GROUPRT,64BIT>
        inet 192.168.1.10 netmask 0xffffff00 broadcast 192.168.1.255
```

If the interface shows `UP` and `RUNNING` entries, try to **ping** the interface again. If this is successful, try to **ping** another address on the same subnet. A **ping** failure here indicates an external network problem.

Use the **arp** command to make sure you have the complete IP address for the target machine. For example:

```
# arp -an
```

The **arp** command looks for the physical adapter address. This command might show an incomplete address. For example:

```
? (9.3.187.187) at (incomplete)
```

This could be due to an unplugged machine, a stray address with no machine at that particular address, or a hardware problem (such as a machine that connects and receives packets but is not able to send packets back).

Look for errors on the adapter card. For example:

```
# netstat -v
```

The **netstat -v** command shows statistics for the Ethernet, Token Ring, X.25, and 802.3 adapter device drivers. The command also shows network and error logging data for all device drivers active on an interface including:

```
No Mbufs Errors, No Mbuf, Extension Errors, and Packets Transmitted and Adapter
Errors Detected.
```

Check the error log by running the **errpt** command to ensure that there are no adapter problems.

Verify that the adapter card is good by running diagnostics. Use the Web-based System Manager Devices application, the **smit diag** fast path, or the **diag** command.

If the **arp -a** command shows a large table, you may need to increase the arp table. The arp size is determined by two network running options, arptab_bsiz and arptab_nb. To see whether the arp table is sized appropriately, run:

```
# no -a | grep arptab
arptab_bsiz = 7
arptab_nb = 25
```

Multiple arptab_bsiz by arptab_nb; this will be the current size of the arp table in entries, if the **arp -a** output shows the number of entries.

To make changes permanent, you will need enter the changes in the /etc/rc.net file then perform a system reboot.

Ethernet interface problems

Some Ethernet adapters may be used with either the transceiver that is on the card or with an external transceiver. Verify that the jumpers are set correctly (see your adapter manual for instructions). The remainder simply require the appropriate connector type setting.

If the network interface has been initialized, the addresses correctly specified, and you have verified that the adapter card is good:

- Verify that you are using a T-connector plugged directly into the inboard/outboard transceiver.
- Make sure you are using an Ethernet cable. (Ethernet cable is 50 OHM.)
- Make sure you are using Ethernet terminators. (Ethernet terminators are 50 OHM.)
- Ethernet adapters can be used with either the transceiver that is on the card or with an external transceiver. There is a jumper on the adapter to specify which you are using. Verify that your jumper is set correctly (see your adapter manual for instructions).
- Verify that you are using the correct Ethernet connector type (twisted-pair is TP, thin is BNC and thick is DIX). If you change this connector type, use the Web-based System Manager, **wsm**, or the SMIT fast path **smit chgenet** to set the Apply Change to Database Only field. (Check the field in Web-based System Manager or set to yes in SMIT.) Restart the machine to apply the configuration change.

Token-ring interface problems

If you cannot communicate with some of the machines on your network, even though the network interface has been initialized, the addresses correctly specified, and you have verified that the adapter card is good:

- Check to see if the hosts with whom you cannot communicate are on a different ring. If they are, use the Web-based System Manager fast path, **wsm**, or the SMIT fast path **smit chinet** to check the Confine BROADCAST to Local Token-Ring field. The field should not be checked in Web-based System Manager and should be set to no in SMIT.

- Check to see whether the token-ring adapter is configured to run at the correct ring speed. If it is configured incorrectly, use the Web-based System Manager Network application or SMIT to change the adapter ring speed attribute. When TCP/IP is restarted, the token-ring adapter will have the same ring speed as the rest of the network.

Note: Running at the wrong speed will cause problems for all machines on the same ring.

ATM or ATMLE interface problems

The ATM interface is for use with 100 Mbits/sec and 155 Mbits/sec ATM connections.

If you are unable to communicate with any network devices through an ATM interface:

- In AIX 5L Version 5.1, it is possible for an ATM station to be part of multiple Logical IP Subnetworks. In this case, multiple interfaces are associated with a device. This requires that an interface be specifically added and a device name be assigned to it. Under normal circumstances, you do not need to delete or add a network interface manually. However, some problem determination procedures might require you to do so. In this case, use the Web-based System Manager **wsm**, or the SMIT fast path **smit inet** to delete and re-add the appropriate interface.
- Check the interfaces for the presence of both ATM LAN emulation and classic IP interfaces with the **netstat -in** command. If both are configured and are required, you need to ensure that each configured interface has a unique IP address. A common problem is for users to configure the at0 interface and the ATMLE interfaces en0 or tr0 with the same address.
- If you are using an ATM switch, check to make sure there is a proper connection to the switch (usually indicated by a port light on the switch). To identify cable problems, look for wire fault errors in the error log with the **errpt |grep atm** command. If the connectors on your Fibre cables are not keyed or connected with a plastic cover, try reversing the connectors on one end.
- Verify the switch configuration (if you are using one) with the switch administrator, because many varied problems occur when the switch is incorrectly configured.
- Verify your ATM LANE CLIENT information with the **lecstat** command:

```
lecstat [-acqrstv] <device name>
```

Where:

-a Requests all the LE Client information. Does not reset statistics counters or toggle trace.

-c Requests the configuration.

-q Requests the LE_ARP cache.

-r Resets the statistics counters after reading.

-s Requests the statistics counters.

-t Toggles full debug trace on/off.

-v Requests the list of virtual connections.

- AIX 5L Version 5.1 adds token ring emulation and IP packet fragmentation support for MPOA. You can verify the MPOA Client information with the **mpcstat** command:

```
mpcstat [-aceimrstv] <device name>
```

Where:

-a Requests all the following MPOA Client information. Does not reset statistics counters or toggle trace.

-c Requests the configuration.

-e Requests the egress (incoming) cache.

-i Requests the ingress (outgoing) cache.

-m Requests the list of MPOA Servers in use.

-r Resets the statistics counters after reading.

-s Requests the statistics counters.

-t Toggles full debug trace on/off.

-v Requests the list of shortcut connections.

- Make sure you have the latest ATM and ATMLE fileset PTFs installed on your IBM @server pSeries or RS/6000 client, as many switch **ping** problems are defects and can be solved by upgrading the filesets to their latest PTF levels.

  The filesets consist of the ATM device driver, the ATMLE LAN device driver, and the common ATM filesets.

ATM LAN emulation problem debugging steps

If you are unable to **ping** the switch or local ATMLE host, run the **entstat -d entx** or **tokstat -d tokx** command. These commands check if the ATMLE interface has registered with the ATM switch and also what Emulated LAN (ELAN) Name and MAC Address is being used.

In the `General Statistics:` section of the **entstat** or **tokstat** command output, check the driver flags for correct operation:

- The `Driver Flags:` should be similar to the following:

```
Driver Flags: Up Broadcast Running
        Simplex AlternateAddress 64BitSupport
```

  If the Up or Running flag is missing, there is no contact with the ATM switch.

  If the Limbo flag is present, that means the client lost contact with one or more ATMLE servers and is attempting network recovery.

  If the Dead flag is present, a hard failure has occurred, and the ATMLE client is no longer operational.

- Check the error log for additional error messages.

  The following examples show the **entstat** command outputs for both a failure to register and a successful switch registration.

  The following is an example of the **entstat -d ent0** command output following the failure of the IBM @server pSeries or RS/6000 ATMLE client to register with the ATM switch:

```
ATM LAN Emulation Specific Statistics:
--------------------------------------
Emulated LAN Name: ZTrans_Lab_Eth
Local ATM Device Name: atm0
Local LAN MAC Address: 08.00.5a.99.89.c4
Local ATM Address:
47.00.91.81.00.00.00.00.00.04.15.00.00.40.00.00.03.75.43.00
Auto Config With LECS: Yes
LECS ATM Address:
00.00.00.11.00.00.00.00.00.00.00.00.00.00.00.00.00.00.00.00
LES ATM Address:
00.00.00.00.00.00.00.00.00.00.00.00.00.00.00.00.00.00.00.00
General Errors: 287                          Address Deregistrations: 0
Control Timeout (sec): 120                   LE_ARP Rsp Timeout (sec): 1
Max Unknown Frame Count: 1                   Flush Timeout (sec): 4
Max Unknown Frame Time (sec): 1              Path Switch Delay (sec): 6
VCC Activity Timeout (sec): 1200             VCC Avg Rate (Kbps): 25600
```

The following ATM Addresses should be listed:

- Local ATM Address of the IBM @server pSeries or RS/6000 ATMLE client. Bytes 14 through 19 contain the MAC address that was entered through SMIT.

- The Lan Emulation Configuration Server (LECS) ATM Address if using Auto Configuration. This will contain either an ATM address with a different switch prefix (bytes 1 through 13), or it may contain the following well-known ATM address as defined by the ATM Forum:

  ```
  47.00.79.00.00.00.00.00.00.00.00.00.00.A0.3E.00.00.01.00
  ```

- The Lan Emulation Server (LES) ATM Address. The thirteen byte prefix (bytes 1 through 13) should match that of the local ATM address that is assigned to the RS/6000 Lan Emulation Client (LEC).

If the Local ATM Address and/or the LES ATM Address contain mostly zeros, the ATM switch registration has failed, as in the preceding **entstat** example.

Failure to register can be caused by any one of the following:

- The UNI version of the ATM adapter does not match that of the switch.
- The PDU size of the ATM adapter is different to that of the switch.
- The IBM @server pSeries or RS/6000 interface to the ATM switch connection is broken.
- The LES/LECS ATM Address is bogus or entered incorrectly, or if the well-known address was used (ATM Address field is blank), the ATM switch does not support the well-known address.
- The Emulated LAN Name is not recognized at the ATM switch or there was no Emulated LAN Name entered in the Add ATM LE Client SMIT panel, and the switch expected one.

The following is an example of the **entstat -d ent0** command output following a successful registration of an IBM @server pSeries or RS/6000 ATMLE client to the ATM switch:

```
ATM LAN Emulation Specific Statistics:
--------------------------------------
Emulated LAN Name: ZTrans_Lab_Eth
Local ATM Device Name: atm0
Local LAN MAC Address: e0.00.5a.99.89.c4
Local ATM Address: 47.00.05.80.ff.e1.00.00.00.f2.0f.28.f7.08.00.5a.99.89.c4.00
Auto Config With LECS: Yes
LECS ATM Address: 47.00.79.00.00.00.00.00.00.00.00.00.00.a0.3e.00.00.01.00
LES ATM Address: 47.00.05.80.ff.e1.00.00.00.f2.0f.28.f7.00.20.48.0f.28.f7.e0
```

If the ATMLE client registers, but still fails to **ping**:

- Check to see that the ELAN name listed in the **entstat** or **tokstat** command matches the correct network address.

This problem can occur if the ELAN name is recognized by the ATM switch that allows the client to register, but the name is assigned to a different subnet. The ELAN names are listed in the LECS/LES depending on how the ATM switch vendor implements ATMLE configuration.

If you have another ATMLE client on the same subnet, **ping** this and check whether the ELAN name is different from the problem ATMLE.

- Check the ARP table for remote IP address and MAC address.
- Try to **ping** the switch port instead of the ATMLE client. If the **ping** to the switch works, the switch may have a problem.
- Check whether the ATM adapter and device driver are working as follows:

```
# atmstat -d atm0 > /tmp/atmstat.out
```

Wait 10 seconds, then run the command again, and append the output to the same file:

```
# atmstat -d atm0 >> /tmp/atmstat.out
```

Edit the /tmp/atmstat.out file and check the following parameters under the Receive Statistics column:

- Packets and Cells received: These two parameters should show an increase in the second **atmstat**, which means the adapter and device driver are working.

No increase in either parameter means the adapter is not able to receive ATM cells.

If either number is not increasing, the adapter and/or the device driver may be hung. Try powering down and rebooting, if this is possible, to clear any hang conditions.

ATM Classic IP problem debugging steps

The debugging steps for classic IP problems are dependent on whether the connection is a Permanent Virtual Circuit (PVC) or Switched Virtual Circuit (SVC).

For PVC connections, verify that you are using the correct Virtual Path Indicator (VPI):Virtual Channel Indicator (VCI) pair, VPI:VCI, with the **smit lsatmpvc** SMIT fast path.

For SVC connections, ensure that the ARP server address is correctly entered for the ARP client. The following three examples of the **arp -t atm -a** command show typical ARP server registration failures and a good registration output.

The first entry in the **arp** output is the local at0 IP address and its 20 byte ATM address.

- The IP address should match that of at0, and the ATM address should contain the MAC address of the atm0 (or atmx) in bytes 14 through 19.
- If the MAC address, the entire ATM address, or the IP address is zeros or incorrect, registration with the switch did not take place.

  Check the configuration of at0 with the **smit chinet** SMIT fast path and ensure the ATM address has not been entered incorrectly.

The second entry in the **arp** output is the IP address and the ATM address of the ARP server.

Example 1: The ATM client did not register with the switch.

```
# arp -t atm -a
at0(198.179.228.31)     0.0.0.0.0.0.0.0.0.0.0.0.0.0.0.0.0.0.0.0
  IP Addr        VPI:VCI Handle ATM Address
  ?(198.179.228.6)          N/A     N/A
0.0.0.0.0.0.0.0.0.0.0.0.0.0.0.0.0.0.0.0
```

Possible causes of a failure to register are: hardware, wrong or incorrectly entered ATM address, or switch configuration.

Example 2: The ATM client registered with switch, but was unable to contact the ARP server.

```
# arp -t atm -a
at0(146.146.75.239)
  39.9.85.11.11.11.11.11.11.11.11.1.1.0.4.ac.ad.28.6a.0
IP Addr        VPI:VCI Handle ATM Address
  ?(0.0.0.0)       N/A     N/A
  39.9.85.11.11.11.11.11.11.11.11.1.1.0.20.35.99.7.33.0
```

Possible causes of being unable to contact the ARP server are: UNI version incorrect or ARP server not recognizing auto-detect, ARP server down or having problems, or different PDU sizes.

Example 3: The ATM client has registered with the switch and made contact with the ARP server.

```
# arp -t atm -a
at0(9.3.35.157) 47.0.5.80.ff.e1.0.0.0.f2.f.28.f7.8.0.5a.99.89.c4.0
  IP Addr        VPI:VCI Handle ATM Address
  flute.austin.ibm.com(9.3.35.150)        0:41   3
47.0.5.80.ff.e1.0.0.0.f2.f.28.f7.0.20.48.f.28.f7.0
  horn.austin.ibm.com(9.3.35.154)         0:43   4
47.0.5.80.ff.e1.0.0.0.f2.f.28.f7.8.0.5a.99.88.cc.0
```

If you are receiving output similar to Example 3, try a different port on the ARP server/ATM switch (check the LED on port); also check the UNI version and PDU size using **smit chg_atm** to ensure they match those of switch.

If the remote host is able to **ping** the IBM @server pSeries or RS/6000 ATM client through the ARP server, try manually adding the remote client ARP entry into the ARP table, as shown below.

For SVC clients:

```
arp -t atm -s svc  <20 byte atm address of remote host>
```

If the ATM client **arp** command output continues to show no registration or no ARP server contact, then run the **atmstat** command to verify the adapter and device driver:

```
# atmstat -d atm0 > /tmp/atmstat.out
```

Wait 10 seconds, then run the command again, and append the output to the same file:

```
# atmstat -d atm0 >> /tmp/atmstat.out
```

Edit the /tmp/atmstat.out file and check the following parameters under the Receive Statistics column:

- Packets and Cells received: These two parameters should show an increase in the second **atmstat**, which means the adapter and device driver are working.

No increase in either parameter means the adapter is not able to receive ATM cells.

If either number is not increasing, the adapter and/or the device driver may be hung. Try powering down and rebooting, if this is possible, to clear any hang condition.

If the problem cannot be determined at this point, you may need to place a support call using local reporting procedures.

X.25 interface problems

This section contains specific debugging information for X.25 TCP/IP interfaces and assumes that the basic TCP/IP network debugging in Section 7.2.1, “Selective host network problems” on page 197 through Section 7.2.4, “Routing problem debugging” on page 202 has been done.

To simplify the X.25 TCP/IP problem determination, you may find it useful to disable any external name resolution and suppress any default gateways. This will avoid any discrepancies that there might be with /etc/hosts.

Note that /etc/hosts is always used by the **x25ip** command when it is executed by /etc/rc.net during the initialization of the system, even if you have a name server.

If you are unable to **ping** your remote X.25 host (see Section 7.4.6, "ping" on page 228 for **ping** command examples), proceed with the following steps:

1. Use the **lsx25** command to see if your TCP/IP X.25 interface (xs0) and your X.25 port (sx25a0) are configured and available. If they are not, you need to configure them. If either the X.25 port or TCP/IP X.25 interface will not configure, see Chapter 9 "X.25 Problem Determination" section in the *AIXLink/X.25 LPP Cookbook,* SG24-4475, for more information on debugging the X.25 LPP.
2. Verify with the SMIT fast path **smit chinetsx25** that the IP-to-NUA translation table entry for the remote host is correct, then do the same verification on the remote host.
3. Refresh the X.25/IP translation table using the **x25ip** command without any arguments, then run the **ping** command again.

If you are still unable to **ping** the remote system, you need to make sure you have routes set up for the X.25 interface (for example, xs0). If the routes seem correct, you need to use the **x25mon** command to monitor the packet level flow as follows:

```
# x25mon -f -p -n sx25a0
```

In another panel or session, **ping** the remote host. If you do not get the expected result, there are four possible scenarios:

1. No error message, nothing transmitted.

   You have a gateway that **ping** used to send your packets. Verify with **netstat -r** (not with **ifconfig**) that the X.25 connection is active. Recheck the static routes and, if necessary, remove and replace the X.25 routes that have a G flag in the **netstat** output.
2. Error message, nothing transmitted.

   If the error message is:

   ```
   sendto: Network is unreachable
   ```

   Or:

   ```
   sendto: No route for this host
   ```

   You have a problem either with the attachment definition or with the route.

If the error message is:

```
ping: sendto: Can't assign requested address
Sendto: The socket name is not available
```

There is a problem with the x25ip translation table. Change it with **smit chinetsx25** or add a correct entry, if necessary, with **smit mksx25**.

3. No error message, the trace shows attempts to establish a virtual circuit.

   If you see in the trace a series of call packets showing unsuccessful attempts to open a virtual circuit, you have an X.25 protocol problem. Refer to X.25 LPP documentation for the CCITT Cause and Diagnostic code in Appendix D, or the "X.25 Protocol Problems" Chapter 9 in the *AIXLink/X.25 LPP Cookbook*, SG24-4475.

   If the incoming call is rejected by the remote system with the diagnostic 241, calling address missing, the calling address was not in the translation table. Add it and use **x25ip** on the remote host to regenerate it.

4. No error message, data transmitted but nothing received.

   In this case, a virtual circuit is established and data packets are sent to the remote host but the remote host does not reply. The packets are correctly transmitted to the remote host, but the remote host IP address they carry does not match the actual IP address of the remote host. Change the IP address of the remote host so it is the same on the remote host as on the local host.

7.3 Common TCP/IP problems

The following sections contain some of the more commonly encountered problems that occur with TCP/IP and other related protocols.

7.3.1 Problems with packet delivery using a bridge

If you cannot communicate between a token-ring and an Ethernet network using a bridge, and you have verified that the bridge is good, check the MTU values of both adapters. The MTU values must be compatible to allow communication. A machine drops packets if the incoming packet (including headers) is greater than the adapter's MTU values. For instance, a 1500-byte packet sent over the bridge collects an 8-byte LLC header, making the total packet size 1508. If the receiving machine MTU is set to 1500, a packet of 1508 bytes is dropped.

7.3.2 LED 581 hang

During the machine boot, LED 581 is shown during the time that the configuration manager configures TCP/IP and runs /etc/rc.net to do specific adapter, interface, and host name configuration.

This problem can be either a system or a network problem that happens because TCP/IP waits for replies over some interfaces (token ring, for example). If there are no replies, it eventually times out on the attempt and marks the interface as down. This timeout period varies and can range from around three minutes to an indefinite period.

The following problem determination procedure is used to verify that the methods and procedures run by /etc/rc.net are causing the LED 581 hang:

1. Boot the machine in Service mode.
2. Move the /etc/rc.net file:

   ```
   # mv /etc/rc.net /etc/rc.net.save
   ```

3. Reboot in Normal mode boot to see if the system continues past the LED 581 and allows you to log in.

> **Note:** The above steps assume that neither DNS or NIS is configured.

If you determine that the procedures in /etc/rc.net are causing the hang, that is, the system continued past LED 581 when you performed the steps above, the problem may be one of the following:

- Ethernet or token-ring hardware problems.

  Run diagnostics and check the error log.
- Missing or incorrect default route.
- Networks not accessible.

  Check that gateways and name servers, are up and available.
- Bad IP addresses or masks.

  Use the **iptrace** and **ipreport** commands for problem determination.
- Corrupt ODM.

  Remove and recreate network devices.
- Premature name or IP address resolution.

  Either named, ypbind/ypserv, or /etc/hosts may need correction.
- Extra spaces at the ends of lines in configuration files.

Use the vi editor with the set list subcommand to check files, such as the /etc/filesystems file, for this problem.

- /usr file system may be full.
- Bad LPPs.

  Reinstall the LPP.

A specific LED 581 hang case occurs when ATMLE is being used with a DNS. If you are experiencing this problem, you can either work around the problem by adding a `host=local,bind` entry to /etc/netsvc.conf file or by adding the following lines to the /etc/rc.net file:

```
####################################################################
# Part III - Miscellaneous Commands.
####################################################################
# Set the hostid and uname to `hostname`, where hostname has been
# set via ODM in Part I, or directly in Part II.
# (Note it is not required that hostname, hostid and uname all be
# the same).
export NSORDER="local"              <<============NEW LINE ADDED HERE
/usr/sbin/hostid `hostname`               >>$LOGFILE 2>&1
/bin/uname -S`hostname|sed 's/\..*$//'` >>$LOGFILE 2>&1
unset NSORDER                       <<============NEW LINE ADDED HERE
####################################################################
```

7.3.3 Telnet or rlogin problems

If you can **ping** both ways between the source and target systems but cannot **telnet** or **rlogin**, the following explanations can be useful in solving problems with the **telnet** or **rlogin** command.

telnetd daemon debugging

If the inetd daemon could execute the telnet service but you still cannot connect using the **telnet** command, there may be something wrong with the telnet interface.

- Verify that telnet is using the correct terminal type.

  Check the $TERM variable on your machine:

  ```
  # echo $TERM
  ```

  Log in to the machine to which you are trying to attach and check the $TERM variable:

  ```
  # echo $TERM
  ```

- Use the telnet interface's debugging capabilities by entering the **telnet** command without flags.

  ```
  # telnet
  tn>
  ```

  – Enter **open** *host* where host is the name of the machine.

  – Enter Ctrl-T.

  – At the tn> prompt, enter **debug** for debugging mode.

- Try to connect to another machine using the telnet interface:

  ```
  # telnet power
  Trying...
  Connected to power
  Escape character is '^T'.
  ```

  Watch the display as the various commands scroll up the screen. For example:

  ```
  SENT do ECHO
  SENT do SUPPRESS GO AHEAD
  SENT will TERMINAL TYPE (reply)
  SENT do SUPPORT SAK
  SENT will SUPPORT SAK (reply)
  RCVD do TERMINAL TYPE (don't reply)
  RCVD will ECHO (don't reply)
  RCVD will SUPPRESS GO AHEAD (don't reply)
  RCVD wont SUPPORT SAK (reply)
  SENT dont SUPPORT SAK (reply)
  RCVD do SUPPORT SAK (don't reply)
  SENT suboption TELOPT_NAWS Width 80, Height 25
  RCVD suboption TELOPT_TTYPE SEND
  RCVD suboption TELOPT_TTYPE aixterm
  ...
  ```

- Check /etc/termcap or /usr/lib/terminfo for the aixterm definition. For example:

  ```
  # ls -a /usr/lib/terminfo
  ```

- If the aixterm definition is missing, add it by building the ibm.ti file. For example:

  ```
  # tic ibm.ti
  ```

  The **tic** command is a terminal information compiler.

The telnet login process

There can be many things that can cause telnet to hang. The last thing that shows up on the terminal panel can point to what is causing the problem.

Below is the normal output that is displayed to the screen when telnetting into AIX:

```
telnet 10.11.12.13
Trying...
Connected to 10.11.12.13
Escape character is '^]'.

telnet (host name of machine)

AIX Version 5
(C) Copyrights by IBM and by others 1982, 2000.
login: tonya
password:
```

Below are some things to check to troubleshoot telnet problems.

- The telnet process can hang at `Trying...`

  Most likely, it is a routing problem either on the client, server, or some device between the two machines.

  Work through Section 7.2, "Problem isolation steps for TCP/IP network problems" on page 196 to solve this problem.

- The second place where telnet can hang is at the `Escape Character is '^]'` line. If telnet comes back with `Connection closed` after `Escape character is '^]'`, then it is possible that the telnet server has tcp wrappers installed. Check the /etc/inetd.conf file and the path for the telnet line should look like the following:

  ```
  /usr/sbin/telnetd
  ```

  If it is not like the above line, then tcp wrappers are not supported on AIX. Also, the /etc/security/login.cfg file may have a invalid entry. Check the default stanza and make sure there is not a herald = line there. If there is, remove it and try to telnet into the machine again.

If the server cannot provide reverse name resolution with the client's IP address, there will be around a 75-second delay before getting a login prompt. If this is happening:

- **cat** the /etc/resolv.conf file on the server to see if the file exists.
- If the file is there, move the /etc/resolv.conf file to a new file name and then try to telnet back into the AIX box and check for the 75-second delay again. If a login prompt comes back quickly, then there is a problem connecting with the nameserver. It could then be a routing problem or a DNS server problem.

ping the nameserver IP addresses in the /etc/resolv.conf file. If you can successfully ping them, then there is not a problem with the routing between the AIX box and the nameservers and you should then look into name resolution problems.

If the telnet connection hangs at this line indefinitely, then it is possible the inetd subsystem is not working properly.

- Type **refresh -s inetd**. It should say:

  ```
  The request for subsystem refresh was completed successfully.
  ```

  If the refresh hangs for some time and comes back with `0513-056 time out waiting for command response`, then the inetd subsystem may not be working correctly and should then be killed nicely. Run **ps -ef | grep inetd** and do a **kill -15** on the process ID on the line that has /usr/sbin/inetd. Once inetd has been killed, type **startsrc -s inetd**. If inetd starts, try to **telnet** into the machine. If inetd does not start up successfully, or if **telnet** still hangs indefinitely, run **kill -15** on the PID of inetd again. Back up the original /etc/inetd.conf file to a new file name by typing:

  ```
  # mv /etc/inetd.conf /etc/inetd.conf.backup
  ```

  The original template is in /usr/lpp/bos.net/inst_root/etc/. You can copy it by typing:

  ```
  # cp /usr/lpp/bos.net/inst_root/etc/inetd.conf /etc/inetd.conf
  ```

  Run **startsrc -s inetd** and you should now be able to telnet into the machine

If telnet is hanging at `telnet` *host name of machine*, then:

- It is possible that the /etc/utmp file is corrupted.
- Type **who** and see if entries are out of order or format.
- Output of **who** might want to be backed up by typing **who > /etc/who.backup**.
- You can clean out the file by typing **cat /dev/null > /etc/utmp**.
- If telnet does still not work and still hangs at telnet (host name), then the /etc/utmp file may have to be created from scratch.

  To backup and create a new /etc/utmp file:

  ```
  # mv /etc/utmp /etc/utmp.backup
  # touch /etc/utmp
  # chmod 644 /etc/utmp
  # chown root:system /etc/utmp
  ```

  telnet should now work to the system.

If telnet is hanging after entering the password for the user, then it is possible that there might be some authentication problems for that particular user or invalid files:

- If the user does not see the Message of the Day file, then that file may have an invalid entry or may be corrupted. Run **mv /etc/motd /etc/motd.backup** and then try to **telnet** back into the machine and you should get a prompt.
- If the user does see the Message of the Day output, then there may be an invalid /etc/passwd file, invalid profile file, /etc/profile, or /etc/environment file.
- If root can login to the system just fine, then it is possible that NIS is running on the system, and can be checked by running **cat /etc/passwd | grep +**.

7.3.4 Dynamic Host Configuration Protocol (DHCP) problems

If you are unable to obtain an IP address from a system with DHCP configured:

- The most common problem is an incorrect DHCP configuration. For configuration assistance, refer to the redbook, *Beyond DHCP Work your TCP/IP Internetwork with Dynamic IP*, SG24-2580.
- Check if the interface to be configured was specified in the /etc/dhcpcd.ini file. You also can check it by using the SMIT fast path **smit dhcp**.
- Check if there is a server on the local network or a relay agent configured to get the requests off the local network.
- Check if the client dhcpcd daemon is running:

  ```
  # lssrc -s dhcpcd
  ```

  If it is not running, start it:

  ```
  # startsrc -s dhcpcd
  ```

- Check if the server dhcpsd daemon is running:

  ```
  # ps -ef | grep dhcpsd
  ```

  If the server dhcpsd daemon is not running, check if the bootpd and dhcpsd (DHCP server) are running at the same time. They cannot be running at the same time, because they use the same service port. To solve this, comment out, with #, the bootps line in the /etc/inetd.conf file and refresh the inetd subsystem:

  ```
  # vi /etc/inetd.conf
  ```

  Put a # in front of the line:

  ```
  bootps dgram   udp     wait    root    /usr/sbin/bootpd .......
  ```

  Save the file and refresh the inetd daemon:

  ```
  # refresh -s inetd
  ```

dadmin

The **dadmin** command lets the DHCP administrator query and modify the state of his DHCP servers' databases. It gives the administrator the ability to locally or remotely query the DHCP server for the status of an IP address, query for a pool of IP addresses, query for a client, delete an IP address mapping, refresh the server, and change the server's tracing level.

7.3.5 snmpd not responding to queries

If snmpd is not responding to queries and there are no log messages received, the packet might be too large for the kernel User Datagram Protocol (UDP) packet handler. If this is the case, increase the kernel variables udp_sendspace and udp_recvspace by issuing the following commands:

```
# no -o udp_sendspace=65535
# no -o udp_recvspace=65535
```

The maximum size for a UPD packet is 64 KB. If your query is larger than 64 KB, it will be rejected. Split the packet into smaller packets to avoid this problem.

7.3.6 X.25 function keys not working properly

When using **telnet** or **rlogin** over X.25, the remote system does not always respond correctly to use of the function keys, especially if using Esc-1 instead of F1.

The ESCDELAY environment variable controls the timeout period, after which the screen handling applications will consider the Esc key to be separate from the following 1.

The ESCDELAY variable only works if the application is written to Curses or Extended Curses. When running over X.25, the Esc key is often put by IP into a separate data packet from the following key. The gap between the two data packets on the receiving system is often further apart than the default timeout. The default value of ESCDELAY (or if it is not set at all) is 500.

To see if this is the reason your function keys are not working correctly, try setting ESCDELAY to a very high value as follows:

1. Insert the following in the /etc/environment file:

   ```
   ESCDELAY=5000
   ```

2. Log completely out of the system, then back in to make sure the new ESCDELAY value is set.

3. Verify using the following command:

```
# echo $ESCDELAY
```

Once your test is completed, remember to either adjust the value down to a more reasonable value (between 1000 and 2000) or, if your problem is not resolved, remove this line completely from the /etc/environment file. If setting this ESCDELAY parameter does not fix your problem, then your application is not written to Extended Curses and the application must be modified to await the entire escape sequence. For example, the AIX SMIT application is written to Curses, but it will work over a slow network regardless of ESCDELAY, because SMIT was written to wait indefinitely for the entire escape sequence. Thus, even though the **iptrace** command output clearly shows the separation of the Esc and the remainder of the escape sequence, the Esc keys works correctly in SMIT.

7.4 TCP/IP network configuration issues

The following sections discuss a selection of configuration issues that can affect network performance.

7.4.1 Maximum Transmission Unit (MTU)

Each device has an MTU and will not transmit packets larger than this without fragmenting. For example:

- If packets are larger than this, they will be fragmented before they are sent.
- Packets crossing a router may be fragmented for the destination network.
- Machines with different MTU sizes may have difficulty communicating.
- If traffic is predominantly local, use the largest MTU supported by your LAN type. This minimizes fragmentation of packets, which is costly.

TCP establishes a Maximum Segment Size (MSS) that the two hosts agree on during the handshaking protocol. This MSS will not be greater than the smallest MTU, and defaults to 512 bytes (the tcp_mssdflt value can be displayed from the network options).

UDP does not establish a connection between two hosts.

You also need to satisfy the sometimes conflicting goals of setting the MTU size to the maximize packet size while at the same time trying to minimize fragmentation.

7.4.2 Path MTU (PMTU) and multipath routing

Path maximum transfer unit (PMTU) discover is used to determine the largest packet that can be sent over a particular network. It is enabled by default in AIX 5L Version 5.1. It should be disabled for multipath routing.

Multipath routing allows a system to be configured with more than one route to the same destination. Different network segments share and balance the network traffic. Multiple routes allow the network subsystem to route traffic to the same segment by using different interfaces. Alternate routes are necessary to enable dead gateway detection (DGD)

The following scenario illustrates the problem with PMTU discover when used with multipath routing:

- Whenever packets go out of the network a separate host route is cloned for the path. Cloned routes are created by copying the parent route and adding specific information unique to the route's destination, including the smallest MTU discovered in the path to host. A cloned route has the same cost and is more specific than the original route.
- All traffic will use the cloned route and therefore will use the same gateway.
- Round robin cycling will not be used

To enable round robin cycling between equal cost routes to the same network, disable PMTU discover for the following network option parameters:

- tcp_pmtu_discover
- udp_pmtu_discover

Example 7-3, shows lines added to the /etc/rc.net file to disable PMTU discover.

Example 7-3 PMTU

```
if [ -f /usr/sbin/no ] ; then
/usr/sbin/no -o tcp_pmtu_discover=0
/usr/sbin/no -o udp_pmtu_discover=0
```

Note:

- Path MTU discovery cannot be used on duplicate routes, including those configured for group routing.
- Enabling path MTU discovery sets the value of the arpqsize option of the no command to a minimum value of 5. This value is not decreased if path MTU discovery is subsequently disabled.

7.4.3 mbufs

To check that enough memory (mbufs) is available for networking activities, use the **netstat -m** and **netstat -i** commands.

A non-zero requests for mbufs denied value in the **netstat -m** output indicates a possible lack of network memory. Other possible causes of non-zero in this field are:

- Heavy network activity is going on and packets are being dropped.
- A network application with a socket leak can exhaust the supply of mbufs.
- More physical memory may need to be added to the machine.

Check the Oerrs column of the **netstat -i** command output. If the number in the Oerrs column exceeds 1 percent of that in the Opkts column for any interface, the TRANSMIT queue size (xmt_que_size) for the adapter should be increased.

If the number of Oerrs exceeds 1 percent of the Ipkts, use the **netstat -m** command as above to check for a possible lack of memory problem.

The network options parameter thewall specifies the maximum amount of memory allocated to the network buffer pools of mbufs and mclusters. To check the value, use the **no -a | grep thewall** command; the value shown is in KBs.

Refer to Section 7.4.4, "thewall" on page 228 for more information.

7.4.4 thewall

thewall is not a settable attribute in AIX 5L Version 5.1. It is merely there for information's sake.

7.4.5 TCP/IP problem isolation commands

The following sections contain summaries and usage examples of some useful TCP/IP problem isolation commands.

7.4.6 ping

The **ping** command is used for investigating basic point-to-point network connectivity problems, answering questions about whether the remote host is attached to the network, and whether the network between the hosts is reliable. Additionally, **ping** can indicate whether a host name and IP address is consistent across several machines. See the following example for usage:

```
ping <host name>
```

or

<address>

```
# ping tonya
PING tonya.au.ibm.com: (9.3.187.200): 56 data bytes
64 bytes from 9.3.187.200: icmp_seq=0 ttl=255 time=1 ms
64 bytes from 9.3.187.200: icmp_seq=1 ttl=255 time=2 ms
^C
----bern PING Statistics----
4 packets transmitted, 4 packets received, 0% packet loss
round-trip min/avg/max = 1/1/2 ms
```

ping -c *num* sends num packets.

Control size of packets sent with **ping** *<host> <size>*.

The **ping** command normally sends 56 bytes of data plus the IP header, for a total of 64 bytes. Using different values can help determine if there are problems with fragmentation. Try values slightly less than, equal to, and greater than the MTU

The **ping** command uses echo request and echo reply ICMP messages, which is part of the IP layer, in the data portion of IP datagrams.

ICMP messages are also used to indicate if a destination for a packet is unreachable, if the packet should be redirected to another router (for more efficient routing called ICMP redirect), and can indicate other types of errors as well.

7.4.7 rup

The **rup** command queries a host for its up time. The **rup** command:

- Uses broadcast on all interfaces by default.
- Uses RPC over UDP.

The **rup** command is useful to find out whether name service and interfaces work in one command. It also tells you how long the machines have been up and whether they are busy.

A remote host responds only if it is running the rstatd daemon, which is defined in the /etc/inetd.conf file and started from the inetd daemon.

7.4.8 traceroute

The **traceroute** command shows the route that IP packets take to a network host.

- If the command seems to be hang, be patient. It does a lookup for each gateway found in the path the name-server address-to-name resolution.
- Not all routers support **traceroute**.

The **traceroute** command is intended for use in network testing, measurement, and management. It should be used primarily for manual fault isolation. Because of the load it imposes on the network, the **traceroute** command should not be used during normal operations or from automated scripts.

7.4.9 netstat

The **netstat** command with various flags is useful in the debugging of most network problems. **netstat** collects and displays a large amount of network related statistical and configuration information, including:

- Active sockets

  Displayed with the **netstat -f** *<family>* command.

  Where <family> is:

  – `inet` for Internet sockets

  – `unix` for UNIX sockets

  – `ns` for Xerox Network System sockets

  The output format is family specific.

  The default display (no flags) shows active sockets for all families.

- Interfaces

  The state and usage of all configured interfaces are displayed with the **netstat -in** command as shown in Example 7-4.

Example 7-4 netstat -in

```
# netstat -in
Name  Mtu   Network     Address            Ipkts Ierrs    Opkts Oerrs  Coll
tr0   1492  link#2      0.60.94.8a.d3.58   908307     0   90635     0     0
tr0   1492  9.3.187     9.3.187.184        908307     0   90635     0     0
vi0   0     link#3                              0     0       0     0     0
vi0   0     9.3.187     9.3.187.184             0     0       0     0     0
lo0   16896 link#1                          89764     0   89764     0     0
lo0   16896 127         127.0.0.1           89764     0   89764     0     0
lo0   16896 ::1                             89764     0   89764     0     0
```

For each interface, **netstat -in** shows:

- Name (asterisk indicates the interface is down)
- MTU
- Link layer address (<link# line>)
- IP network
- IP address
- Input packets and errors
- Output packets and errors

- Routing tables

  Displayed with the **netstat -rn** command, as shown in the following example:

```
# netstat -rn
Routing tables
Destination      Gateway           Flags    Refs      Use  If    PMTU Exp
Groups

Route Tree for Protocol Family 2 (Internet):
default          9.3.187.129       UGc        0         0  tr0      -   -
9.3.1.2          9.3.187.129       UGHW       0         2  tr0      -      1
9.3.187/24       9.3.187.184       U          6     75532  tr0      -   -
9.3.187.184      127.0.0.1         UH        26     88838  lo0      -   -
9.3.240.111      9.3.187.129       UGHW       3      9527  tr0   1492   -
127/8            127.0.0.1         U          3       384  lo0      -   -

Route Tree for Protocol Family 24 (Internet v6):
::1              ::1               UH         0         0  lo0 16896   -
```

  The route tree for each protocol family is shown.

  The **netstat -rn** command will be faster, as the host name lookup are eliminated.

- Protocol statistics

  The **netstat -s** command displays protocol statistics for IP, ICMP, IGMP, TCP, and UDP. The data shown includes information on errors, fragmentation, redirects, packets sent and received, and packets dropped and discarded.

  It also shows TCP connections established, timed out, and UDP datagrams received and sent.

  To display a single protocol, use **netstat -p <protocol>**, as shown in the following terminal output:

```
# netstat -p udp
```

```
udp:
269378 datagrams received
0 incomplete headers
0 bad data length fields
0 bad checksums
7 dropped due to no socket
268931 broadcast/multicast datagrams dropped due to no socket
0 socket buffer overflows
308 datagrams output
```

- Network adapter device driver statistics

  The **netstat -v** command shows device driver statistics for all installed network adapters.

  If you only want the output of a specific adapter type, you can use the **stat** commands instead of **netstat -v**; refer to Section 7.4.14, "The stat commands" on page 235 for details.

- Network memory usage statistics

  The most useful statistics in the output of the **netstat -m** command are the counters that show the requests for mbufs denied and non-zero values in the failed column. If the requests for mbufs denied is not displayed, then this must be an SMP system running AIX Version 4.3.2 or later; for performance reasons, global statistics are turned off by default. To enable the global statistics, set the **no** parameter extendednetstats to 1. Use the command:

  ```
  # /usr/sbin/no -o extendednetstats=1
  ```

  A system reboot is required, before you reboot, include the following lines in /etc/rc.net, as shown in Example 7-5.

Example 7-5 `extendednetstats`

```
####################################################################
if [ -f /usr/sbin/no ] ; then
/usr/sbin/no -o extendednetstats=0 >>/dev/null 2>&1
fi
```

  If you do set the **no** parameter extendednetstats to 1, you should refer to other considerations as mentioned in Chapter 9, "Analyzing network performance", in *AIX 5l Version 5.1 Performance Management Guide*, which can be found at:

  `http://publibn.boulder.ibm.com/cgi-bin/ds_form?lang=en_US&viewset=AIX`

- Protocol Control Block (PCB) addresses

  The **netstat -A** command is used to show the address of any PCB associated with the sockets. The -A flag is normally only used for low-level debugging purposes.

7.4.10 arp

Address Resolution Protocol (ARP) maps IP addresses to hardware addresses. For example:

- To display the local machine's cache of ARP translations, use the **arp -a** command.
- IP addresses only have meaning to IP. The data-link level of the Internet network layer use the hardware address of the adapter itself. Each hardware address is unique.
- ARP translates IP addresses to hardware addresses and vice-versa. It works by using a broadcast asking for the owner of a particular IP address.

7.4.11 iptrace and ipreport

The **iptrace** command traces all packets to and from a machine. For example:

- This command generates very detailed output that is viewed by using the **ipreport** command.
- It can be a useful tool for finding lower level communication errors needed for detailed debugging of network problems. It is not really needed for general use, because interpretation of the output requires a detailed knowledge of TCP/IP.

Specify the source and or destination host with the -s <source> and -d <dest> flags to narrow down the problem. The following flags are also useful in reducing the amount of captured data, greatly simplifying analysis of the output:

-a Excludes ARP packets.

-P *<protocol_list>* Gathers data only for a specified protocol.

-i *<interface>* Gathers data for a specific interface.

-L *<log_size>* Specifies the trace file size.

The following changes have been made in AIX 5L Version 5.1:

- A new flag -L has been added to **iptrace**. It is used to specify the trace file size. Once the trace file reaches the number of bytes specified with the -L flag, it will be renamed to *filename*.old and a new trace file will be started. The trace file will also be renamed to *filename*.old when **iptrace** is started.
- The -P flag has been modified to accept a comma separated list of protocols to trace.
- The -p flag has been modified to accept a comma separated list of ports to trace.

The following example illustrates how to trace all traffic sent and received from host taboo through the en0 interface and place formatted output into a file:

```
# iptrace -i en0 -d taboo -b /tmp/trace.raw
```

Reproduce the problem:

```
# ps -ef | grep iptrace
# kill <iptrace PID>
# ipreport -rns /tmp/trace.raw > /tmp/trace.out
```

Note: Never use **kill -9 <iptrace PID>** to kill the process in the above example.

7.4.12 tcpdump

The **tcpdump** command prints out detailed packet headers for TCP:

- It allows very detailed analysis, again useful for expert network debugging.
- It allows you to specify pattern matching to narrow the information shown.

The following example prints out all packets arriving or departing from host taboo:

```
# tcpdump -I host taboo
```

7.4.13 no

The **no** command changes or displays network options.

The **no -a** command displays the values of all the network parameters defined in the system.

- In AIX 5.1, when the **no** command is used to modify a network option, it will log a message to the syslog using the LOG_KERN facility. See Example 7-6.

Example 7-6 syslog.out sample

```
# cat /etc/syslog.conf
user.info           /tmp/syslog.out
# no -o tcp_sendspace=16384
# no -o tcp_sendspace=32768
# cat /tmp/syslog.out
Aug 16 14:46:43 F80right no[475374]: Network option tcp_sendspace was set to
the value 16384
Aug 16 14:46:50 F80right no[475376]: Network option tcp_sendspace was set to
the value 32768
```

- The **no -o** command allows you to change selected settings or values within the kernel. It allows the changes to take effect immediately, but the changes only last until the next system boot. For example, to change the `tcp_sendspace` value to 64 MB, the following command syntax is used:

```
# no -o tcp_sendspace=32768
```

  To maintain the settings across system boots, the specific **no** commands need to be appended to the /etc/rc.net file as shown below:

```
##########################################################
if [ -f /usr/sbin/no ] ; then
        /usr/sbin/no -o tcp_sendspace = 16384
        /usr/sbin/no -o tcp_recvspace = 16384
fi
```

System values should only be changed after referring to tuning information in AIX documentation or under the direction of support personnel.

7.4.14 The stat commands

Instead of using the **netstat -v** command, you can use a **stat** command for the particular interface. These commands reside in the /usr/sbin directory and include the following:

- **entstat** *<ent#>*
- **tokstat** *<tok#>*
- **atmstat** *<at#>*

> **Note:** Use the -d flag for detailed device specific data.

7.4.15 Virtual IP addresses

This capability allows for the definition of a virtual IP address for a host. From a TCP connection standpoint, it decouples the IP address associated with physical interfaces. As a result, the user connection should not be affected if the interface go down.

Virtual IP addresses (VIPA) have the following attributes:

- The application binds to a virtual IP address.
- It can be brought up or down without affecting real interfaces.
- When a failure is detected, the network traffic can be re-routed to a different real interface. If the re-routing occurs quickly enough, sessions will not be lost.

VIPA can be configured with the **mkdev** command or **smit mkinetvi** command. See Example 7-7 for an example.

Example 7-7 VIPA configuration

```
# mkdev -c if -s VI -t vi -a netaddr='9.3.187.184' -a \
> netmask='255.255.255.0' -w 'vi0' -a state=up
vi0 Available
# netstat -in
Name  Mtu   Network     Address            Ipkts Ierrs    Opkts Oerrs  Coll
tr0   1492  link#2      0.60.94.8a.d3.58    36778     0      557     0     0
tr0   1492  9.3.187     9.3.187.184         36778     0      557     0     0
vi0   0     link#3                              0     0        0     0     0
vi0   0     9.3.187     9.3.187.184             0     0        0     0     0
lo0   16896 link#1                            468     0      468     0     0
lo0   16896 127         127.0.0.1             468     0      468     0     0
lo0   16896 ::1                               468     0      468     0     0
# ifconfig vi0
vi0: flags=84000041<UP,RUNNING,64BIT>
        inet 9.3.187.184 netmask 0xffffff00
```

7.5 NIS and NIS+ troubleshooting

> **Note:** LOG_START cannot be disabled. This implies a mask range from 0x0800 through 0x1FFF.

This section covers the tools and methods used to troubleshoot NIS problems. Additional information on RPC debugging can be found in Section 7.6, "NFS troubleshooting" on page 248.

7.5.1 Troubleshooting tools for NIS

The following sections contain a selection of networking commands that can be used as NIS troubleshooting tools.

ping

The **ping** command is a general purpose tool for investigating point-to-point connectivity problems.

If the **ping** command hangs or has long response times, then there is a low-level connectivity problem. This should be resolved before debugging NIS problems any further.

For more detail on the **ping** command, refer to Section 7.4.6, "ping" on page 228.

rpcinfo

The **rpcinfo** command is an analog of **ping** that queries RPC servers and their registration with the portmapper, thereby verifying that a remote machine is capable of replying to an RPC request.

The **rpcinfo** command can be used to detect:

- Dead or hung servers caused by improper configuration or a failed daemon.
- RPC program version number mismatches between client and server.
- Renegade RPC servers (NIS servers that do not have valid maps for the domain they are serving).
- Broadcast-related problems.

The **rpcinfo -p** command takes a remote host name and queries the portmapper on the host for all registered RPC services:

- Output from the **rpcinfo** command shows the RPC program and version numbers, the protocols supported, the IP port used by the RPC server, and the name of the RPC service.
- Service names come from the rpc.bynumber NIS map. If no name is printed next to the registration information, the RPC program number does not appear in the map.
- Missing RPC service names could indicate a corrupted or incomplete rpc.bynumber NIS map.

When working toward diagnosing any RPC-related problem, verify that the remote portmapper is alive and returning valid RPC registrations.

- If the portmapper on the remote machine has died or is not accepting connections for any reason, **rpcinfo** times out attempting to reach it and reports the error. This indicates a low-level problem in the network.

If you are debugging in a heterogeneous environment and running multiple versions of each RPC service, it is possible to get RPC version number mismatch errors.

These problems affect NIS and diskless client booting; they are best sorted out by using the **rpcinfo** command to emulate an RPC call and by observing server responses.

For example, perform a broadcast and then watch the order in which responses are received. The **rpcinfo -b** command sends a broadcast request to the specified RPC program and version number:

```
# rpcinfo -b ypserv 1
9.3.187.184 austin
```

```
9.3.187.185 sydney
9.3.187.186 napoli
```

In this example, all NIS servers on the local network answer the **rpcinfo** broadcast request to the null procedure of the **ypserv** daemon. If austin should not be the NIS server and clients bind to it, the network will be prone to periods of intermittent failure.

A renegade NIS server may be the first to answer a ypbind broadcast for NIS service. Its lack of information about the domain makes the client machine unusable.

Failure to fully decommission a host as an NIS server (leaving empty NIS map directories, for example) may cause this problem.

The **rpcinfo** command helps to determine why a particular client cannot start the NIS service. If no host replies to the **rpcinfo** command request, then the broadcast packet is failing to reach any NIS servers. If the NIS domain name and the broadcast address are correct, then it may be necessary to override the broadcast-based search and give ypbind the name and address of a valid NIS server by issuing a **ypset** command.

Sometimes, just looking at the list of servers that respond to a request may indicate a problem if you notice that one of the servers should not be answering the broadcast.

Like **ping**, the **rpcinfo** command provides a measure of basic connectivity at the session layer in the network protocol stack. Pinging a remote machine ensures that the underlying physical network and IP address handling are correct: using the **rpcinfo** command to perform a similar test verifies that the remote machine is capable of replying to an RPC request. This includes validation of the integrity of the network and that there is an RPC service registered on the other machine.

ypmatch

As a diagnostic tool, the **ypmatch** command can be used to see if a change to a map has taken effect and identify NIS maps that are out of synchronization after a map transfer has been requested or scheduled.

Generally, building a new map will push the map to other servers with the **yppush** command.

To check for map consistency, issue the **ypmatch** command on several clients and then the server. Verify that the same results are returned.

If not, a map inconsistency exists. Try pushing the maps to servers with the **yppush** command.

Often, NIS map changes may not propagate as quickly as desired, even though the change has been pushed with the **yppush** command.

ypwhich

The **ypwhich** command is used to verify an NIS server for a client, as shown in the following example:

```
# ypwhich
taboo
```

If a host name is passed as a parameter, the **ypwhich** command queries the named host for its current binding. If the **ypwhich** command cannot resolve the host name into an IP address, it reports an error as follows:

```
# ypwhich tonya
ypwhich: can't find tonya
```

Note: An IP address may be used in place of a host name.

The **ypwhich -x** command prints the table of nicknames:

```
stepiii $ ypwhich -x
Use passwd for map passwd.byname
Use group for map group.byname
Use networks for map networks.byaddr
Use hosts for map hosts.byaddr
Use protocols for map protocols.bynumber
Use services for map services.byname
Use aliases for map mail.aliases
Use ethers for map ethers.byname
```

The **ypwhich -m** command examines the NIS master server name embedded in the NIS map DBM file:

```
# ypwhich -m
auto.master stargate
auto.src stargate
rpc.bynumber stargate
protocols.bynumber stargate
auto.projects stargate
auto.mail stargate
auto.home stargate
```

If you have concerns about data disappearing from NIS maps, dump the entire map (including keys) using the **makedbm -u** command:

```
taboo $ /usr/etc/yp/makedbm -u ypservers
taboo
mighty
```

```
tiny
YP_LAST_MODIFIED 0706832572
YP_MASTER_NAME taboo
taboo $
```

The master map information is useful if you have changed NIS master servers and need to verify that client maps are built correctly and synchronized with the new server.

Querying client bindings individually is useful for debugging client problems.

In addition to providing NIS server binding information, the **ypwhich** command examines the NIS map information, the master server for a map, the list of all maps, and map nickname translations.

7.5.2 Troubleshooting examples with NIS

When debugging a network problem:

- Think about potential causes of the problem.
- Work your way through the protocol layers to ensure you do not miss a low-level problem that is posing as a high-level failure.

For example, if your attempts to bind to an NIS server are failing:

- Test the network using the **ping** command.
- Test the ypserv processes using the **rpcinfo** command.
- Finally, check the binding itself with the **ypset** or **ypwhich** commands.

yppush hangs making new maps

If you find the **yppush** command hangs when adding new NIS maps after initial maps have been transferred to a slave server, you need to:

1. Make the new map(s) with the NOPUSH option set to 1.

   ```
   make NOPUSH=1 <new_mapname>
   ```

   Failure to use the NOPUSH option will cause the command to hang.

2. Update the slave servers by running **ypxfr** on each one. This only applies if the new map does not already exist on the slave server.

Note: In AIX 5L Version 5.1:

- When a password is changed on the NIS client, the yppasswdd daemon directly updates the password maps and pushes the new maps to the NIS master. This results in a performance improvement when updating the NIS maps.
- **yppush** now pushes in parallel (up to 30 slaves at a time).

Client broadcasts do not bind

The most common problem occurring at an NIS client node is for a command to hang.

Sometimes a command appears to hang, and a message similar to the following appears on the console:

```
NIS: server not responding for domain <aussie>. Still trying
```

This error message indicates that the ypbind daemon on the local machine is unable to communicate with a ypserv daemon serving the wigwam domain.

Normally, this condition is temporary; the messages go away when the NIS server machine reboots and the ypserv daemon restarts or when the load on the NIS server and the network decreases.

If you are getting a `server not responding for domain` message, one of the following situations might exist:

- The domain name on the NIS client machine is not set or is set incorrectly.

  Clients must use a domain name that the NIS servers know.
- Your local network may not have an NIS server machine.

  In this circumstance, all other NIS clients on your network show the same or similar problems.
- The NIS server may not be up and running or it may be overloaded.

  If there is not a backup server in the broadcast subnet, all clients will hang on NIS query until the server recovers or the load reduces.
- The broadcast mask may be set incorrectly.

  Configuration errors in setting up the network or broadcast mask can also keep the broadcasts that **ypbind** uses from reaching a server.

If a server is unreachable due to some catastrophic failure, it may be necessary to temporarily start up a new server for the domain so the clients can be entered with logins.

The ypwhich command is inconsistent

When you use the **ypwhich** command repeatedly at the same client node, the response varies because the status of the NIS server changes. This is normal.

- The binding of NIS client to NIS server changes over time on a busy network. Whenever possible, the system stabilizes so that all clients get acceptable response time from the NIS servers.
- The source of an NIS service is not important because an NIS server machine often gets its own NIS services from another NIS server on the network.

A common cause of concern is when an NIS server that is also running as an NIS client is bound to some other server. It seems intuitive that the machine would bind to itself, but this is often not the case. The client is indiscriminate as to the server it binds to.

Very large maps are not supported

The NIS architecture does not scale well. 2 GB maps are the absolute maximum.

Large DBM databases are very slow and inefficient. When map sizes approach 2 GB, the DBM routines can fail with fseek() errors that cause map creation to fail. Prior to reaching this size, however, the performance has usually degraded to the point where using the maps is no longer practical.

Routers, network devices, and NIS binding

NIS binding is normally done through broadcasts.

Broadcasting is the primary way for NIS clients to bind to a server and for NIS slaves to bind to a master for map transfers. If the clients fail to bind, and there are bridges or routers between the machines seeking to bind, the problem may be that the hardware cannot pass through the broadcast packets necessary for the binding.

The **ypset** command can help get around this, but has the disadvantage that it is not secure. The best solutions in these situations are to have a server machine bridging the two networks or to break the network into two separate domains (perhaps duplicates of one another).

Group membership wrong for new group changes

Usually, this problem occurs because the netid map is incorrect.

Since it contains a mapping of groups by user, the netid map will yield incorrect results if it is not rebuilt whenever the passwd and group maps are changed.

To avoid this problem, do not make the group map by itself.

mkdbm fails with large NIS map entries

The design of DBM limits entries to 1024 bytes or less as follows:

The sum of DBM key + data must be < = 1024 bytes.

The most common problem caused by this is when a large group entry is rejected by DBM because there are too many users in one group, causing **mkdbm** to fail.

The problem is usually seen in group map entries and has two workarounds:

- Make two or more groups with the same GID.
- Add users with the *large group* as their primary group, then delete the user names from the group entry in /etc/group.

7.5.3 Troubleshooting examples for NIS+

Here are some troubleshooting examples for NIS+.

User cannot log in

There are many possible reasons for a user being unable to log in:

- The user forgot the password.
- Mistyped password.
- The user's password privileges have expired.
- An inactivity maximum has been set for this user, and the user has exceeded it.

Edit the /usr/lib/security/methods.cfg configuration file. (Add them, if they do not exist.) The following lines must exist and not be commented in these files:

```
NISPLUS
  program=/usr/lib/security/NISPLUS
```

and

```
/etc/security/user
```

User cannot remote log in to remote domain

User tries to **rlogin** to a machine in some other domain and is refused with a `Permission denied` type of error message. To **rlogin** to a machine in another domain, a user must have local credentials in that domain.

Run **nismatch** *username.domainname.cred.org_dir* in the other domain to see if the user has a LOCAL credential in that domain. If not, do the following:

- Go to the remote domain and use **nisaddcred** to create a LOCAL credential for the user in that domain.

A NISPLUS user requires DES credentials in their home domain to have proper NISPLUS authentication.

Slow performance and system hang problems

When someone has issued an **nisping** or **nisping -C** command, or the rpc.nisd daemon is performing a checkpoint operation and the system seems to hang, do not reboot. Do not issue more **nisping** commands. You may have corrupted information in the NIS+ domain.

After issuing an **nisping** or **nisping -C** command, the server can become sluggish and not immediately respond to other commands. In a large namespace, **nisping** commands can take a noticeable amount of time to complete. Delays caused by **nisping** commands are multiplied if you, or someone else, enter several such commands at one time. Do *not* reboot. This kind of problem solves itself. Wait until the server finishes performing the command.

During a full master-replica resync, the involved replica server is taken out of service until the resync is complete. Do *not* reboot. Wait for the resync to complete.

Namespace administration problems

This covers problems that may be encountered in the course of routine namespace administration work. This set of problems can cause the following symptoms:

- Illegal object type for operation message
- Other "object problem" error messages
- Initialization failure
- Checkpoint failures
- Difficulty adding a user to a group
- Logs too large/lack of disk space/difficulty truncating logs
- Inability to delete groups_dir or org_dir

Illegal object problems

If a problem is caused by an illegal object, the system displays the `Illegal object type for operation` or other messages that indicate an *object* problem. There are a number of possible causes for such an error message:

- You have attempted to create a table without any searchable columns.
- A database operation has returned the status of DB_BADOBJECT.
- You are trying to add or modify a database object with a length of zero.
- You attempted to add an object without an owner.
- The operation expected a directory object, and the object you named was not a directory object.
- You attempted to link a directory to a LINK object.
- An object that was not a group object was passed to the **`nisgrpadm`** command.
- An operation on a group object was expected, but the type of object specified was not a group object.
- An operation on a table object was expected, but the object specified was not a table object.

nisinit fails

Make sure that:

- You can ping the NIS+ server to check that it is up and running as a machine.
- The NIS+ server that you specified with the -H option is a valid server and that it is running the NIS+ software.
- rpc.nisd is running on the server.
- The nobody class has read permission for this domain.
- The netmask is properly set up on this machine.

Checkpoint keeps failing

If checkpoint operations with a **`nisping -C`** command consistently fail, make sure you have sufficient swap and disk space. Check for error messages in syslog. Check for core files that are filling up space.

Cannot add user to a group

A user must first be an NIS+ principal client with a local credential in the domain's cred table before the user can be added as a member of a group in that domain. A DES credential alone is not sufficient.

Logs grow too large

Failure to regularly checkpoint your system with **nisping -C** causes your log files to grow too large. Logs are not cleared on a master until all replicas for that master are updated. If a replica is down or otherwise out of service or unreachable, the master's logs for that replica cannot be cleared. Thus, if a replica is going to be down or out of service for a period of time, remove it as a replica from the master by running **nisrmdir -f -s** for all directories, including groups_dir and org_dir.

Cannot truncate transaction log file

Check to make sure that the file in question exists, is readable, and that you have permission to write to it. You can use:

- **ls -l /var/nis/trans.log** to display the transaction log
- **nisls -l** and **niscat** to check for existence, permissions, and readability
- syslog to check for relevant messages

Most likely, you cannot truncate an existing log file for which you have the proper permissions because of lack of disk space. (The checkpoint process first creates a duplicate temporary file of the log before truncating the log and then removing the temporary file. If there is not enough disk space for the temporary file, the checkpoint process cannot proceed.) Check your available disk space and release additional space if necessary.

Domain name confusion

Domain names play a key role in many NIS+ commands and operations. To avoid confusion, you must remember that except for root servers, all NIS+ masters and replicas are clients of the domain above the domain that they serve. If you treat a server or replica as if it were a client of the domain that it serves, you may get `Generic system error` or `Possible loop detected in` *namespace directoryname*:*domainname* error messages.

For example, the machine aladin might be a client of the subwiz.wiz.com domain. If the master server of the subwiz.wiz.com subdomain is the machine merlin, then merlin is a client of the wiz.com domain. When using, specifying, or changing domains, remember these rules:

- Client machines belong to a given domain or subdomain.
- Servers and replicas that serve a given subdomain are clients of the domain above the domain they are serving. The only exception is that the root master server and root replica servers are clients of the same domain that they serve. In other words, the root master and root replicas are all clients of the root domain.

Thus, in this example domain, the fully qualified name of the aladin machine is aladin.subwiz.wiz.com. The fully qualified name of the merlin machine is merlin.wiz.com. The name merlin.subwiz.wiz.com causes an error because merlin is a client of wiz.com, not of subwiz.wiz.com.

Inability to delete org_dir or groups_dir

Always delete org_dir and groups_dir before deleting their parent directory. If you use **nisrmdir** to delete the domain before deleting the domain's groups_dir and org_dir, you will be unable to delete either of those two subdirectories.

Namespace database problems

This covers problems related to the namespace database and tables, which result in error messages with operative clauses, such as:

- `Abort_transaction: Internal database error`
- `Abort_transaction: Internal Error, log entry corrupt`
- `Callback: - select failed`
- `CALLBACK_SVC: bad argument`

Multiple rpc.nisd parent processes

Indications that you have multiple independent rpc.nisd daemons running are database and transaction log corruption error messages that contain the terms:

- `Corrupt log`
- `Log corrupted`
- `Log entry corrupt`
- `Corrupt database`
- `Database corrupted`

In normal operation, rpc.nisd may spawn child rpc.nisd daemons. However, if two parent rpc.nisd daemons are running at the same time on the same machine, they overwrite each other's data and corrupt logs and databases. (Normally, this could only occur if someone starts rpc.nisd by command.)

To check whether this is the problem, run **ps -ef | grep rpc.nisd**. If you have more than one parent rpc.nisd entry, you must kill all but one of them. Use **kill -9** *process-ID*, then run the **ps** command again to make sure it has died. (If you started rpc.nisd with the -B option, you must also kill the rpc.nisd_resolv daemon.)

If an NIS+ database is corrupt, you must restore it from your most recent backup that contains an uncorrupted version of the database. You can then use the logs to update changes made to your namespace since the backup was recorded. However, if your logs are also corrupted, you must re-create any namespace modifications made since the backup was taken.

7.5.4 Automountd debugging

The automountd daemon is an RPC server that processes and answers requests from the local AutoFS file system kernel extension. It uses local files or name service maps to locate file systems to be mounted.

You can run automountd in mode. See Example 7-8.

Example 7-8 automountd

```
# cat /etc/syslog.conf
*.debug /tmp/syslog.out
# refresh -s syslogd
# automount
# stopsrc -s automountd
# startsrc -s automountd -a "-d -d -d"
<create the problem>
review /tmp/syslog.out for automountd debug messages
```

7.6 NFS troubleshooting

Troubleshooting for NFS problems involves understanding the strategies for tracking NFS problems, recognizing NFS-related error messages and selecting the appropriate solutions. When tracking down an NFS problem, isolate each of the three main points of failure to determine which is not working:

- The server
- The client
- The network itself

7.6.1 Identifying hard-mounted and soft-mounted file problems

When the network or server has problems, programs that access hard-mounted remote files fail differently from those that access soft-mounted remote files. If a server fails to respond to a hard-mount request, NFS prints the message:

```
NFS server hostname not responding, still trying
```

Hard-mounted remote file systems cause programs to hang until the server responds because the client retries the mount request until it succeeds. Use the -bg flag with the **mount** command when performing a hard mount, so if the server does not respond, the client will retry the mount in the background.

If a server fails to respond to a soft-mount request, NFS prints the message:

```
Connection timed out
```

Soft-mounted remote file systems return an error after trying unsuccessfully for a while. Unfortunately, many programs do not check return conditions on file system operations, so you do not see this error message when accessing soft-mounted files. However, the NFS error prints on the console.

7.6.2 Identifying NFS problems checklist

If a client is having NFS trouble, do the following:

- Verify that the network connections are good.
- Verify that the inetd, portmap, and biod daemons are running on the client.
- Verify that a valid mount point exists for the file system being mounted.
- Verify that the server is up and running by running the following command at the shell prompt of the client:

  ```
  # /usr/bin/rpcinfo  -p  f80right
  ```

If the server is up, a list of programs, versions, protocols, and port numbers is printed, similar to the following:

```
program vers proto   port  service
100000    4   tcp     111  portmapper
100000    4   udp     111  portmapper
100001    3   udp   32773  rstatd
100002    1   udp   32774  rusersd
100008    1   udp   32775  walld
100012    1   udp   32776  sprayd
150001    1   udp   32777  pcnfsd
100068    5   udp   32778  cmsd
100083    1   tcp   32769  ttdbserver
100024    1   tcp   32772  status
100021    4   udp   32845  nlockmgr
100021    4   tcp   32773  nlockmgr
100003    2   udp    2049  nfs
100003    3   tcp    2049  nfs
100005    1   udp   33259  mountd ................
```

If a similar response is not returned, log in to the server at the server console and check the status of the inetd daemon.

- Verify that the mountd, portmap and nfsd daemons are running on the NFS server by entering the following commands at the client shell prompt:

```
# /usr/bin/rpcinfo  -u  server_name  mount
# /usr/bin/rpcinfo  -u  server_name  portmap
# /usr/bin/rpcinfo  -u  server_name  nfs
```

If the daemons are running at the server, the responses returned can be seen in Example 7-9.

Example 7-9 rpcinfo command

```
# /usr/bin/rpcinfo  -u f80right mount
program 100005 version 1 ready and waiting
program 100005 version 2 ready and waiting
program 100005 version 3 ready and waiting
# /usr/bin/rpcinfo  -u f80right portmap
program 100000 version 2 ready and waiting
program 100000 version 3 ready and waiting
program 100000 version 4 ready and waiting
# /usr/bin/rpcinfo  -u f80right nfs
program 100003 version 2 ready and waiting
program 100003 version 3 ready and waiting
```

- Verify that the /etc/exports file on the server lists the name of the file system that the client wants to mount and that the file system is exported. Do this by entering the command:

```
# showmount -e server_name
```

This command lists all the file systems currently exported by the server_name.

7.6.3 Asynchronous write errors

When an application program writes data to a file in an NFS-mounted file system, the write operation is scheduled for asynchronous processing by the biod daemon. If an error occurs at the NFS server at the same time that the data is actually written to disk, the error is returned to the NFS client and the biod daemon saves the error internally in NFS data structures. The stored error is subsequently returned to the application program the next time it calls either the fsync or close functions. As a consequence of such errors, the application is not notified of the write error until the program closes the file. A typical example of this event is when a file system on the server is full, causing writes attempted by a client to fail.

7.6.4 Common NFS error messages

Here are some error codes that can be generated while using NFS.

- `mountd will not start`

  Name resolution of loopback may be the problem. It must resolve exactly the same using IP and name. Furthermore, it should return loopback is 127.0.0.1, not localhost is 127.0.0.1. If it returns localhost is 127.0.0.1, change the order of the entry in /etc/hosts to read:

  ```
  127.0.0.1 loopback localhost
  ```

  If using DNS, set the /etc/netsvc.conf to `hosts=local,bind`.

- `... not in hosts database`

  On a network without Network Information Service (NIS), this message indicates that the host specified in the **mount** command is not in the /etc/hosts file. On a network running NIS, the message indicates that NIS could not find the host name in the /etc/hosts database or that the NIS ypbind daemon on your machine has died. If the /etc/resolv.conf file exists so that the name server is being used for host name resolution, there might be a problem in the named database.

  Check the spelling and the syntax in your **mount** command. If the command is correct, your network does not run NIS, and you only get this message for this host name, check the entry in the /etc/hosts file.

  If your network is running NIS, make sure that the ypbind daemon is running by entering the following at the command line:

  ```
  # ps -ef
  ```

  You should see the ypbind daemon in the list. Try using the **rlogin** command to log in remotely to another machine, or use the **rcp** command to remote-copy something to another machine. If this also fails, your ypbind daemon is probably stopped or hung. If you only get this message for this host name, check the /etc/hosts entry on the NIS server.

- `mount: ... server not responding: port mapper failure - RPC timed out`

  Either the server you are trying to mount from is down or its port mapper is stopped or hung. Try restarting the server to activate the inetd, portmap, and ypbind daemons.

  If you cannot log in to the server remotely with the **rlogin** command but the server is up, check the network connection by trying to log in remotely to some other machine. Also, check the server network connection.

- `mount: ... server not responding: program not registered`

  This means that the **mount** command got through to the port mapper, but the rpc.mountd NFS mount daemon was not registered.

- `mount: access denied ...`

  Your machine name is not in the export list for the file system you are trying to mount from the server.

Note: In AIX 5L Version 5.1, you can now allow root access by netgroup.

  You can get a list of the server exported file systems by running the following command:

  ```
  # showmount -e hostname
  ```

  If the file system you want is not in the list, or your machine name or netgroup name is not in the user list for the file system, log in to the server and check the /etc/exports file for the correct file system entry. A file system name that appears in the /etc/exports file, but not in the output from the **showmount** command, indicates a failure in the mountd daemon. Either the daemon could not parse that line in the file, it could not find the directory, or the directory name was not a locally mounted directory. If the /etc/exports file looks correct and your network runs NIS, check the ypbind daemon on the server. It may be stopped or hung.

- `mount: ...: You are not allowed`

  You must have root authority or be a member of the system group to run the **mount** command on your machine, because it affects the file system for all users on that machine. NFS mounts and unmounts are only allowed for root users and members of the system group.

7.6.5 Identifying the cause of slow access times for NFS

If access to remote files seems unusually slow, ensure that access time is not being inhibited by:

- A runaway daemon
- A bad tty line
- A similar problem

Checking processes

On the server, enter the following at the command line:

```
# ps -ef
```

If the server appears to be operating correctly and other users are getting timely responses, make sure your biod daemons are running. Try the following steps:

- Run the **ps -ef** command and look for the biod daemons in the display.

If they are not running, then try:

- Stop the biod daemons that are in use by issuing the following command:

```
# stopsrc -s biod -c
```

- Start the biod daemons by issuing the following command:

```
# startsrc -s biod
```

To determine if one or more biod daemons are not responding, the user can run **nfsstat -c** several times during the period when they suspect that one or more biod daemons are hung. If there is no noticeable change in the number of Remote Procedure Call (RPC) client reads or writes, one or more of the biod daemons are not performing their task. You can determine only that one or more biod daemons are inactive; you cannot determine which one is inactive.

7.6.6 Checking network connections

If the biod daemons are working, check the network connections. The **nfsstat** command determines whether you are dropping packets. Use the **nfsstat -c** and **nfsstat -s** commands to determine if the client or server is retransmitting large blocks. Retransmissions are always a possibility due to lost packets or busy servers. A retransmission rate of five percent or more is considered high.

The probability of retransmissions can be reduced by changing communication adapter transmit queue parameters. The System Management Interface Tool (SMIT) can be used to change these parameters.

7.6.7 Setting MTU sizes

To set MTU size, use the Web-based System Manager, or the SMIT fast path **smit chif**. Select the appropriate adapter and enter an MTU value in the Maximum IP Packet Size field.

The **ifconfig** command can be used to set MTU size (and must be used to set MTU size at 8500). The format for the **ifconfig** command is:

```
# ifconfig trn NodeName up mtu MTUSize
```

where trn is your adapter name, for example, tr0.

7.6.8 Fixing hung programs

If programs hang during file-related work, the NFS server could have stopped. In this case, the following error message may be displayed:

```
NFS server hostname not responding, still trying
```

The NFS server (host name) is down. This indicates a problem with the NFS server, the network connection, or the NIS server.

Check the servers from which you have mounted file systems if your machine hangs completely. If one or more of them is down, do not be concerned. When the server comes back up, your programs continue automatically. No files are destroyed. If a soft-mounted server dies, other work is not affected. Programs that time out while trying to access soft-mounted remote files fail with the error message, but you are still able to access your other file systems.

If all servers are running, determine whether others who are using the same servers are having trouble. More than one machine having service problems indicates a problem with the nfsd daemons on the server. In this case, log in to the server and run the **ps** command to see if the nfsd daemon is running and accumulating CPU time. If not, you might be able to stop and then restart the nfsd daemon. If this does not work, you have to restart the server.

Check your network connection and the connection of the server if other systems seem to be up and running.

7.6.9 Permissions and authentication schemes

Sometimes, after mounts have been successfully established, there are problems in reading, writing, or creating remote files or directories. Such difficulties are usually due to permissions or authentication problems. Permission and authentication problems can vary in cause, depending on whether NIS is being used and secure mounts are specified.

The simplest case occurs when non-secure mounts are specified and NIS is not used. In this case, user IDs (UIDs) and group IDs (GIDs) are mapped solely through the server /etc/passwd file and client /etc/group file. In this scheme, for a user named B to be identified both on the client and on the server as B, the user B must have the same UID number in the /etc/passwd file. Example 7-10 shows how this might cause problems.

Example 7-10 UIDs

```
User  B  is  uid  200  on  client  foo.
User  B  is  uid  250  on  server  bar.
User  G  is  uid  200  on  server  bar.
```

The /home/bar directory is mounted from server bar onto client foo. If user B is editing files on the /home/bar remote file system on client foo, confusion results when he saves files.

The server bar thinks the files belong to user G, because G is UID 200 on bar. If B logs on directly to bar by using the **rlogin** command, he may not be able to access the files he just created while working on the remotely mounted file system. G, however, is able to do so because the machines arbitrate permissions by UID, not by name.

The only permanent solution to this is to reassign consistent UIDs on the two machines. For example, give B UID 200 on server bar or 250 on client foo. The files owned by B would then need to have the **chown** command run against them to make them match the new ID on the appropriate machine.

Because of the problems with maintaining consistent UID and GID mappings on all machines in a network, NIS or NIS+ is often used to perform the appropriate mappings so that this type of problem is avoided.

7.6.10 Name resolution on an NFS server

When an NFS server services a mount request, it looks up the name of the client making the request. The server takes the client Internet Protocol (IP) address and looks up the corresponding host name that matches that address. Once the host name has been found, the server looks at the exports list for the requested directory and checks the existence of the client name in the access list for the directory. If an entry exists for the client and the entry matches exactly what was returned for the name resolution, then that part of the mount authentication passes.

If the server is not able to perform the IP address-to-host-name resolution, the server denies the mount request. The server must be able to find some match for the client IP address making the mount request. If the directory is exported with the access being to all clients, the server still must be able to do the reverse name lookup to allow the mount request.

The server also must be able to look up the correct name for the client. For example, if there is an entry in the /etc/exports file similar the following:

```
/tmp -access=taboo:tonya
```

the following corresponding entries exist in the /etc/hosts file:

```
9.3.187.200 taboo.domain.name.com
9.3.187.190 tonya.domain.name.com
```

Notice that the names do not correspond exactly. When the server looks up the IP address-to-host-name matches for the hosts taboo and tonya, the string names do not match exactly with the entries in the access list of the export. This type of name resolution problem usually occurs when using the named daemon for name resolution. Most named daemon databases have aliases for the full domain names of hosts so that users do not have to enter full names when referring to hosts. Even though these host-name-to-IP address entries exist for the aliases, the reverse lookup might not exist. The database for reverse name lookup (IP address to host name) usually has entries containing the IP address and the full domain name (not the alias) of that host. Sometimes the export entries are created with the shorter alias name, causing problems when clients try to mount.

7.6.11 Mounting from NFS servers that have an earlier version of NFS

When mounting a file system from a pre-Version 3 NFS server onto a Version 3 NFS client, a problem occurs when the user on the client executing the mount is a member of more than eight groups. Some servers are not able to deal correctly with this situation and deny the request for the mount. The solution is to change the group membership of the user to a number less than eight and then retry the mount. The following error message is characteristic of this group problem:

```
RPC:     Authentication error; why=Invalid client credential
```

7.6.12 Problems that occur if the NFS kernel extension is not loaded

Some NFS commands do not execute correctly if the NFS kernel extension is not loaded. Some commands with this dependency are: **nfsstat**, **exportfs**, **mountd**, **nfsd**, and **biod**. When NFS is installed on the system, the kernel extension is placed in the /usr/lib/drivers/nfs.ext file. This file is then loaded as the NFS kernel extension when the system is configured. The script that does this kernel extension loads the /etc/rc.net file. There are many other things done in this script, one of which is to load the NFS kernel extension.

Note:

- It is important to note that Transmission Control Protocol/Internet Protocol (TCP/IP) kernel extension should be loaded before the NFS kernel extension is loaded.
- The **gfsinstall** command is used to load the NFS kernel extension into the kernel when the system initially starts. This command can be run more than once per system startup and it will not cause a problem. The system is currently shipped with the **gfsinstall** command, used in both the /etc/rc.net and /etc/rc.nfs files. There is no need to remove either of these calls.

7.7 Problems with a SLIP network interface

In general, the most effective method for debugging problems with a Serial Line Interface Protocol (SLIP) interface is to retrace your configuration, verifying each step. However, you can also:

- Verify that the slattach process is running and using the correct tty port by issuing the **ps -ef** command. If it is not, run the **slattach** command.
- Verify that the point-to-point addresses are specified correctly by entering the **smit chinet** fast path. Select the SLIP interface. Make sure that the internet address and destination address fields are correct.

If the modem is not functioning correctly:

- Make sure that the modem was installed correctly. See the modem installation manual.
- Verify that any flow control the modem does is turned off.

If the tty is not functioning correctly, verify that the tty baud rate and modem characteristics are set correctly in the configuration database by entering the **smit tty** fast path.

7.8 Asynchronous Point-to-Point Protocol (PPP) debugging

This section contains debugging information for AIX PPP client and server connections. The PPP subsystem provides an alternative to SLIP. PPP provides a standard method for transporting multiprotocol datagrams over point-to-point media. PPP is comprised of three main layers:

- A method for encapsulating multiprotocol datagrams. PPP supports the TCP/IP network layer protocols.
- A Link Control Protocol (LCP) for establishing, configuring, and testing the data-link connection. PPP implements this through streams kernel extensions.
- A family of Network Control Protocols (NCPs) for establishing and configuring different network layer protocols. PPP supports Internet Protocol Control Protocol (IPCP) for negotiating a TCP/IP connection.

7.8.1 AIX as a PPP client (outgoing calls)

In order to dial out with PPP, there must be a tty defined for the modem port with Enable LOGIN set to `disable` and FLOW CONTROL to be used set to `rts`. To test the tty, you first of all need to ensure that BNU utilities are installed, check for the bos.net.uucp fileset on the system, and then execute the **cu -ml ttyXX** command. Refer to the following cu example for the session flow:

```
taboo@planet:/home/taboo > cu -ml tty8
Connected
at
OK
~[planet].
The connection is ended.
```

> **Note:** Do not proceed with further PPP debugging until the modem responds as above. If additional debug output is needed, use **cu -dml ttyXX**.

Another useful tool in PPP debugging is syslogd. If this has not already been set up as part of the initial PPP configuration, you need to set it up now. The following setup example can be used as a guide:

1. Add the following line to the /etc/syslog.conf file:

   ```
   *.debug   /tmp/ppp
   ```

2. Create the file /tmp/ppp and set the permissions so it can be written to:

   ```
   >/tmp/ppp
   chmod +w /tmp/ppp
   ```

3. Tell syslogd that /etc/syslog.conf has been updated. Execute the following command:

   ```
   # refresh -s syslogd
   ```

Also check that the /etc/uucp/Devices file contains the following line:

```
Direct tty## - baud_rate direct
```

Where tty## is the tty created above and baud_rate is the baud rate set for that tty.

Try to start the PPP subsystem, use the SMIT ppp screen or execute the following command from the command line:

```
# startsrc -s pppcontrold
```

Note: Any changes to the link control configuration require that the PPP subsystem (pppcontrold) be stopped and restarted. Use either SMIT or **stopsrc -cs pppcontrold** to stop the subsystem.

Use the following commands to check that the PPP subsystem started:

- **# netstat -in** (to see whether pp# network interfaces have been created). Before a connection is established, the IP address of PPP interfaces will be 0.0.0.0.
- **# lssrc -s pppcontrold** (to see whether PPP is running).

If PPP is not running, there may be problems in the link control configuration (check with **smit ppp**), or PPP fileset updates are needed. To provide more detailed debugging output from the **pppcontrold** command, you can send signal 30 as follows:

```
# lssrc -s pppcontrold
```

Note the Process ID (PID):

```
# kill -30 <pppcontrold_PID>
```

Where pppcontrold_PID is the PID number of **pppcontrold** returned by the **lssrc** command.

This will append a message indicating that debugging has been activated on the /tmp/ppp file that was set up with syslogd configuration. Diagnostic output can later be switched off by using **kill -31** *<pppcontrold_PID>*. This option can be used when the PPP connection is being established and thereby provide protocol, addressing, PAP/CHAP, and other information.

If the link is not started when the **pppattachd** command runs:

- Check the route tables on both systems.
- Ensure that the dial string from the Chat Script matches the modem requirements.

The **pppattachd** command calls the pppdial program, which uses the chat script to do the actual dial-out. Refer to the following for a sample dial-out command:

```
/usr/sbin/pppattachd client tty8 connect "/usr/sbin/pppdial -v -f
CHAT_SCRIPT_FILE"
```

- After issuing the **pppattachd** command, the progression of the dial-out can be watched by executing the following command:

  ```
  # tail -f /tmp/ppp
  ```

Where /tmp/ppp is the file set up with syslogd to which the debug output has been directed.

The following configuration files also contain useful data for connection problem determination:

- /etc/ppp/if_conf

  Contains PPP IP interface configuration.
- /etc/ppp/lcp.conf

  Contains configuration information set in the LCP configuration panels.
- /etc/ppp/if_link.map

  Contains the correlation of interfaces to LCP network connection blocks.
- /etc/ppp/attXXX.pid

  Contains process ID files for the async attachments.

Chat scripts

The pppdial program called by the **pppattachd** command uses a UUCP chat dialog to establish a connection with the remote system. The following example shows a simplified chat script file with explanatory notes to assist with PPP troubleshooting:

```
''
ATDT555-5555
CONNECT
''
in:
myuserid
word:
mypassword
```

On a line-by-line basis, the above script means:

- Expect nothing.
- Send the modem `ATDT555-5555` (to make the modem dial this number).
- Expect CONNECT from modem.
- Send nothing.
- Expect [log]in: (the login prompt sent by the remote system).
- Send my user ID.
- Expect [pass]word: (the password prompt sent by the remote system).
- Send my password.

Authentication problems

The specific reason for failure to authenticate when using PAP or CHAP security authentication protocol is normally shown in the syslogd log file (/tmp/ppp in the examples).

If you are using CHAP authentication, note that Microsoft uses a CHAP algorithm that differs from that of AIX. The Windows 95/Windows NT CHAP protocol is incompatible with AIX.

If using PAP, use the following simplified authentication setup procedure to see if authentication works. In the PAP Authentication SMIT panel:

- The remote host name is the name of the authenticator from the peer's perspective.
- A * for remote host name indicates any authenticator.

On the server machine, run:

```
smitty ppp
  PAP  Authentication
   Add a User
            User name             [david]
            Remote host name      [*]
            Password              [david]
```

To verify the pap user has been created, run:

```
# vi /etc/ppp/pap-secrets
```

Look for david * david in the file:

```
# cd /home/goliath
```

Where goliath is the user created for login on the server. Then run:

```
# vi .profile
```

Add the following line:

```
# exec /usr/sbin/pppattachd server authenticate pap 2>/dev/null
```

On the client machine, run:

```
smitty ppp
PAP  Authentication
   Add a User
          User name             [david]
          Remote host name      [*]
          Password              [david]
```

Use the following command to connect as the client:

```
# /usr/sbin/pppattachd client /dev/tty# peer pap USERNAME connect \
"/usr/sbin/pppdial -v -f CHAT_SCRIPT_FILE"
```

Where USERNAME is the name of the PAP user and CHAT_SCRIPT_FILE is the full path name of your chat script file.

Dial from the client, get the link established, and the authentication should work. If not, check the syslogd output file.

7.8.2 AIX as a PPP server (incoming calls)

In order to accept incoming calls with PPP, there must be a tty defined for the modem port with Enable LOGIN set to `enable`, `delay`, or `share`, and FLOW CONTROL to be used set to `rts`. Refer to Section 7.8.1, "AIX as a PPP client (outgoing calls)" on page 258 for tty test details.

Also, set up syslogd, as was done in the client section.

Verify that the PPP subsystem is active on this server system with the following commands:

- **`# lssrc -s pppcontrold`**

  This should show as active.
- **`# ps -ef | grep ppp`**

  There should be a pppcontrold process running.
- **`# ifconfig pp0`**

  The pp0 interface should display the correct IP address.

If you are unable to login after establishing the connection, check that the user is a member of the UUCP group.

Also check the users .profile for the first line as follows (for ksh):

```
# exec /usr/sbin/pppattachd server 2>/dev/null
```

7.8.3 PPP and snmp

PPP can interact with the TCP/IP SNMP daemon to report PPP link layer configuration information as well as information about active Link Control Protocol (LCP) interfaces. Providing that both the TCP/IP SNMP and the SNMP management software are configured correctly, PPP SNMP enables:

- Retrieval of PPP Link Configuration information (Maximum Receive Unit size, Asynchronous Character Mapping, and so on)

- Setting of PPP Link Configuration information
- Retrieval of LCP interface information for active LCP links
- Changing of the state of active LCP links can be changed to "down" by setting the appropriate ifAdminStatus Management
- Information Base (MIB) object

7.8.4 Enabling PPP SNMP

By default, SNMP for PPP is disabled. To enable PPP SNMP, you can use the Web-based System Manager, **wsm**, or use the following procedure. You must have root privileges to perform this procedure.

> **Note:** The following procedure assumes that PPP Link Configuration is already set.

Start the SMIT Interface and display the Change/Show a Link Configuration screen by entering:

```
# smit chglcp
```

Then:

- Toggle the Enable PPP SNMP subagent field to `yes`.
- Accept your changes and exit SMIT.

PPP SNMP is *not* enabled until PPP is restarted.

If PPP is currently running, then:

- Stop PPP using the **smit stopppp** fast path
- Periodically check to see if the subsystem has completed shutdown by entering:

  ```
  # lssrc -s pppcontrold
  ```

The amount of time it takes to completely stop the subsystem is dependent on the number of links defined in the PPP configuration. The subsystem is completely shut down when the output of this command shows a status of inoperative. You should start PPP using the **smit startppp** fast path.

7.9 Sendmail troubleshooting

AIX 5L Version 5.1 now runs Sendmail 8.11.0. The /etc/sendmail.cf file has moved to /etc/mail/ sendmail.cf. The /etc/aliases file has moved to /etc/mail/aliases. Before AIX 5L Version 5.1, root was owned by bin.bin. If sendmail (running as root) had a problem sending mail, it could not write to /dead.letter. Therefore, an error mail would be sent. In AIX 5L Version 5.1, root is now owned by root.system. Now that sendmail (running as root) can write to /dead.lettor, root users might stop seeing an error mail for problems. Instead, the error mail will be in /dead.letter.

The debugging -d switch allows you to observe the detailed inner workings of the sendmail program. Here we cover only some of the more common debugging issues.

7.9.1 Local mail delivery

Before trying to send or receive mail on the network, be sure local mail is working. Try mailing from the command line using **mail -v** which gives verbose output. See Example 7-11 for details of the output.

Example 7-11 local mail

```
# mail -v tonya
Subject: test
this is a test
.
Cc:
tonya... Connecting to local...
tonya... Sent
# mail -u tonya
Mail [5.2 UCB] [AIX 4.1]  Type ? for help.
"/var/spool/mail/tonya": 1 message 1 new
>N  1 root              Wed Sep  5 14:55  10/340  "test"
? 1
Message  1:
From root Wed Sep  5 14:55:25 2001
Date: Wed, 5 Sep 2001 14:55:25 -0500
From: root
To: tonya
Subject: test

this is a test
```

7.9.2 Network mail delivery

If local mail is working fine, but you are having trouble sending or receiving mail to another machine, check the following:

- Name resolution problems often cause sendmail problems.
- The debugging -d switch allows you to observe the detailed inner workings of the sendmail program.

Sendmail will attempt to define the variables Dw, Dm, and Cw automatically in memory by default. Dw, Dm and Cw represent, respectively, your host name, domain name and host aliases. This is done in a two-step process:

- The product of the **hostname** command is used to define the Dw variable.
- Then a gethostbyname system call is used by sendmail to find a domain name and any aliases, which are used to define the Dm and Cw variables.

Most problems with sending and receiving mail occur when these variables are defined incorrectly. These problems can be caused by incomplete entries in /etc/hosts, or incorrect information in the DNS server.

A sendmail debug option may be used to display these definitions (Dm and Cw). Enter the following command to view the System Identity section:

```
# sendmail -d0.1
```

Sendmail is built to work with DNS for resolving host names. If a system is not configured for DNS, that is, the /etc/resolv.conf file does not exist, then sendmail must be told not to use the DNS by creating the file /etc/netsvc.conf with an entry as follows:

```
hosts=local
```

If NIS is used, then the entry should read either `hosts=local,nis` or `hosts=nis,local`.

Because sendmail is built to use a DNS, sendmail also expects the host name to have a domain name. Edit the /etc/hosts file and give the local systems host name a domain name, so 9.3.187.189 taboo will become:

```
9.3.187.189 taboo.lab.net taboo
```

The short name taboo was moved to the alias position.

When a workstation that is behind a firewall needs to send and receive Internet mail, the DS and DM variables are used. The comments for the DS entry describe the server defined there as a Smart Relay. A Smart Relay is a system that has access to a working DNS, and has Internet connectivity so that it is able to make a network connection and deliver the mail. Typically, the DS is a firewall, or a system that is trusted by the firewall.

8

X11 and graphics

This chapter describes graphics components and how to handle problems related to them.

8.1 Handling graphics devices

Before running any graphics software or application, the underlying hardware components must be in place.

These components must be correctly configured and the capabilities of the hardware understood. Often a graphics problem may be isolated because some underlying hardware does not support a graphics feature called at some higher level.

If you suspect a problem at this level, use the following checklist:

1. Configure the hardware correctly.

   If you have moved the hardware, ensure you do not have conflicting ODM entries for the same hardware in different slots or that the adapter is mis-seated. It is true that some older 3D graphics adapters did require multiple slots; however, all of the graphics adapters sold in the last three years or more are single slot.

   Refer to Section 8.1.1, “Removing devices” on page 269, and Section 8.1.2, “Hot plugging” on page 269 for more information.

2. Install the correct device drivers.

   Without the required software support filesets, your hardware will not function.

   Install these as required for your hardware via the **smit devinst** fast path to install device support filesets. Select, from your installation media, the applicable filesets from the list.

   A fresh installation will automatically install required filesets; however, the addition of new devices not present at initial AIX installation will require additional device support filesets to be installed.

   If the device support software requires modules to be loaded into the kernel, often a system reboot will be required.

3. Run advanced diagnostics against the hardware.

   If you have installed the required diagnostics software for your hardware, run the **diag** command and select Advanced Diagnostics and then Problem Determination. If your devices support a diagnostic module, test it from diagnostics. Ensure you are not currently running the X server, as this often conflicts with the diagnostic routines.

   You may also boot the machine in Service mode boot and load diagnostics from a Diagnostic CD-ROM. Refer to Chapter 5, “Hardware problem determination” on page 115 for more information.

4. Compare with another workstation.

   Try to isolate a problem with a specific graphics device by substituting it with another device or similar device, if possible.

   Note in your problem report if the problem appears on all hardware used or only a specific adapter or other graphics hardware.

8.1.1 Removing devices

Often, if an adapter is removed or moved to other location in the machine, the ODM may not reflect the correct status if the **diag -a** command is not run. This command prompts you to remove missing devices from ODM or add newly detected devices. Generally, use this to remove old devices in old locations and indicate the new device is valid for a new location.

Failure to do this may require a manual check of the output of the **lscfg** command against what is presently in each slot in the machine. If conflicting or overlapping devices are present, often the case with multi-slot graphics adapters, the results are unpredictable.

8.1.2 Hot plugging

Physically disconnecting and reconnecting the keyboard, mouse, tablet, LPFKs, and dials to a workstation after they have been configured with power turned on may cause problems, even though the devices may appear to function correctly. This is especially true for the keyboard.

If you physically detach a device from the workstation, then either reboot the machine, or:

1. Reconnect the device.
2. Unconfigure the device using the **rmdev** command.
3. Reconfigure the device using the **mkdev** command.

8.2 X11 component isolation

Using X11 implies the use of two main components: an X server and an X client. The X server drives the screen or display output and input from devices such as a keyboard and mouse.

Therefore, the task to isolate graphic related problem starts with isolating the problem to one of the following applicable components:

- X server

- X client or application
- Transport between the X client and X server

8.3 X server

Before you can start an X client, the client must have an X server to connect to. The X server may execute on the same machine as the client or on another machine.

8.3.1 Start X server

Locating the source of the problem depends on how the X server is started.

For a non-Xstation, the process /usr/lpp/X11/bin/X is started together with some initial clients, as shown below:

- CDE

  AIX 5L uses graphical boot by default when a graphics monitor is detected on a machine.

  You can disable graphical boot without disabling CDE by running:

  ```
  # /usr/dt/bin/dtconfig -enograph
  ```

  If CDE is not working properly, it is a good idea to boot up your workstation without CDE.

  To enable a graphical boot, run:

  ```
  # /usr/dt/bin/dtconfig -e
  ```

  The default startup script for the X server is /usr/lpp/x11/defaults/xserverrc.

- XDM

  XDM is also known as the X display manager. Its major function is to provide X login. The default startup configuration file to start the XDM Xserver is /usr/lpp/X11/lib/X11/xdm.

- Startup script

  User can start the X server with the **startx** or **xinit** commands.

- Xstation

  Once an Xstation boots, it is already running the X server. X clients can begin to connect straight away.

8.3.2 Failure to start

Prior to starting the X server process, it is assumed the graphics screen can produce a character login or prompt. If you are not at this stage, perform hardware diagnostics and general problem reporting first.

Before attempting to perform problem diagnosis on an X11 startup problem, try starting the X server using the default configuration files. The files used will depend on how the X server is configured to start. This will isolate the problem to a genuine X server problem, not a configuration problem.

If the X server fails to start, check these points:

1. The AIXwindows Runtime Environment fileset, X11.base.rte, is installed and at the correct level:

   ```
   # lslpp -l X11.base.rte
   ```

   Verify the X server file exists and has execute permissions:

   ```
   # ls -al /usr/lpp/X11/bin/X
   -rxwr-xr-x 1 bin bin 2611202 OCT 21 1998 /usr/lpp/X11/bin/X
   ```

   Use the **lppchk** command to check the fileset for missing files or incorrect size files:

   ```
   # lppchk -c X11.base.rte
   lppchk:0504-206 File /usr/lpp/X11/bin/X could not be located.
   ```

   The easiest and fastest way to recover the situation mentioned above is to back up all your graphic configuration files, if you have made any changes on it, then reinstall the relevant filesets.

2. Libraries and device drivers installed.

   The X server may call other libraries or device drivers when executed.

   Try to execute the X server manually to check for error messages. If it does not load, you may see errors similar to the following example:

   ```
   # /usr/lpp/X11/bin/X
   exec():0509-036 Cannot load program /usr/lpp/X11/bin/X because of the
   following errors:
   0509-023 Symbol aixgsc in ksh is not defined
   0509-026 System error:cannot run a file that does not have a valid format
   ```

   In our example, a symbol, `aixgsc`, cannot be found in any libraries on the system. Knowledge of the symbols within libraries is required to locate the symbol.

3. Wrong display.

   The X server maybe running correctly but on the wrong display. Use the **lsdisp** command to display all available adapters and the **chdisp** command to modify the current display.

   For example, to permanently change the display to use the other graphics adapter, first list the available devices, then change it, and then reboot the system:

```
# lsdisp
DEV_NAME SLOT BUS ADPT_NAME DESCRIPTION
======== ==== === ========= ===========
wga0     0J   sys POWER_Gt1x POWER Gt1x Graphics Adapter
bbl0     0J   buc GXT150    GXT150 Graphics Adapter
Default display = wga0
# chdisp -p bbl0
# shutdown -Fr
```

   If you have only one display, remember to change the cabling so the output is shown correctly.

4. Logging errors.

   Examine the system error log, as shown in Section 2.3, "Error log management" on page 22, and examine the specific /tmp/xlogfile X log file for messages that appear when an attempt to start the X server is made.

8.3.3 Hung or stopped server

If the X server starts executing but then terminates or stops abnormally, check against the following symptoms.

You may see the following symptoms, indicating an X server problem:

- The screen blanks out and returns to a login prompt.
- A core file is created.
- The cursor appears frozen.
- All panels are no longer refreshed.

  Attempting to click on icons does not open any X clients, such as a panel. If you can still select panels, obscured parts, when revealed, are no longer redrawn for all panels.
- You are unable to bring up another aixterm.

The following indicates that the problem is something other than an X server problem:

- You can still start X clients remotely.

- Power management.

  Check the power indicator LED on the physical monitor you are viewing. If the power led has switched to standby mode, typically indicated by a non-green led, this is merely the power management subsystem conserving power.

- The cursor responds to the mouse.

Server terminates

When the X server core dumps, it creates a core file. If there is sufficient space and you have write authority, then the core file exists in the directory where you started the X server.

If a core file exists, the following steps can help locate which function caused the core dump:

1. Use **cd** to change to the directory that contains the core file.
2. Invoke:

   ```
   dbx /usr/lpp/X11/bin/X core
   where > coredump_x.log
   quit
   ```

   Ensure the core file actually came from the X process. When you run **dbx**, it will display the executable name like this: (X). If it is not (X), you have the wrong core file.

Server hangs

If you are experiencing a hang, execute the following:

1. Telnet into the hung machine from another machine.
2. Invoke:

   ```
   # ps -ef | grep X
   ```

   This generates, for example:

   ```
   userid 11634 11377 0 09:35:30 pts/1 0:33 /usr/lpp/X11/bin/X -x dps -D
   /usr/lib/X11/rgb
   ```

   The first number, in this case 11634, is the process ID.

3. Invoke:

   ```
   # dbx -a pid
   ```

   Where pid is the process ID associated with the X process. Therefore, in this example, you would issue:

   ```
   # dbx -a 11634
   ```

4. To find the location of the hang, type:

   ```
   where > hang_x.log
   detach
   pg hang_x.log
   ```

   The **kill -9 11634** command would terminate the X server when hung.

   However, ensure you have collected all of the necessary information for reporting the problem before killing the X server.

   With applications that also use the X server (such as graPHIGS remote nucleus), the dbx trace can be valuable input as well. Follow the same procedures listed above to obtain a dbx trace for the application you were running at the time the hang occurred. Instead of **grep X**, **grep** the name of the application. Also, to avoid overwriting your hang_x.log file, issue the **dbx** subcommand:

   ```
   where > hang_app.log
   ```

   Ensure that the time stamp on the file(s) you are including with your problem report have the appropriate time stamp (that is the time at which the failure occurred):

   ```
   # ls -l file
   ```

   Where file is xlogfile, core, or any other pertinent file.

8.4 Connecting X clients to the X server

The DISPLAY environment variable indicates what server a client will connect to and the transport method it will use.

If this is incorrectly specified, this can often stop an application from starting or achieve less than optimal performance.

8.4.1 The DISPLAY variable

An X client knows what X server to connect to by the value of the DISPLAY environment variable.

This variable has the general form:

```
[TCP/IP host]: display#[.screen#]
```

Where TCP/IP host is the TCP/IP host name defined for the X server, display# is a number representing the display number, and [. screen#] optionally indicates a screen within the display.

For example, to display X clients on the first display on the TCP/IP host mercury, set DISPLAY as follows:

```
mercury:0
```

For the Korn shell (/bin/ksh), the command to set the variable for your current process is:

```
# export DISPLAY=mercury:0
```

For the C shell (/bin/csh), the syntax to set the variable is:

```
# setenv DISPLAY mercury:0
```

For the Bourne shell (/bin/bsh), the syntax to set the variable is:

```
# DISPLAY=mercury:0
# export DISPLAY
```

The remaining examples in this section assume the use of the Korn shell.

The current setting of the variable can be found with the command:

```
# echo $DISPLAY
```

Before resetting the variable, write down the current setting.

8.4.2 X transport

The transport mechanism between an X client and X server allows X clients to execute on remote hosts or on the same machine as the X server.

The transport method is implicitly defined by the value of the DISPLAY environment variable or the X client code specifying the parameter directly to the OpenDisplay routine.

This flexible mechanism has three forms:

- Shared Memory Transport (SMT)

  This is the fastest transport method and only available for clients running on the same host as the X server process. To set the DISPLAY variable, omit the host name portion, for example:

  ```
  # export DISPLAY=:0
  ```

- UNIX sockets

  This is only applicable to for clients running on the same host as the X server process. To set the DISPLAY variable, use the following syntax:

  ```
  # export DISPLAY=unix:0
  ```

- TCP sockets

  This is applicable to clients executing remotely, for example, on a Xstation. To set the DISPLAY variable, use a valid TCP/IP host name, for example:

  ```
  # export DISPLAY=ted:0
  ```

8.4.3 Testing client/server connectivity

Test the validity of your DISPLAY variable by executing a simple well-known client.

For example, if your application does not seem to connect to your X server, execute:

```
# xsetroot -solid white
# xsetroot -solid red
```

Does your X server screen change color?

If it does not, check each of the following:

- DISPLAY not set or malformed

  Run:

  ```
  # echo $DISPLAY
  ted2
  # xsetroot -solid white
  1356-265 xsetroot: Unable to open display: ted2.
  ```

  In this example, the DISPLAY variable is not set correctly. It is missing `:0` at the end.

- Invalid DISPLAY host name

  Run:

  ```
  # echo $DISPLAY
  bogus:0
  # xsetroot -solid white
  1356-265 xsetroot: Unable to open display: bogus:0.
  # ping bogus
  0821-062 ping: host name bogus NOT FOUND
  ```

  In this example, the TCP/IP host name component of the DISPLAY variable refers to a host that does not exist.

- Client hangs

  Run:

  ```
  # xsetroot -solid white
  1356-265 xsetroot: Unable to open display: rally:0.
  ```

In this example, there is a long pause or hang after running the **xsetroot** command. Attempt to **ping** the host and check if the X server is running on that host. Perhaps your client does not have a route to the X server.

- Connection refused

  Run:

```
# xsetroot -solid white
Xlib: connection to "mossad:0.0" refused by server
Xlib: Client is not authorized to connect to Server
1356-265 xsetroot: Unable to open display: mossad:0.
```

  The X server maintains an access control list, allowing certain hosts to be denied access. For a machine running an X server on AIX, the default access control list disables all other hosts.

  To enable all hosts to connect, use the **xhost** command. For example, run the following command on the same host as the X server is running:

```
# xhost +
```

  The syntax to allow host specific access is as follow:

```
# xhost +<hostname>
```

  The **xhost** command is part of the X11.apps.config fileset, which, depending on the level of AIX you are running, may not be installed by default.

- Missing output

  Run:

```
# xsetroot -solid white
```

  If the command executes without error and without delay, yet the result is not visible, ensure you are viewing the correct screen. If you are using multiple graphics adapters in your machine and/or multiple X servers, you may be looking at the wrong screen.

  Note: For CDE environment users, this command will only affect the first workspace. Ensure you select the first workspace from the switch area.

8.4.4 Failed X client start

Now that you have verified the functionality of the X server, run your application in place of the well-known X client above.

If this fails to start, check the following symptoms:

- X protocol error messages

  Run:

```
# ./my_app
X Error of failed request: BadWindow (invalid Window parameter)
Major opcode of failed request: 1 (X_CreateWindow)
Resource ID in failed request: 0x200003e8
Serial number of failed request: 3
Current serial number in output stream: 5
```

  This indicates a run-time error received by the client application.

  For example, an inappropriate operation is performed on the X resource or a requested resource is not available.

  The above example shows the output from the default X error handler. A user application may call a custom error handler by using the function XSetErrorHandler().

  Function isolation is aided by the client application calling XSynchronize() to enable the X server's synchronization of an X protocol request and the X server's completion of the request. This ensures that the application will terminate at the point of the X call causing the problem, rather that after the event due to the X servers buffering of requests.

- exec format errors

  Run:

```
# ./my_app
exec(): 0509-036 Cannot load program ./my_app because of the following
errors:
0509-022 Cannot load library libXm.a[shr4.o].
0509-026 System error: A file or directory in the path name does not exist.
```

  or

```
# ./my_app
exec(): 0509-036 Cannot load program ./my_app because of the following
errors:
0509-023 Symbol _XmStrings in ksh is not defined.
0509-023 Symbol XmStringLtoRCreate in ksh is not defined.
0509-026 System error: Cannot run a file that does not have a valid form
```

  These examples indicate an installation problem; either the libraries referenced by the executable at load time are missing or the version of the libraries is downlevel.

  In the first case, the libXm.a library is missing. It must be installed for the application to run.

In the second case, symbols cannot be located in the libraries found on the machine. Check with the supplier of the client software to find out what libraries the symbols are expected to be in and what version should be installed. Generally, specific knowledge of the location of the symbols within libraries is required. Refer to Section 9.2.4, “Library problems” on page 288 for more information on determining the missing libraries.

8.5 X kernel extension

The functionality of the X server is extended with the addition of X extensions.

8.5.1 Loading an X extension

The method to load an X extension will depend on the method used to start the X server. /usr/lpp/X11/defaults/xserverrc controls the loading of X extensions and other customizations. Refer to *AIX 5L Differences Guide*, SG24-5765, for every new X extension that is included in the new release. For CDE, also refer to Section 8.6.2, “Login screen does not appear” on page 281.

8.5.2 Installing verification commands

The commands **xrdb -symbols** and **xdpyinfo** enable you to check for loaded X extensions. The **xrdb** command is part of the X11.apps.rte fileset. The **xdpyinfo** command is part of the X11.samples.apps.clients fileset.

8.5.3 Checking X extensions

With **xrdb**, check for the -DEXT_ entries. For example:

```
# xrdb -symbols
-DHOST=ted2 -DSERVERHOST=ted2 -DSRVR_ted2 -DDISPLAY_NUM=0 -DCLIENTHOST=bob3
-DCLNT_bob3 -DVERSION=11 -DREVISION=0 -DVENDOR="International Business
Machines" -DVNDR_International_Business_Machines -DRELEASE=5 -DNUM_SCREENS=1
-DEXT_SCREEN_SAVER -DEXT_SHAPE
-DEXT_XTestExtension1 -DEXT_xColormapExtension
-DEXT_aixCursorExtension -DEXT_XAixExtension
-DEXT_xDirectAccessExtension -DEXT_XInputExtension
-DSCREEN_NUM=0 -DWIDTH=1280 -DHEIGHT=1024 -DX_RESOLUTION=3596
-DY_RESOLUTION=3606 -DPLANES=8 -DBITS_PER_RGB=8 -DCLASS=PseudoColor
-DCLASS_PseudoColor=33 -DCOLOR -DCLASS_PseudoColor_8=33
-DCLASS_DirectColor_8=34
```

If you are using **xdpyinfo**, check the loaded extensions list. For example:

```
# xdpyinfo | pg
```

```
.
.
number of extensions: 8
XInputExtension
xDirectAccessExtension
XAixExtension
aixCursorExtension
xColormapExtension
XTestExtension1
SHAPE
SCREEN-SAVER
.
```

Some APIs may require that extensions to the X server are loaded before running an application.

Check your API below and verify that the extension is loaded:

- OpenGL
  - abx (xAncillaryBufferExtension)
  - mbx (Multi-Buffering)
  - GLX (GLX)
- graPHIGS
  - xgpshm (GP-MIT-SHM)
- PEX
  - mbx (Multi-Buffering)
  - pex (X3D-PEX)

8.6 CDE problem determination

CDE is the default graphic interface on AIX 5L.

8.6.1 CDE log files

If you run into a problem with CDE, the first place you should look is the log files:

- /var/dt/Xerrors
- $HOME/.dt/startlog
- $HOME/.dt/errorlog
- /tmp/xlogfile

/var/dt/Xerrors contains errors that occur when the Login Server is started. The location of this log file can be changed using the Dtlogin.errorLogFile resource in /usr/dt/config/Xconfig.

Session Manager logs problems with session startup in the $HOME/.dt/startlog file.

Various desktop applications log errors to $HOME/.dt/errorlog. For example, errors that occur when an action is loaded will be logged in $HOME/.dt/errorlog.

X logs errors to /tmp/xlogfile.

It is important that you look at these log files to diagnose problems. We list common problems you may meet and their solutions.

8.6.2 Login screen does not appear

This can happen when customizations to the X servers file were made, but the command does not execute properly.

Check the log files and confirm that X or xinit will start. If X or xinit will not start, go to Section 8.3.1, “Start X server” on page 270.

Next, look for /etc/dt/config/Xservers and see if it was customized. If it was, verify that the command will execute from an low function terminal (LFT). If not, look for customizations made directly to /usr/dt/config/Xservers. Customizations of the /usr/dt files are discouraged because they may be overwritten at the next upgrade of CDE. The default /usr/dt/config/Xservers file contains the following line:

```
:0 Local local@console /usr/lpp/X11/defaults/xserverrc -T -force :0
```

To start the X server, the Login Manager then executes:

```
/usr/lpp/X11/defaults/xserverrc -T -force :0
```

The **xserverrc** executable is a shell script, so customizations to the start of X could be made directly to the xserverrc file. If no changes to either of the Xservers files are detected, then check to make sure the /usr/lpp/X11/defaults/xserverrc file is executable by all users. File mode 755 is recommended. Also, you can run the script manually to see if there are errors in the script:

```
ksh -x /usr/lpp/X11/defaults/xserverrc -T -force :0
```

8.6.3 Problem with login

The first step here is to check the log files for information. If you cannot get enough information from log files, you may try to run Login Manager in debug mode. If the problem is on the console, start dtlogin remotely:

```
/usr/dt/bin/dtlogin -debug 10|tee /tmp/<logfile>
```

If you have to run dtlogin in debug mode, you must first stop all current dtlogin processes. Be sure all CDE users are logged out before killing the dtlogin process, or you may cause your users to lose data.

If X terminates, then you must kill dtlogin, then issue the following command to restart the desktop:

```
dtlogin -daemon; exit
```

8.6.4 CDE hangs

Network interface parameters (such as the host name and IP address) of a machine should never be changed while CDE is running.

Always exit from the desktop and stop desktop processes to modify network interfaces. If CDE is not halted before something like the host name is changed, exit from CDE and see if you can run **smit mktcpip** to stop and restart the network connection. If this still fails, reboot the machine.

8.6.5 The DT messaging system could not be started

You may get this message in a dialog box when attempting to login to CDE:

```
The DT messaging system could not be started. Login using failsafe, check
hostname at these locations:
/etc/src.sh
/etc/hosts
/usr/adm/inetd.sec
```

AIX only uses the /etc/hosts file, but this message is generic for all of the CDE platforms, so do not be surprised to see files mentioned that do not exist.

The message may indicate:

- Host name changed while still running CDE.
- Multiple machines on the network have the same host name.
- If you do not use DNS, you may:
  - Set /etc/netsvc.conf to read /etc/hosts:

    ```
    hosts = local,bind,nis
    ```

   - Set /etc/hosts to recognize both the short name and the fully qualified name of your machine:

     ```
     9.3.187.211 itsosrv1.austin.ibm.com itsosrv1
     ```

   - Make sure **smit mktcpip** and **hostname** both show the same fully qualified name for your machine.

- If you update /etc/netsvc.conf and /etc/hosts, check your host name. If the problem still occurs, modify /etc/hosts by adding your host name as an alias to the loopback interface line and commenting out the original name to address mapping, as below:

  ```
  127.0.0.1 loopback localhost itsosrv1 # loopback (lo0)
  #9.3.187.211 itsosrv1.austin.ibm.com itsosrv1
  ```

  Then rename /etc/netsvc.conf to /etc/netsvc.conf.old and reboot the machine.

8.7 Client libraries

X releases contain two numbers: The version number indicating major protocol or standards revisions and a release number indicating minor changes.

8.7.1 X11R6

At the time of writing, the latest version is X11 Release 6, also known as X11R6. The latest release of OSF/MOTIF is V2.1 (based on X11R5). Major revisions of X are incompatible, but there is backward compatibility with minor releases within major revision categories. AIX 5L runs on X11R6 and Motif 2.1.

8.7.2 X11R6 enhancements

Compared to X11R5, X11R6 has a lot of enhancements. Refer to the *AIX Version 4.3 Differences Guide*, SG24-2014, for more details.

8.7.3 X11/Motif compatibility fileset

Users installing AIX 5L who are concerned about binary compatibility with prior versions of AIX Version 4 should install the compatibility filesets offered on the installation media.

These filesets offer commands, library versions, symbolic links, and other items that, when added to the system, make it look more like the old version system from an application point of view.

While some of these filesets increase disk requirements (substantially, in the case of the AIXwindows X11R3, X11R4, and X11R5 compatibility packages) and contain obsolete functions, the compatibility filesets increase portability in an environment with machines running mixed levels of AIX. Installing the compatibility filesets is highly recommended.

If you performed a migration installation, these filesets will already be installed.

The X11 and Motif compatibility filesets are shown in Table 8-1.

Table 8-1 X11 and Motif compatibility filesets

Fileset name	Description
X11.compat.lib.Motif10	Motif 1.0 Libraries Compatibility
X11.compat.lib.Motif114	Motif 1.1.4 Libraries Compatibility
X11.compat.lib.X11R3	X11R3 Libraries Compatibility
X11.compat.lib.X11R4	X11R4 Libraries Compatibility
X11.compat.lib.X11R5	X11R5 Libraries Compatibility

9

User applications troubleshooting

This chapter attempts to help you perform problem determination on user applications. We will concentrate on problems concerning the application or AIX system administrator, not application development, which means we will not discuss debugging of the program. The problems that can affect user applications are almost as varied and numerous as the applications themselves. There are a huge number of third party applications, including many Linux programs, for the AIX 5L platform from many different vendors. In addition, some systems are running inhouse applications, developed by the user of a system to perform a customized task.This chapter cannot detail every single problem with every application but, instead, will mention some of the most common problems that can be encountered. As most users interact with applications, rather than the AIX operating system itself, when something goes wrong, it is most often first noticed because of strange behavior from an application.

In general, the causes of user application problems can be divided into three distinct categories:

- Problems with the application

  It may be that the problem is entirely within the user application. In this case, the AIX operating system is functioning correctly. The starting point is investigating the system and application log, usually in the /var file system. If you are a developer, you should debug with tools similar to adb or dbx, or the Integrated Development Environment's debugger. Refer to *AIX 5L Version 5.1 General Programming Concepts: Writing and Debugging Programs*, which can be found at:

  `http://publibn.boulder.ibm.com/cgi-bin/ds_form?lang=en_US&viewset=AIX`

- Problems with the system

  In some cases, there may be an underlying problem with the hardware or operating system that affects the application. Use error logs or crash the dump to determine the cause of the problem. (In AIX 5L, the **crash** command is dropped; use the **kdb** command instead, which is called the kernel debugger.)

- User error

  In some cases, a user may perceive a problem that does not exist, for example, when trying to get the application or AIX operating system to perform a task for which it is not designed.

We will assume that user error has been eliminated as one of the steps in the problem determination process so far. In other words, the user is having a problem doing something that was previously working correctly.

9.1 Problem determination approach

The basic approach that can be taken when looking at user application problems is as follows:

- Can you start the application?
- Are you starting the correct application?
- Is the application configured correctly?
- Does the user running the application have the correct permissions?
- Does the system have enough free resources?
- Are any other processes that are required, such as background daemons, already running?

9.2 Application startup problems

The reasons for the failure of an application to start are many and varied. Some of the most common problems are listed here and should be investigated as part of the problem determination process.

9.2.1 PATH problems

There are three methods by which a user normally starts an application from a shell. The first is to use an absolute path name to specify the executable or shell script to run. For example:

```
# /usr/bin/ls
```

The second is to use a relative path to invoke the application. For example:

```
# ../../bin/ls
```

The third is to just enter or use the name of the application. In this case, the users command shell will search the list of directories specified in the PATH environment variable for the named application. If it finds an executable that matches, it will invoke it.

9.2.2 Permissions problems

All of the three methods described above will only work if the user invoking the command has the appropriate permissions. In each case, the user must have execute permission for the application itself and all directories on the path specified to the application. If the application is a shell script, the user must also have read permission for the application itself.

9.2.3 Name conflict

Depending on how your system is configured, you may have multiple versions of the same user application command. To determine which application will be started when you use the PATH environment variable, use the **whence** shell command. For example:

```
# whence ls
/usr/bin/ls
```

This indicates that the shell has parsed the PATH environment variable, and the first instance of the **ls** command that it can execute is /usr/bin/ls. Make sure you are starting the correct application.

You can search for any other instances of an application with the same name by using the **find** command. For example:

```
# find / -name ls -type f -print
/usr/bin/ls
```

> **Note:** In AIX 5L, basic Linux commands are located in the /opt/freeware/bin directory to avoid conflicts with AIX binaries, and linked to /usr/linux/bin. If you want to run Linux commands, use the full path for the commands or put the directory /opt/freeware/bin in PATH variables. But do not set it prior to the /usr/bin, which is for normal AIX commands, because it may cause conflicts with or malfunctions in some AIX applications.

9.2.4 Library problems

Once you have determined that you are invoking the correct application, you need to make sure that it can actually start. In order to start, executables should be able to resolve all of their internal symbols. All executables need to resolve symbols from the kernel when they start. Also, the processes need to resolve symbols from one or more shared objects. You have symbol resolution problems if you get a message similar to either of the following:

```
exec(): 0509-036 Cannot load program clear because of the following errors:
        0509-022 Cannot load library libdbl.a[shr.o].
        0509-026 System error: A file or directory in the path name does not
exist.
```

or

```
exec(): 0509-036 Cannot load program myapp because of the following errors:
0509-023 Symbol _XmStrings in ksh is not defined.
0509-023 Symbol XmStringLtoRCreate in ksh is not defined.
0509-026 System error: Cannot run a file that does not have a valid form
```

To determine which shared objects the executable will look for at invocation, use the **dump** command with the -H option, as shown in Example 9-1.

Example 9-1 Sample dump command output

```
# dump -H mcat

mcat:

                        ***Loader Section***
                      Loader Header Information
VERSION#          #SYMtableENT      #RELOCent         LENidSTR
0x00000001        0x00000071        0x000002a5        0x0000002e

#IMPfilID         OFFidSTR          LENstrTBL         OFFstrTBL
0x00000003        0x00002a74        0x000000a7        0x00002aa2


                        ***Import File Strings***
INDEX  PATH                          BASE                MEMBER
0      /usr/lib:/lib
1                                    libc.a              shr.o
2                                    libnsl.a            shr.o
```

This command prints the header section of the executable. The important part of the output is contained in the Import File Strings section at the end. The entry for index 0 shows the library search path that was used to compile the executable. This is the path that the system loader will use to search for the specified shared objects. This built-in path can be extended by the use of the LIBPATH environment variable. Similar in format to the PATH environment variable, it specifies the list of directories to be searched for shared objects when trying to start an executable.

Subsequent entries list the archive libraries and shared objects that the executable requires to be available at load time to complete the symbol resolution process.

If you get an error message similar to the one described above, you should check to see that the shared objects the executable will look for at start time exist in one of the directories specified in the built in library path.

Missing shared object

If you receive an error message stating that a particular library could not be loaded, for example:

```
exec(): 0509-036 Cannot load program clear because of the following errors:
        0509-022 Cannot load library libapp.a[shr1.o].
```

```
        0509-026 System error: A file or directory in the path name does not
exist.
```

Then there are a number of possible explanations for the problem. The first step for resolution is to determine if the archive library mentioned exists on the system. Take, for example, the output shown in Figure 9-1 on page 295. The first step is to search the system for the missing library. If the library exists, but it is not in one of the directories listed in the INDEX 0 entry, then you may need to set the LIBPATH environment variable to include the directory name. If the executable has the setuid bit enabled, then it will only look in directories listed in the INDEX 0 entry. It will ignore the LIBPATH environment variable. In this case, you should either copy the library to one of the directories listed in the INDEX 0 entry, or create a symbolic link.

If you find the library, you should check that it contains the particular shared object that the executable requires. This can be done with the **ar** command. For example:

```
# ar t libapp.a | grep shr1.o
shr1.o
```

You can find what the library archive contains using the following command:

```
# ar -tv <libname.a>
```

If you can find the library on the system, you should check that the user invoking the executable has read permission on the library.

If you cannot find the library on the system, then you may need to reinstall the user application or install additional AIX components to solve the problem.

> **Note:** For GNU software, we can use the libtool. The **libtool** command is a GNU software package which helps develop and maintain shared libraries. It simplifies the use of shared libraries by hiding the complexity. The tool is fully integrated with the GNU autoconf and automake utilities.

9.2.5 Licensing and environment problems

This section covers licensing and environment problems.

Licensing problems

Many applications use a licensing system to control their usage. Ensure that you have an appropriate number of application licenses for the machine in question.

If the application uses a nodelock license, ensure that the user invoking the application has permission to read the nodelock license file. If the system is using the LUM license system, the nodelock file is /var/ifor/nodelock.

To configure a LUM nodelock server, run:

```
#/var/ifor/i4cfg -a n -S a
#/var/ifor/i4cfg -start
```

The first command configures the local machine as a nodelock license server and sets the option that the LUM daemons should be automatically started when the system boots. The second command starts the LUM daemons. To check the license daemon running, run the following command:

```
#/var/ifor/i4cfg -list
```

If you did not add the license to the LUM server, enroll the product license as follows:

```
#/var/ifor/i4blt
```

and follow the LUM manual at the site:

```
ftp://ftp.software.ibm.com/software/lum/aix/doc/V4.6.0/lumusg.pdf
```

Ensure that the system date and time configuration is accurate. Sometimes, the system date and time can drift, or become out of date, if the system lithium battery fails. The correct system date and time can be significant if a remote license server is being used.

Environment problems

You should ensure that the user starting the application is doing so from the correct environment. Many applications require particular environment variables to be configured before working correctly. Check that any configuration scripts run by the user at login time are present and contain the correct information. The main AIX files to check are /etc/profile, /etc/environment, and the $HOME/.profile of the individual user. Depending on the application, there may be many more configuration files.

9.2.6 Binary compatibility and Linux application affinity

The AIX operating system provides upwards binary compatibility between releases. That is, an executable produced on a particular version of AIX will also work on subsequent versions of AIX, providing some other criteria are met.

AIX 5L Version 5.1 binary compatibility: 32-bit applications from AIX Version 4 releases

AIX Version 4.1, 4.2, or 4.3 applications written for RS/6000 POWER-, POWER2-, POWER3-, and PowerPC-based models can be executed on AIX 5L Version 5.1, without recompilation, for the same and newer models in that processor family (POWER, POWER2, POWER3, or PowerPC). The exceptions to this statement would be:

- Applications compiled using POWER2, POWER3, or PowerPC specific compiler options but executed on models other than POWER2, POWER3, or PowerPC, respectively.
- Applications using non-shared compiles of AIX shared libraries.
- Applications using features explicitly described as non-portable by IBM in the AIX Version 4 or 5L reference manuals.
- Applications using undocumented AIX internal features.
- X11R5 Server Extensions Applications compiled on AIX Version 5.1 will not operate properly on systems running any level of AIX Version 4.

Any program that must run in all environments (POWER, POWER2, POWER3, and PowerPC (601 and newer PowerPC processors)) must be compiled using the common mode option of the compiler. Programs compiled to exploit POWER2 or POWER3 technology must be run on the same processor type. Programs compiled to exploit PowerPC-based technology must be run on PowerPC-based processors. Existing binaries need not be recompiled to operate on the target processors.

AIX 5L Version 5.1 binary compatibility: 64-bit applications from AIX Version 4 releases

64-bit applications produced using AIX Version 4 will not execute on AIX 5L Version 5.1. These applications will need to be recompiled from the source on AIX 5L Version 5.1 to execute on this version of AIX. 64-bit applications produced using AIX 5L Version 5 on any of the 32-bit or 64-bit processor models will execute without recompilation on the 64-bit processor models. 32-bit applications produced using AIX 5L Version 5 on either 32-bit or 64-bit processor models will execute without recompilation on both models.

X11R5/X11R6 compatibility issues on AIX 5L Version 5.1

The AIX 5L Version 5.1 X-server uses the X-Consortium release 6 of X (commonly known as X11R6). The libraries shipped by IBM with X11R6 are backward compatible and the client applications that access these libraries work as on AIX Version 4. As on AIX Version 4, IBM will also ship X11R3, X11R4, and X11R5 compatibility installation options for maximum customer flexibility.

The broad majority of applications using X fall into this category and will not see any difficulty. However, a small minority of X-applications use the loadable extension facility provided by the X-server.

The X-server allows for the addition of new functionality through its extension mechanism. For each extension, part of the extension is loaded into the X-server before it can be executed. X11R6 has modified how this mechanism works in the course of improvements to X, and it is this part of the extension that must be made compatible with X11R6 to execute properly. All extensions supplied by IBM have been made compatible. In some circumstances, a customer may have an extension which will not work with X11R6, for example, a customer:

- Has a sample extension downloaded from the X-Consortium ftp site
- Develops his own extension
- Uses a third-party extension

In these cases, the extensions will need to be made compatible with X11R6 before they will execute properly. Customer-developed extensions and sample X-consortium extensions will need to be recompiled with the X11R6 environment. For third-party extensions, the customer should contact the vendor for a X11R6 compatible update.

Customers using non-IBM display adapters may also be using vendor-supplied software specific to those devices that uses X11R6 Server capabilities. If so, this software must be compatible with X11R6 to operate properly. The customer should contact the particular vendor of the display adapter for this software.

IBM provides the *AIX 5L Porting Guide* with AIX 5L Version 5.1 to assist customers and vendors developing adapters or extensions for AIX.

Between AIX Versions 3 and 5L Version 5.1

All AIX applications using AIX Version 3 Release 3.2 or greater for POWER-, POWER2-, and PowerPC-based models that are written in accordance with the guidelines in this announcement and other AIX announcements will run on AIX 5L Version 5.1 without recompilation for those same models. The exceptions to this statement would be applications compiled using POWER2 or PowerPC specific compiler options but run on models other than POWER2 or PowerPC or applications using:

- Their own loadable kernel extensions
- Certain High Function Terminal control interfaces
- X11R3 Input Device interfaces
- The CIO LAN device driver interface
- SCSI Device configuration methods (IHVs)

- The nlist() interface
- DCE threads

Applications created on a system using AIX 5L Version 5.1 may not function properly on a system using AIX Version 3. Applications must have been created using the AIX shared libraries for these binary compatibility statements to apply.

Linux application affinity

AIX affinity with Linux uses an Application Programming Interface (API) approach to provide Linux application interoperability. This approach is not an environment or an additional operating system layer of wrapper in which to run Linux applications. It is the integration of Linux compatible APIs and header files into AIX 5L Version 5.1 Thus, recompiled Linux applications are native AIX applications and have access to all the RAS abilities of AIX. Hence, we get a tighter integration of the application to the operating system than the one achieved with an Application Binary Interface (ABI) approach, such as another layer and wrapper method.

To make AIX more compatible with Linux applications, we must use two complementary methods: using the AIX Toolbox for Linux Applications, and including additional Linux-compatible APIs and commands in AIX 5L.

The AIX Toolbox for Linux Applications contains a collection of open source and GNU software built for AIX Version 4.3.3 and AIX 5L on IBM @server pSeries and RS/6000 systems. These tools provide the basis for the development environment of choice for many Linux application developers. All the tools are packaged using the easy-to-install RPM format. If you install the whole toolbox, at time of the writing of this redbook, you will need 400 - 500 MB hard disk capacity. If you are interested in learning more about Linux affinity, refer to the redbook *Running Linux Application on AIX*, SG24-6033.

For a complete and updated list of all the tools contained in the Toolbox and to check the availability of software for a specific platform, visit the following Web site:

`http://www.ibm.com/servers/aix/products/aixos/linux/index.html`

When you have a plan to port Linux application onto an Itanium™-based platform to POWER platform or vice versa, there are some possible problems:

- Endian problem

  Little-endian describes a computer architecture in which bytes at lower addresses have lower significance. The Itanium-based architecture uses little-endian. Big-endian describes a computer architecture in which the most significant byte has the lowest address. The POWER architecture uses big-endian.

Although both PowerPC and Itanium-based architectures support big-endian (BE) and little-endian (LE) implementations, the endianness of AIX 5L Version 5.1 running on Itanium-based systems and POWER systems is different. AIX 5L Version 5.1 for Itanium-based systems is little-endian, and AIX 5L Version 5.1 for Power systems is big-endian. In order for an application or a device driver to use the same source code base on both platforms, it must either be endian neutral, or use conditional compilation to select the appropriate code modules. A program module is considered endian neutral if it retains its functionality while being ported across platforms of different endianness. In other words, there is no relation between its functionality and the endianness of the platform it is running on.

Refer to Figure 9-1 for more information on this subject.

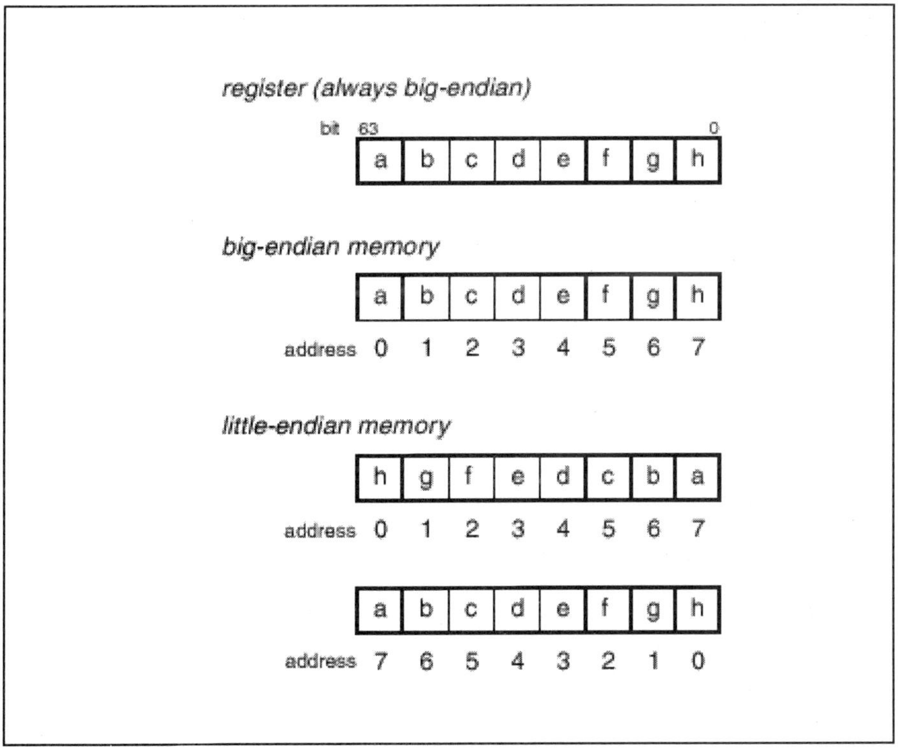

Figure 9-1 Endian diagram example

- POSIX compliant

  AIX is POSIX and UNIX98 compliant while Linux is not currently compliant. Coding applications that meet these standards will help ensure that applications can be ported to AIX

AIX Toolbox for Linux applications

The installation of the toolbox requires AIX Version 4.3.3 or newer. You can use either AIX 5L without additional PTFs or AIX Version 4.3.3 with fixes from APAR IY15017. You can download them from:

```
http://techsupport.services.ibm.com/rs6000/support
```

and then search for IY15017 in the APAR database. Follow the instructions for downloading and installing the fixes. You should also check for the latest available maintenance level at:

```
http://techsupport.services.ibm.com/server/support?view=pSeries
```

To separate the files belonging to the toolbox from the base operating system and other installed software, it is recommended that you create a new file system (/opt/freeware) at this time.

Installing the RPM package.

Run the following:

```
#installp -qacXgd rpm.rte rpm.rte (Install RPM Package Manager From AIX CD)
#export MANPATH=$MANPATH:/opt/freeware/man (to refer to the linux command man
page)
#rpm -ivh info-* gett* qzip* popt* rpm* tar* unzi* gcc* gdb* (Install the
packages you want from Toolbox CD or ftp downloaded packages)
#rpm -qa (verify the installation)
```

You might get the errors when installing RPM packages:

- `Out of Filesystem Space`

  This can happen because, unlike **installp**, RPM cannot automatically increase the size of a file system during the install. If we enlarge the file system and try to issue the same command again, it fails, because some of the RPMs to be installed are already installed. RPM does not attempt to install any of the packages. Unfortunately, the error messages do not explicitly say that the install failed, only which files are already installed. To deinstall the packages, you can use the command **rpm -e** or (preferably) execute the destroy RPMS script, which removes all RPMS installed on the system and is provided by the toolbox CD-ROM under the directory tools and Web site at:

  ```
  ftp://ftp.software.ibm.com/aix/freeSoftware/aixtoolbox/tools/destroyRPMS
  ```

- `Corrupt Package files`

  Another likely reason for an RPM install to fail is the presence of a corrupt package file. The **rpm -ivh** shows the initial (not very meaningful) error message that results from having a corrupt package file, and how to get more information about what caused the error by using **rpm -ivv** instead of **rpm -iv**. The important lines are the two which show differing package sizes.

GNUpro development environment

The GNUPro development environment images are now available as RPM installable packages. They contain the gcc compiler, gcc C++ compiler, gdb debugger and associated utilities, such as ar, nm, and readelf. For an installation of all images of the GNUPro Toolkit, we need 80 MB of disk space. The installation is performed by using the **rpm -ivh** command, as shown in the following:

```
# rpm -ivh gcc-2.9.aix43.010216-1.aix5.1.ppc.rpm
# rpm -ivh g++-2.9.aix43.010216-1.aix5.1.ppc.rpm
# rpm -ivh binutils-2.9.aix43.010216-1.aix5.1.ppc.rp
# rpm -ivh gdb-2.9.aix43.010216-1.aix5.1.ppc.rpm
```

Rebuilding and updating a package with RPM

First install the wget SRPM (this means the Source RPM to install source files instead of binaries) from the toolbox with the command:

```
# rpm -iv /cdrom/SRPMS/wget/wget-1.5.3-1.src.rpm
```

Now change to the directory /opt/freeware/src/packages/SPECS and rebuild the original wget package with the command:

```
# rpm -ba wget.spec (we use the b option for build and the a option for all)
```

This should generate the following RPMs:

- wget-1.5.3-1.src.rpm in /opt/freeware/src/packages/SRPMS/
- wget-1.5.3-1.aix4.3.ppc.rpm in /opt/free-ware/src/packages/RPMS/ppc/

Now, we want to update the source code of wget to a newer level. Instead of the Version 1.5.3 that is currently provided by the Toolbox, we want to use Version 1.6, which is available from the GNU FTP servers at:

```
ftp://prep.ai.mit.edu/pub/gnu/wget/
```

It is a simple process to get this new version. Just download the new software (archive wget-1.6.tar.gz) to /opt/freeware/src/packages/SOURCES and change the line:

```
%define version 1.5.3
```

in the wget.spec file to:

```
%define version 1.6
```

and rebuild by issuing the command:

```
# rpm -ba wget.spec
```

This should generate the following RPMs:

- wget-1.6-1.src.rpm in /opt/freeware/src/packages/SRPMS/
- wget-1.6-1.aix4.3.ppc.rpm in /opt/freeware/src/packages/RPMS/ppc/

The new version can now be installed with one of these commands:

```
# rpm -Uv /opt/freeware/src/packages/RPMS/ppc/wget-1.6-1.aix4.3.ppc.rp
# rpm -Fv /opt/freeware/src/packages/RPMS/ppc/wget-1.6-1.aix4.3.ppc.rp
```

using the option -Uv for upgrade and -Fv for freshen.

> **Note:** If large packages are to be built, the /var file system should have enough free space. Because rpm temporarily uses RPM_BUILD_ROOT, which is located in the /var, we recommend having 150 MB available.

9.3 Application resource monitoring

When an application is extremely resource intensive, more and more the resources of system are quickly exhausted. This section covers application resource problems on the whole. This topic is more of a performance topic, but it is worth mentioning as a troubleshooting method. We do not mention specific details.

9.3.1 Resource problems

You may run into resource limits when trying to run an application. There are two types of resource limits that can be encountered. You may encounter system resource limits, where the resources of the system itself become exhausted by an application. The main system resources that can become exhausted are CPU, memory, and disk space.

If an application makes large memory requests, then the system may eventually run out of paging space. If this condition occurs, then an entry is made in the error log recording the problem. If the condition continues, the system will eventually start terminating processes in an attempt to alleviate the situation.

The system monitors the number of free paging-space blocks and detects when a paging-space shortage exists. When the number of free paging-space blocks falls below a threshold, known as the paging-space warning level, the system informs all processes, except kernel processes (kprocs), of this condition by sending the SIGDANGER signal. If the shortage continues and falls below a second threshold known as the paging-space terminate level, the system sends the SIGKILL signal to processes that are the major users of paging space and that do not have a signal handler for the SIGDANGER signal.

The other system resource that can become quickly exhausted is disk space. If an application produces output to files, then it may eventually cause a file system to become full.

In addition to experiencing system resource problems, the user invoking the application may have restricted access to the system resources. For example, the user may have a disk quota on a particular file system that, if exceeded, may cause an application to terminate. In this case, it is not the system resource that has become exhausted, but an user allowed usage of the system resource.

As with disk space, a user's memory usage can be restricted. There are many different uses for system memory, and each type of usage can be controlled on an individual basis with the **ulimit** command. Depending on the version of AIX you are running, you may see a different output from the **ulimit -a** command, which lists the resources that can be controlled, and the limits for the current user. For example:

```
# ulimit -a
time(seconds)         unlimited
file(blocks)          2097151
data(kbytes)          131072
stack(kbytes)         32768
memory(kbytes)        32768
coredump(blocks)      2097151
nofiles(descriptors)  2000
```

The main limits that can have an impact on the normal running of an application are file, data, stack, memory, and nofiles. Exceeding any of these limits may cause an application to terminate abnormally. The hard limits for each parameter can be set on a per-user basis by the root user and are stored in the configuration file /etc/security/limits.

If you suspect a resource problem of this nature, try changing the **ulimit** values for the user to unlimited, indicated with the value `-1`, and retrying the application.

Finding memory-leaking programs

A *memory leak* is a program error that consists of repeatedly allocating memory, using it, and then neglecting to free it. A memory leak in a long-running program, such as an interactive application, is a serious problem, because it can result in memory fragmentation and the accumulation of large numbers of mostly garbage-filled pages in real memory and page space. Systems have been known to run out of page space because of a memory leak in a single program.

A memory leak can be detected with the **svmon** command, by looking for processes whose working segment continually grows. A leak in a kernel segment can be caused by an mbuf leak or by a device driver, kernel extension, or even the kernel. To determine if a segment is growing, use the **svmon** command with the -i option to look at a process or a group of processes and see if any segment continues to grow.

Identifying the offending subroutine or line of code is more difficult, especially in AIXwindows applications, which generate large numbers of malloc() and free() calls. C++ provides a HeapView Debugger for analyzing/tuning memory usage and leaks. Some third-party programs exist for analyzing memory leaks, but they require access to the program source code.

Some uses of the realloc() subroutine, while not actually programming errors, can have the same effect as a memory leak. If a program frequently uses the realloc() subroutine to increase the size of a data area, the working segment of the process can become increasingly fragmented if the storage released by the realloc() subroutine cannot be reused for anything else.

Use the disclaim() system call and free() call to release memory that is no longer required. The disclaim() system call must be called before the free() call. It wastes CPU time to free memory after the last malloc() call, if the program will finish soon. When the program terminates, its working segment is destroyed and the real memory page frames that contained working segment data are added to the free list.

The following **svmon** command will show the memory usage of processes:

```
# svmon -P 43622 -i 1 3
Pid Command          Inuse      Pin     Pgsp  Virtual   64-bit    Mthrd
   43622 myprog 3951      1585      2340    10109          N          N

    Vsid      Esid Type Description                        Inuse   Pin Pgsp Virtual
       0         0 work kernel seg                          2659  1583 2275   4726
   1c01c         d work shared library text                 1132     0   65   5283
    a16b         2 work process private                       77     2    0     77
    50a5         1 pers code,/dev/hd2:6244                    57     0    -      -
   13052         f work shared library data                   23     0    0     23
    9069         - pers /dev/hd2:21013                         2     0    -      -
```

```
2183          - pers /dev/hd4:492                        1    0    -    -
```

9.3.2 Resource Monitoring Control

In AIX 5L Version 5.1, a new Resource Monitoring and Control (RMC) subsystem is available that originated as the Reliable Scalable Cluster Technology (RSCT) on the IBM SP platform. This subsystem allows you to associate predefined responses with predefined conditions for monitoring system resources. This tool is useful for resource problem determination.

The Monitoring application offers a comprehensive set of monitoring and response capabilities that let you detect, and in many cases correct, system resource problems, such as a critical file system becoming full. You can monitor virtually all aspects of your system resources and specify a wide range of actions to be taken when a problem occurs, from simple notification by e-mail to recovery that runs a user-written script. You can specify a multiple number of actions to be taken in response to an event.

As a system administrator, you have a great deal of flexibility in responding to events. You can respond to an event in different ways based on the day of the week and time of day. The following are some examples of how you can use monitoring:

- You can be alerted by e-mail if /tmp is unmounted during working hours, but you can have the problem logged if /tmp is unmounted during nonworking hours.
- You can be notified by e-mail when /var is 80 percent full.
- You can run a user-written script automatically when an application program, such as a communication daemon inetd failed.
- You can be informed when available system memory is too low.

The major components of RSCT Resource Monitoring and Control are the Resource Monitoring and Control (RMC) subsystems and certain resource managers. These are described in the following sections.

A *resource manager* is a stand-alone daemon. The resource manager contains definitions of all resource classes that the resource manager supports. A *resource class* includes a description of all attributes, actions, and other characteristics of a resource class.

These resource classes are accessible and their properties can be manipulated by the user through the Web-based System Manager or through the command line. At the time of writing, SMIT is not supported.

The following resource managers are provided:

- Audit Log resource manager (IBM.AuditRM):Provides a system-wide facility for recording information about the system's operation, which is particularly useful for tracking subsystems running in the background.
- Event Response resource manager (IBM.ERRM):Provides the ability to take actions in response to conditions occurring on the system.
- File System resource manager (IBM.FSRM):Monitors file systems.
- Host resource manager (IBM.HostRM):Monitors resources related to an individual machine. The types of values that are provided relate to load (processes, paging space, and memory usage) and status of the operating system. It also monitors program activity from initiation until termination.

Among the above lists, FSRM and HostRM will be one of the choices for monitoring in case resource problems occurred.

The basic function of RMC is based on two keywords: *conditions* and *responses*. To provide you a ready-to-use system, 84 conditions and eight responses are predefined for you. You can use them as they are, customize them, or use them as templates to define your own conditions and responses. To monitor a condition, simply associate one or more responses with the condition.

A condition monitors a specific property, such as total percentage used, in a specific resource class, such as JFS. You can monitor the condition for one or more, or all the resources within the monitored property, such as /tmp, or /tmp and /var, or all the file systems. Each condition contains an event expression to define an event and an optional rearm expression to define a rearm event. When a condition is met, the associated event responds and monitored resources have returned to an acceptable state, then the rearm event runs. The event expression is a combination of the monitored property, mathematical operators, and some numbers, such as PercentTotUsed > 90 in the case of a file system. The rearm expression is a similar entity, for example, PercentTotUsed < 85.

If you want to monitor your program, use the IBM.Program resource class. This resource class can monitor a set of processes that are running a specific program or command whose attributes match a filter criterion. The filter criterion includes the real or effective user name of the process, arguments that the process was started with, and so on. The primary aspect of a program resource that can be monitored is the set of processes that meet the program definition. A client can be informed when processes with the properties that meet the program definition are initiated and when they are terminated. This resource class typically is used to detect when a required subsystem fails so that recovery actions can be performed, or the administrator can be notified, or both.

All the executables and related items are installed into the /usr/sbin/rsct directory, while the log files and other temporary data are located in /var/ct. In /etc/inittab file, the RMC subsystem ID is ctrmc. There is another method to invoke RMC subsystem; use the **/usr/sbin/rsct/bin/rmcctrl** command with the proper option.

To start the RMC subsystem, run:

```
# /usr/sbin/rsct/bin/rmcctrl -s
0513-059 The ctrmc Subsystem has been started. Subsystem PID is 257
```

Here is an example for the application monitoring named Myapp. If Myapp is down, the system broadcasts and sends a mail to root.

First, make a condition on the resource class IBM.Program. In this example, the condition name is `Myapp Program is down`.

```
# mkcondition -r IBM.Program -e "Processes.CurPidCount<=0" -E
"Processes.CurPidCount>1" -s 'ProgramName=="Myapp"' "Myapp Program is down"
```

The ProgramName is the same real process name that we find out by using **ps lx** or **ps -o comm**. Note that the program name displayed by **ps** when the -f flag or -o args is specified may not be the same as the base name of the file containing the program, and Processes must have a minimum duration (approximately 15 seconds) to be monitored by the IBM.Program resource class. If a program runs for only a few seconds, all processes that run the program may not be detected.

We trigger two responses to the condition that Myapp is down:

```
# mkcondresp "Myapp Program is down" "Critical notifications" "E-mail root
anytime"
```

At present, the condition we made is not monitored:

```
# lscondition | grep Myapp
"Myapp Program is down"          "Not monitored
```

Turn the condition on by running the **startcondresp** command:

```
# startcondresp "Myapp Program is down" "Critical notifications" "E-mail root
anytime"
```

Then intentionally kill the program Myapp, just for testing:

```
# lscondresp "Myapp Program is down"
Displaying condition with response information:

condition-response link 1:
        Condition = "Myapp Program is down"
        Response  = "E-mail root anytime"
```

```
        State     = "Active"

condition-response link 2:
        Condition = "Myapp Program is down"
        Response  = "Critical notifications"
        State     = "Active"
```

You may see following messages on the screen and get the mail:

```
Broadcast message from root@unix (tty) at 19:57:04 ...

Informational Event occurred for Condition Myapp Program is down on the
resource ProgramName == 'Myapp' of the resource class Program at Friday
08/31/01 19:57:0
```

For further information, use the *Resource Monitoring and Control Guide and Command Reference*, found at:

http://publibn.boulder.ibm.com/cgi-bin/ds_form?lang=en_US&viewset=AIX

9.4 System hang detection

System hang management allows users to run mission critical applications continuously while improving application availability. System hang detection alerts the system administrator of possible problems and then allows the administrator to log in as root or to reboot the system to resolve the problem.

It relies on a new daemon named shdaemon, which runs at the highest priority (0 priority) and a corresponding configuration program named shconf.

The system hang detection alerts the administrator and allows the system to perform several actions when a hang is suspected.

A hang is defined as a situation where no process at or below the threshold priority has been scheduled during the specified timeout. For example, the default value of the `Action log an error in error log` is a 60 priority level and two minutes of timeout. If there are no running or ran processes of lower priority than 60 during two minutes, then shdaemon will log the following error to the error log file:

```
A HANG PRIORITY PROBLEM IS DETECTED.
```

You can set the priority level lower and timeout for fast detection. (In AIX 5L Version 5.1, the priority level has the range of 1-255, in which a greater number means a lower priority. The shdaemon has the highest priority level, namely 0.)

At this point, the possible actions are:

1. Log the error in the Error Logging file
2. Display a warning on a console with or without reboot
3. Start an interactive command interpreter
4. Execute a shell script.

The user is able to program a priority level and a time-out detection value (in minutes) that is associated with these actions.

> **Note:** Once an action has been launched due to a hang, the same action cannot be launched for the same type of hang as long as this action is in progress or the hang has not been recovered.

The user can specify the five actions described below and can specify the priority level to check (the timeout while no process or thread executes at a lower or equal priority) the terminal device for the warning action and the getty action:

- Log an error in the errlog file.
- Display a warning message on the system console (alphanumeric console) or on a specified TTY.
- Reboot the system.
- Give a special getty to allow the user to log in as root and launch commands.
- Launch a command.

There are two ways to configure system hang detection.

9.4.1 Option 1: Using SMIT

The SMIT method is shown in Example 9-2.

The fast path for this menu is **smit shd**.

Example 9-2 SMIT system hang detection configuration.

```
      Change/Show Characteristics of Priority Problem Detection

Type or select values in entry fields.
Press Enter AFTER making all desired changes.

                                                        [Entry Fields]
  Enable Process Priority Problem                      enable                +
  Log Error in the Error Logging                       disable               +
    Detection Time-out                                [2] #
    Process Priority                                  [60] #
  Display a warning message on a console               disable               +
```

```
    Detection Time-out                                [2] #
    Process Priority                                  [60] #
    Terminal Device                                   [/dev/console]
  Launch a recovering login on a console              enable           +
    Detection Time-out                                [2] #
    Process Priority                                  [56] #
    Terminal Device                                   [/dev/tty0]
  Launch a command                                    disable          +
    Detection Time-out                                [2] #
    Process Priority                                  [60] #
    Script                                            [/]
  Automatically REBOOT system                         disable          +
    Detection Time-out                                [5] #
    Process Priority                                  [39] #

F1=Help             F2=Refresh          F3=Cancel           F4=List
F5=Reset            F6=Command          F7=Edit             F8=Image
F9=Shell            F10=Exit            Enter=Do
```

The first entry enables the shd daemon, and the other entries present the five actions that have their timeout and priority, respectively. Furthermore, there is a terminal device and script to run during the time of system hang.

9.4.2 Option 2: Using the command line interface

To configure the system hang detection, use the **shconf** command. The usable flags are:

```
shconf [ -d ] [ -R |-D [ -O] | -E [ -O ] | [ [ -a Attribute ] ...] -l prio
[ -H ]
```

The only existing detection name is *prio*, which means that the system hang daemon will always compare the priorities of all running processes to a set threshold, and will take one of the five supported actions, each of a different priority, when the entire system fails to run a process below the specified priority any time in the timeout period.

- The -d flag displays the current status of the shdaemon.
- The -R flag restores the system default values.
- The -D and -E flags display either the default or the effective values of the configuration parameters.
- The -H flag adds an optional header to this output.
- The -O flag, together with either the -D or -E flags (in this case, the -H flag is not allowed), allow you to request a more concise output. It displays two lines:

one with the colon-separated names, and one with the colon-separated values of the configuration parameters.

- The -a flag, and a name/value pair, allows you to change the parameter values.

After installing of AIX 5L Version 5.1, the output of the **shconf** command appears as follows:

```
# shconf -d
sh_pp=disable
# shconf -E -l prio -H
attribute  value        description

sh_pp      disable      Enable Process Priority Problem
pp_errlog  disable      Log Error in the Error Logging
pp_eto     2            Detection Time-out
pp_eprio   60           Process Priority
pp_warning disable      Display a warning message on a console
pp_wto     2            Detection Time-out
pp_wprio   60           Process Priority
pp_wterm   /dev/console Terminal Device
pp_login   enable       Launch a recovering login on a console
pp_lto     2            Detection Time-out
pp_lprio   56           Process Priority
pp_lterm   /dev/tty0    Terminal Device
pp_cmd     disable      Launch a command
pp_cto     2            Detection Time-out
pp_cprio   60           Process Priority
pp_cpath   /            Script
pp_reboot  disable      Automatically REBOOT system
pp_rto     5            Detection Time-out
pp_rprio   39           Process Priority
```

The ss_pp parameter determines the availability of the system hang detection feature. Enabling it with the default configuration may generate the following error:

```
# shconf -l prio -a sh_pp=enable
1735-033 shconf: Unable to configure the emergency login.
1735-022 shconf: Configuration method error.
```

You have to disable the pp_login action, enable the system hang detection, and then configure the desired actions. The output of these commands appears as follows:

```
# shconf -l prio -a sh_pp=disable
1735-023 shconf: Priority Problem Conf has changed.

# shconf -l prio -a pp_login=disable
```

```
1735-023 shconf: Priority Problem Conf has changed.

# shconf -l prio -a sh_pp=enable
1735-023 shconf: Priority Problem Conf has changed.
1735-023 shconf: WARNING: Priority Problem Detection is enabled with all
actions disabled.

# shconf -l prio -a pp_errlog=enable
1735-023 shconf: Priority Problem Conf has changed.
```

10

Performance problems

This chapter describes what to do if you suspect a performance problem. The causes of performance problems can generally be divided into three types:

- Resource constraint problems

  A resource constraint problem arises when the applications running on a system try to consume more resources than are available. The three resources that can become exhausted are:

  - CPU
  - Memory
  - I/O (Disk and network)

- Software problems

  A performance problem can be caused by an underlying problem with the application or operating system. The problems can be one of two types:

  - Incorrect configuration

    This is where the application or operating system is functioning correctly as configured, but the configuration is inappropriate for the system. Generally, this tends to lead to a resource constraint problem.

  - Software bug

    This is where the application or operating system does not function as it should.

- Hardware problems

  Problems with hardware devices can cause a degradation in application and system performance.

Most common performance problems are caused by resource constraints. The first step in examining a potential performance problem is to monitor the resources in use by the system. If you can determine that there is no resource constraint, then you should perform hardware diagnostics to determine if you have a hardware problem that is affecting system performance. Refer to Chapter 5, “Hardware problem determination” on page 115 for more information.

If, after checking the system resources and hardware, you still have a problem, then you will need to collect some data before reporting the problem to IBM.

10.1 Performance bottlenecks

A performance bottleneck is the slowest component in a computer environment. This can either be a system resource, such as CPU, memory, or disk, or it could be the network. There is always a bottleneck, because some resource will always be the slowest. The question is whether this bottleneck is a problem on a daily basis.

The sequence of measuring system performance is extremely important. You should always follow the specified path, which is: CPU, Memory, I/O, and Network (see Figure 10-1).

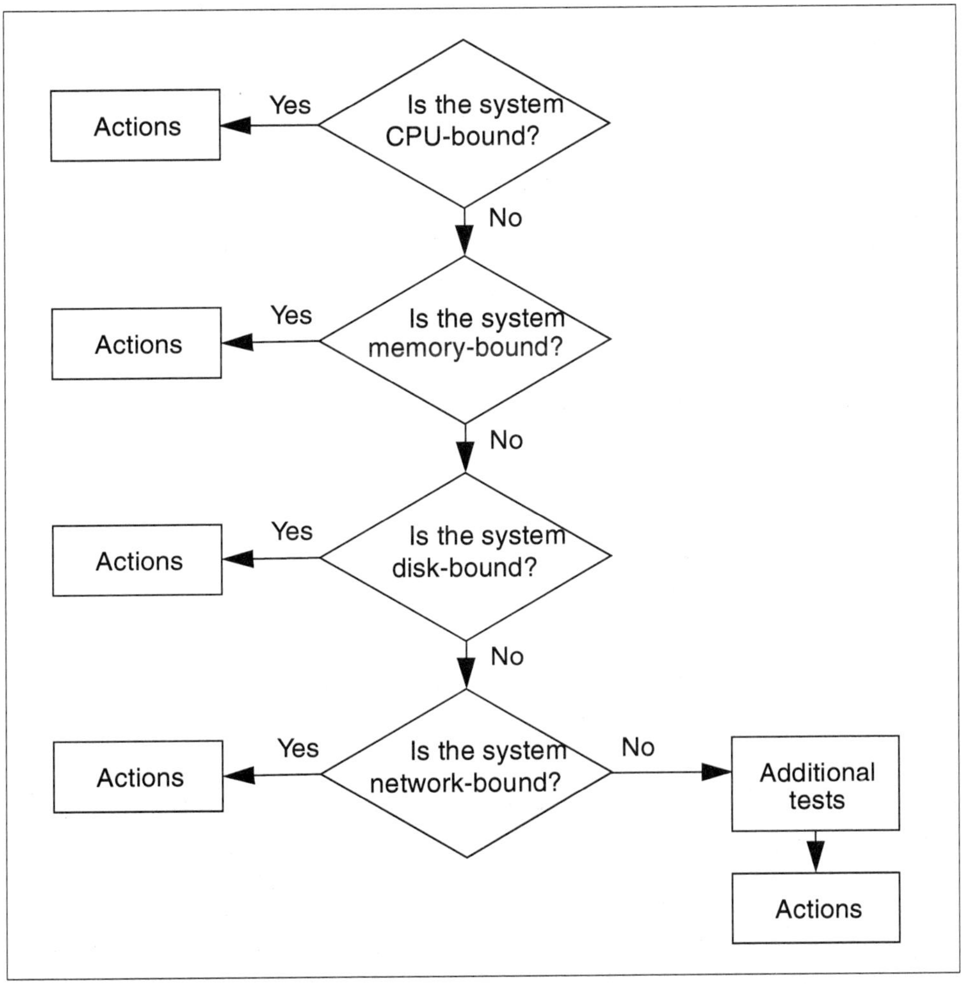

Figure 10-1 Bottleneck determining process

10.2 Monitoring performance

Due to the heritage of UNIX, AIX provides many tools for monitoring CPU, memory performance usage, and disk usage. If the system appears to be having performance problems, you must identify the bottleneck. Monitoring tools can also be used to detect cases where you are not aware of a problem. Making changes could result in overall better system performance. However, sometimes it could degrade the system performance. Therefore, changing should be carefully done over a long period of time.

In this section, we describe some monitoring tools, how they work, and what they mean.

Before using some commands, you need to install the performance agent package named perfagent.tools and the base accounting package named bos.acct. Use the following commands to check whether these filesets are installed:

```
# lslpp -h perfagent.tools
# lslpp -h bos.perf.perfstat
# lslpp -h bos.acct
# lslpp -h bos.sysmgt.trace
```

In AIX 5L Version 5.1, the base performance tools are repackaged and moved from the perfagent.tools to the bos.perf.tools fileset. You can use the following command to check this fileset:

```
# lslpp -h bos.perf.tools
  Fileset          Level     Action        Status        Date          Time
  ----------------------------------------------------------------------------
Path: /usr/lib/objrepos
  bos.perf.tools
                   5.1.0.0   COMMIT        COMPLETE      08/15/01      15:04:01
                   5.1.0.1   COMMIT        COMPLETE      09/04/01      17:16:07
```

10.2.1 Monitoring CPU

This section shows the CPU monitoring tools and how to interpret their output.

High CPU percentage for kproc processes

When you examine the output of the **ps** command and look at the CPU usage numbers in the column header %CPU, these figures are the percentage of CPU time consumed by that process since it was started. The CPU percentage reported for kproc processes may seem high. The kproc processes are part of the kernel and are started when the AIX system boots. Some kprocs are the idle processes that run when the system is idle. Since this process just indicates the idle time of the system, the high CPU percentage does not indicate a problem and no action is required. Depending on the number of CPUs and the exact software configuration of your system, you may see between two and thirty kproc processes.

The formula for computing the %CPU value is:

%CPU = CPUTime(pid) / (currentTime - startTime(pid)) * 100.0

This equation gives the true percentage of CPU that a process has consumed over its lifetime. On unburdened systems, kproc processes will use 50 percent or more of CPU. Since this computation is based on lifetime statistics, it will be slow to rise and slow to fall. In AIX 5L Version 5.1, the **ps** command can display a real name of the kernel process instead of "kproc" (see Example 10-1).

Example 10-1 Display the current status of processes

```
# ps ug | pg
USER          PID %CPU %MEM   SZ  RSS    TTY STAT    STIME  TIME COMMAND
root        16388 25.0  8.0   40 21092     - A       Aug 29 11992:23 wait
root        24582 25.0  8.0   40 21092     - A       Aug 29 11988:36 wait
root        40970 25.0  8.0   40 21092     - A       Aug 29 11987:12 wait
root        32776 25.0  8.0   40 21092     - A       Aug 29 11981:11 wait
root       417904  0.0  1.0 1664 1692      - A      Aug 29 21:30 dtgreet
root       106574  0.0  0.0  336  340      - A      Aug 29  0:52 /usr/sbin/syncd
root            0  0.0  8.0   52 21104     - A       Aug 29  0:50 swapper
root       426102  0.0  1.0 4156 3172      - A      Aug 29  0:47 /usr/lpp/X11/bin
root            1  0.0  0.0  868  880      - A      Aug 29  0:18 /etc/init
root        73746  0.0  8.0  112 21164     - A       Aug 29  0:16 gil
root        65552  0.0  8.0   48 21100     - A       Aug 29  0:04 netm
root       172090  0.0  1.0 1684 1784      - A      Aug 29  0:03 /usr/sbin/snmpd
root       196678  0.0  1.0 1988 1584      - A      Aug 29  0:02 sendmail: accept
root       327766  0.0  1.0 1592 1684      - A      Aug 29  0:01 /usr/sbin/rsct/b
```

Additionally, you should see that adding up the numbers in the %CPU column does not yield 100 percent. For example, process A may have been using 80 percent of the CPU for its first hour. Then process B is started at a higher priority and consumes 80 percent. Process A still runs, but now only gets 5 percent of the CPU slices. The %CPU, as shown by **ps ug**, will gradually decline for process A, starting from 80 percent and eventually leveling off near 5 percent. For a while, both process A and B will show %CPU of 80 percent.

Using the vmstat command

The **vmstat** command reports statistics about processes, virtual memory, paging activity, faults, CPU activity, and disk transfers. Options and parameters recognized by this tool are indicated by the usage prompt:

```
# vmstat [ -fsiIt ] [Drives] [ Interval [Count] ]
```

This command displays one line of output every five seconds. A sample output is shown is Example 10-2.

Example 10-2 Output of vmstat command

```
# vmstat 5
kthr     memory             page              faults        cpu
----- ----------- ------------------------ ------------ -----------
 r  b   avm   fre  re  pi  po  fr   sr  cy  in   sy  cs us sy id wa
 0  0 32426 211973  0   0   0   4   89   0 104  170  16  3  1 94  3
 0  0 32428 211966  0   0   0   0    0   0 429  634  65  0  0 99  0
 0  0 32429 211965  0   0   0   0    0   0 429  643  61  0  0 99  0
 1  1 33098 207955  0   2   0   0    0   0 608 1291 220 22  4 33 41
 1  1 33100 205000  0   0   0   0    0   0 620 1167 185 31  4 26 38
 0  2 33101 202345  0   3   0   0    0   0 619 1109 227 21  4 21 54
 1  1 33103 200509  0   0   0   0    0   0 648 1005 270 22  3 26 50
 0  2 33104 199460  0   0   0   0    0   0 691  891 337 16  2 26 55
 0  2 33105 197843  0   0   0   0    0   0 622  968 231 17  3 25 55
 0  2 33106 195751  0   0   0   0    0   0 605 1001 203 21  3 26 50
 1  1 33107 192793  0   0   0   0    0   0 587 1132 187 24  4 25 48
 1  1 33108 189109  0   0   0   0    0   0 579 1290 180 29  3 25 43
 1  1 33109 185135  0   0   0   0    0   0 577 1564 176 34  5 25 37
 2  0 33110 182504  0   0   0   0    0   0 531 2899 114 58  6 25 12
 3  0 33111 181553  0   3   0   0    0   0 484 2350  68 71  4 24  1
 3  0 33112 180034  0   0   0   0    0   0 505 2278  59 70  6 25  0
 2  0 32666 215430  0   2   0   0    0   0 493 1751  69 43  5 51  1
 0  0 32445 233677  0   2   0   0    0   0 433  676  67  1  1 97  0
 0  0 32446 233676  0   0   0   0    0   0 429  599  60  0  0 99  0
 0  0 32447 233672  0   0   0   0    0   0 431  592  62  0  0 99  0
```

Columns under kthr

The columns under the kthr heading in the output provide information about the average number of threads on various queues.

r
: The r column indicates the average number of kernel threads on the run queue at one-second intervals. This field indicated the number of runable threads. If each one executes for a complete or partial time slice, the number of runable threads could easily exceed 100.

b
: The b column shows the average number of kernel threads on the wait queue (blocked) at one-second intervals (awaiting resource, awaiting input/output).

Columns under cpu

You need to pay attention to the numbers under the cpu label (last four columns) for CPU statistics. These columns are:

us
: User CPU utilization percentage

sy System CPU utilization percentage

id Percentage CPU idle

wa I/O wait percentage

The sum of all four of these columns will equal 100 percent. If id (idle) is consistently zero, or user + system is greater than 80 percent, then the workload may be CPU bound.

If the wa (percent I/O wait) is non-zero, some of the workload may be I/O limited (in AIX 4.3.3 and later, this is also true for NFS-mounted disks). Refer to Section 10.2.3, "Monitoring I/O" on page 327. Also note the pi and po activity under page. Page in and page out activity can indicate thrashing.

The other columns under the memory, page, and faults headings will be described in Section 10.2.2, "Monitoring memory" on page 319.

Using the sar command

The **sar** command gathers statistical data about the system. The system maintains a series of system activity counters which record various activities and provide the data that the **sar** command reports. The **sar** command does not cause these counters to be updated or used; this is done automatically, regardless of whether or not the **sar** command runs. It merely extracts the data in the counters and saves it, based on the sampling rate and number of samples specified to the **sar** command. An example of the **sar** command is given in Example 10-3.

Example 10-3 Monitoring CPU Usage: sar command

```
# sar -u 1 5

AIX f50left 1 5 000321944C00     09/07/01

17:31:59    %usr    %sys    %wio   %idle
17:32:00       0       0       0     100
17:32:01      12       7       0      81
17:32:02      12       3       0      84
17:32:03       0       0       0     100
17:32:04       0       0       0     100

Average        5       2       0      93
```

The CPU usage report from **sar** is a good place to begin narrowing down whether a bottleneck is a CPU problem or an I/O problem.

The **sar** command reports either systemwide CPU statistics or statistics for each individual processor. This command is useful on SMP systems.

Useful flags

-P Proc ID, ... | ALL Reports per-processor statistics for the specified processors. By specifying the ALL keyword, statistics for each individual processor and an average for all processors is reported.

-c Shows the system call rate. If the fork/s column is high, then further investigation using the **trace** command is needed.

-q Shows the run-queue size and the swap-queue size.

An example output of the **sar** command with options is given in Example 10-4.

Example 10-4 The sar commands with options

```
# sar -P ALL 1 3

AIX f50left 1 5 000321944C00     09/07/01

22:03:19 cpu    %usr     %sys     %wio    %idle
22:03:20  0        1        2        0       97
          1        0       11        0       89
          2        1       23        0       76
          3       24       55       21        0
          -        7       23        6       64
22:03:21  0        0        2        0       98
          1        0        6        0       94
          2        1       33        0       66
          3       26       50       24        0
          -        7       23        6       64
22:03:22  0        8       14        9       70
          1        1       12        1       86
          2        0       23        0       77
          3       19       39       17       25
          -        7       22        7       65

Average   0        3        6        3       88
          1        0        9        0       90
          2        1       26        0       73
          3       23       48       21        8
          -        7       23        6       64
# sar -c 1 3

AIX f50left 1 5 000321944C00     09/07/01

22:03:30 scall/s sread/s swrit/s  fork/s  exec/s rchar/s wchar/s
22:03:31   67106   32880   32772    0.00    0.00 6184387 5723448
22:03:32   65437   32591   32592    0.00    0.00 5692669 5692730
22:03:33   65977   32721   32722    0.00    0.00 5715768 5715361
```

```
Average    66172   32730   32695    0.00    0.00 5863430 5710504
# sar -q 1 3

AIX f50left 1 5 000321944C00    09/07/01

22:03:38 runq-sz %runocc swpq-sz %swpocc
22:03:39     1.0      100
22:03:40     2.0      100
22:03:41

Average      1.5       62
```

Starvation

If the system appears to be having performance problems and responding very slowly, check for threads showing high CPU usage and high priority. These threads could be "starving" the CPU.

To see if you have that kind of threads, use the **ps -el** command, as shown in Example 10-5.

Example 10-5 Checking for threads showing high CPU usage

```
# ps -el | pg
       F S UID   PID  PPID   C PRI NI ADDR    SZ     WCHAN   TTY  TIME CMD
  200003 A   0     1     0   0  60 20 17037  812                -  0:00 init
   40001 A   0  3278     1   0  60 20 32a3   952                -  0:00 httpd
  240401 A   0  3390     1   0  60 20 130f3   80                -  0:00 ssa_daemon
  240001 A   0  3662  6456   0  60 20 31e3  1624                -  0:32 dtgreet
  240001 A   0  4464  4936   0  60 20 161b6 5120 30ffd910       -  0:05 X
   40001 A   0  4936     1   0  60 20 a1aa   420                -  0:00 dtlogin
  240001 A   0  5210     1   0  60 20 12212  328 30066fd8       -  0:27 syncd
  240001 A   0  5536  6740   0  60 20 b46b  3144 702cbc6c       -  0:03 i4lmd
  340001 A   0  5962  6740   0  60 20 6346  1568 ea0025a0       -  0:00 rmcd
  240001 A   0  6222  6740   0  60 20 19259  720                -  0:00 portmap
   40001 A   0  6456  4936   0  60 20 71c7   576 30d5bec0       -  0:00 dtlogin
  240001 A   0  6740     1   0  60 20 15055  684                -  0:00 srcmstr
....
       1 A   0 13680 18814 44 133 39 12bf2  140 30d5b02c pts/2  0:00 dd
  240001 A   0 13938     1  0  60 20 f30f   736 7007e844  lft0  0:00 getty
```

In the output of the **ps -el** command, look at the TIME column (total CPU used), the C column (processor utilization used for scheduling), and the PRI column (priority). To get real-time execution for a critical application, use the **nice** command. The application can run at a high fixed priority (low number). This is a trade-off decision to make, based on workload and priorities.

Emulation and alignment detection

In AIX 5L Version 5.1, new tools were added in the perfagent.tools fileset; in addition to the existing **emstat** command, **alstat** will count alignment interrupt, while **emstat** will display emulation statistic.

The **emstat** command works similarly to the **vmstat** command, in that you specify an interval time in seconds, and optionally, the number of intervals. For example:

```
# emstat 2 5

  Emulation  Emulation
  SinceBoot      Delta
    8845591          0
    8845591          0
    8845591          0
    8845591          0
    8845591          0
```

Once emulation has been detected, the next step is to determine which application is emulating instructions. One way is to run the **trace** command and analyze this trace output file and find the emulating application.

The **alstat** command displays alignment exception statistics. Alignment exceptions may occur when the processor cannot perform a memory access due to an unsupported memory alignment offset (such as a floating point double load from references may be corrected by some processors and does not generate an alignment exception):

```
# alstat 2 5

  Alignment  Alignment
  SinceBoot      Delta
    8845591          0
    8845591          0
    8845591          0
    8845591          0
    8845591          0
```

Monitoring CPU usage

Use the **time** command to understand the CPU usage of a particular program:

```
# time my_program
real 0m11.44s
user 0m0.04s
sys 0m0.03s
```

The **time** command shows the amount of real time (user-perceived clock time) and the amount of CPU time (user + sys) that a program consumes.

The difference between the real time that a program takes to finish and the CPU time it consumes can be explained by either other programs running and taking the CPU resource, or by I/O that the program has to wait for before it can continue.

10.2.2 Monitoring memory

When you monitor memory related resources, you need to know some of the following factors.

Real size of memory

Before using any other memory measuring tools, it is important to know how much memory you have. To check how much memory you have, use the following command:

```
# bootinfo -r
1048576
```

or

```
# lsattr -El sys0 -a realmem
realmem 1048576 Amount of usable physical memory in Kbytes False
```

The output displays the amount of usable physical memory in the system. Divide the answer by 1024 to get the answer in MB. The word `False` at the end of the line indicates that the attribute cannot be changed by the **chdev** command. Unfortunately, the only way to increase the value is to insert more memory.

Paging space

To see the usage of paging space, enter:

```
# lsps -s
```

The output will be similar to the following:

```
Total Paging Space   Percent Used
      512MB              12%
```

Rules for calculating paging space requirements

There is no right amount of paging space for a system. Paging space requirements are unique for each system, depending on the applications that are running, the number of active users, and other factors.

There are several general rules that can help determine how much paging space is needed:

- Rule 1

  For systems with less than 64 MB of RAM, the installation process creates paging space equal to two times (2X) the memory:

  ```
  Page space = 2 * RAM
  ```

  For systems with 64 MB to 256 MB of RAM, the following paging space equation applies:

  ```
  Page Space = RAM size + 16 MB
  ```

  For systems with more than 256 MB of RAM, use the following equation:

  ```
  Page Space = 512 + ( RAM - 256 ) * 1.25
  ```

- Rule 2

  Systems with large amounts of memory typically do not need such large amounts of paging space. In a persistent storage environment, in which the machine hosts a few small programs and a large amount of data, the system may need less than one times (1X) its RAM size for paging space. For example, a 1 GB database server that runs on an IBM @server pSeries or RS/6000 system with 256 MB of RAM and uses only 50 MB of working storage does not need 256 MB of paging space, or even 512 MB of paging space. It needs only the amount of paging space that allows all the working storage to be paged out to disk, because the 1 GB database is mostly persistent storage and requires little or no paging space.

  > **Note:** Starting with AIX Version 4.3.2 and Deferred Page Space Allocation, this guideline may tie up more disk space than actually necessary; refer to the *AIX 5L Version 5.1 Performance Manage Guide* or visit:
  >
  > http://publib.boulder.ibm.com/doc_link/en_US/a_doc_lib/aixbman/prftungd/2365c77.htm

- Rule 3

  If a disk drive containing an active paging space logical volume is removed from the system, the system will crash.

Considerations when creating or enlarging paging space

Do not put more than one paging space logical volume on a physical volume.

All processes started during the boot process are allocated paging space on the default paging space logical volume (hd6). After the additional paging space logical volumes are activated, paging space is allocated in a round robin manner in 4 KB chunks. If you have paging space on multiple physical volumes and put more than one paging space on one physical volume, you are no longer spreading paging activity over multiple physical volumes.

Avoid putting a paging space logical volume on the same physical volume as a heavily active logical volume, such as that used by a database.

It is not necessary to put a paging space logical volume on each physical volume.

Make each paging space logical volume roughly equal in size. If you have paging spaces of different sizes, and the smaller ones become full, you will no longer be spreading your paging activity across all of the physical volumes.

Do not extend a paging space logical volume onto multiple physical volumes. If a paging space logical volume is spread over multiple physical volumes, you will not be spreading paging activity across all the physical volumes. If you want to allocate space for paging on a physical volume that does not already have a paging space logical volume, create a new paging space logical volume on that physical volume.

For the best system performance, put paging space logical volumes on physical volumes that are each attached to a different disk controller.

Determining if more paging space is needed

Allocating more paging space than necessary results in unused paging space that is simply wasted disk space. But if you allocate too little paging space, a variety of unpleasant symptoms may occur on your system. To determine how much paging space is needed, use the following guidelines:

- Enlarge the paging space if any of the following messages appear on the console or in response to a command on any terminal:

  ```
  INIT: Paging space is low
  ksh: cannot fork no swap space
  Not enough memory
  Fork function failed
  fork () system call failed
  Unable to fork, too many processes
  Fork failure - not enough memory available
  Fork function not allowed. Not enough memory available.
  Cannot fork: Not enough space
  ```

- Enlarge paging space if the %Used column of the **lsps -s** output is greater than 80.

Use the following commands to determine if you need to make changes regarding paging space logical volumes:

```
#iostat
#vmstat
#lsps
```

If you wish to remove a paging space from the system, or reduce the size of a paging space, this should be performed in two steps. The first step in either case is to change the paging space so that it is no longer automatically used when the system starts. This is done with the **chps** command, for example:

```
# chps -a n paging00
```

Once this has been done, you need to reboot the system, since there is no way to dynamically bring a paging space offline. Once the system reboots, the paging space will not be active. At this point, you can remove the paging space logical volume.

If you wanted to reduce the size of the paging space, you should remove the logical volume, and then create the new paging space with the desired size. The new paging space can be created activated without having to reboot the machine using the **mkps** command.

> **Note:** In AIX 5L Version 5.1, a new command, **swapoff**, allows you to deactivate a paging space. The -d flag, for the **chps** command, provides the ability to decrease the size of a paging space. For both commands, a system reboot is no longer required. Refer to Chapter 7 of the *AIX 5L Version 5.1 System Management Guide: Operating System and Device* or visit:
>
> http://publibn.boulder.ibm.com/doc_link/en_US/a_doc_lib/aixbman/baseadmn/baseadmntfrm.htm

Using the svmon command

The **svmon** command can be used to determine roughly how much memory the system is using. For example:

```
# svmon
                size       inuse        free         pin     virtual
memory        262119       30048      232071       11712       32473
pg space      131072       14567

                work        pers        clnt
pin            11712           0           0
in use         17928       12120           0
```

Memory columns

The columns grouped in the memory heading have the following meanings:

size This shows total size of memory in 4 KB pages.

inuse This shows the number of pages in RAM that are in use by a process plus the number of persistent pages that belonged to a terminated process and are still resident in RAM. This value is the total size of memory minus the number of pages on the free list.

free This shows the number of pages on the free list.

pin This shows the number of pages pinned in RAM (a pinned page is a page that is always resident in RAM and cannot be paged out).

virtual This shows the number of pages allocated in the system virtual space.

Pg space columns

The columns grouped in the pg space heading have the following meanings:

size This is total size of paging space in 4 KB pages.

inuse This is total number of allocated slots.

Pin columns

The columns grouped in the pin heading have the following meanings:

work This shows the number of working pages pinned in RAM.

pers This shows the number of persistent pages pinned in RAM.

clnt This shows the number of client pages pinned in RAM.

In use columns

The columns grouped in the in use heading have the following meanings:

work This shows the number of working pages in RAM.

pers This shows the number of persistent pages in RAM.

clnt This shows the number of client pages in RAM (client page is a remote file page).

The memory usage of a specific process

To find out how much memory a process is using, enter the command shown in Example 10-6 on page 324.

Example 10-6 The memory usage of a specific process

```
# svmon -P 17908
-------------------------------------------------------------------------------
     Pid Command          Inuse      Pin     Pgsp  Virtual   64-bit    Mthrd
   17908 -ksh              3185     1622     1983     8414        N        N

    Vsid      Esid Type Description              Inuse   Pin Pgsp Virtual
       0         0 work kernel seg                2693  1620 1894  4520
   1c01c         d work shared library text        385     0   28  3792
    b0ab         1 pers code,/dev/hd2:6244          55     0    -     -
    6be6         2 work process private             30     2   53    77
    5be5         f work shared library data         18     0    8    25
   17077         - pers /dev/hd2:21059               2     0    -     -
    5485         - pers /dev/hd4:494                 2     0    -     -
```

To see the number of working pages unique to this process' private stack and data use in all of virtual memory, look at the work type and description private. The **svmon** output may also list several shared segments. For a complete picture, determine which segments are unique to an individual process and which are shared with other programs. Multiply the values by 4096 to get the number of bytes in memory the process is using. The number 4096 comes from the fact that each page is 4 KB in size. You can also divide the number of pages by 256 in order to get megabytes.

Using the vmstat command

To see how much of memory used, use **vmstat** again. For a sample output, refer to Example 10-2 on page 314.

Let us look at the columns under memory, page, and faults.

Columns under memory

The information under the memory heading provides information about real and virtual memory:

avm The avm column gives the average number of pages allocated to paging space. In AIX, a page contains 4096 bytes of data. This stands for Active Virtual Memory and not Available Memory. The avm is the number of 4 K pages that are in use in paging space. Prior to AIX Version 4.3.2, the same idea is reflected in the PERCENT USED column of the **lsps -s** command.

Note: Starting with AIX Version 4.3.2, there is a slight change in reporting this value. The **vmstat** command reports the amount of virtual memory actually accessed because with deferred page space allocation policy, the paging space may not get touched.

fre The fre column shows the average number of free memory frames. A frame is a 4096-byte area of real memory. If the fre value is substantially above the MAXFREE value (which is defined as MINFREE plus 8), then it is unlikely that the system is thrashing (continuously paging in and out). However, if the system is thrashing, be assured that the fre value is small. Most UNIX and AIX operating systems will use nearly all available memory for disk caching, so you need not be alarmed if the fre value oscillates between MINFREE and MAXFREE.

Columns under page

The information under the page heading includes information about page faults and paging activity:

re The re column shows the number (rate) of pages reclaimed.

pi The pi column details the number (rate) of pages paged in from paging space. One theory is that five page-ins per second should be the upper limit. Use this theoretical maximum as a reference but do not adhere to it rigidly. This field is important as a key indicator of paging space activity. If a page-in occurs, then there must have been a previous page-out for that page. It is also likely in a memory-constrained environment that each page-in will force a different page to be stolen and therefore paged out.

po The po column shows the number (rate) of pages paged out to paging space.

fr The fr column details the number (rate) of pages freed. If the fr/po ration is less than h (system wide thrashing parameter modified by **schedtune**), then you are probably thrashing.

sr The sr column details the number (rate) of pages scanned by the page-placement algorithm. Lots of page in and outs and high CPU wa (wait on I/O) times indicated you could be thrashing. Thrashing means that you might have a lack of memory.

cy
: The cy column provides the rate of complete scans of the Page Frame Table. The cy shows how many times (per second) the page-replacement code has scanned the Page Frame Table. Since the free list can be replenished without a complete scan of the PFT, and because all of the **vmstat** fields are reported as integers, this field is usually zero

Columns under faults

The information under the faults heading in the **vmstat** output provides information about process control:

in
: The in column shows the number (rate) of device interrupts. This column shows the number of hardware or device interrupts (per second) observed over the measurement interval. Examples of interrupts are disk request completions and the 10 millisecond clock interrupt. Since the latter occurs 100 times per second, the in field is always greater than 100.

sy
: The sy column details the number (rate) of system calls. Resources are available to user processes through well-defined system calls. These calls instruct the kernel to perform operations for the calling process and exchange data between the kernel and the process. Since workloads and applications vary, and different calls perform different functions, it is impossible to say how many system calls per second are too many.

cs
: The cs column shows the number (rate) of context switches.

Memory related problem

Processes requesting additional memory are killed once the system runs low on paging space. The system appears hung as new processes and telnet connections are terminated. The error messages like `Not enough memory` or `Fork function failed` are generated. There are three ways to resolve this situation:

1. Add additional paging space.

2. Memory leak

   Systems often have plenty of paging space (sometimes three to four times RAM), and can still run out. This could be due to a memory leak. The question then is which process is causing the memory leak. Refer to "The memory usage of a specific process" on page 323.

3. Maximum process

   The system may be reaching its maximum number of processes allowed per user, or maxuproc. Depending on what maxuproc is set to (default is 40), if a user already has maxuproc number of processes, the system will not allow that user to fork anymore processes.

10.2.3 Monitoring I/O

The I/O subsystem is a very slow resource compared with CPU or memory. For better performance of the I/O subsystem, you need to consider the following factors.

Hard disk management consideration

Performance can be improved by putting more than one physical volume in a volume group. The idea is to get the volume group's journaled logical volume on one physical disk, and then place high activity file systems on a separate disk in the volume group. Low activity file systems should be placed on the hard disk containing the journaled logical volume.

High usage logical volumes can be spread across multiple physical disks. This allows parallel reading of the disks and speed I/O access to the logical volume. Large files that are heavily used and not accessed sequentially, such as database files, should be spread across more than one physical volume.

Depending on whether speed or reliability is your priority, there can be several ways to define a hard disk. If high reliability is your priority, use mirroring. If sequential access speed is your priority, use striping. Striping allows a sequential read of a file to read from more than one disk at a time, speeding the access. For random access speed, distribute files across multiple disks.

Disk I/O pacing

Disk I/O pacing allows the system administrator to balance I/O intensive workloads with other system activity. Pacing will slow down the rate of an I/O intensive task, allowing I/O to be more quickly available to other tasks. This can be controlled by high and low water marks. The default value of I/O pacing is 0. It means no pacing. A process cannot exceed the high water mark pending writes to a file. If it tries to do more than this, it is put to sleep until the number of writes is less than or equal to the low water mark. This is important for an HACMP or I/O intensive system.

The values can be changed using with Web-based System Manager, SMIT, or the command line.

Option 1: Using Web-based System Manager

Follow the step to change the I/O pacing values:

1. On the start panel of Web-based System Manager, double-click the System Environment icon on the right frame and then double-click the Settings icon. Then select the Operating System icon in the panel (Figure 10-2).

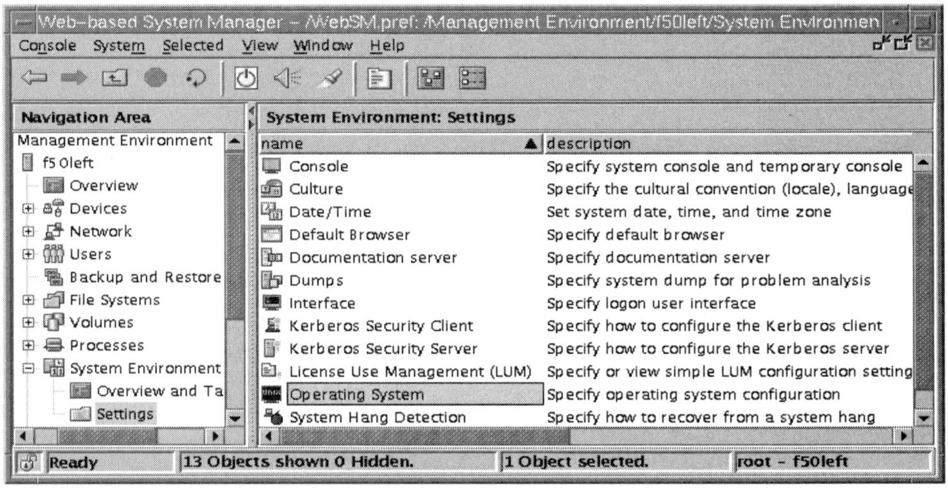

Figure 10-2 System Environment Settings panel

2. On the device sys0 properties panel, select the Attributes tab. You can change the high and low water mark values in this panel (Figure 10-3).

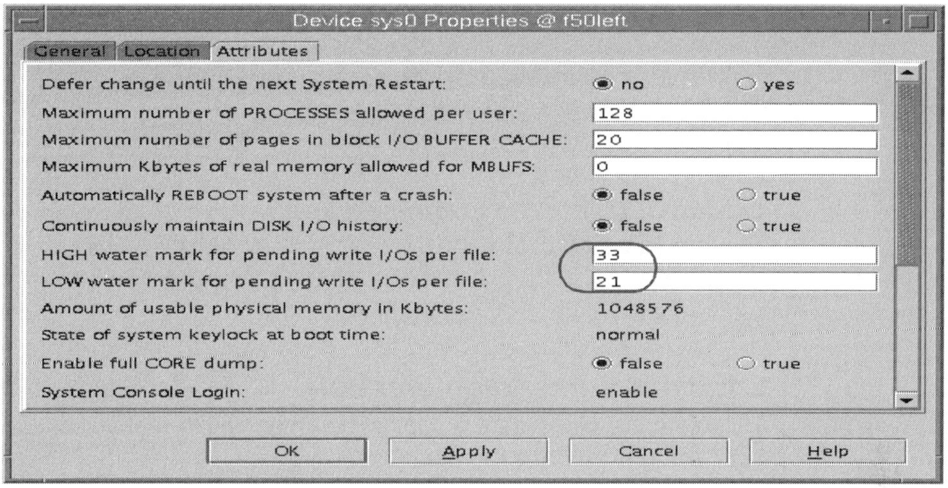

Figure 10-3 Device sys0 properties panel

Option 2: Using SMIT

To change the I/O pacing value by using SMIT, select the following sequence:

System Environments -> **Change/Show Characteristics of Operating System**

or use the SMIT fast path **`smitty chgsys`**.

After selecting this sequence, you can see the screen shown in Example 10-7.

Example 10-7 Change / Show Characteristics of Operating System

```
                Change / Show Characteristics of Operating System

Type or select values in entry fields.
Press Enter AFTER making all desired changes.

                                                        [Entry Fields]
  Maximum number of PROCESSES allowed per user        [128]                 +#
  Maximum number of pages in block I/O BUFFER CACHE   [20]                  +#
  Maximum Kbytes of real memory allowed for MBUFS     [0]                   +#
  Automatically REBOOT system after a crash            false                +
  Continuously maintain DISK I/O history               false                +
  HIGH water mark for pending write I/Os per file     [33]                  +#
  LOW water mark for pending write I/Os per file      [21]                  +#
  Amount of usable physical memory in Kbytes           1048576
  State of system keylock at boot time                 normal
  Enable full CORE dump                                false                +
  Use pre-430 style CORE dump                          false                +
  CPU Guard                                            disable              +
```

```
  ARG/ENV list size in 4K byte blocks                   [6]                +#

F1=Help             F2=Refresh          F3=Cancel           F4=List
F5=Reset            F6=Command          F7=Edit             F8=Image
F9=Shell            F10=Exit            Enter=Do
```

Option 3: Using the command line

Run the following command:

```
# chdev -l sys0 -a maxpout='33' -a minpout='21'
sys0 changed
```

Logical volume fragmentation

To look at the placement of logical volumes within a physical volume, use the **lslv** command. For example:

```
# lslv -p hdisk0 hd1
```

The above command will output the numbered partitions of logical volume hd1 that are contained in hdisk0.

The partitions shown are either USED, FREE, or numbered as part of hd1.

If the numbered partitions are scattered around, it may indicate fragmentation has occurred.

To reorganize a logical volume or volume group, use SMIT to run the **reorgvg** command. Select the following sequences:

Physical & Logical Storage -> **Logical Volume Manager**-> **Volume Groups** -> **Set Characteristics of a Volume Group**-> **Reorganize a volume group**

or use the fast path **smit reorgvg**.

To reorganize a file system, back up the files to another file system, unmount the mount point, remake the file system, remount the mount point, and then restore the files.

> **Note:** Do this very carefully, or you can lose data.

The **defragfs** command can also be used to increase a file system's contiguous free space.

File fragmentation

To see if a particular file is fragmented, use the **fileplace** command. For example:

```
# fileplace -pv /home/my_file
```

This command indicates the number of separate sections that make up the file. It also indicates the space efficiency of the file placement.

Disk I/O activity

The **iostat** command will provide data on the activity of physical volumes, but not file systems or logical volumes. Remember that the first set of data displayed by **iostat** represents a summary of all activity since system startup. If activity for a disk is greater than 70 percent, then that disk will suffer performance problems.

To see how much disk I/O activity is taking place, enter:

```
# iostat -a 2
```

This shows the output every two seconds (see Example 10-8). In AIX 5L Version 5.1, the -a flag provides an adapter basis sum of activities.

Example 10-8 Output of the iostat command

```
# iostat -a 2

tty:        tin          tout   avg-cpu:  % user    % sys       % idle    % iowait
            0.2          16.1               2.0       1.4        94.8       1.9

Adapter:                      Kbps        tps     Kb_read    Kb_wrtn
scsi1                         90.7        22.7    3243813       3722

Disks:          % tm_act      Kbps        tps     Kb_read    Kb_wrtn
hdisk2             0.6        90.6        22.6    3242736       2184
hdisk0             0.0        0.0         0.0        1077         36
hdisk3             0.0        0.0         0.0           0          0
hdisk4             0.0        0.0         0.0           0          0
hdisk1             0.0        0.0         0.0           0       1502

Adapter:                      Kbps        tps     Kb_read    Kb_wrtn
scsi0                         0.0         0.0           0          0

Disks:          % tm_act      Kbps        tps     Kb_read    Kb_wrtn
cd0                0.0        0.0         0.0           0          0

tty:        tin          tout   avg-cpu:  % user    % sys       % idle    % iowait
            0.0         430.7               9.5      21.3        63.5       5.7

Adapter:                      Kbps        tps     Kb_read    Kb_wrtn
```

```
scsi1                        5415.8      1354.0       11644          0

Disks:          % tm_act      Kbps        tps     Kb_read   Kb_wrtn
hdisk2            35.3      5415.8      1354.0       11644          0
hdisk0             0.0         0.0         0.0           0          0
hdisk3             0.0         0.0         0.0           0          0
hdisk4             0.0         0.0         0.0           0          0
hdisk1             0.0         0.0         0.0           0          0

Adapter:                      Kbps        tps     Kb_read   Kb_wrtn
scsi0                          0.0         0.0           0          0

Disks:          % tm_act      Kbps        tps     Kb_read   Kb_wrtn
cd0                0.0         0.0         0.0           0          0

tty:       tin         tout    avg-cpu:  % user    % sys     % idle    % iowait
           0.0         431.6              7.2      21.7       65.5        5.6
:
```

The first set of output is cumulative since boot time.

Look at the %iowait numbers to see if a large amount of waiting on I/O is going on. Look at each individual disk listed to see if there is a balance of disk activity between the different disks. The columns KB_read and KB_wrtn show the kilobytes read and written to the disk. Also look at the %tm_act (time active or percentage utilization of the disk) to see if a particular disk is a bottleneck. In that case, some data from the disk should be redistributed. If any single disk averages more than 35 percent busy, it is a sign that it is a bottleneck to the system and should be tuned. An average physical volume utilization greater than 25 percent across all drives indicates a need for more physical disks.

We also see the CPU numbers, %user (cpu time spent in user mode), %sys (percent of CPU time spent in kernel mode), %idle (percent of time CPU spent idle with no outstanding local disk requests), and %iowait (percent of time CPU spent idle but with outstanding I/O requests), should be less than 20 percent. On multiprocessor systems, CPU statistics are calculated as averages among all processors.

Using the lvmstat command

The **lvmstat** command generates reports that can be used to change logical volume configuration to better balance the input/output load between physical disks. To use the **lvmstat** command, you must have root user authority.

The -e flag enables the statistics collection for a volume group or a logical volume.

For example, if you want to collect the statistics for rootvg, then run the following command:

```
# lvmstat -v rootvg -e
```

Run the following command to display the history of all the partitions of logical volume hd2:

```
# lvmstat -l hd2 | pg

Log_part  mirror#  iocnt   Kb_read   Kb_wrtn       Kbps
      77        1   4097     16388         0       0.43
      76        1   4096     16384         0       0.43
      78        1   4096     16384         0       0.43
      79        1   4096     16384         0       0.43
      80        1   4096     16384         0       0.43
      81        1   4096     16384         0       0.43
      82        1   4096     16384         0       0.43
      83        1   4096     16384         0       0.43
      84        1   4096     16384         0       0.43
      85        1   4096     16384         0       0.43
      86        1   4096     16384         0       0.43
```

Run the following command to display the history of top five logical volumes of volume group rootvg:

```
# lvmstat -v rootvg -c 5

Logical Volume         iocnt   Kb_read   Kb_wrtn       Kbps
  hd4                 137946    551876       100      14.58
  hd2                    104        31       468       0.01
  hd6                     89         0       356       0.01
  hd8                     65        44       272       0.01
  hd9var                  15         0        88       0.00
```

Run the following command to disable statistics collection for rootvg:

```
# lvmstat -v rootvg -d
```

Using the filemon command

The filemon tool collects and presents trace data on the various layers of file system utilization, including the logical file system, virtual memory segments, LVM, and physical disk layers. Data can be collected on all the layers, or layers can be specified with the -O layer option. The default is to collect data on the VM, LVM, and physical layers. Both summary and detailed reports are generated.

The usage of the **filemon** command is as follows:

```
# filemon [-i file] [-o file] [-d] [-v] [-u] [-O opt]
   -i file: open input file (default is real-time trace)
```

```
-o file: open output file (default is stdout)
-d: deferred trace (until `trcon')
-T num: set trace kernel buf sz (default 32000 bytes)
-P: pin monitor process in memory
-v: verbose mode (print extra details)
-u: print unnamed file activity via pid
-O opt: other monitor-specific options.
   valid -O options: lf,vm,lv,pv,all
   lf: monitor logical file I/O
   vm: monitor virtual memory I/O
   lv: monitor logical volume I/O
   pv: monitor physical volume I/O
   all: short for lf,vm,lv,pv (default is: vm,lv,pv)
```

Normally, The **filemon** command runs in the background while other applications are running and being monitored. When the **trcstop** command is issued, the **filemon** command stops and generates its report. You may want to issue **nice -n -20 trcstop** to stop the **filemon** command because the **filemon** command is currently running at priority 40.

> **Note:** The **filemon** command will only collect data for those files opened after the **filemon** command was started, unless you specify the -u flag. Normally, only the top 20 logical files and segments are reported unless the -v (verbose) flag is used.

Creating additional log logical volumes

Placing the log logical volume on a physical volume different from your most active file system logical volume will increase parallel resource usage. You are allowed to have a separate log for each file system.

When creating your logical volumes, remember that the performance of drives differs.

Try to create a logical volume for a hot file system on a fast drive.

Disk and SCSI performance issues

Discussions of disk, logical volume, and file system performance sometimes lead to the conclusion that the more drives you have on your system, the better the disk I/O performance. This is not always true. Since there is a limit to the amount of data that can be handled by the SCSI adapter, the SCSI adapter can become a bottleneck.

If all your disk drives are connected to one SCSI adapter, and your hot file systems are on separate physical volumes, you may benefit from using multiple SCSI adapters. The performance improvement will depend on the type of access.

To see if a particular adapter is saturated, use the **iostat** command and add up all the Kbps amounts for the disks attached to a particular SCSI adapter. For maximum aggregate performance, the total of the transfer rates (Kbps) must be below the SCSI adapter throughput rating. In most cases, use 70 percent SCSI adapter throughput capacity.

Asynchronous I/O

An application's processing cannot continue until the synchronous I/O operation is complete. In contrast, asynchronous I/O operations run in the background and do not block the user application.This improves performance, because I/O operations and applications processing can run simultaneously.

Many applications, such as databases and file servers, take advantage of the ability to overlap processing and I/O. These asynchronous I/O operations use various kinds of devices and files.

You can change attributes relating to asynchronous I/O using the **chdev** command or SMIT. Likewise, you can use SMIT to configure and remove (unconfigure) asynchronous I/O. Alternatively, you can use the **mkdev** and **rmdev** commands to configure and remove asynchronous I/O. To start SMIT at the main menu for asynchronous I/O, enter **smit aio**.

The default minimum number of servers configured when async I/O is enabled is 1. This is the minservers attribute. There is also a maximum number of async I/O servers that can get created that is controlled by the maxservers attribute. This has a default value of 10. If the number of async I/O requests is high, then the recommendation is to set maxservers to at least 10*(number of disks accessed asynchronously), and minservers should be maxservers /2.

10.3 Monitoring network performance

Several tools can measure network statistics and give a variety of information, but only part of this information is related to performance tuning. See Chapter 7, "TCP/IP and networking problem solving" on page 195 for more information.

To enhance performance, you can use the **no** (network options) command and the **nfso** command for tuning NFS options. You can also use the **chdev** and **ifconfig** commands to change system and network parameters.

10.3.1 Using the netpmon command

The **netpmon** command uses the trace facility to obtain a detailed picture of network activity during a time interval. Because it uses the trace facility, the **netpmon** command can be run only by a root user or by a member of the system group.

The usage of the **netpmon** command is as follows:

```
# netpmon -v -o nmon.out
<run application programs and commands here>
trcstop
```

After stop the tracing, all the specified reports are generated. The output of the **netpmon** command is composed of two different types of reports: global and detailed.

10.4 The topas monitor

The **topas** command reports vital statistics about the activity on the local system in a character terminal. It requires AIX Version 4.3.3 or later.

topas updates the screen to show the current state of the system (see Example 10-9). In the upper left is the same information that is given from the **sar** command. The middle of the left side shows the same information as the **iostat** command. The right side of the screen shows the same information from the virtual memory manager. In AIX 5L Version 5.1, **topas** displays the Workload Manager information, the CPU, disk, and block I/O usage for each class.

To exit from the topas, press the q key. The h key is also available for help.

Example 10-9 topas monitor

```
Topas Monitor for host:     f50left                 EVENTS/QUEUES     FILE/TTY
Tue Sep 11 17:27:32 2001    Interval: 2             Cswitch       63  Readch 3509.2K
                                                    Syscall     1684  Writech1159.0K
Kernel     4.4     |#                             | Reads        881  Rawin        0
User      51.6     |###############               | Writes       290  Ttyout       0
Wait       0.0     |                              | Forks          0  Igets        0
Idle      43.7     |############                  | Execs          0  Namei       31
                                                    Runqueue     3.1  Dirblk       0
Network  KBPS    I-Pack  O-Pack    KB-In  KB-Out    Waitqueue    0.0
tr0       0.0       1.0     0.5      0.0     0.0
lo0       0.0       0.0     0.0      0.0     0.0    PAGING            MEMORY
                                                    Faults        92  Real,MB   1023
Disk     Busy%     KBPS     TPS  KB-Read KB-Writ    Steals         0  % Comp    13.3
hdisk2    51.0   1158.5    72.8      0.0  1158.5    PgspIn         0  % Noncomp 33.1
hdisk0     0.0      0.0     0.0      0.0     0.0    PgspOut        0  % Client   0.5
```

```
                                                 PageIn        0
WLM-Class (Active)      CPU%     Mem%  Disk-I/O%  PageOut     289  PAGING SPACE
Unmanaged                  0        5          0  Sios         73  Size,MB     512
Unclassified               0       23          0                   % Used     11.0
                                                  NFS (calls/sec)  % Free     88.9
Name              PID CPU% PgSp Class             ServerV2      0
compress        27116 26.7  0.9 System             lientV2      0   Press:
compress         3650 26.7  0.9 System             erverV3      0   "h" for help
compress        17660 26.7  0.9 System             lientV3      0   "q" to quit
```

10.5 Workload management

Workload management simply means assessing the components of the workload to determine whether they are all needed as soon as possible. Usually, there is work that can wait for a while. You can run programs at a specific time. For example, the cron daemon can be used to spread out the workload by running a different times. Also, you can run the program with a lower priority. In this way, the system administrator can control workload of the system.

AIX Workload Manager (WLM) is an operating system feature introduced in AIX Version 4.3.3. The WLM is designed to give the system administrator control over how the scheduler and Virtual Memory Manager (VMM) allocate CPU, physical memory, and I/O resources to processes. It can be used to prevent different jobs from interfering with each other and to allocate resources based on the requirements of different groups of users.

You can find more information about WLM in *AIX 5L Workload Manager (WLM)*, SG24-5977.

In AIX 5L Version 5.1, there is a new interface for generating reports on WLM activities. The **wlmmon** and **wlmperf** commands generate resource usage reports of system WLM activity. The **wlmperf** command, which is part of the Performance Toolbox (PTX), can generate reports from trend recordings made by the PTX daemons for periods covering minutes, hours, days, weeks, or months. The **wlmmon** command, which ships with the base AIX, generates reports only for the latest 24-hour period and has no usage options. Three types of visual reports can be generated:

- Snapshot Display
- Detailed Display
- Tabulation Display

The type of report can be customized to cover specified WLM classes over specific time periods. In addition, the WLM activity from two different time periods can be compared (trended) for any chosen display type.

These reports are generated from data that is collected using the same mechanism as the **wlmstat** command. However, the **wlmmon** and **wlmperf** commands use recordings made by a daemon that must operate at all times to collect WLM data. For the **wlmmon** command, this daemon is called xmwlm, and ships with the base AIX. For the **wlmperf** command, this daemon is called xmtrend, and ships with the PTX.

10.6 Reporting performance problems to IBM

If, after examining the system resources, there does not appear to be a resource constraint, and successfully testing the system hardware, then you may need to report the performance problem to IBM.

To report performance related problems, you need to gather some data using the **perfpmr** shell script:

```
# perfpmr.sh 600
```

When collection is completed, **tar** the containers of the collection directory to a file. Then send the collected data to IBM.

There is an internal version of **perfpmr** that can be downloaded from an anonymous ftp server. The following URL can be used:

```
ftp://ftp.software.ibm.com/aix/tools/perftools/perfpmr
```

Download the fileset that relates to the version of AIX you are running. See the README file contained in the package for further instructions.

10.7 Other tools

There are many other tools that can be used to determine what is causing the system performance degradation. Some of them are in the fileset perfagent.tools:

acctcms Produces command usage summaries from accounting records.

acctcom Displays selected process accounting record summaries.

accton Performs process-accounting procedures.

alstat Shows alignment exception statistics. New in AIX 5L Version 5.1.

bf, bfrpt Reports on memory access by applications. Withdrawn in AIX 5L Version 5.1.

emstat Shows emulation exception statistics.

fdpr Optimizes executable modules.

filemon Monitors the performance of the file system, and reports the I/O activity on behalf of logical files, virtual memory segments, logical volumes, and physical volumes.

fileplace Displays the placement of file blocks within logical or physical volumes.

gennames Gathers all the information necessary to run the **tprof**, **filemon**, **netpmon**, or **pprof** commands in off-line mode.

gprof Displays call graph profile data.

lockstat Reports on kernel lock contention. Withdrawn in AIX 5L Version 5.1.

locktrace Controls kernel lock tracing. New in AIX 5L Version 5.1.

mmtu Displaying, adding, and deleting Maximum Transfer Unit (MTU) values used for path MTU discovery. This command only applies to AIX Version 4.2.1 or later.

netpmon With a moderate, network-oriented workload, **netpmon** increases overall CPU utilization by 3 to 5 percent. In a CPU-saturated environment with little I/O of any kind, **netpmon** slowed a large compile by about 3.5 percent.

netstat Most of the variations of this command use fewer than 0.2 seconds of CPU time.

nfsstat Most of the variations of this command use fewer than 0.1 seconds of CPU time.

no Configures network options.

prof Displays object file profile data.

pprof Reports CPU usage of all kernel threads over a period of time.

PDT Performance Diagnostics Tool. This tool is installed as part of bos.perf.diag_tool and configured to send daily reports about system parameters and performance data to help monitor the system. Configure PDT by running /usr/sbin/perf/diag_tool/pdt_config as root. Select option 4, modify/enable PDT collection, then select 7 to exit.

renice Alters priority of running processes.

rmss Simulates a system with various sizes of memory for performance testing of applications.

sar Collects, reports, or saves system activity information.

stem Allows insertion of user-supplied instrumentation code at the entry and exit points of existing program and library subroutines. Withdrawn in AIX 5L Version 5.1

stripnm Displays the symbol information of a specified object file.

syscalls Records and counts system calls. Withdrawn in AIX 5L Version 5.1

timex Reports, in seconds, the elapsed time, user time, and system execution time for a command.

topas Reports selected local system statistics.

tprof Since **tprof** uses **trace**, it causes some system overhead. **tprof** only enables one trace hook, however, so its overhead is less than that of a full trace. For example, **tprof** degraded the performance of a large compile by less than 2 percent.

trace The overhead added by **trace** varies widely, depending on the workload and the number of hook IDs being collected. As an extreme case, a long-running, CPU-intensive job in an otherwise idle system took 3.2 percent longer when **trace** was running with all hooks enabled.

`trcnm` Generates a kernel name list.

truss Traces a process's system calls, received signals and incurred machine faults. New in AIX 5L Version 5.1.

11

Event tracing

This chapter describes the concept of trace and how to use it for gathering and reporting system events.

11.1 Introduction

The trace system is a tool allowing you to capture the sequential flow of system activity or system events. Unlike a stand-alone kernel dump that provides a static snapshot of a system, the trace facility provides a more dynamic way to gather problem data.

Trace can be used to:

- Isolate and understand system problems.
- Observe system and application execution for measuring system performance.

The events that are traced are time stamped as they are written to a binary trace file named /var/adm/ras/trcfile.

There are events pre-defined in AIX and included in selected commands, libraries, kernel routines, kernel extension routines, and interrupt handlers. A user can define their own trace events in application code.

The trace facility generates a large amount of data. For example, a trace session capturing one second of events from an idle system gathered four thousand events in the trace. This value depends on what events you trace and the CPU performance of the system.

11.2 Installing trace

The trace facility and commands are provided as part of the Software Trace Service Aids fileset named bos.sysmgt.trace.

To see if this fileset is installed, use the following command:

```
# lslpp -l | grep bos.sysmgt.trace
```

If a line is produced which includes bos.sysmgt.trace, then the fileset is installed; otherwise, you must install it from your installation media.

11.3 Taking a trace

Before tracing events, a strategy for what to trace and when to trace is important.

Follow these steps to gather a useful trace:

1. Select the required hook IDs for tracing.

2. Enable trace.
3. Recreate the problem.
4. Disable trace.
5. Generate the trace report.

11.3.1 Hook IDs

The events traced are referenced by hook identifiers.

Each hook ID uniquely refers to a particular activity that can be traced.

When tracing, you can select the hook IDs of interest and exclude others that are not relevant to your problem. A trace hook ID is a three-digit hexadecimal number that identifies an event being traced. Trace hook IDs are defined in the /usr/include/sys/trchkid.h file.

The currently defined trace hook IDs can be listed using the **trcrpt** command. (See Example 11-1.)

Example 11-1 Displays the list of hook IDs

```
# trcrpt -j | sort | pg
001 TRACE ON
002 TRACE OFF
003 TRACE HEADER
004 TRACEID IS ZERO
005 LOGFILE WRAPAROUND
006 TRACEBUFFER WRAPAROUND
:
```

11.3.2 Selecting trace events

All trace events may not be required for general cases. You can choose specific events of interest. For example, to investigate the problem of the mbuf activity, the event ID you may want to trace is 254. This can get this by running:

```
# trcrpt -j | grep MBUF
```

In AIX 5L Version 5.1, trace now supports the concept of event group. An event group is a collection of event IDs related to a specific topic. The concept of an event group makes choosing the appropriate event IDs much easier. For example, the group proc contains trace hook IDs 134, 135, and 139. These hook IDs correspond to the appropriate system calls. This allows hooks to be turned on or off at once when starting a trace. The currently defined event groups can be listed using the **trcevgrp** command. (See Example 11-2.)

Example 11-2 Display event groups

```
# trcevgrp -l | pg
tidhk - Hooks needed to display thread name (reserved)
        106,10C,134,139,465
gka - GENERAL KERNEL ACTIVITY (files,execs,dispatches) (reserved)
        106,10C,134,139,465,107,135,15b,12e,116,117,200,20E,20F
gkasc - GENERAL KERNEL ACTIVITY + SYSTEM CALLS (reserved)
        106,10C,134,139,465,107,135,15b,12e,101,104,116,117,200,20E,20F
fop - FILE OPENS (reserved)
        15b,107
fact - FILE ACTIVITY (open,close,read,write) (reserved)
        106,134,139,107,135,15b,12e,19c,163
proc - EXECS, FORKS, EXITS (reserved)
        134,139,135
:
```

There is a new **trcevgrp** command to list and manage event groups in AIX 5L Version 5.1 (Refer to the *AIX 5L Version 5.1 Commands Reference* or visit:

http://publib.boulder.ibm.com/doc_link/en_US/a_doc_lib/cmds/aixcmds5/trcevgrp.htm)

Sometimes, the specific hook IDs for a trace will be indicated by the developer of the code that has a problem. Specific calls recording an event are present.

Refer to the person supporting the specific code with a problem for a list of useful hook IDs or event groups to use.

Doing a blanket method of selecting all events is not useful because the trace log files will quickly fill and overwrite previous entries. Additionally, this generates lots of unwanted data that becomes difficult to manage.

11.3.3 Timing the trace

Carefully selecting the time to trace is important. You may only have a short period of time when you can gather a useful trace. Selecting this time wisely will ensure the problem is not missed during the trace session.

If tracing is stopped prematurely, the problem may not show up in the trace. The problem may have been recorded, but then overwritten as the trace log file fills up.

The recommended method to trace only the data required is to start and stop the trace on the command line.

For example, to trace a user program named myprogram and look at files it opened the (hook ID is 15b), run the commands:

```
# trace -a -j 15b; ./myprogram; trcstop
```

By limiting the period of the trace to include only the period of execution of the problem command, you are much more likely to capture the sequences of events leading up to the problem.

Ideally, you may write a shell script to trace your problem. This allows you to easily reproduce the trace session, so you can concentrate on reproducing the problem, not managing the timing of the trace. (See Example 11-3.)

Example 11-3 Sample shell script

```
#!/bin/ksh
# This is a script to trace the problem
# now we start trace
trace -a -j 15b
# Now we run the command
./myprogram
# Now we stop trace
trcstop
exit
```

Also, you can start and stop the trace in a program or use your own trace hook ID. Sometimes, you should use error notification to stop the trace or force a dump; refer to Chapter 4, “Error Notification”, in *AIX 5L Version 5.1 General Programing Concepts: Writing and Debugging Programs* or visit the following Web site:

http://publibn.boulder.ibm.com/doc_link/en_US/a_doc_lib/aixprggd/genprogc/genprogctfrm.htm

11.3.4 Starting a trace

Trace can be started in background mode or interactive mode.

Interactive mode tracing

If the **trace** command is issued without the -a option, it runs in interactive mode; the **trace** command returns a -> prompt. You can issue subcommands and regular shell commands from the trace subcommand mode by preceding the shell commands with an exclamation mark (!). For example, the trcon subcommand starts the collection of trace data, the trcoff subcommand stops tracing, and the quit subcommand exits **trace** command by stopping.

Background mode tracing

There is normally no need to run the **trace** command in the interactive mode, since the entire system is being traced, not just the commands started from that shell.

trace can be run in the background by using the -a option. Once trace has been started this way, you can use the **trcon**, **trcoff**, and **trcstop** commands to start tracing, stop tracing, or exit the trace session.

Using the trace buffer

Trace uses in-memory buffers to save the trace data. There are three methods of using the trace buffers:

- Alternate mode (the default)

  All trace events will be recorded in the trace log file.

- Circular mode (-l)

  The trace events wrap within the in-memory buffers and are not captured in the trace log file until the trace data collection is stopped.

- Single mode (-f)

  The collection of trace events stops when the in-memory trace buffer fills up and the contents of the buffer are captured in the trace log file.

It is often desirable to specify the buffer size and the maximum log file size. The trace buffers require real memory to be available so that no paging is necessary to record trace hooks. The log file will fill to the maximum size specified, and then wrap around, discarding the oldest trace data. The -T size and -L size flags specify the size of the memory buffers and the maximum size of the trace data in the log file in bytes.

The trace command syntax

```
trace [ -a [ -g ]][ -f | -l ][-b | -B][-c][-C [ CPUList | all ]] [ -d ]
[ -h ][-j Event [ ,Event ]][-k Event [ ,Event ]][-J Event-group
[,Event-group ]] [ -K E vent-group [,Event-group ]] [ -m Message ][-n ]
[ -o Name ][ -o- ][ -p ][ -s ][ -L Size ][ -T Size ]
```

Useful flags

-d — Sets up trace daemon, but does not start actual tracing (the **trcon** command starts the actual tracing).

-L ***size*** — Sets the trace file maximum size (default is 1 MB).

-T ***size*** — Sets the trace buffer size (default is 128 KB).

-o ***name*** — Uses name as the trace file (if name is "-", writes data to stdout).

-s — Causes trace to stop if trace file is full (default is to wrap the file when it fills up).

-j ***event[, event...]*** — Specifies trace events to be included.

-k ***event[, event...]*** — Specifies trace events to be excluded.

-J ***event group[, event group..]*** — Specifies trace event groups to be included (new in AIX 5L Version 5.1).

-K ***event group[, event group...]*** — Specifies trace event groups to be excluded (new in AIX 5L Version 5.1).

The SMIT panel for **trace** makes specifying these options much easier.

You can use SMIT or the command line interface to start **trace**.

Option 1: Using SMIT

1. You can go the START trace screen by selecting the following sequence:

   Problem Determination -> **Trace** -> **START Trace**

   or use the SMIT fast path **smitty trcstart**.

   Example 11-4 shows the SMIT START Trace panel.

Example 11-4 SMIT panel for START Trace

```
                                 START Trace

Type or select values in entry fields.
Press Enter AFTER making all desired changes.

                                                       [Entry Fields]
  EVENT GROUPS to trace                              []                        +
  ADDITIONAL event IDs to trace                      []                        +
  Event Groups to EXCLUDE from trace                 []                        +
  Event IDs to EXCLUDE from trace                    []                        +
  Trace MODE                                         [alternate]               +
  STOP when log file full?                           [no]                      +
  LOG FILE                                           [/var/adm/ras/trcfile]
```

```
  SAVE PREVIOUS log file?                               [no]            +
  Omit PS/NM/LOCK HEADER to log file?                   [yes]           +
  Omit DATE-SYSTEM HEADER to log file?                  [no]            +
  Run in INTERACTIVE mode?                              [no]            +
  Trace BUFFER SIZE in bytes                            [131072]        #
  LOG FILE SIZE in bytes                                [1310720]       #
  Buffer Allocation                                     [automatic]     +

F1=Help             F2=Refresh          F3=Cancel           F4=List
F5=Reset            F6=Command          F7=Edit             F8=Image
F9=Shell            F10=Exit            Enter=Do
```

2. Select the event group from the EVENT GROUPS to trace field; you can use the F4 key to display the possible event group list.

   Example 11-5 shows the SMIT EVENT GROUPS panel.

Example 11-5 SMIT panel for EVENT GROUPS

```
                          EVENT GROUPS to trace

Move cursor to desired item and press F7. Use arrow keys to scroll.
    ONE OR MORE items can be selected.
Press Enter AFTER making all selections.

[TOP]
  tidhk - Hooks needed to display thread name (reserved)
  gka - GENERAL KERNEL ACTIVITY (files,execs,dispatches) (reserved)
  gkasc - GENERAL KERNEL ACTIVITY + SYSTEM CALLS (reserved)
  fop - FILE OPENS (reserved)
  fact - FILE ACTIVITY (open,close,read,write) (reserved)
  proc - EXECS, FORKS, EXITS (reserved)
  procd - EXECS, FORKS, DISPATCHES (reserved)
  filephys - FILE ACTIVITY (with physical file system) (reserved)
[MORE...53]

F1=Help                 F2=Refresh              F3=Cancel
F7=Select               F8=Image                F10=Exit
Enter=Do                /=Find                  n=Find Next
```

3. Optionally, select the specific trace events from the ADDITIONAL event IDs to trace list.

   Example 11-6 shows the event ID options.

Example 11-6 Selecting event ID

```
                         ADDITIONAL event IDs to trace

Move cursor to desired item and press F7.
    ONE OR MORE items can be selected.
```

```
Press Enter AFTER making all selections.

[MORE...68]
  13A FSTAT SYSTEM CALL
  13B FSTATFS SYSTEM CALL
  13E FULLSTAT SYSTEM CALL
  14C IOCTL SYSTEM CALL
  14E KILL SYSTEM CALL
  152 LOCKF SYSTEM CALL
  154 LSEEK SYSTEM CALL
> 15B OPEN SYSTEM CALL
[MORE...194]

F1=Help                 F2=Refresh              F3=Cancel
F7=Select               F8=Image                F10=Exit
Enter=Do                /=Find                  n=Find Next
```

4. Select the appropriate trace mode and modify the other fields. Once you make your selection, press the Enter key. The trace starts.
5. If you set the Run in INTERACTIVE mode field to `yes`, you will see the panel shown in Example 11-7.

Example 11-7 Interactive tracing in SMIT

```
                                 COMMAND STATUS

Command: running       stdout: yes           stderr: no

Before command completion, additional instructions may appear below.

->!ls
```

6. You get the interactive mode, as denoted by the -> prompt. Use the trace subcommand (such as !) to trace the selected system event. Use the quit subcommand to stop the trace.

Option 2: Using the command line

To trace the OPEN() SYSTEM CALL event when running the **ls** command in interactive mode, issue the following commands:

```
# trace -j 15b
->!/usr/bin/ls
->quit
```

To trace the same command in background mode, issue the following commands:

```
# trace -a -j 15b
/usr/bin/ls
```

```
# trcstop
```

To trace the same command in background mode with circular trace buffer, issue the following command:

```
# trace -a -l -j 15b
```

To trace the same command in background mode with single trace buffer, issue the following command:

```
# trace -a -f -j 15b
```

Note: In AIX 5L Version 5.1, the maximum trace buffer size for -f flag is 536870368 bytes. The max buffer size for the other options is unchanged.

11.3.5 Collecting trace data for analysis

To gather the required files for analysis and write to the tape device /dev/rmt0, run the following command:

```
# snap -Dg -o /dev/rmt0
```

You can ignore any messages regarding the dump device if your trace data does not relate to a system dump.

Send the tape to your support organization.

11.3.6 Tracing fatal problems

If the problem you are tracing crashes the system, increase the size of the trace buffer and log files. The trace buffer remains in kernel memory and can be extracted from the kernel dump.

This is the general outline:

1. Check the size of the dump device.

   The dump device will require sufficient space for the extra trace buffer that will be dumped. For example, if you specify a 6 MB trace buffer, the dump device must cater to an extra 6 MB.

2. Start trace with large buffers.

   For example, to have a 6 MB trace buffer in kernel memory and a 12 MB log file to trace some networking hook IDs, run the following command:

   ```
   # trace -a -j 251,252,253,254 -L 12000000 -T 6000000
   ```

   Ensure the size of trace log directory is enough. The default trace log file is /var/adm/ras/trcfile.

3. Recreate the problem that crashes the system.
4. Extract the trace buffer from the kernel dump.

   For example, with the kernel dump file in the current directory, run the following command to extract the trace buffer into a file trcfile.dump:

   ```
   # trcdead -o trcfile.dump dump
   ```

5. You can run a report against this extracted file, for example:

   ```
   # trcrpt trcfile.dump
   ```

11.4 Generating a trace report

The raw /var/adm/ras/trcfile trace file that contains system events needs to be translated into a usable format for viewing. The **trcrpt** command formats the output.

11.4.1 Running trcrpt command

The **trcrpt** command is used to generate a readable trace report form the log file generated by the **trace** command.

The trcrpt command syntax

```
trcrpt [ -c ][-C [ CPUList | all ]] [ -d List ][ -D Event-group-list ]
[ -e Date ][ -G ][ -h ][ -j ][ -k List ][ -K Group-list ][-n Name ][ -o File ]
[ -p List ][ -r ][ -s Date ][ -t File ][-T List ][ -v ][-O Options ][ -x ]
[ File ]
```

Useful flags

-d *List* Includes only list hook IDs.

-D *Event group list* Limits the report to hook IDs in the event group list (new in AIX 5L Version 5.1).

-k *List* Excludes list hook IDs.

-K *Group list* Excludes hook IDs in the event group list from the report (new in AIX 5L Version 5.1).

-T *List* Includes only events for the kernel thread IDs in list.

-T *!List* Excludes events for those kernel thread IDs in list.

-s *Date* Starts the report at date.

-e *Date* Ends the report at date.

-p *List* Reports the process IDs for each event specified by the List variable.

-O *Options* Allows more detailed options, separated by commas.

- **ids=[on | off]** Displays hook IDs in report's first column.
- **pid=[on | off]** Displays process IDs for each line of report.
- **tid=[on | off]** Displays thread IDs for each line of report.
- **cpuid=[on | off]** Displays CPU IDs for each line of report.
- **svc=[on | off]** Displays system call names for each line.
- **exec=[on | off]** Displays exec path names.
- **timestamp=[0| 1| 2| 3]** Displays elapsed time since trace started.
  - **0** Elapsed time in nanoseconds, plus deltas in microseconds.
  - **1** Elapsed time only in microseconds.
  - **2** Same as 0, except for deltas in milliseconds.
  - **3** No time stamps.
- **starttime= *seconds*** Starts the report at seconds after the starting time in the trace file.
- **endtime= *seconds*** Ends the report at seconds.
- **2line=[on | off]** Breaks report lines into two per trace event.

You can run the **trcrpt** command through SMIT or on the command line interface.

Option 1: Using SMIT

Execute the following fast path to display the SMIT panel for trace reporting:

```
# smitty trcrpt
```

You can change major options values and select specific event IDs.

Example 11-8 shows the SMIT Trace Report panel.

Example 11-8 SMIT panel for Trace Report

```
                              Generate a Trace Report

Type or select values in entry fields.
Press Enter AFTER making all desired changes.

                                                           [Entry Fields]
  Show exec PATHNAMES for each event?                    [yes]                 +
  Show PROCESS IDs for each event?                       [no]                  +
  Show THREAD IDs for each event?                        [no]                  +
  Show CURRENT SYSTEM CALL for each event?               [yes]                 +
```

```
  Time CALCULATIONS for report                          [elapsed only]          +
  Event Groups to INCLUDE in report                     []                      +
  IDs of events to INCLUDE in report                    []                      +X
  Event Groups to EXCLUDE from report                   []                      +
  ID's of events to EXCLUDE from report                 []                      +X
  STARTING time                                         []
  ENDING time                                           []
  LOG FILE to create report from                        [/var/adm/ras/trcfile]
  FILE NAME for trace report (default is stdout)        []


F1=Help             F2=Refresh          F3=Cancel           F4=List
F5=Reset            F6=Command          F7=Edit             F8=Image
F9=Shell            F10=Exit            Enter=Do
```

Option 2: Using the command line

To output a formatted trace report to the /tmp/trcrpt.out file, run the following command:

```
# trcrpt -o /tmp/trcrpt.out
```

11.4.2 Filtering the trace report

Often, the output of the trace report file is very large.

Despite selecting a narrow time period to do your trace, the system may be tracing other unrelated events from the execution of other threads or interrupt handlers.

Reducing the size of the output to the events of interest is useful for problem management. The output can be reduced by specifying the process ID of the application having the problems.

For example, to create a trace report for the process ID 8002, run the following command:

```
# trcrpt -O'svc=on timestamp=3' -p 8002 > /tmp/trcrpt.out
```

11.4.3 Running trace report on a different system

To examine the /var/adm/ras/trcfile trace file on another machine, like dump analysis, you must also include the kernel namelist file, /etc/trcfmt, to interpret address of kernel symbols correctly.

For example, run the **trcnm** command and redirect the output into a file:

```
# trcnm > trace.nm
```

Copy the following files from the system where the trace was run to a temporary directory on the analysis machine:

- /var/adm/ras/trcfile
- /etc/trcfmt

If you are reading a tape written with the **snap** command, restore it from tape device /dev/rmt0 with the command:

```
# tar -xvf /dev/rmt0
```

The **trcrpt** command can use the -n and -t flag to specify the kernel namelist and trace format file:

```
# trcrpt -n trace.nm -t trcfmt -o trace.out
```

11.4.4 Analysis of trace report

The trace facility is useful for gauging performance characteristics of a program by examining the time stamps of system calls. It is also useful for examining the precise sequential flow of system activity in a multithreaded and possibly multiprocessor environment.

For example, to obtain captures from the execution of the **ls** command, run the following command:

```
# trace -a -J proc -j 15b -o trc_raw;ls /usr;trcstop
```

The -J proc option traces the event group for process management events, and the -j 15b option traces the system call open().

The **trcrpt** command reads the trace log specified by the parameter, formats the trace entries, and writes a report to standard output. (See Example 11-9.)

Example 11-9 Trace report output

```
# trcrpt -O "exec=on,pid=on,timestamp=1"  trc_raw

Internet Address: 0903BBC8 9.3.187.200
The system contains 4 cpus, of which 4 were traced.
Buffering: Kernel Heap
This is from a 32-bit kernel.
Tracing only these hooks, 134,135,139,15b

trace -a -J proc -j 15b -o trc_raw

ID  PROCESS NAME  PID    I  ELAPSED    APPL SYSCALL KERNEL  INTERRUPT

001 --1-          19358     0.000000                TRACE ON channel 0
                                                    Fri Aug 24 20:53:36 2001
```

```
135 trace          20544    0.007045       exit wait_status=0000 lockct=0001
139 ksh            20126    0.007045*      fork:   pid=20546 tid=26355
15B ksh            20546    0.013109       open fd=3 RDONLY
134 ksh            20546    0.014565       exec:   cmd=ls /usr pid=20546
tid=26355
15B ls             20546    0.036225       open fd=3 RDONLY
135 ls             20546    0.047027       exit wait_status=0000 lockct=0001
139 ksh            20126    0.047027*      fork:   pid=20548 tid=26357
15B ksh            20548    0.052349       open fd=3 RDONLY
134 ksh            20548    0.054156       exec:   cmd=trcstop pid=20548
tid=26357
15B trcstop        20548    0.069096       open fd=3 RDONLY
15B trcstop        20548    0.079511       open fd=3 RDONLY
15B trcstop        20548    0.080269       open fd=4 RDONLY
002 trcstop        20548    0.080309              TRACE OFF channel 0000 Fri
Aug 24 20:53:36 2001
```

The header of the trace report shows basic system information and the trace options of the trace.

We can see the fork() and exec() of the **ls** command. We can measure the time of each event. Based on this, we can find the performance characteristic of the **ls** command and understand the flow of system activity.

12

Printing problems

The goal of this chapter is to provide the system administrator with some tools and tips that will help turn the art of printer troubleshooting into a science. Problems with printing may be as minor as minor cosmetic blemishes on the output to as major as checks that have failed to print. Where you look for problems depends on such factors as the type of printer and the type of file to be printed, the way in which the printer is connected to the server.

This chapter is divided into three sections:

- Common troubleshooting techniques
- Troubleshooting specific to System V printing
- Troubleshooting specific to PowerPC printing

The procedure of problem determination can be reduced to a few steps:

1. Isolate the problem
   - Determine the system and subsystem where the problem exists.
   - Determine if the problem is hardware or software.
   - Determine if the problem is local or remote.
   - Is data getting to the printer?
2. Identify the cause of the problem
   - Is the printer plugged in with the proper pinouts?

- Is the data formatted properly by the right formatter and filter?
- Are the right flags being used?
- Is the printer properly configured?

3. Improve the situation
   - Try a different printer, adapter, or cable.
   - Use a more appropriate virtual printer or printer type.
   - Use different print flags.
4. Test the solution
   - Test with other print files.
   - Have other users test for problems.
   - Make sure you did not create a new problem.

The rest of the chapter lists some of the most common printing problems, and provides information to help you isolate the problem, identify the problem, improve the situation, and test the solution.

12.1 Common troubleshooting checklist

This section is organized in terms of the problems that typically occur when trying to print documents. In each case, the areas common to both print subsystems will be explored.

12.1.1 Checklist for local printing problems

The following list is a high level overview of things that you might check if jobs are not printing on local printers. More details are given in the rest of the chapter.

- Is the printer functioning?
  - Is the printer turned on?
  - Does the printer have a message on the display or blinking lights?
  - Can it print a test page?
  - Can you print from other systems?
  - Are the cables tight, the correct type, and the correct length?
  - Is the cable good? Test it on another system.
- Is the device set up properly?
  - Redirect output directly to the device file, for example, using the **cat** command.
  - Are the baud rate, handshaking, and port number right for serial?
  - Try a different port on the computer.
- Is the printer or virtual printer setup properly?
  - Does the printer match the defined types and data streams in the printer/queue setup?
  - Does the printer point to the right device?
  - Is the user allowed to print to the printer or form? (System V)
  - Are the print flags valid for the virtual printer or interface script?
  - Is the printer accepting jobs and enabled? Use the **lpstat** command with the right flags.
  - Is the printer name spelled correctly on the print command line?
  - Do you get command line, mail, or logged messages?
- Is the qdaemon (PowerPC) or lpsched (System V) running? To find out, run the appropriate command:
  - System V: **lpstat -r**

– PowerPC: `lssrc -s qdaemon`

12.1.2 Checklist for remote printing problems

The following list is a high level overview of things that you might check if jobs are not printing on remote printers. More details are given in the rest of the chapter.

- Is lpd or lpNet running on the server? To find out, run the appropriate command:
  - System V: `lpstat -r`
  - PowerPC: `lssrc -s lpd`
- Does the client have the right host name and remote queue specified?
- Do both the client and host names exist in a DNS or common /etc/hosts files?
- Does the client have permission to print to the server?
  - System V: Check the servers and clients Systems file.
  - PowerPC: Check the servers /etc/hosts.lpd file for the system name.
  - Does the name in this file match the DNS entry? Test the IP address and fully qualified and short names.
- Does the user on the client have permission to print to the printer?
- System V: Check the printers users.allow file or run `lpstat -p printer -l` for the correct permissions. Use all!all for all remote users.
- PowerPC: Use the rembak and lpd debug log features.
- System V: Check the /etc/lp/logs/lpNet log.
- Use `iptrace` to check the job as it goes over the network.
- Disable server queue.
  - Make sure the job is queued on the server while the queue is disabled.
  - Check the Job Description File (JDF) in the /var/spool/lpd/qdir directory or request log for command line flags.
- If the job queues when the queue is disabled, but does not print when the queue is enabled:
  - Make a copy of the file and use local procedures.
  - Use the flags in the JDF or request log to print.

12.1.3 Check the obvious

To cover the bases, check the obvious:

- Make sure the printer is turned on and is online.
- Make sure the cable is attached to the printer and the computer.
- Make sure the LAN cables are plugged into both the printer server (computer) and the printer. Check that you can ping the printer from the AIX server.

12.1.4 Nothing prints on local printers

One of the most aggravating situations is to print a job, go to the printer, and find that the output is missing. Where can you go from there?

My job is missing, but others are printing

The problem may have nothing to do with the printer. Someone else may have accidently picked up the printout. This tends to happen more often when banners are not being used, or when the banner is the same color as the output.

Multiple queues with one disabled or down

Is it possible that the queue is backed up with a large number of jobs, or a single very large job? Sometimes a large job will cause a queue to go down, or disable. When you set up multiple queues or virtual printers to print to the same printer, it may be possible that one of these queues is disabled while other queues are still printing.

Are you printing text to a PostScript printer?

While some printers are able to sniff the type of print data stream and automatically select the right internal mechanism for printing, very often when a printer is told that a job is PostScript, it will print nothing if it is sent a plain ASCII text file or a PostScript job that is improperly formatted. Check the printer to see if the files that are printing are valid PostScript jobs.

How large is the failing job?

If the job that is not printing is much larger than the jobs that are printing, there could be several reasons for the job failing to print. Some of these reasons are:

- The job is being spooled, and there is not enough spool space. See "Is there enough space in the spool file system?" on page 367.
- The job is being sent to a network print server that does not have a large enough buffer. If you are using a network print server device, such as the Axis, HP JetDirectEX or Intel NetPort box, the internal buffer space of the box may limit the size of the file you can print. Check to see if the job can print if

the printer is attached to a local parallel or serial port. If you determine the job is too large, try to print the job in sections.

- The printer memory is not large enough to handle the print job. If the AIX file system is large enough and you can print small jobs, the problem may be in the printer. See if you can break the job into smaller pieces. Try to establish the limits of the printer by testing with files of different sizes. It may be possible to add more memory to the printer.

Is the job accessible to the print service?

AFS/DFS print files that are accessible to the user sometimes may not be accessible to the print service. If you are trying to print files that are mounted from a remote system and they will not print, even though similar files print on your local system, try moving the file to /tmp and printing it from there. If this works, you will either have to use this as a workaround or change the permissions on how the files are exported from the server.

Did you send the job to the right printer or queue?

Often printer names can be confusing and similar. Make sure you are printing to the right queue and that the printer destination is at the location where you are trying to pick up the output.

Nothing prints, but the lights on the printer flash or change

With this symptom, you know that at least something is getting to the printer, but for some reason the printer is rejecting the jobs.

Does the printer support the data stream of the print file?

As described in the previous section, one of the most common causes for this problem is printing plain ASCII text files to a PostScript queue. Many users have the misconception that laser printers can automatically print any kind of file that is sent to it.

Is the print job too large for the printer?

This case was already covered. However, it is possible that an large job is in front of the queue and blocking all jobs. If you have the queue set to automatically retry, you could see the spooler try over and over to try to send the job to the printer without success.

Is there bad wiring to the printer?

Some cases of bad wiring will still allow a signal to go to the printer. Some of these cases are cables that are too long, or that are missing some of the signal pins necessary for full communications. See the section below on "Is the printer properly connected to the computer?" on page 364.

Are the port settings right?

Printers that are connected through serial cables can cause problems that are hard to detect when the serial port settings of the computer adapter and the printer serial port do not fully match. Typical settings include the baud rate, the number of data bits, the parity, and the number of stop bits. Often, when the baud rate is wrong, you will get garbage characters like upside down question marks printed, but sometimes nothing will print.

Some printers, such as Printronix and IBM 6400 series printers, have a setting on the printer to determine the meaning of some of the serial lines. On these printers:

- Make sure that RTS is always TRUE.
- Make sure that DTR is controlled by BUFFER FULL.

Nothing is reaching the printer

In some situations, there is no evidence that the print job has reached the printer. For locally attached printers, this may be hard to determine, because some printers give no indication when a print job arrives that they cannot handle. In these situations, you will have to review "Nothing prints, but the lights on the printer flash or change" on page 362.

For network printers, you should always use a network tracing technique, as described in Section 12.2.7, "Using iptrace to trace network printing" on page 382.

Some of the common problems associated with jobs never reaching the printer are discussed in the rest of this section.

Is the job still in the queue?

If **lpstat** shows that the job is still in the print queue, there are usually two situations.

1. The job is next in line, but the queue is down, disabled, running, or in a wait state.

   If the queue or printer is down or disabled, this indicates that the print system had problems sending the job to the printer. Common causes of this problem are:

   - Bad cable connection
   - Bad permissions on files or directories
   - Mismatch on network protocols
   - Files that are too large to print
   - Printer is turned off or off line

- The right size of paper was not requested

The steps that you should take to diagnose this symptom are:

- See if you can **cat** or **copy** the file directly to the device or network printer. This will isolate the problem to either the print device or to the print spooler. If you find the problem is with the device or the network connection, then you will not have to perform the rest of the diagnostic steps listed here, but can go directly to improving the situation by fixing the cabling, device, or actual problems with the printer.
- See if root can print the file. This will test for some file permission problems but not all. If only root can print, then you will need to check for file permission problems. Use **tcbck**, but be careful to not use the automatic fix flag, as this can introduce more problems than it fixes.
- Check to make sure that the remote printer server is using the same port numbers. A common mistake is to set up a network printer using the JetDirect protocol, when it expects the LPR/LPD remote protocol. Another problem may be using the wrong port number for a terminal server that accepts print jobs. One trick for printers that support the JetDirect protocol is to telnet to port 9100 and type data to see if it will print when you exit by pressing the designated escape character (usually Ctrl-]).
- Check the file size and file system sizes using **df** and **ls -l**.

2. The job is not first in the queue.

   It is possible that someone else's job is causing the problem. In this case, make sure you are using the same procedure, but testing with the job that is causing the problem.

Is the printer properly connected to the computer?

First, make sure the printer and the computer are connected by a cable. This can be a real problem when going through a patch panel or switching box.

Make sure that the same type of interface is used on the computer and the printer. A mistake that some people make is to assume that since both the printer and the computer adapter breakout box (such as a 128-port RAN) both have RJ-45 connectors that they can simply attach a cable between the two and make a connection. Unfortunately, the RJ-45 on the printer is usually an Ethernet connection, while that on the RAN is a serial connection, and the two will always fail to communicate. Some people make a similar mistake in connecting serial and parallel cables.

What type of cable is being used? Even though many buildings are wired with CAT 5 networking cable, do not assume that this can be used without special consideration being given to attaching serial printers. The RS/232 standard says that you should use standard shielded twisted pair cable for serial communications. CAT 5 cables do not meet this requirement. If you have to use a CAT 5 cable, make sure the proper pairs of wires are paired together to avoid crosstalk. Pay particular attention to pairing a ground signal with the data signal.

Getting the pinouts right can be a difficult exercise. For example, the IBM 64-port adapter, 128-port adapter, and 7318 terminal server all use RJ-45 connectors, but each of them uses different RS/232 pinouts. Make sure that you are using the right pinouts from the device reference guides.

Some printers use the SSD line (pin 11 on a db25 connector in DTE mode) to do hardware flow control. This line must be pinned to DCD on the IBM @server pSeries or RS/6000 adapter port.

Some printers (for instance, Epson FX1050, HP LaserJet 4M, HP LaserJet 4plus, and HP DeskJet) treat the RTS signal as a flow control signal. This signal is normally connected to the IBM @server pSeries or RS/6000 CTS line. AIX requires that the CTS signal be a sign that the printer is turned on and functional. If this signal goes false while printing, the PowerPC queue will go DOWN. For these printers, special cables are needed to wrap the RTS signal to CTS on the computer end of the cable.

The length and quality of the cable can have a huge effect on the ability to print. If the printer and adapter both support RS/232D, then quality print cables can allow the printer to be up to 200 feet from the computer. If either only supports RS/232C, then the distance should be limited to 50 feet. For parallel printing, the standard recommends 6-foot cables. Since cables are sold in lengths that exceed the standard, pay special attention to these limits.

Are the port settings right?

Serial port settings, such as baud rate, data bits, stop bits, and flow control method can be set at both the printer and the computer device setup. Make sure that you check that these setting match on both ends.

Does the printer device exist?

If for some reason the printer device is removed, sometimes a regular file can get created in the /dev directory. When this happens, the print jobs can fill up the file rather than being directed to a printer. To see if this might be the case, use the `ls -l /dev/lp#` command to make sure that each file permission starts with the 'c' for "character special device." To identify the special device file that is associated with a traditional print queue in AIX, use the **lsque** to find the queue device name and the **lsquedev** to find the associated special file. Then use the **ls -l** command on that file, as shown in Example 12-1.

Example 12-1 lsque and lsquedev command

```
$ lsque -q asc
asc:
        device = lp0
$ lsquedev -q asc  d lp0
lp0:
        file = /dev/lp0
        header = never
        trailer = never
        access = both
        backend = /usr/lib/lpd/piobe
$ ls -l /dev/lp0
crw-rw-rw-   1 root     system    24,  0 Oct 19 09:56 /dev/lp0
```

If the file listing does not start with crw, then make sure that the device is properly created. This may require removing the file and re-adding the device.

For the printer in System V printing, use the **lpstat** command with -t:

```
$ lpstat -t | grep ps1
device for ps1: /dev/lp0
$ ls -l /dev/lp0
crw-rw-rw-   1 root     system    24,  0 Oct 19 09:56 /dev/lp0
```

The following shows the output from an incorrect entry of a normal (non-device driver) file:

```
-rw-rw-rw    1  lp      lp         53455  Oct 19 09:57 /dev/lp1
```

Is the printer attached to the correct device?

From the last section, you should be able to find the device attached to a queue or printer. It is important to make sure that the device is on the adapter that you expect and at the right port. To find the device location, use the **lsdev** command, as shown here:

```
# lsdev -Cc printer
lp0 Available 01-D0-00-00 Lexmark Optra laser printer
lp1 Available 00-00-0P-00 HP LaserJet 4m
```

In this case, the lp0 location number starts with 01. This indicates that the device is one of the bus 01 of the computer. The lp1 printer device indicates that it is attached to the main parallel port. The location code varies between models, but can always be used to find the location of the adapter and port on that adapter. Make sure the printer is on the right port.

In some cases, you may find that the output that you printed went to someone's terminal screen or to a different printer. This can be a problem after restoring a mksysb tape for a system with 128-port adapters when the RANs have been added in different order. The problem is caused by the order in which the new devices are added in *walk the bus* order on restoring the mksysb tape. In this case, the safest alternative may be to remove and re-add devices.

Can you print directly to the print device?

One way to isolate the problem between the print service and the device, cable, and hardware side is to **copy** or **cat** the file directly to the device file. If the printer is an ASCII text or PCL printer, then redirect the **lptest** command to the printer as follows:

```
# splp -p+ lp0
# lptest 10 10 > /dev/lp0
```

If the printer is a PostScript, then use the **cat** command with a small PostScript file that you know works. Our suggestion is that you use one of the header files, such as H.ps. For example:

```
# cat /usr/lib/lpd/pio/burst/H.ps > /dev/lp0
```

If this prints, this indicates the problem is with the print service. If the command hangs and then returns the error message when you press Ctrl-C:

```
ksh: /dev/lp0: 0403-005 can't create the specified file
```

This usually indicates that either the printer is not turned on, or that there is a cable problem. With serial printers, this usually indicates that there is no signal coming from the printer to the computer CTS signal pin.

Is there enough space in the spool file system?

To find the space in the file system in KBs and the size of the file. See how much space is left in the /var, /tmp, and /etc file systems. If the space in /var is smaller than the file you are trying to print, increase the file system size using the **smitty chjfs** fast path. Commands to check the size of the file systems and file are:

```
# df -k
# ls -l full-path-name-to-file
```

Make sure to look at the space that is left in the file system and not the percentage left. Be sure to check that you have not run out of i-nodes. In some situations, there is space left, but no i-nodes available, so new files cannot be created under /var.

The file space issue is most important in two cases.

1. When you are spooling files

   Spooling files makes a copy of the file before it is sent to the printer. For PowerPC based printing, files are spooled to /var/spool/lpq/qdaemon, while in System V, they are spooled to /var/spool/lp/tmp. If you expect a lot of large files, then we recommend that you create a separate file system and link the spool directory. This gives you the advantage of being able to reduce the size of the file system much easier than reducing the size of /var.

2. When the server is receiving files from a remote client.

   Files received by the lpd daemon in PowerPC printing are received in /var/spool/lpd and stored there until they print. If you receive too many files, or if the files are too large, you can run out of space in this directory as well. This is harder to link, because the PowerPC print subsystem permanent files are stored in subdirectories with this as the parent directory.

Nothing prints, but you get an error message

The error messages that you get back from the print command that you use will usually be different for the two print subsystems and will be covered in the separate sections later in this chapter.

12.1.5 The output is garbled or incomplete

This section is designed to help you fix problems once there is ink on the paper. This may range from legible text with minor flaws in formatting to a few garbled characters on the page.

Are the port settings correct?

If all you see are a few upside down question marks, and other characters that do not look like real text, this may indicate a bad baud rate setting if you are on a serial connection. Make sure the baud rate set on the printer and that set on the computer match. If you are going through a modem or a multiplexer, then you may also have to match the baud with these devices.

Are the tabs set correctly?

You would see this problem most often in printing text documents with tables. Confirm this is the problem by creating a couple lines of text in a file with columns of different length separated by tabs. If this prints incorrectly, then you can change the tab setting for the virtual printer, or for the physical printer. In some serial printers, you may need to use the **stty -tabs** command.

Does only the first line print or do you see stairsteps?

This problem occurs most often when you have set to print PCL or text in passthrough mode and neither the printer nor the print subsystem are set to add carriage returns to line feeds. To test to see if this is the problem, use the **lptest** command to generate a small file and pipe to the print command.

```
# lptest 5 5 | lp -d text01
!"#$%
     "#$%&
          #$%&'
               $%&'(
                    %&'()
```

If the output is in stairsteps, as shown here, then you need to set the print spooler, filter, or printer to add carriage returns. With the virtual printer, you can make sure that the command that sets the carriage control tells the printer to add the carriage returns.

Lines only at the top of the page or zig-zagging down the page indicate that there are no carriage returns at the end of the line. Usually this means that the file was printed without formatting or using the pass-through mode.

For PCL printers, the quickest fix is to add the command to the setup to tell the printer to add its own carriage returns.

Set this in PowerPC printing with the virtual printer attribute:

```
ct=/033&k2g
```

Set this in System V printing with an echo statement in the interface script:

```
echo "\033*k2g"
```

The more correct answer for PCL printers is to set the printer as content type pcl, and use the /usr/lib/lp/bin/pcl. Register the printer with:

```
# lpfilter -f pcl -F /etc/lp/fd/pcl.fd
```

Once you have done this, the pcl filter will add carriage returns to line feeds.

Does the printer print correctly for a while then malfunction?

There are two cases when you will see the printer print correctly for a while, then skip some output and then usually print correctly again for a while.

The first case is when the flow control (serial handshake) is not set up properly between the computer and the printer. This is only a problem with RS/232 attached printers, because RS/422, parallel, and network printing all have flow control built in to the protocol or hardware.

For RS/232 attached printers, we recommend that you use hardware flow control whenever possible. With hardware flow control, when the print buffer on the printer reaches a high water mark, the printer signal on a line, such as DTR, drops. When this happens, if this signal line is attached to the AIX DCD signal, the AIX computer will stop sending data until the line is asserted once again. Because this is handled in hardware, the printing stops immediately. As soon as the printer empties the buffer to a low water mark by printing the information from the buffer, the DTR signal is asserted, and AIX starts sending data once again. The important consideration in hardware flow control is to recognize which signal line is used by the printer to indicate buffer flow and make sure that line is attached to the DCD signal line on the AIX side. In the rare instance when a printer is set up as a TTY device, RTS-CTS flow control should be used.

When the computer printing is setup with software flow control (also called XON/XOFF flow control), the printer signals that the buffer has reached its low water mark by sending an XOFF character on the printer TxD line, which is received on the computer RxD line. The computer may wait, continue to send data a character at a time until it receives a number of XOFF characters before stopping the data flow. Once the printer buffer is down to the low water mark, the printer sent an XON signal to tell the computer to resume sending data. This procedure has an built-in delay and with slow printers can cause buffer overflow and lost data. You may be able to change the print output buffer size on the device driver or set parameters to reduce the delay in responding to the XOFF, but we recommend that you change to hardware flow control if you possibly can. To change the number of XOFF characters that the driver looks for, change the RECEIVE trigger level in **smitty devices** for the printer from 3 to 1.

For slow parallel printers and plotters, there is a SMIT parameter called Microseconds to delay between characters that can help avoid this type of problem. To change the transmit buffer size for a serial printer, use **smitty devices** and change the printer's TRANSMIT buffer count.

Are there problems printing graphics?

If you are trying to print graphics files directly, then you need to find a filter that will convert the graphics to either PCL or PostScript, or use a program like a browser or xv to view the graphics file and print from there. This is usually a good solution for printing to PostScript printers.

If the graphics are in a PostScript document, then the problem probably lies in an incompatibility between the application that created the data and the printer, or you have passed the PostScript file through an ASCII text filter that has split the file based on width or added extra characters.

If the file is a formatted PCL file, the most common problem is that when the file is printed though an ASCII text queue, the line width is truncated by the text filter. It is important to print these files in passthrough mode and tell the printer to add carriage returns to line feeds.

Is the printer type correct?

Printing with the wrong printer type for the data stream can cause several different but equally undesirable results. All laser printers cannot be PostScript printers. PostScript is often an add-on option for a laser or other printer.

Does PostScript print out like a program listing?

If the output on the printer looks like a plain text file viewed using the `pg` or `more` command, then, most likely, the problem is that either the printer does not support PostScript, or you have sent the PostScript file to an ASCII printer or queue, which has sent commands to the printer to tell the printer to print text. In the first case, you can fix the problem by using a PostScript printer, or in some cases using a filter like GhostScript to convert the PostScript to PCL or other format. In the second case, you can fix the problem by creating a PostScript queue for PostScript print jobs.

Do you have unexpected symbols in the output?

In this case, much of the output prints fine, but there are control characters either at the beginning or throughout the text. Control characters for one printer may print as symbols on another. A good example would be printing a file created for an Epson InkJet printer on an HP InkJet printer. This is especially true if the file was created in a Windows application where sometimes the characters are printed as graphics. In files created on AIX, if you use the wrong virtual printer for PowerPC printing, or the wrong printer type in System V printing, then the control characters set to initialize the printer could also exhibit this behavior.

12.1.6 The output spacing is bad

The output contains the expected text and may be readable, but the text appears in an unexpected format, such as:

- Double spaced
- No left margin
- Lines only at the top of page, or zig-zagging down page
- Incorrect printer type

Double spaced

If your output is double spaced, this usually indicates that you have printed a file that already contains carriage returns at the end to a virtual printer or System V printer that adds carriage returns to line feeds. The solutions to this problem is to print in pass-through mode, or to use a filter to strip the existing carriage returns before submitting the job to the print processing.

No left margin

If you print a file that starts with tabs at the beginning of some lines, but these lines are printing at the left margin, then the tabs are not being correctly converted to spaces or not handled properly by the printer. This problem is unlikely to occur on PowerPC based printing because the default is to map tabs to eight spaces. In System V, if the printer's tab settings are not correct, they should set every eight spaces. You can have the System V print service not send tabs by using the -tabs stty option as follows:

```
# lpadmin -p printer-name -o stty=-tabs
```

12.1.7 The output prints with the wrong font

The size and type of font is dependent on several issues:

- Is the file PostScript or formatted PCL?
- What is the default font for the printer?
- What fonts are installed on the printer?
- Does the interface program or printer backend set the font?
- What is the LANG variable set to?

Is the file PostScript or formatted PCL?

With PostScript or formatted PCL files, the fonts are often specified inside the document. It may be that the font requested is not available on the printer. Potential solutions are to change the font in the document, downloading the font to flash memory on a semi-permanent basis, or downloading the font with the print job.

For PostScript fonts, the font is specified in a statement like this:

```
/Times-BoldItalic findfont
```

Since PostScript files contain only ASCII text, you can edit and change this with an editor to a font that is available on your printer.

What is the default font for the printer?

If the interface program or printer backend do not set the font, then the default font for the printer will be used. The method to check the default font will be different for different printers. See the printer's technical reference manual for more details. Another option is to add a command to set the font to the interface script or backend program. When using System V printers, this can be done with an **echo** statements in the interface script similar to the following:

```
echo "\033(s3T"
echo "\033(s15H"
```

For the PowerPC print subsystem, when using virtual printers, the font setting is a part of the virtual printer setup. Normally there will be a limited selection of the available fonts. For PCL printers, the available fonts are usually defined by the mU, eP, or eT attribute of the virtual printer. It is always possible to add a font command at the end of the printer initialization attribute ci.

Does the interface program or printer backend set the font?

In UNIX print subsystems, the character sets, styles, and fonts can be set once at the beginning by the interface program or printer backend.

In System V, the fonts are set by the interface script. For the standard interface script, the CHARSET environment variable is used to determine the required character set. If CHARSET is enabled, then it is passed to the lp.set filter as the fifth parameter. The lp.set then checks to see if the character set exists in the printer terminfo database and if it does, it will output the command string from the database to initialize the printer. This will only work with TERM types where the character set is defined. When using manufacturer scripts or interfaces built on the /usr/lib/hpnp/hpnplS.model, the character set is chosen by echoing a command sequence. For example, in the hpnplS.model script, the following line selects the character set:

```
echo "\033)0B\c"
```

The command used to set the pitch to 12 cpi is:

```
echo "\033(s12H\033)s12H\c"
```

To make changes to character sets not supported by the script, you will have to add changes to the interface script. In this case, the user chooses the pitch with the **lp -o pitch=condensed** or similar command.

In PowerPC virtual printers, the printer is initialized by the ci attribute sequences. These are set from SMIT, the Web-based System Manager, or **lsvirprt**. Users can select the print style and pitch with the **qprt -s style -p pitch** flags. To support font sizes or styles not supported by the virtual printer requires special customization. For PCL printers, this is usually done with the mU attribute.

What is the LANG variable set to?

For the PowerPC print subsystem using virtual printers, the installation LANG variable will set the input translation table for the particular virtual printer. This will show up in the _X attribute. For example:

```
# lsvirprt -q asc -d lp0 -a X
Name     Description                                        Value
_X       CODE PAGE of print file                            ISO8859-1
```

The default codepage for the US is ISO8859-1. One of the problems that people experience is that files with box characters do not print the boxes correctly when this codepage is used. To print a simple ASCII text file that contains line drawing characters, specify the IBM850 codepage by changing the X attribute, or using the following command:

```
$ qprt -XIBM850 -Ptext /tmp/testfile
```

12.1.8 The print job requests the wrong paper size

For PCL or other ASCII printers, make sure the default paper size is set right in the virtual printer or interface script. Next, make sure the command for the paper size is not embedded in the file. For PostScript files, the paper size is often defined inside the print file itself, and there is little you can do in the virtual printer or interface script to change it. You should go back to the application that creates the file.

12.1.9 Network print jobs fail to print

When printing to network print servers and network printers, the goal of troubleshooting is to isolate the problem to the print client or server and then to do local problem determination.

Print jobs still queued on local queue

Since the job is still queued on the local (client) queue, then you can assume that the job was rejected by the remote (server) system, or that the system could not be reached.

Can the client reach the server?

Before looking specifically at the printing subsystem, you should make sure that you have a good network connection between the client and the server. You should be able to ping the server from the client both by address and by name.

If you can not ping by both address and name, then printing is not going to work. If you cannot even ping by address, then fix the networking problem or make sure both the client and server are turned on and that you can ping the client from the server.

Are there any name resolution problems?

Because the rembak client and the lpd server may do a gethostbyname call, it is important that both the client and the server can recognize each other not only by address but also by name. If you are using DNS, then use the **nslookup** command to check the name lookup both by address and by name.

If you are not using a Domain Name Server (DNS), then use the **host** command instead of **nslookup**.

If you fail to get the same results from the address and the name, or if you do not get a name at all, then either add the names to the DNS, or to the /etc/hosts file.

Is the lpd daemon turned on the server?

If the server is an AIX system running the PowerPC print subsystem, then you can check to see if lpd is running by using the following command:

```
# lssrc -s lpd
```

If it is not enabled, then turn it on with:

```
# startsrc -s lpd
```

or from the SMIT menu for managing a remote printer subsystem.

If the server is an AIX system running the System V print subsystem, then first check to see that the scheduler is running with the **lpstat** command:

```
# lpstat -r
```

If this is running, then use **ps** as follows:

```
# ps -ef | grep lpNet
```

Make sure that the lpd server is accepting jobs on other servers.

Does the client have permission to print to the server?

For PowerPC servers, this means that the /etc/hosts.lpd file on the server contains an entry for the client, or has the + symbol to allow all clients. Check the server manuals for setting client permissions for other print servers. For System V printers, the allow=all only allows local users. To allow all remote users, set the allow value to all!all.

Does the network protocol match?

If the server is a network printer, then make sure that it supports LPD printing, or that you are using the appropriate type of printing on AIX to support the protocol to talk to that printer.

Collect error messages and logs

Look for error messages that may indicate a problem. In the PowerPC print subsystem, you can turn on logging with remote computing to help solve these problems.

Do a network trace to see if there are any identifying error messages in the output. For a network trace, see the Section 12.2.7, "Using iptrace to trace network printing" on page 382.

Check to see if the user received e-mail or a message

Often the text of the mail will give the information required to diagnose the problem.

Is there enough space on the server?

Some jobs are rejected by the server because there is not enough room to store the file. In this case, the file may be so large that a trace is nearly impossible. This problem is probably most easily identified if only large print jobs do not get moved to the remote server system.

Are the permissions for LPD correct on the server?

We have seen cases where the permissions for the lpd daemon or spool directory have been changed by mistake, and the daemon was unable to save files. Check that both the user ID that is running lpd and the file permissions on the /var/sbin/lpd daemon and the /var/spool/lpd directory.

Does iptrace show error messages?

Sometimes the server will send back a text error message that can be seen in the iptrace file that will help to identify the cause of the problem.

Does iptrace show negative acknowledgements?

After each request by the client, the server should return a single byte with a zero value. This can be seen in the **iptrace** output. If this value is non-zero, then the client is sending an error message back (sometimes called a negative acknowledgement or NACK) to the server. The PowerPC print subsystem will assume this means the client is not ready, and will change the queue status to DOWN. The System V print subsystem will retry after a specified timeout period for a specified number of tries based on the values in the Systems file

Is the timeout value set for System V remote printing?

When using remote printing, with the System V print subsystem, make sure that you have set a timeout value for the system you are printing to with the **lpsystem** command to set the timeout to two minutes:

```
# lpsystem -T 2 -p printer-name
```

Print jobs backing up on remote queue

If the print job backs up on the remote queue, then the connection between the client and the server was successful. In this case, you have a local printing problem on the server system.

Print jobs disappear

When the job seems to just disappear, this can be caused by flags that are accepted by the remote system lpd, but are incompatible with the printer or virtual printer on the server, or it can be a file that is incompatible with the printer on the server.

Disable the queue on the remote system

By disabling the queue on the remote system, you can find out several things. First, you can make sure that the print job has actually been queued on the server. If it has not, then you can use **iptrace** to see if it ever left the client. If it was transferred, but is no longer queued, then the lpd daemon may have some problems passing the job to the print subsystem. If the trace shows the job never left the client, then you have isolated the problem to the client.

If the file is queued on the server, then you can check to see if the flags passed to the server are valid, and if the file will print to the queue when submitted locally.

Are the flags correct?

This is a good time to play "capture the flag," as described in the individual print subsystem sections. There are two places to get the flags. The first is from the control file in the **iptrace**. The second is from the request description file. In PowerPC printing, this file is the job description file in /var/spool/lpd/qdir. In System V printing, the flag can be found in the request file in /var/spool/lp/tmp/*printer-name*/*printid*-0.

Does the file print correctly locally on the server?

The name of the copy of the file on the AIX server can also be found in the same request description files described in the previous section. Copy this file to /tmp/testfile. Now enable the queue on the server. The print job should disappear again, or you have discovered a timing problem. Now print a copy of the file you saved to /tmp/testfile without any flags. If this prints ok, then you know the file prints ok and you can try the file with the flags you found in the previous step. Often you will need to use the -o flag with enq or lp to use the captured flags. If the file does not print, then you have a local printing problem with that file and you can use the local print troubleshooting steps elsewhere in this chapter.

12.2 Common troubleshooting techniques

This section describes some of the common print troubleshooting techniques that you can use on AIX. While the previous sections of this chapter are problem oriented, this section is tool oriented.

12.2.1 Using lptest to generate print files

The **lptest** command is an excellent tool for generating a known output that can be printed. It generates a test pattern to standard output and can be used by piping the output to a print command, or redirecting it to a device. The syntax of the command is:

```
$ lptest columns lines
```

For example, to generate a file 20 lines wide by 5 lines long, use the following command:

```
$ lptest 20 5
!"#$%&'()*+,-./01234
"#$%&'()*+,-./012345
#$%&'()*+,-./0123456
$%&'()*+,-./01234567
%&'()*+,-./012345678
```

This command is useful for making sure a printer has the right print width and page length because you can generate exactly the number of rows and columns that should fit on a page. In other cases, you can generate a small number of short rows to see if there is any stair step effect on the printer.

To test printing, use pipe for the output to the print command:

```
$ lptest 10 5 | lp -d laser1
```

To output directly to the print device, use the following command:

```
$ lptest 15 5 > /dev/lp17
```

12.2.2 Use enscript to generate PostScript

The **enscript** command must be installed from the bos.txt.ts fileset. This command generates PostScript files from ASCII text files. You can combine it with the output from **lptest** with **enscript** for testing PostScript printers. Use the -d flag to specify the print queue. For example:

```
$ lptest 10 10 | enscript -d ps1
```

The **enscript** command can be used to provide additional capabilities, such as page titles, special fonts, and 2-up printing.

12.2.3 Use splp to look at printer devices

The **splp** command gives you the characteristics of the printer device. For a serial printer, it also gives the port characteristics, such as baud rate. If you are having problems with files "catted" directly to the port, try setting the device driver to passthrough with:

```
# splp -p+ lp0
```

An example of **splp** output from a parallel printer follows:

```
# splp lp0
device = /dev/lp0       (+ yes      ! no)
CURRENT FORMATTING PARAMETERS (ignored by qprt, lpr, and lp commands)
Note: -p + causes the other formatting parameters to be ignored.
-p !    pass-through?                    -c +    send carriage returns?
-l 64   page length (lines)              -n +    send line feeds?
-w 80   page width (columns)             -r + carriage rtn after line feed?
-i 0    indentation (columns)            -t !    suppress tab expansion?
-W !    wrap long lines?                 -b +    send backspaces?
-C !    convert to upper case?           -f +    send form feeds?
CURRENT ERROR PROCESSING PARAMETERS
-T 300  timeout value (seconds)          -e !    return on error?
```

12.2.4 Printing to a file

Printing to a file is one of the most useful techniques for testing how the print interface programs, backends, and filters change a print file. Because this is done differently, it will be discussed separately with each print subsystem. See Section 12.3.7, "Printing to a file" on page 393 and Section 12.4.5, "Printing to a file with PowerPC printing" on page 408 for details.

12.2.5 Printing directly to the device special file

If the queue is continuously going to a down or disabled state, the problem may be in the cabling or the device driver. To print a file directly to the device, you can use the **cat** command and simply redirect the output to the device, as shown here:

```
# cat /etc/hosts > /dev/lp32
```

If this hangs, then the printer connection may be bad, including missing signals. If you press Ctrl-C, and the screen message that returns refers to `Can't create device`, this is an indication that the serial connection is not receiving a signal on the computer CTS line. Try wrapping back RTS to CTS with a jumper to see if this solves the problem. If it does, then fix the wiring.

If you get a message back that the device is busy, use the **fuser** command to find the process that has the printer open, as follows:

```
# fuser /dev/lp12
```

When printing formatted files to the device, you may need to use splp to place the driver in passthrough mode, as described above.

Some applications open the file /dev/lp## directly and print to the file. This should work, but will probably put a lock on the file, so the print scheduler will not be able to use the print device.

12.2.6 Printing directly to network printers

This section discusses problems associated with printing directly to network printers.

Printing directly to an LPD attached printer

You can use **rembak** to print directly to the LPD on another system, but only if you are the root user or a member of the printq group. Save the file that you want to print, and use the -S flag to designate the server IP address and the -P flag to specify the printer name on the server. The **rembak** command cannot act like a filter, as it will not accept standard input. For example, to print to host net27 with a queue name of ASCII, only root can use the following command:

```
# /usr/lib/lpd/rembak -S net27 -P ASCII /tmp/testfile
```

Printing directly to an HP JetDirect attached printer

AIX contains two commands to print to HP JetDirect printers. For the PowerPC print subsystem, /usr/lib/lpd/pio/etc/piohpnpf will be used to send jobs to the printer. For the System V print subsystem, /usr/lib/hpnp/hpnpf will be used to send the jobs. The only flag needed for testing is the -x flag, to designate the host name or IP address of the printer or JetDirect box port 0. This will send data to port 9100. The following shows sample commands for each print subsystem:

```
# lptest 10 10 | /usr/lib/lpd/pio/etc/piohpnpf -x laser42.biguys.myco.com
# lptest 20 10 | /usr/lib/hpnp/hpnpf -x laser42.bigguys.myco.com
```

Telnet to JetDirect printers

For true HP JetDirect printers or print servers, you can telnet to port 9100 (or the appropriate port). You do not have to login, but can type text directly. Once you are done, type the escape control sequence given (usually Ctrl-[) and the printer will print. For example:

```
# telnet 150.1.1.4 9100
# Trying...
Connected to 150.1.1.4
Escape character is '^]'
Testing to see if this prints
Line two
^] - Press the ctrl-] key
telnet> quit
Connection closed
```

This should print the following:

```
Testing to see if this prints
Line two
```

12.2.7 Using iptrace to trace network printing

The two most used network tracing tools on AIX are **iptrace** and **tcpdump**. While **tcpdump** is useful for determining the protocols and amount of data going over the network, **iptrace** is the most useful for printing, because you can see both the handshaking as well as the actual data as it passes between the client and the server. It is also the only tool that can be used to capture the LPR control file being sent to the server.

To run **iptrace** for printing, you should first know which TCP/IP port that the transfer will use. When using standard remote printing, the well known printer port 515 will always be used. For using the HP JetDirect protocol, the port number will be 9100, except for JetDirect EX boxes with multiple ports, which will use ports 9101 and 9102. For terminal servers, you will usually find the port number during the setup. The format of the **iptrace** command that you should use for tracing printing is:

```
# iptrace -p port-number -a -b -s client-name -d server-name file-name.trc
```

Try to print with as small a job as you can, and still observe the problem, to reduce the size of the file. Once the test job has been transferred, check to see that the file has increased in size over the 11 byte beginning size. If it has not grown in size, then you probably have multiple interface adapters and may need to use the -i flag to specify a particular adapter. Assuming that the file has grown in size, find the process ID of the **iptrace**, and then use **ipformat** to format the output. The following shows a sample capture of standard remote printing between host prtsrv and netprt01:

```
# iptrace -p 515 -a -b -s prtsrv -d netprt01 /tmp/test.trc
print from the users application
# ps -ef | grep iptrace
root 12908  6970   0   14:41:51   -    0:11   iptrace
# kill 12908
# ipreport -n /tmp/test.trc > /tmp/test.rpt
# pg /tmp/test.rpt
```

12.2.8 Capturing files

Files can be captured many places along the path between the job submitter and the printer. This is necessary to find where errors may be occurring.

Capturing the file before it goes through the queue

It is often important to know if the problem is with the file, the print settings, or with the virtual printer. The user may not actually know what the file looks like. This is especially true if the job is created by an application that sends the job to the printer. These steps show how to capture the input file when using the PowerPC print subsystem:

1. Disable the queue:

```
# disable testq
```

2. Submit the job to the queue. Usually this would be from an application. For example, you would use the following print command in Netscape:

```
# lpr -P testq
```

   Check to make sure the job is queued:

```
# lpstat -vtestq
Queue   Dev   Status    Job Files              User PP %   Blks  Cp Rnk
------- ----- --------- --- ------------------ ---------- ---- -- ----
testq   lpx   DOWN
              QUEUED     66 STDIN.76636        root          1   1   1
```

3. Find the file name of the spooled file from the job description file:

```
# ls /var/spool/lpd/qdir
n0root:local$#@!iXyb
n0root:testq$#@!kRMc
n0root@rs9220a.itsc.austin.ibm.com:kristin$#@!iGUb
```

4. Tail the qdir file to get the spool file name:

```
# tail /var/spool/lpd/qdir/n0r00t:test*
-Ptestq

STDIN.76636
root
rs9220b
0
/var/spool/qdaemon/t01kRMa 2
```

5. Copy the file to /tmp/testfile. The last line of the file contains the file name:

```
# cp /var/spool/qdaemon/t01kRMa /tmp/testfile
```

Examine the file and print it with different flags. If printing remotely, you may want to compare it to the file once it reaches the server.

Capturing a file after it goes through the queue

To capture the file after it goes through the queue, print to a file, as described in the sections for the individual print subsystems.

Capturing a file as it goes over the network

The **iptrace** command can be used to capture the file and the flags as the file moves across the network from the client to the server. This can help determine if the entire file is being sent to the server, and what flags were sent. See Section 12.2.7, "Using iptrace to trace network printing" on page 382 for details.

Capturing a file on the remote system

If the remote system or server is running AIX, then you simple disable the queue on the remote system and capture it, as described in "Capturing the file before it goes through the queue" on page 383. If it is a different type of server, you will have to use tools from that server, or simply use the **iptrace** as it goes to the server.

12.2.9 Capture the flag

Often a flag that is not compatible with the system can cause a file to simply disappear. This happens when printing from applications, mainframe print methods in VMS and OS/400, or, often, from PC based lpr clients. To capture the flags, disable the queue and print the file or from the application. Then look at the job control file.

System V flags

In System V printing, the flags can be found in the request file in /var/spool/lp/tmp/*hostname*/*printid*-0 (see Example 12-2).

Example 12-2 System V flags

```
# disable junk
# lp -d junk -m -L C -o land /etc/motd
# ls /var/spool/lp/tmp/aix4prt/264-0
/var/spool/lp/tmp/aix4prt/264-0
# cat /var/spool/lp/tmp/aix4prt/264-0
C 1
D junk
F /etc/motd
N M
O land locale=C flist='/etc/motd:880'
P 20
t simple
U heidi
s   0000
```

The flags can be interpreted as shown here:

- C: The number of copies to print

- D: The requested print queue
- F: The file to be printed
- N: Mail back when printed
- O: The -o and other options
- P: Print priority
- t: Content type
- U: User sending the job

PowerPC flags

PowerPC flags can be found in the job description file located in /var/spool/lpd/qdir. For example:

```
# qprt -z+ -T"This title" -p12 -Pjunk /etc/motd
# ls -l /var/spool/lpd/qdir
total 3
-rw-rw----   1 root     printq        1304 Nov 13 09:56 n0root:junk$#@!nP7b
# cat /var/spool/lpd/qdir/n0r*
-TThis title-Pjunk

This title
root
aix4prt
0
$#@!-z
$#@!+
$#@!-p
$#@!12
/etc/motd 0
```

The flags that are listed under the environment variables are flags that are defined for the **enq** command. See the **enq** man pages for details. In this example, they are the title and the print queue:

```
-TThis title-Pjunk
```

The other flags are those sent through **enq** as -o options. These show up in lines starting with $#@!. In this example, these are:

```
$#@!-z
$#@!+
$#@!-p
$#@!12
```

This command is equivalent to:

```
enq -o -z -o + -o p -o 12 -T"This title" -Pjunk
```

The other method to capture flags is to use **iptrace**, or the lpd logging function in PowerPC lpd. In this case, you need to understand the flags that are supported by the LPD RFC-1179. The flags always appear in the control file of the trace. The flags not defined by the standard are shipped as either -o options for BSD and ATT type traces, or special AIX flags for AIX only printing. The following shows an example of the control file:

```
00000000     48616978 34707274 0a50726f 6f740a66     |Haix4prt.Proot.f|
00000010     64664134 36366169 78347072 740a5564     |dfA466aix4prt.Ud|
00000020     66413436 36616978 34707274 0a4e2f76     |fA466aix4prt.N/v|
00000030     61722f74 6d702f70 696f726c 66625f31     |ar/tmp/piorlfb_1|
00000040     36393534 0a2d6f2d 640a2d6f 700a2d6f     |6954.-o-d.-op.-o|
00000050     2d6a0a2d 6f300a2d 6f2d4a0a 2d6f300a     |-j.-o0.-o-J.-o0.|
00000060     2d6f2d5a 0a2d6f30 0a2d4e31 0a2d5a72     |-o-Z.-o0.-N1.-Zr|
00000070     6f6f7440 61697834 7072740a 2d74726f     |oot@aix4prt.-tro|
00000080     6f744061 69783470 72740a2d 542f7661     |ot@aix4prt.-T/va|
00000090     722f746d 702f7069 6f726c66 625f3136     |r/tmp/piorlfb_16|
000000a0     3935340a                                |954.            |
```

The first few flags in the file above are flags from the standard:

- Haix4prt: Client host name
- Proot: User submitting job
- fdfA466aix4prt: Temporary file name to store data
  - f: Identifies file as a plain text or formatted file
  - dfA: Identifier that this is the data file
  - 466: Job number on the client
  - aix4prt: Client host name
- UdfA466aix4pr: Unlink this File when done (says this is temporary file)

The other flags in the control file are divided between other flags, for example, flags that start with a -o, and **enq** flags. **enq** flags are the flags found with **man enq**. Many of the -o or other flags are actually virtual printer or **qprt** flags when used between two AIX systems, but are transferred as other flags because LPD on the server passes the flags to **enq** to start the print process on the AIX server.

The following shows how the flags are logged when lpd logging is turned on, as described in "Remote printing logs" on page 406:

```
lpd[56734] doit: cfn=[cfA929tesch.972600121].
lpd[56734] doit: get a line [Htesch].
lpd[56734] doit: get a line [Proot].
lpd[56734] doit: get a line [fdfA929tesch].
lpd[56734] doit: get a line [UdfA929tesch].
lpd[56734] doit: get a line [NSTDIN.6404].
```

12.2.10 Using the script shell to capture user input

When using any command from the command line that gives more output than a single screen will hold, use the **script** command to capture your keystrokes and the program output. This can be quite useful if you are running a printer install script, such as /usr/lib/hpnp/hpnpcfg. To use **script**, follow these instructions:

1. Start the script shell and designate a log file:

   ```
   # script /tmp/hpnpcfg.log
   ```

2. Run the command that you want to diagnose:

   ```
   # /usr/lib/hpnp/hpnpcfg
   ```

3. After the program exits, exit the script by typing `exit`.

   ```
   # exit
   Script command is complete on Mon Oct 23 19:17:23 CST 2000
   ```

4. Print out the log or page it to the screen:

   ```
   # lp -d net12 /tmp/hpnpcfg.log
   ```

12.2.11 Using fuser to find processes

The **fuser** command gives a list of the process IDs associated with a file. Because device drivers are represented by files in UNIX, it is possible to find the process that is currently printing to a device by using **fuser**, as shown here:

```
# fuser /dev/lp0
/dev/lp0:     12808   45590
# ps -ef | grep 12808
    root 12808  7756   0 13:46:36      -  0:00 /usr/lib/lpd/piobe /etc/motd
    root 45590 12808   0 13:46:36      -  0:00 /usr/lib/lpd/pio/etc/pioout
```

This can be useful when trying to free a hung printer queue.

12.2.12 Using the echo statement in shell scripts

Much of System V printing is done through shell scripts, and simple shell scripts can be written for PowerPC printing to diagnose things, such as bad flags being passed. Because the standard out of the shell script is often directed to the printer or to an unknown locations, when using the echo statement, direct it to a known file. For System V, an example is given in Section 12.3.10, "Troubleshooting System V interface scripts" on page 396.

12.2.13 Special considerations for some RS/232 adapters

Here we discuss some special considerations for some RS/232 adapters.

16-port adapter considerations

The 16-port adapter uses a breakout box that has 25-pin connectors. The pinouts for these connectors satisfy the requirements for printing because Txd, Rxd, DCD, and DTR are all present. In the cases where users try to use CTS flow control, there will be problems, because the CTS signal is not brought out to the breakout box. The CTS signal tells AIX that the printer is turned on. The CTS signal is wrapped back, and AIX may not be able to tell if the printer has been turned off. This is especially true when using software flow control.

128-port adapter considerations

The 128-port adapter breakout boxes are called Remote Asynchronous Nodes (RANs). The connectors are RS/45 connectors similar to those used in networking.

One of the problems with using the 128-port adapter is that the RJ/45 connectors use a unique pinout for the RS/232 signal lines that is different from the 64-port adapter and the 7318 network terminal server that IBM used to sell. It is important that you check the pinouts carefully when adding devices on 128-port adapters.

The second problem with 128-port adapters is that the DCD signal is on the outside pin of the 10-bin RJ/45 connector. This is the signal that the AIX device driver uses for hardware flow control. Since 10-bin RJ/45 connectors are hard to find at times, people use 8-bin connectors, which do not contain the DCD pin. Through software control, the DSR signal (pin 2) can be made to act like DCD and the hardware flow control will still work. For this to work, you must set Use Alternate RJ 45 pinouts to `Yes` in SMIT.

Attaching printers with four wires

When buildings are pre-wired with cables containing only four wires, there are often problems attaching serial printers. First of all, unless you do special wiring to insure that the DTR signal from the printer attaches to the DCD signal on the AIX system, there will be no hardware flow control. Second, the CTS signal on the AIX side will need to have a wrap cable from the AIX RTS signal or the port will not be able to open and you will get the `Can't create` error message when catting to the file. In the case, the queue would always go down.

The second option that some people use is to add the printer as a TTY device with clocal turned on. In this case, you will use software flow control. The only problem that we have seen with this setup is that the queue does not know when the printer has been taken off line, and jobs can be lost because XOFF may not be sent or seen.

12.3 Troubleshooting for System V printing

This section lists the troubleshooting techniques that only apply to System V printing on AIX.

12.3.1 File permission problems

Some of the key permissions you will want to check are:

- Are the permissions for lpsched and lpNet set to ----s--x--- owned by root:lp?
- Are the default filters in /usr/lib/lp/bin set to executable?
- Is the interface program executable?
- Are the device file attributes allowing users to print?

12.3.2 Is the print service active?

To see if the scheduler is running, use the **lpstat** command with -r:

```
# lpstat -r
scheduler is running
```

For printing to remote servers, check that lpNet is also started:

```
# ps -ef | grep lpNet
```

If the scheduler is not running, try to restart it with:

```
# /usr/lib/lp/lpsched
```

You do not have to separately start lpNet, as lpsched starts it automatically.

Before making major changes, disable the scheduler with **lpshut**.

If the daemons are not active, double check the permissions on files, and make sure that you check any changes you made during since it was last active.

12.3.3 Does the printer have the right attributes?

It is important the printer setup have the right attributes both for the local printer device as well as for the printer spooler attributes.

Printer device

Check the communications attributes of the serial or parallel device driver to make sure they match those of the printer.

System V defined printer attributes

System V attributes that must match the printer include:

- Printer type
- Printer interface
- Content type

Other printer attributes that you need to pay attention to are the permissions for the printer and for forms set with the allow and deny flags in **lpadmin**. The default allow for a printer is all, but that is only good for local users. See the **lpadmin** man pages for the syntax for allowing remote user permissions. The setting for all users on all systems is all!all.

12.3.4 Logs and status files

There are a number of places to check for logs.

Check the mail

Check your mail to see if you have received any mail messages from the lp user. These will give you a place to start looking for the problem. An example error message is shown in Example 12-3.

Example 12-3 Example of error message

```
From lp Tue Oct 24 09:33:01 2000
Received: (from lp@localhost)
 by rs9220b.itsc.austin.ibm.com (AIX5.0/8.9.3/8.9.3) ID JAA61332
 for root@rs9220b; Tue, 24 Oct 2000 09:33:01 -0600
Date: Tue, 24 Oct 2000 09:33:01 -0600
From: lp
Message-Id: <200010241533.JAA61332@rs9220b.itsc.austin.ibm.com>
To: root@rs9220b.itsc.austin.ibm.com
Content-Length: 173
Status: RO

Subject: Status of lp request hp1-357

 Your request hp1-357 destined for hp1
 encountered an error while printing on printer hp1.
Printing stopped with an exit code of 1.
```

In this case, the problem was with an unsupported LANG variable and the message was not much help, but in other instances, this message can be very helpful.

Check the logs in /var/lp/logs

There are three files in this directory:

- requests
- lpsched
- lpNet

The requests file gets updated every time someone attempts to print. It contains the default flags, and other information, as shown in the sample log entry in Example 12-4.

Example 12-4 Sample log entry

```
= hpl-357, uid 0, gid 0, lid 0, size 110, Tue Oct 24 09:32:59 2000
z hpl
C 1
D hpl
F /var/spool/lp/tmp/rs9220b/357-1
O locale=en_US flist=':110'
P 20
t simple
U root
r
s 0x0100
```

This shows the ownership of the user who printed, the date the job was printed, the job ID, the priority, and the content type. This also shows the location of the file being printed. This does not tell you as much about what is wrong, as it does tell you how the print job was submitted. For example, this **lp** command used the -r flag when it was submitted.

The lpsched log tells you when lpsched was started and stopped, and any errors that have occurred in forking child processes or in executing interface scripts (see Example 12-5).

Example 12-5 lpsched log entry

```
Thu Oct 12 18:55:36 2000: UX:lpsched: INFO: Print services stopped.
Thu Oct 12 18:55:44 2000: UX:lpsched: INFO: Print services started.
Thu Oct 12 23:12:30 2000: UX:lpsched:
   ERROR: 0920-281 Received unexpected signal 33; terminating.
Fri Oct 13 08:39:32 2000: UX:lpsched: INFO: Print services started.
Fri Oct 13 11:08:28 2000: UX:lpsched:
   ERROR: 0920-271 Failed to fork child process
          (Resource temporarily unavailable).
Thu Oct 12 18:55:36 2000: UX:lpsched: INFO: The network process has terminated.
```

The lpNet log shows you when network programs such as lpNet are forked, and when connections are made with remote systems. This log shows the events when we tried to cancel a job that was not printing on a remote system (see Example 12-6).

Example 12-6 lpNet log entry

```
10/24/00 10:37 c 12972 rs1230a.myco.com lpd retrying connection to
rs1230a.myco.com
10/24/00 10:45 c 58614 rs1230a.myco.com ERROR:
   class=Fatal, type=Unix, trace=(contimeout/setjmp), Interrupted system call
10/24/00 10:45 c 58614 rs1230a.myco.com Abnormal process termination.
10/24/00 10:47 p 61398 <none> Got a hit.
10/24/00 10:47 p 61398 <none> Got a hit. lpExec
10/24/00 10:47 p 61398 <none> Started child for rs1230a.myco.com, pid = 50990
10/24/00 10:47 p 61398 <none>  Into Polling loop.
10/24/00 10:47 c 50990 rs1230a.myco.com lpd starting (active)
```

Checking the pstatus file

The /var/spool/lp/system/pstatus file contains a status stanza for each of the printers. This file often has a line with the last failure as shown here:

```
==========
net12
enabled accepting
972671048 971311069
NAK'd by remote lpd: waiting auto retry
new destination
```

12.3.5 Is the LANG variable set right?

If you try to print from a locale that has not been fully installed on your system, you may get errors, such as the one shown below:

```
# lptest 10 10 | lp -d hp1
UX:lp: ERROR: 0920-054 There is no filter to convert the file content.
    TO FIX: Use the lpstat -p -l command to find a
        printer that can handle the file type
        directly, or consult with your system
        administrator.
```

However, if you simply add the -L C flag, the file prints with no errors:

```
# lptest 10 10 | lp -L C -d hp1
request ID is hp1-362 (standard input)
```

12.3.6 Cancelled remote jobs still queued

When a remote printer is set up, and for some reason it stops printing when you cancel a job, the job is still visible to **lpstat** but shows a canceled status, as shown here:

```
# lpstat -o all
net12-359          root          110   Tue Oct 24 10:16:50 2000 canceled
```

In this case, you will probably have to shut down the scheduler and restart, although it may be possible to kill the **lpNet** command that is hanging that port.

12.3.7 Printing to a file

By printing to a file, you can see exactly what the virtual printer has added to the file that is being printed. With the **lpadmin** command, you can specify an output file with the -v option. The following procedure explains how you could use this to diagnose a problem:

1. Create a file in the /dev directory. The file must have permissions for the user doing the testing to use, therefore you can set the permissions accordingly:

   ```
   # touch /dev/lpx
   # chmod 600 /dev/lpx
   # chown lp:lp /dev/lpx
   ```

2. Create a printer to a file using the printer type, interface type, and content type that you want to diagnose:

   ```
   # lpadmin -m standard -T hplaserjet -I simple -p fileq -v /dev/lpx
   ```

   This may give an error if the lpx permissions are set to 777 or something else, but that is not a problem. For PostScript queues, you will need to specify type PS-b, because this uses lp.cat, while PS uses postio, which will not print to a file, but only to a printer.

   ```
   # lpadmin -m PS -T PS-b -I PS -p fileps -v /dev/lpx
   ```

3. Give the commands to have the printer accept jobs and enable the printer:

   ```
   # accept fileq
   UX:accept: INFO: destination "fileq" now accepting requests
   # enable fileq
   UX:enable: INFO: printer "fileq" now enabled
   ```

4. Print to the fileq printer with a test job and make sure there is data in the file:

   ```
   # lptest 5 5 | lp -d fileq -L C
   request ID is fileq-594 (standard input)
   # ls -l /dev/lpx
   -rw-rw-rw-   1 lp      lp            222 Nov 01 12:34 /dev/lpx
   # cat /dev/lpx
   ```

When looking at the file, it may be useful to use **vi** and the **od** command to look at escape sequences.

12.3.8 Cleaning up and starting over

It should not be necessary to clear out all the queues and start over, but you might have a need for this if you clone a system.

Resetting the print subsystem job number

The job number for the local jobs is stored in /spool/tmp/*host-name*/.SEQF and contains four fields separated by colons, as shown here:

```
1:999:1:598
```

The first two numbers are the limits of the job numbers. The next number shows where this job sequence started, and the last number (598) is the number of the next print request. To change the sequence number, just change this last value, and recycle the print subsystem with **lpshut** and **lpsched**.

Cleaning out old print files

If you are just having problems you may want to start out by cleaning out the job request files. First check to see the job names and cancel them, as shown here:

```
# lpstat -o
# cancel fileps-124
```

If you are not able to cancel the files, then remove the individual files from the /spool/tmp/*host-name* directory and the /var/spool/lp/requests/*host-name* directory.

Cleaning out old printers

Try to use **lpadmin** first to remove the queues using the -x flag

```
# lpadmin -x fileps
```

Check to see if the file was not removed and if it was not, then remove the directory files and the interface program:

```
# lpstat -p fileps -l
# rm -R /etc/lp/printers/fileps
# rm /etc/lp/interfacers/fileps
```

Remove the temporary files

The temporary message files and such sometimes build up in the /var/spool/lp/tmp and /var/spool/lp/temp directories and subsequent subdirectories. Use **ls -lR /var/spool/lp/tmp** to look for file that might be left over.

Remove the old log files

The log files are stored in /var/lp/logs. We would make a backup copy of the logs and then copy /dev/null on top of each of the files to zero them or simply redirect nothing, as shown here:

```
# > /var/lp/logs/lpNet
# > /var/lp/logs/lpsched
# > /var/lp/logs/requests
```

12.3.9 Stopping unwanted header pages

In System V printing, the banners are controlled by the interface script, the printer setup, and the command line flags.

Configuration banner selection

When creating the printer, specify no banners. If you are creating or modifying a printer with **lpadmin**, use the -o nobanner flag to specify that you do not want banners.

The configuration file in /etc/lp/printers/printer-name/configuration may show:

```
Banner: on:Always
```

The Always forces a banner page no matter what the user sends on the **lp** command line. After you run **lpadmin -o nobanner**, this line will change to:

```
Banner: on
```

This does not turn off banners, but allows the user to select to not have banners by using the -o nobanner flag to the **lp** command.

Command line banner selection

If the administrator has enabled banner select for users with -o nobanner, as described in the previous section, then the user can avoid banners with the **lp -o nobanner** command, as shown here:

```
$ lp -o nobanner -d finetext
```

By default, the **lpr** command will always send a command line flag to have a header page. To avoid this, you can use **lpr -h** for no header.

Interface file banner selection

For local printers, find the interface in /var/spool/lp/admins/lp/interfaces that has the same name of the printers. The script should have a line that starts with nobanner="no". To easily find this in vi, use the **find** command with a carat (beginning of line) as follows:

```
/^nobanner
nobanner="no"
```

Change this to:

```
nobanner="yes"
```

12.3.10 Troubleshooting System V interface scripts

Many of the System V interface programs are scripts. This makes it easy for you to use the **echo** command to investigate problems, and even to determine the order of events for local programs, or to determine where formatting errors might be occurring.

Each local printer has an interface program in /etc/lp/interfaces based on one of the model scripts. For example, if your printer is named hp1, the interface will be /etc/lp/interfaces/hp1. To see if the hp1 script is called, edit the script, and after the line that starts with the word trap, enter these two lines:

```
date >> /tmp/hp1.log
echo "entered hp1" >> /tmp/hp1.log
```

Set the permission on /tmp/hp1.log, so all users can write:

```
# chmod 755 /tmp/hp1.log
```

Now print to the hp1 queue, and check the log:

```
Fri Oct 27 13:33:40 CST 2000
entered hp1
```

This shows that the script is invoked. Now you can try to use this to find problems that you have. For example, if you issue the following **lp** command, you may want to know if the problem is from the **lp** command, or from the interface script:

```
# lp -o cpi=17 -d hp1 /etc/motd
UX:lp: ERROR: 0920-056 The following options can't be handled:
        -o cpi=
    TO FIX: The printer(s) that otherwise qualify
        for printing your request can't handle
        one or more of these options. Try
        another printer, or change the options.
```

Checking the log, you will find that the entry was not logged, so the problem occurs prior to reaching the interface script, and therefore it is likely that terminfo was not checked.

You can also use this method to verify the command line arguments that have been passed to the script or to check the environment variables that have been set and passed by **lpsched**. Adding the lines in bold to the script can help show information that was passed:

```
## Check arguments
##########

echo "Arguments are $*" >> /tmp/hp1.log
parse () {
        echo "`expr \"$1\" : \"^[^=]*=\(.*\)\"`"
        echo "`expr \"$1\" : \"^[^=]*=\(.*\)\"`" >> /tmp/hp1.log
```

and

```
printer=`basename $0`
request_id=$1
user_name=$2
title=$3
copies=$4
option_list=$5
echo "printer: $printer" >> /tmp/hp1.log
echo "requist_id: $request_id" >> /tmp/hp1.log
echo "user_name: $user_name" >> /tmp/hp1.log
echo "title: $title" >> /tmp/hp1.log
echo "Number of copies: $copies" >> /tmp/hp1.log
echo "#options: $option_list" >> /tmp/hp1.log

shift 5
files="$*"
echo "Filenames: $files" >> /tmp/hp1.log
```

The following **echo** statements help to diagnose problems with the parameters sent to lp.set and can be placed in the internal_lpset subroutine:

```
internal_lpset () {
echo "Inside internal_lpset" >> /tmp/hp1.log
echo "LPSET parms are $1:$2:$3:$4:$5" >> /tmp/hp1.log
echo "LPSET parms are cpi:lpi:width:length:character set" >> /tmp/hp1.log
```

Test the environment variables somewhere in the script with:

```
env >> /tmp/hp1.env
```

or

```
set >> /tmp/hp1.env
```

These tools can be expanded until you find the problems.

Most of the interface scripts also write to a log file, but the log file is usually removed when the script exits. If you continue to have problems, comment out the statement that removes the temporary log, print, and then check the log file. For example, in the JetDirect backend, uncomment the lines that say:

```
rm -f $LOGFILE
```

12.3.11 Check timeouts in the Systems file for remote queues

Under certain conditions, remote queues may have problems if the timeouts are not properly set. Check the timeouts for the remote queue by checking the /etc/lp/Systems file. The following output does not have timeout numbers, as shown by no numbers:

```
rs1230a.itsc.austin.ibm.com:x:-:bsd:-:-:-:-:-:
```

The following file shows a timeout value of 1 minute with 2 retrys:

```
rs1230a.itsc.austin.ibm.com:x:-:bsd:-:1:2:-:-:
```

If timeout is not set, set the timeout with **lpsystem**, as shown here:

```
# lpsystem -T 2 rs1230a.itsc.austin.ibm.com
```

12.3.12 Is /etc/lp/Systems file entry correct?

The /etc/lp/Systems file must contain the full name that the **lpNet** command gets when doing a get host by name. In testing, we found that if you simply put the IP address in this file that we could send jobs to the system, but not receive them. Only after entering the fully qualified domain name were we able to receive print jobs. The entry looked like this:

- The first line was replace by the second shown below:

  ```
  rs1290a:x:-:bsd:-:1:2:-:-:ibm4312
  rs1290a.itsc.austin.ibm.com:x:-:bsd:-:1:2:-:-:ibm4312
  ```

- You can also look at the Systems settings for a specific setting with **lpsystem**:

  ```
  # lpsystem -l rs1290b
  System:                      rs1290b
  Type:                        bsd
  Connection timeout:          1 minutes
  Retry failed connections:    after 1 minutes
  Comment:                     jetdir
  ```

12.3.13 Example: solving a remote printing problem

This section shows a troubleshooting example for both an outgoing and an incoming LPD print job.

Example: Missing outgoing network print jobs

Symptoms: Jobs to the remote printer are queued, but continue in a running state. When you try to cancel them, they stay in the **lpstat** output, but show as canceled. Running the **lpstat -o net12** command for printer net12, there was a several second delay, and then no output printed.

After stopping the scheduler and restarting, we cleared the /etc/lp/logs/lpNet flag, and re-ran the **lpstat -o net12** command; we get the following output to the **lpNet** log:

```
10/27/00 11:12 p  7888 <none> Got a hit.
10/27/00 11:12 p  7888 <none> Got a hit. lpExec
10/27/00 11:12 p  7888 <none> Started child for rs1230a.itsc.austin.ibm.com,
pid = 19322
10/27/00 11:12 p  7888 <none>  Into Polling loop.
10/27/00 11:12 c 19322 rs1230a.itsc.austin.ibm.com lpd starting (active)
```

When we check the process table for process 19322, we get:

```
# ps -ef | grep 19322
root 19322  7888   0 11:12:19      -  0:00 lpNet
```

This is a child process forked by the parent lpNet, as shown by this **ps** command:

```
# ps -ef | grep lpNet
    root  7888 45298   0 10:59:18      -  0:00 lpNet
    root 19322  7888   0 11:12:19      -  0:00 lpNet
```

The lpNet parent is owned by process 45298, which is the scheduler:

```
# ps -ef | grep 45298
    root  7888 45298   0 10:59:18      -  0:00 lpNet
    root 45298     1   0 10:59:18      -  0:00 /usr/lib/lp/lpsched
```

We checked the /etc/lp/Systems file to see if the server was entered:

```
$ cat /etc/lp/Systems
9.19.129.12:x:-:bsd:-:3:10:-:-:
rs1230a.itsc.austin.ibm.com:x:-:bsd:-:1:2:-:-:
```

We checked the configuration file to see if the server name matched:

```
$ cat /etc/lp/printers/net12/conf*
Banner: on:Always
Content types: simple
Printer type: hplaserjet
```

```
Remote: rs1230a.itsc.austin.ibm.com!TEXT
Range: 3,8
Form feed: on
```

The match showed the server name was the same in both files.

We checked the connection to the host:

```
$ ping rs1230a
0821-062 ping: host name rs1230a NOT FOUND
```

We checked the host list and found the host name for the printer had been changed without our knowledge to rs1290a, so we used the **lpadmin** command to change the server name, but received the message:

```
UX:lpadmin: ERROR: 0920-195 System "rs1290b" does not exist.
    TO FIX: Use the "lpsystem -l" command to list
        all known systems.
```

We ran the **lpsystem** command to add the new host, and re-ran the **lpadmin** command to change the server.

```
# lpadmin -s rs1290a -p net12!TEXT
```

After making this change, the **lpstat -o net12** command returned immediately, but the file in the queue still did not print. We recycled the print service with **lpshut** and **lpsched**, but the file did not print. Next, we tried to disable the printer, but the message said the printer was already disabled. We enabled the printer, and the job printed.

Example: Missing inbound network print job

Symptom: A job was printed from an AIX Version 4.3.3 server to the AIX 5L System V print queue, but disappeared without printing. The AIX Version 4.3.3 lpd log shows that the job was successfully sent, and the /etc/lp/logs/netLP file shows:

```
11/01/00 14:42 p 19414 <none> Got a hit.
11/01/00 14:42 p 19414 <none> Got a hit. listenBSD
11/01/00 14:42 p 19414 <none>  Into Polling loop.
11/01/00 14:42 c  9190 matt.dfw.com lpd starting (passive)
11/01/00 14:42 c  9190 matt.dfw.com matt.dfw.com requests recv job hp1
11/01/00 14:42 c  9190 matt.dfw.com lpd exiting, status=0
```

This appears to have been a successful receipt of the job to queue hp1, but nothing shows on the printer, in the interface echo logs, or in the /var/lp/logs/lpsched or /var/lp/logs/requests files. The **lpstat -o** command shows that no jobs are queued.

We disabled the queue, and repeated the test print from the remote client, but again nothing was queued. Suspecting a problem with locale, because we often have to use the **lp -L C** command to print, we tried starting **lpsched** with the locale set to C instead of en_US, as follows:

```
# lpshut
# export LANG=C
# /usr/lib/lp/lpsched
```

This did not resolve or change the problem in any way.

We checked the /var/spool/lp/system/pstatus file and it read:

```
==========
hp1
disabled accepting
973111581 972921654
unknown reason
Testing the printer
```

The test user on the client received this mail message:

```
Subject: printer job

Your printer job
could not be printed.

Reason for failure:

UX:lpd: ERROR: 0920-053 You are not allowed to use the destination
        "hp1".
    TO FIX: Use the lpstat -p command to list all
        known printers; you can use those marked
        "available".
```

The **lpstat -p** command showed the queue hp1 was available.

```
# lpstat -p | grep hp1
printer hp1 disabled since Wed Nov  1 14:46:21 2000. available.
```

We checked the allow file for the printer:

```
# cat /etc/lp/printers/hp1/users.allow
all
```

The **lpadmin** command says that to receive jobs from remote systems that this file needs to be all!all. We changed the file with:

```
# lpadmin -u allow:all!all -p hp
```

We recycled the scheduler and can now print from the remote client.

12.3.14 Troubleshooting HP JetDirect printing

When printing to a network printer with the HP JetDirect print protocol, there are some default tools for debugging.

Check for /tmp/hpnpf.* log files

```
# ls -l /tmp/hpnpf.*
-rw-r--r--   1 lp      lp           280 Nov 15 16:40 /tmp/hpnpf.41480
# cat /tmp/hpnpf.41480
wsm1-331       /etc/lp/interfaces/model.orig/wsm1 | /usr/lib/hpnp/hpnpf -x
rs1290b
wsm1-331       Do not have access
wsm1-331       Do not have access
wsm1-331       Do not have access
wsm1-331       Do not have access
wsm1-331       Do not have access
wsm1-331       5 errors logged for wsm1-331; errors no longer logged
```

The `Do not have access` is an indication that the printer may be offline. The JetDirect protocol does *not* use the lpsystem information in any way. At this point, check to see if the printer is available using **ping**. Then telnet to port 9100. If you get the following error, then check the printer:

```
# telnet 9.3.240.52 9100
Trying...
telnet: connect: A remote host refused an attempted connect operation.
```

Stair step output on PCL printers

The default printer that you create with type simple will give stair step output. The key to getting this to work right on PCL printers is to set the content type for the printer to pcl, and registering the pcl filter. To register the pcl filter, use the following command:

```
# lpfilter -f pcl -F /etc/lp/fd/pcl.fd
```

12.4 Troubleshooting for PowerPC printing

The following section includes troubleshooting tips that only apply to the PowerPC print subsystem.

12.4.1 File permission problems

The only time you are likely to have problems with file permissions is when an overaggressive system administrator has made changes manually, or someone has run **tcbck** with the flags set to automatically fix problems. Symptoms of the problem are:

- Only root can print.
- Cannot print from some directories.

Use **tcbck** to find out what files appear to have the wrong permissions, and change them manually. A checklist of common print permission errors is given in the troubleshooting chapter of the *AIX 5L Version 5.1 Guide to Printers and Printing*, found at:

```
http://publibn.boulder.ibm.com/cgi-bin/ds_form?lang=en_US&viewset=AIX
```

12.4.2 Is the print service active?

To determine if the qdaemon and lpd are active, you can use the **lssrc** command, as shown here:

```
# lssrc -s qdaemon
# lssrc -s lpd
```

Starting the print services

To restart either daemon, use the **startsrc** command:

```
# startsrc -s qdaemon
# startsrc -s lpd
```

Be sure to check again to make sure that the daemons have stayed active.

The qdaemon will not stay active

A frequent problem that occurs when administrators manually edit the /etc/qconfig file is that the qdaemon finds syntax errors in the file and will not remain active. If this is the case, make a backup copy of /etc/qconfig, and then start removing queues from the end one at a time, try to restart the qdaemon after removing each queue. A queue consists of two paragraphs or stanzas of information: the queue stanza, which points to the queue device stanza. Make sure that there is a queue device for each queue stanza. Make sure that all lines begin with a tab, except for the lines defining the queue or queue device names, and these must start in column zero.

Extraneous files in qdir

Another problem that can cause errors and problems with the qdaemon are extraneous files in the /var/spool/lpd/qdir directory. If there are any files in this directory other than job description files for active queues, these files should be removed.

The dummy queue device

When queue devices are removed while jobs are queued, sometimes you will end up with a queue with a dummy queue device. To fix this, remove the queue stanza from /etc/qconfig, and remove any virtual printer files, status files, and job description files associated with that queue.

12.4.3 Does the printer have the right attributes?

Setting up a printer with the wrong attributes can cause problems with flow control and formatting. It is important that you match the printer to one similar in capabilities in AIX. Both the attributes of the printer device and the virtual printer are important.

Printer device

When adding a printer that is locally attached using either RS/232 or parallel interfaces, there are a number of attributes that need to be set.

RS/232 attached printers

For RS/232 attached printers, the baud rate, number of data bits, parity setting, and number of stop bits must all match those set on the printers. In addition, the size of the buffer can be important, because with some slow printers the data may be sent faster than the printer can accept the data and so fast that it cannot set the flow control. The other RS/232 setting that must match is the flow control. Although hardware flow control is recommended, either hardware or software flow control can be used. The important thing is that it must be set the same on both the printer and the computer device settings.

Parallel attached printers

About the only setting that can really affect the outcome of parallel attached printers is the delay with which the printers respond to the hardware handshake lines. For slow printers and plotters, the value for `Delay between characters` can be increased in the printer devices section.

Virtual printers

While device attributes can determine whether something can print, the virtual printer attributes will have a large effect on the output that actually appears on the printed page. Because a virtual printer does printer initialization with print commands that are unique to the data stream supported by the printer, it is important that you select a virtual printer that uses the same data stream that your printer expects.

Other things that must match are the page width and length, especially when printing text files.

12.4.4 Logs and status files

When you are having printing related problems, there are messages and log files that can help resolve the problem. This section describes a number of the places you might look for diagnostic information.

Command line error messages

When you print, the first opportunity for error comes from using illegal command flags or values for those flags. An example of using the wrong flag is shown here:

```
# cd /tmp
# cat cmderr.txt
# lp -p69 -P3130pcl /etc/motd
lp: illegal option -- p
usage: lp [-cmsw] [-dDestination] [-nNumber] [-oOption]
          [-tTitle] [-] File ...
          Prints a file in a format suitable for sending to a line printer.
```

Mail messages

Often, either the qdaemon or the piobe backend will mail messages to the user submitting the job and the root user, describing problems that occur.

Messages to the console

Often, the message that a queue has gone down or other errors will be printed to the user's login terminal.

Virtual printer error message files

When errors occur with parameters for flags within the virtual printer, an error file is created in /var/spool/lpd/pio/@local. The files begin with msg and then contain a number, a period, and the queue name and device name.

For example, this command with an illegal pitch:

```
# qprt -p15 -P3130pcl /etc/motd
```

produced this error message in msg1.3130pcl:@aus3130b:

```
-------------------------------------------------------------
Thu Oct 26 13:23:07 2000 (root)
-------------------------------------------------------------
=====> MESSAGE FROM PRINT JOB 1062 (/etc/motd) <=====
0782-598 The value 1 specified in the validate op V in the
limits field for _p attribute indicates failure
```

Remote printing logs

Both **rembak** and **lpd** have the capability to use log files. This can provide information on what type of errors might have occurred.

Using rembak log files

When creating a queue, this can be added in the field labeled:

```
To turn on debugging, specify output file pathname [/tmp/rem1.log]
```

For later, a -D logfile flag is added to /etc/qconfig, as shown here:

```
backend = /usr/lib/lpd/rembak -D /tmp/remback.log
```

Normally, you will do this by changing a queue device from SMIT.

The output contains a lot of information, and may save you from doing a trace. The part of the output that shows the file being sent is shown in Example 12-7.

Example 12-7 Sample of rembak log file

```
# grep sendjob rem1.log
rembak[56708] sendjob: sendjob starts, jobname=STDIN.46218, current
time=9725985
26.
rembak[56708] sendjob: datafn[0]=dfA069rs9220b, fakedfn=dfA069rs9220b.
rembak[56708] sendjob: ctrlfname=/tmp//rembakOFTyqa, fakecfn=cfA069rs9220b.
rembak[56708] sendjob: State machine starts.....
rembak[56708] sendjob: State 1 - send the "Receive a Print Job" request.
rembak[56708] sendjob: state 3 - Send data file(s), dfcount=1.
rembak[56708] sendjob:  realfn=/var/spool/qdaemon/tOnJiEa,
fakefn=dfA069rs9220b,
 filter=/usr/lib/lpd/aixshort.
rembak[56708] sendjob: State 2 - send control file,
ctrlfname=/tmp//rembakOFTyqa
, fakecfn=cfA069rs9220b.
rembak[56708] sendjob: State 5 - end of job #69 (STDIN.46218).
rembak[56708] sendjob: Delete control file /tmp//rembakOFTyqa.
```

Using lpd log files

When receiving files, the lpd daemon can also make logs of the activity. To turn on lpd debugging, stop the qdaemon and restart with:

```
# stopsrc -s lpd
# startsrc -s lpd -a "-D /tmp/lpddebug"
```

The output from this command is helpful in that it provides information on the control file that was passed to AIX, as well as the **enq** command that lpd generated. Example 12-8 shows some of the output from a sample run.

Example 12-8 Sample of lpd log file

```
lpd[56734] doit: cfn=[cfA929tesch.972600121].
lpd[56734] doit: get a line [Htesch].
lpd[56734] doit: get a line [Proot].
lpd[56734] doit: get a line [fdfA929tesch].
lpd[56734] doit: get a line [UdfA929tesch].
lpd[56734] doit: get a line [NSTDIN.6404].
lpd[56734] doit: exec enq cmd=[/usr/bin/enq -P3130pcl -r -troot@tesch
-Zroot@tes
ch.aix.dfw.ibm.com -N1 -TSTDIN.6404 /var/spool/lpd/dfA929tesch.972600121 ].
```

Job description files

The job description file (JDF) can help find information about the file that is being printed, the user's environment, and the flags that are being passed. In most cases, the information at the end of the file is most useful. For example, the JDF file Example 12-9 shows the **enq** flags, the 'other' flags, and the file being printed.

Example 12-9 Sample of job description file

```
-Ttesting-Ptestq

testing
root
rs9220b
0
$#@!-d
$#@!p
$#@!-p
$#@!17
$#@!-z
$#@!+
$#@!-f
$#@!1
/var/spool/qdaemon/t6FLT7a 2
```

Line descriptions for the file above are:

- The line with -Ttesting-Ptestq shows which of the standard **enq** flags were passed from **qprt** to **enq**.
- The middle lines show the title was testing, printed by root on system rs9220b.
- The lines beginning with $#@! are formatting flags from **qprt**, or **lp -o** that are treated as 'other' flags by **enq**. They are usually virtual printer formatting flags and useful for diagnosing problems where illegal flags are being sent a a job simply disappears. Test these flags individually with **enq -o**. A common problem is the -fl flag; if this is set, make sure the virtual printer has an fl attribute set to %ip.
- The final line in the file is the name of the file being printed. Because this is in /var/spool/qdaemon, the file has been spooled locally. For local jobs that are not spooled, the original file name will show on this line. For jobs received from remote clients, the files will be in /var/spool/lpd.

Status files

Status files are used by **lpstat** and **qchk** to list the status of the file. The files are in /var/spool/lpd/stat, and begin with s.; however, the files are in binary format and cannot be directly accessed. The PID file in this directory does give the process ID of the qdaemon, and the files that begin with p. contain process IDs for processes forked by the qdaemon. For example, before a device timed out on lp0 (because the printer was turned off), the file p.textq.lp0 contained the value 12808. To see what processes are associated with this queue, use the **ps** command, as shown here:

```
# cat plocal.txt
# ps -ef | grep 12808
    root 12808  7756   0 13:46:36      -  0:00 /usr/lib/lpd/piobe /etc/motd
    root 45590 12808   0 13:46:36      -  0:00 /usr/lib/lpd/pio/etc/pioout -A0
-B880 -C14688 -F\14\15
    root 46824 14270   1 13:50:52  pts/1  0:00 grep 12808
```

This shows that the **pioout** command was called by piobe. The **pioout** command is the filter that writes to the local device port.

12.4.5 Printing to a file with PowerPC printing

By printing to a file, you can see exactly what the virtual printer has added to the file that is being printed. In AIX 5L, you have the capability to add printers to a file in the /dev directory.

The following procedure explains how you could use this to diagnose a problem:

1. Create a file in the /dev directory. The file must have permissions for the user doing the testing to use; therefore, you can set the permissions accordingly:

```
# touch /dev/lpx
# chmod 666 /dev/lpx
```

2. Create a queue printing to a file using the printer type you want to diagnose:

```
# smitty mkpq
Choose: file File in the /dev directory
Choose the printer manufacturer
Choose the model of printer
Name of existing file in the /dev directory [lpx]
Enter the queue name testq and press [Enter]
```

3. Test print to the queue:

```
# lptest 5 5 | qprt -P testq
```

4. Examine the file with vi or od (see Example 12-10).

Example 12-10 Sample file as a queue

```
^[%-12345X@PJL SET RESOLUTION = 300
@PJL SET LPAPERSOURCE = TRAY1
@PJL SET PAPER = LETTER
@PJL SET LTRAY1PAPERTYPE = NORMAL
@PJL ENTER LANGUAGE = PCL
^[(s17H^M
^[(s0S^[(s0B^[(s3T^[&l10^[&k0G^[&l8.00C^[(8U!"#$%^M
"#$%&^M
#$%&'^M
$%&'(^M
%&'()^M
^[E^[(s17H^[&l10^[&k0G^[&l6D^[%-12345X
```

5. Compare the output with the printer reference manual.

```
^[ is an escape character
^[%-12345X is a printer reset to start PJL commands
@PJL commands are usually obvious
^[(s17H sets the pitch in characters per inch
^[(s0S sets to simple non-italics style
^[(s0B sets to normal, not-bold
^[(s3T sets the type style to courier
^[&k0G tells the printer not to add carriage returns.
^M is a carriage return
```

This is also a useful technique to see where the virtual printer is placing line feeds by using **lptest 200 1** to output a single line 200 characters long.

This is also useful to see how different command line flags actually affect the command issued to a printer.

12.4.6 Cleaning up and starting over

When jobs seem to be hung and the qdaemon will not start, our recommendation is to see if you can first deal with the problem by finding the offending process.

First try to find the cause of the hang

The process IDs of the processes that have been forked by the qdaemon are stored in files that begin with the letter p in the /var/spool/lpd/stat directory. Start by stopping the qdaemon and checking for existing status process files in this directory. If they still exist, then **cat** the files and use **kill -9** to stop the processes. In many cases, this will fix the problem. After this, use the **fuser** command to see if there are any processes still active on the device that appears hung. For example, if you have jobs that seem to be hung on lp17, then check for processes with:

```
# fuser /dev/lp17
```

If any process is active on this port, this command will give the process ID.

Check to see if any other processes that start with qd or pio are still active:

```
# ps -ef | grep qd
# ps -ef | grep pio
# kill -9 PIDnumbers
```

Another thing that can cause the qdaemon to fail is the presence of extraneous files in /var/spool/lpd/qdir. Make sure that the files in this directory have the format of job description files (JDF). A non JDF file will cause **lpstat** to give an error about a bad queue.

At this point, you may want to cancel jobs that created the problem and restart the qdaemon.

Last resort: Clean out the queueing system

When all else fails and you cannot resolve problems with print jobs that are hung, you can totally clean out the queuing system. This procedure deletes all print jobs and they must be resubmitted. You must be root to perform this task. The steps to follow are:

1. Stop the qdaemon and associated processes:

   ```
   # stopsrc -s qdaemon
   ```

2. Kill all processes associated with the qdaemon. These are normally processes that start with qd, such as qdfork, or pio, such as pioformat or pioout:

```
# ps -ef | grep qd
# ps -ef | grep pio
# kill -9 PIDnumbers
```

   If processes cannot be killed with **kill -9**, you may need to reboot.

3. Clean out the queue status files. This will reset the job numbers unless you preserver /var/spool/lpd/stat/numfile:

```
# rm /var/spool/lp/stat/*
```

4. Remove any spooled jobs:

```
# rm /var/spool/lpd/qdir/*
# rm /var/spool/lpd/qdaemon/*
# rm /var/spool/lpd/df*
```

5. Restart the qdaemon:

```
# startsrc -s qdaemon
```

12.4.7 Checking the flags to enq

In PowerPC printing, all the commands (**qprt**, **lp**, **lpr**, **lpd**, **dtprint**, and so on) all send their output through **enq**. One way to test this is to mount the **echo** command over the **enq** command, as shown here:

```
# mount /bin/echo /bin/enq
```

Now print from the commands and see how this is seen by **enq**:

```
$ qprt -p17 -Ttitle -v8 -Pasc /etc/motd
-o -p -o 17 -T title -o -v -o 8 -P asc /etc/motd
# lp -m -djunk -o land /etc/motd
-C -n -P junk -o land -j -- /etc/motd
# lpr -P junk /etc/motd
-P junk -c -Bgn /etc/motd
```

Note that when you do this, no one will be able to print until you unmount using the following command:

```
# unmount /bin/enq
```

12.4.8 Stopping unwanted header pages

Banner pages for PowerPC printing can be controlled by command line flags to the print commands, configuration of the queue, or customization of the virtual printer file.

Configuration banner selection

Banners are supported by the virtual printer for PowerPC printing. When you create or modify a virtual printer, you can specify if you want header pages, trailer pages, separator pages, any combination, or no banner pages.

To change banner pages, use the **smitty chpq** fast path, select the printer, and then select Change / Show Default Print Job Attributes. Scroll down to the field Separator Pages and press the F4 key. Select None for no banner pages.

This will show up in the queue device stanza for the printer in /etc/qconfig as header and trailer, as shown in this example for the queue asc with queue device lp0:

```
# lsquedev -q asc -d lp0
lp0:
        file = /dev/lp0
        header = never
        trailer = never
        access = both
        backend = /usr/lib/lpd/piobe
```

Command line banner selection

Users can override the banner selection from the configuration file. To turn off banners from the command line with **enq** or **qprt**, use the -Bnn flag, as shown here:

```
$ enq -Bnn -P lj24 /tmp/testfile
$ qprt -Bnn -P lj24 /tmp/testfile
```

The **lpr** command issues a header page by default. To turn off the header page, use the -h flag:

```
$ lpr -h -P lj24 /tmp/testfile
```

Virtual printer banner selection

At times, applications issue the **lpr** command, or you as the administrator have no control of users who want to use the **lpr** command without flags. You can disable all banner pagers from the virtual printer by removing the banner page generation program from the sh virtual printer attribute. Use the **lsvirprt** command to modify the virtual printer for this type of operation.

1. Start lsvirprt:

   ```
   # lsvirprt
   ```

2. Select the desired printer.
3. Set sh to nothing, as shown in Example 12-11 on page 413.

Example 12-11 Virtual printer banner selection

```
4050n            lpx       hplj-4050  (PCL)
To LIST attributes, enter AttributeName1 ... (* for all attributes)
To CHANGE an attribute value, enter AttributeName=NewValue
To FORMAT and EDIT an attribute value, enter AttributeName~v
To EDIT the attribute file, enter ~v
To terminate, press Enter:  sh

Name     Description                                           Value
sh       Pipeline for Header Page                              %Ide/pioburst %F[H
                                                               ] %Idb/H.ascii | %
                                                               Ide/pioformat -@ %
                                                               Idd/%Imm -!%Idf/pi
                                                               ofpcl -J+ -L! %IsH
                                                                -u%IuH

To LIST attributes, enter AttributeName1 ... (* for all attributes)
To CHANGE an attribute value, enter AttributeName=NewValue
To FORMAT and EDIT an attribute value, enter AttributeName~v
To EDIT the attribute file, enter ~v
To terminate, press Enter:  sh=

Name     Description                                           Value
sh       Pipeline for Header Page
```

12.5 Common errors and solutions

This section describes some problems that people often have when configuring AIX printing or printing files. This section also includes examples of errors seen in both the System V print subsystem and the PowerPC print subsystem.

12.5.1 Problem adding a second local printer on the same device

Once you have added a printer to a device line lp0, if you try to add another virtual printer using the **smitty mkpq** fast path, you will get an error message in SMIT that looks like this:

```
Command: failed         stdout: yes          stderr: no
Before command completion, additional instructions may appear below.
Method error (/usr/lib/methods/cfgpp):
        0514-031 A device is already configured at the specified location.
```

This problem can be solved by adding a printer to a file in the dev directory, and specifying the file name as lp0 (or whatever device file name you were trying to use).

12.5.2 Cannot change attributes because device is busy

When trying to change the printer device settings, you may get this error.

```
Command: failed        stdout: yes          stderr: no
Method error (/usr/lib/methods/chggen):
        0514-062 Cannot perform the requested function because the
                 specified device is busy.
```

First, disable the queue, and if the command still fails, use the **fuser** command to see what process is holding the device open:

```
# fuser /dev/lp0
/dev/lp0:     12808   45590
```

Then kill the processes.

12.5.3 Remote job disappears after queue enabled

A common problem with remote jobs disappearing is that they pass flags that are not valid for the virtual printer. The most common problem is the -fl flag. The symptom is that if you disable the queue, the job will be queued, but when you enable it, the job disappears. If you capture the file on the server and print it locally, it prints fine.

While the job is queued, look in the job description file in /var/spool/lpq/dir. If you see a line that contains the following text near the bottom of the file:

```
$#@!-fl
```

The problem is likely that the client is passing the -fl flag, and the server does not have the fl attribute defined in the virtual printer. To fix the problem, use **lsvirprt**, select the virtual printer, and enter:

```
fp=%ip
```

Press Enter to save the **lsvirprt** settings and retry the job.

12.5.4 Bad mandatory environment variable

When printing to a PostScript printer setup with a content type of PS and an interface type of PS, but with a printer type of hplaserjet, the following error is mailed back to the user:

```
Subject: Status of lp request wsm3-336
...
 Reason for failure:

 UX:lp:   ERROR: Bad mandatory environment variable.
```

```
TO FIX: Consult your system administrator.
```

Checking the interface program for the printer shows that this error is generated when the TERM type is not one of the PostScript TERM types of PS, PS-b, PS-r, PS-br, or PSR. To fix the problem, use **lpadmin** to change the printer type to PS-b:

```
# lpadmin -p wsm3 -T PS-b
```

After making this change, you should be able to print.

12.5.5 LOG: is read only

When adding JetDirect printers with the /usr/lib/hpnp/hpnpcfg script using the standard hpnp.model, the following error is mailed back to users who try to print to the queue:

```
Printing stopped with an exit code of 1.

 Reason for failure:
/etc/lp/interfaces/wsm2[44]: LOG: is read only
```

On examining the script /etc/lp/interfaces/wsm2, line 44 contained the following script statement:

```
LOG=/tmp/$PERIPH.$$
```

Further examination indicates that the problem is not with file permissions, but with environment variable permissions. If the line is changed to:

```
LOG1=/tmp/$PERIPH.$$
```

The problem will even cause JetDirect printers that were working before to no longer work. The reason is that the hpnpcfg script sets the LOG environment variable prior to restarting lpsched. When lpsched exec's the interface program, the variable is set in read only mode. The solution to the problem is to stop the scheduler, make sure the LOG is unset in the root environment, and then restart the scheduler:

```
# lpshut
# unset LOG
# /usr/lib/lp/lpsched
```

Although the hpnpcfg script is undocumented and unsupported, a more permanent solution to the problem is to modify the hpnpcfg script; but hpnpcfg calls /usr/lib/hpnp/cfg/option6 to create the printer, and this is where the scheduler is stopped, lpadmin is called to add the printer, and lpsched is called to stop the printer. If you comment out the lines so the scheduler is not stopped and restarted, then the printers will work without manual intervention. The following shows the lines commented out in the option6 shell script:

```
STARTLP=0
#echo /usr/sbin/lpshut | tee -a -- $LOG
#/usr/sbin/lpshut
#if [ $? -eq 0 ]
#then
#  STARTLP=1
#fi
```

12.5.6 No formfeed after banner page

When you add a printer with the hpnpcfg script, if you do not specify the type as pcl, you may not see any pages beyond the header. This is because the simple type is a passthrough type of printing with no modification to the file. This can be fixed by changing the content type to pcl and making sure the pcl filter has been installed as follows:

```
# lpadmin -p printer-name -I pcl
# lpfilter -f pcl -F /etc/lp/fd/pcl.fd
```

Once you make this change, the text files will print fine, but there will be no formfeed after the header page. To add a formfeed, simply change the printer type to hplaserjet, as shown here:

```
# lpadmin -p printer-name -T hplaserjet
```

If this is not a PCL printer, choose an appropriate terminfo type for the option.

13

NIM troubleshooting

This chapter suggests solutions for network boot problems and describes procedures for producing debug output for AIX Network Installation Management (NIM) Base Operating System (BOS) installations.

13.1 Debugging a network boot problem

If a client machine is unable to network boot from its boot server, there may be a problem in one or more of the following stages of the network boot:

- Establishing network communication between the client and server.
- Obtaining the boot image from the server.
- Running the boot image on the client.

13.1.1 Establishing network communication between client and server

- Before initiating the network boot on the client, perform a **ping** test from the client machine to the server (master) machine:

```
# ping f80right
PING f80right.itsc.austin.ibm.com: (9.3.187.184): 56 data bytes
64 bytes from 9.3.187.184: icmp_seq=0 ttl=255 time=10 ms
64 bytes from 9.3.187.184: icmp_seq=1 ttl=255 time=0 ms
64 bytes from 9.3.187.184: icmp_seq=2 ttl=255 time=0 ms
```

- If the **ping** test fails, verify that the client, server, and gateway addresses are specified correctly. Perform the steps mentioned in Section 7.2.1, “Selective host network problems” on page 197.
- If the addresses are correct, try to **ping** the server from a different machine in the client's subnet.
- If the server can be pinged from another machine, the network adapter on the boot client may be faulty.
- If the server cannot be pinged from another machine in the client's subnet, there may be routing problems between the client and the server, or network communications on the server may be faulty. Perform the steps mentioned in Section 7.2.2, “No network access” on page 198

13.1.2 Obtaining the boot image from the server

- If the **ping** test is successful, perform a network boot of the client. When a network boot is initiated on a client, a bootp request packet is sent from the client to the server. The server then replies with a packet to the client. The client machine displays the number of packets sent and received for the bootp request. If a packet is sent from the client, but none is received, another packet will be sent.

Note: Certain switches or routers drop bootp packets; check the settings on your switch or router.

- If bootp packets continue to be sent but not received, the boot server may not be responding to the request.
- From the bootp server, view the /etc/bootptab file on the server. It should contain an entry for the client machine. (See Example 13-1.)

Example 13-1 /etc/bootptab file

```
# cat /etc/bootptab
43p150.itsc.austin.ibm.com:bf=/tftpboot/43p150.itsc.austin.ibm.com:ip=9.3.187.1
89:ht=token-ring:sa=9.3.187.184:sm=255.255.255.0:
```

If an entry does not exist, either the NIM command used to set up the current operation failed, or the machine was reset before the boot operation could occur. Rerun the NIM bos_inst, diag, or maint_boot operation to prepare the server for the client boot request. Use:

```
# smit nim
```

Select the following sequence:

Perform NIM Administration Tasks -> **Manage Machines** -> **Perform Operations on Machines**

If the entry exists in /etc/bootptab, verify that the specified data is correct. If a field contains incorrect data, the information that was used to define the machine or network in the NIM database was probably wrong. Correct this problem by resetting the client machine, correcting the invalid data in the client or network definition, retrying the NIM operation, and rebooting the client.

- If the /etc/bootptab file is correct, verify that the inetd daemon is running:

  ```
  # ps -ef | grep inetd
  root 262208 229458   0   Sep 04      -  0:00 /usr/sbin/inetd
  root 933984 540786   0 11:00:56  pts/3  0:00 grep inetd
  # lssrc -s inetd
  Subsystem         Group            PID     Status
  inetd            tcpip            262208   active
  ```

  If it is not running, start it and retry the network boot from the client. If the inetd daemon is running, it should automatically start the bootpd daemon when the bootp request is received at the server.

- If the bootpd daemon is not started, verify that the bootps entry in the /etc/inetd.conf file is not commented out:

  ```
  # cat /etc/inetd.conf | grep bootps
  ```

```
bootps  dgram   udp     wait    root    /usr/sbin/bootpd        bootpd
/etc/bootptab
```

If it is commented out, uncomment it and restart inetd with:

```
# refresh -s inetd
```

Retry the network boot of the client.

- If a bootp reply is still not received at the client, manually start the bootpd daemon in debug mode:

```
# vi /etc/inetd.conf
```

Comment out the following line:

```
bootps  dgram   udp     wait    root    /usr/sbin/bootpd        bootpd
/etc/bootptab
```

Save changes and exit:

```
# refresh -s inetd
# ps -ef | grep bootpd
```

If it is running, use the **kill -15** command to kill the process:

```
# vi /etc/syslog.conf
```

Comment out the following line:

```
*.debug              /tmp/bootp.log
```

Run the following commands:

```
# touch /tmp/bootp.log
# stopsrc -s syslogd
# startsrc -s syslogd
# bootpd -s -d -d -d &
```

The output will be logged to /tmp/bootpd.log.

- Retry the network boot from the client. If no output is displayed from the running **bootpd** command, (check the /tmp/bootpd.log), the client bootp request is not reaching the server. Verify that the addresses specified in the bootp menus are correct. If they are correct, perform network debugging procedures to determine why the packet is not reaching the server. Follow the steps from Section 7.2, "Problem isolation steps for TCP/IP network problems" on page 196.
- For a sample of /tmp/bootpd.log entries (see Example 13-2).

Example 13-2 /tmp/bootpd.log entries

```
# cat /tmp/bootp.log
Sep 13 10:37:53 F80right syslogd: restart
Sep 13 10:38:18 F80right bootpd[909344]: bootpd 2.1 #77: Tue Jul 16 11:29:48
CDT 1991
Sep 13 10:38:18 F80right bootpd[909344]: bind: Address already in use
```

```
Sep 13 10:40:07 F80right bootpd[499802]: bootpd 2.1 #77: Tue Jul 16 11:29:48
CDT 1991
Sep 13 10:40:07 F80right bootpd[499802]: bind: Address already in use
Sep 13 10:41:56 F80right tftpd[811132]: [00000102] EZZ7053I stopsrc issued
Sep 13 10:41:56 F80right tftpd[827442]: [00000001] EZZ7030I Exiting.
Sep 13 10:42:00 F80right tftpd[811134]: [00000001] EZZ7001I Starting.
Sep 13 10:47:58 F80right bootpd[499832]: bootpd 2.1 #77: Tue Jul 16 11:29:48
CDT 1991
Sep 13 11:02:58 F80right bootpd[499832]: exiting after 15 minutes of inactivity
Sep 13 11:16:57 F80right tftpd[811134]: [00000102] EZZ7053I stopsrc issued
Sep 13 11:16:57 F80right tftpd[802992]: [00000001] EZZ7030I Exiting.
Sep 13 11:17:01 F80right tftpd[802994]: [00000001] EZZ7001I Starting.
Sep 13 11:19:03 F80right tftpd[802994]: [00000102] EZZ7053I stopsrc issued
Sep 13 11:19:03 F80right tftpd[811136]: [00000001] EZZ7030I Exiting.
Sep 13 11:19:08 F80right tftpd[802996]: [00000001] EZZ7001I Starting.
Sep 13 11:25:01 F80right tftpd[802996]: [00000102] EZZ7053I stopsrc issued
Sep 13 11:25:01 F80right tftpd[909438]: [00000001] EZZ7030I Exiting.
Sep 13 11:25:06 F80right tftpd[802998]: [00000001] EZZ7001I Starting.
Sep 13 11:26:05 F80right syslogd: restart
Sep 13 11:26:16 F80right bootpd[934024]: bootpd 2.1 #77: Tue Jul 16 11:29:48
CDT 1991
Sep 13 11:26:16 F80right bootpd[934024]: bootptab mtime is Thu Sep  6 17:09:50
2001
Sep 13 11:26:16 F80right bootpd[934024]: reading "/etc/bootptab"
Sep 13 11:26:16 F80right bootpd[934024]: read 1 entries from "/etc/bootptab"
Sep 13 11:26:16 F80right bootpd[934024]: dumped 1 entries to
"/etc/bootpd.dump".
```

- If the server receives the client bootp request, the running **bootpd** command displays output matching the client data in the /etc/bootptab file. Verify that the specified addresses are correct. This information is sent back to the client in the bootp reply.
- If the client is still not receiving the bootp reply, perform network debugging procedures to determine why the reply packet is not reaching the client. Follow the steps from Section 7.2, "Problem isolation steps for TCP/IP network problems" on page 196.
- After the client receives the bootp reply, it will tftp the boot image from the server.
- The number of tftp packets transferred to the client will be displayed at the client machine.
- The boot image has been successfully retrieved at the client machine when the LED shows 299 on RS6000 platform machines.
- If the tftp of the boot image does not complete successfully, the client may be trying to get the wrong boot image. Verify that the client definition in the NIM

database shows the correct platform and kernel type. Check this from the server:

```
# smit nim
```

Select the following sequence:

Perform NIM Administration Tasks -> **Manage Machines** -> **Change/Show Characteristics of a Machine**

If the data is incorrect, correct it, reset the client machine, rerun the NIM operation, and reboot the client over the network.

- Verify that the /tftpboot directory on the boot server contains a link with the client name to the correct boot image:

```
# ls -l /tftpboot
total 12848
lrwxrwxrwx   1 root     system          27 Sep 06 17:09
43p150.itsc.austin.ibm.com -> /tftpboot/spot1.rs6k.up.tok
-rw-r--r--   1 root     system        1154 Sep 06 17:09
43p150.itsc.austin.ibm. com.info
-rw-r--r--   1 root     system     6571397 Sep 06 17:08 spot1.rs6k.up.tok
```

If the link does not exist, reset the client machine, rerun the NIM operation, and reboot the client over the network.

- If the link with the client name is pointing to the correct boot image and the tftp of the boot image does not complete successfully, the boot image may be corrupted. Recreate the boot image by performing a NIM check operation:

```
# smit nim
```

Select the following sequence:

Perform NIM Administration Tasks -> **Manage Machines** -> **Perform Operations on Machines**

- This should come back with O.K. If the client is not an RS/6000 machine, also make sure the client has the latest version of the firmware installed.

13.1.3 Running the boot image on the client

After the client machine has successfully received the boot image from the server, the most common errors encountered are hangs with the LED showing 608, 611, or 613. Some machines may not have LED displays. Debugging such problems on these machines will require using debug-enabled boot images. For information on building debug boot images, refer to the Section 13.2.2, "Producing debug output from the BOS install program" on page 428.

608

Explanation

tftp retrieve of client info file failure

Action

If a 608 hang is encountered, verify that the ClientName.info file exists in the /tftpboot directory. If it does not exist, retry the NIM operation to create it. If it does exist, verify that tftp access to the /tftpboot directory is not restricted in the /etc/tftpaccess.ctl file. It is also possible that the network adapter was not configured properly in the boot environment. Use the debug-enabled network boot images to look for errors in the boot environment. If the client is not an RS/6000 machine, make sure that it has the latest version of firmware installed.

611

Explanation

Remote mount of NFS file system failure

Action

611 hangs occur when the client machine is unable to mount a resource from a server. Ensure that NFS is running on the resource server. Verify that the resources specified for the operation are exported properly by checking the /etc/exports and /etc/xtab files on the server. Also, confirm that the resources have permissions set correctly for reading. Debug-enabled network boot images can also be used to determine exactly which mount command is failing on the client.

613

Explanation

Failure setting up route tables

Action

613 hangs usually occur because a route is incorrectly defined for a network in the NIM database. Verify that the correct gateways are specified between networks, and all gateways are functional. Use debug-enabled network boot images to determine which routes could not be defined.

For other NIM LED codes, see Table 13-1 for the meaning of the LED codes. If your NIM client does not have an LED display, you can get the LED information by issuing the **lsnim -l NimClientName** command on the NIM server (master). The Web-based System Manager will also display the value of the LED while a NIM process is in progress.

Table 13-1 Overview of relevant NIM LED codes

LED	Description
299	Boot image successfully received at the NIM client.
600	Starting network boot (portion of /sbin/rc.boot).
602	Configuring network parent devices.
603	Script defsys, cfgsys, or cfgbus located in /usr/lib/methods/ failed.
604	Configuring physical network boot device.
605	Configuration physical network boot device failed.
606	Running /usr/sbin/ifconfig on logical network boot devices.
607	/usr/sbin/ifconfig failed.
608	Attempting to retrieve the client.info file with tftp from the SPOT server. A flashing 608 indicates multiple attempts to retrieve the client.info file are occurring.
609	The client.info file does not exist or could not be accessed, or it is zero length.
610	Attempting to mount a remote file system using NFS.
611	The client is unable to mount a remote file system (NIM resource) using NFS.
612	Accessing remote files. Unconfiguring network boot devices.
613	The **route** command failed.
614	Configuration of logical paging devices.
615	Configuration of logical paging device failed.
616	Converting from diskless to dataless configuration.
617	Diskless to dataless configuration failed.
618	Configuring remote (NFS) paging device.
619	Configuration of remote (NFS) paging space failed.
620	Updating special device files and ODM in permanent file system.
622	Control returned to the /sbin/rc.boot program.

LED	Description
623	The BOS installation program has encountered a fatal error.
624	Control passed to the BOS installation program.

13.2 Producing debug output for NIM BOS installations

Due to problems in the network or in the NIM configuration, clients may fail to boot properly and/or install. When this happens, it may be necessary to produce debug information in order to determine the cause of the problem. If a client machine fails to configure properly from the network boot image, debug output from the boot image can be obtained by building the debug-enabled image and attaching a tty to the client system. This will display the commands and output that are run as the client is configured before further processing is done by AIX.

If the system has been booted from the network boot image, but failures are still occurring during a BOS installation, it may be necessary to collect debug information from the BOS install program. The commands and output from the BOS install program will automatically be displayed on the tty if the boot image was built debug-enabled. If the boot image was not built for debugging, output can be obtained by either setting a value in a bosinst.data file or by entering special codes at the installation menus.

When problems arise during a NIM BOS installation, you will most likely get system hangs. Viewing the debug output can be extremely useful, because you will be able to see the commands that failed. The problem may be a misconfiguration of the network adapter or an inability to perform an operation from the client to the server. By examining the debug output, you can see what failed and make corrections to avoid the error in the future.

You will see the **showled** command running in the debug output. This command displays status values on the LEDs on the front of the machine. Frequently, known problems and solutions are referenced by the LED value that is displayed when a problem occurs. Some machines do not have LEDs for displaying such information. Therefore, when debugging problems on such machines, special attention should be given to observing the values that the **showled** commands are displaying.

Obtaining debug information from a network installation can save you time in determining the root cause of a problem. Usually, the problem will be an incorrect definition in the NIM environment that can be found without the debug information. However, with the debug information, you can significantly reduce the scope of the investigation.

13.2.1 Producing debug output from a network boot image

- Create debug versions of the network boot images using the check operation from the Web-based System Manager or SMIT interfaces or by using the following command:

  ```
  # nim -Fo check -a debug=yes SPOTName
  ```

  where SPOTName is the name of your SPOT.

- Get the address for entering the debugger:

  ```
  # lsnim -a enter_dbg SPOTName
  ```

  where SPOTName is the name of your SPOT. The displayed output will be similar to the following:

  ```
  spot1:
  enter_dbg = "chrp.mp 0x001840d4"
  enter_dbg = "chrp.up 0x00160b7c"
  enter_dbg = "rs6k.mp 0x001840d4"
  enter_dbg = "rs6k.up 0x00160b7c"
  enter_dbg = "rspc.mp 0x001840d4"
  enter_dbg = "rspc.up 0x00160b7c"
  ```

  Write down the enter_dbg address for the client you are going to boot. For example, you would write down the address 38ca54. (See Example 13-3 for details.)

Example 13-3 NIM commands

```
# lsnim -l 43p150
43p150:
   class          = machines
   type           = standalone
   platform       = rs6k
   netboot_kernel = up
   if1            = network1 43p150 0 tok0
   ring_speed1    = autosense
   Cstate         = ready for a NIM operation
   prev_state     = BOS installation has been enabled
   Mstate         = currently running
   lpp_source     = lpp_source1
   spot           = spot1
   cpuid          = 000902774C00
   control        = master
   Cstate_result  = reset
# nim -Fo check -a debug=yes spot1
# lsnim -a enter_dbg spot1
spot1:
   enter_dbg = "rs6k.up.tok 0x0038ca54"
```

- Attach a tty device to your client system (port 1).

  To set up the interface system, perform these steps. In the listed commands, the serial port 0 is used. You must create a tty on the Serial port. Use the following command to set up the tty serial port 0:

  ```
  # mkdev -c tty -t 'tty' -s 'rs232' -p 'sa0' -w '0'
  ```

  You will get a response, such as:

  ```
  tty0 available
  ```

  Add the following line to the file /etc/uucp/Devices by using vi:

  ```
  Direct tty0 - 9600 direct
  ```

  Run the following commands to capture the debug output. The script command will log all output to the /tmp/debug.log file, and the **cu** command connects the current session to the serial port:

  ```
  # script /tmp/debug.log
  # cu -ml tty0
  ```

  To disconnect from the NIM client and stop logging, enter the following:

  ```
  ~.
  exit
  ```

- Set up and perform the NIM operation that will require the client to boot over the network. Boot the client over the network.
- After the client gets the boot image from the SPOT server, the debug screen will appear on the tty. At the > prompt, enter the following command:

  ```
  # st Enter_dbg_Value 2
  ```

  Specifying a 2 at the address of the enter_dbg value prints the output to your tty.

- Type g for go and press Enter to start the boot process.
- Use Ctrl-s to temporarily stop the process as you watch the output on the tty. Use Ctrl-q to resume the process.
- To rebuild your boot images in non-debug mode, use the following command:

  ```
  # nim - Fo check SPOTName
  ```

> **Note:** If the boot image is left in debug mode, every time a client is booted from these boot images, the machine will stop and wait for a command at the debugger > prompt. If you attempt to use these debug-enabled boot images and there is not a tty attached to the client, the machine will appear to be hanging for no reason.

13.2.2 Producing debug output from the BOS install program

There are two ways to obtain debug output from the BOS install program. The first involves entering a special value at one of the installation menus. (See Section 13.2.3, "To produce debug output without using a bosinst_data resource" on page 428.) The second method uses a bosinst_data resource to tell the installation program to display debug output. (See Section 13.2.4, "To produce debug output when using a bosinst_data resource" on page 428.)

13.2.3 To produce debug output without using a bosinst_data resource

- To enable debugging for the BOS install program, start by performing all the processing you would normally do to install a client.
- Since you are not using a bosinst_data resource, you will be prompted to supply information about the installation to the BOS install program.
- Select your console.
- Select your language.
- The `Welcome to Base Operating System Installation and Maintenance` menu is displayed. Instead of selecting one of the options, enter `911` at the prompt and press Enter.
- Continue the normal procedure for selecting options and specifying data until the installation begins. Debug output will be sent to the client's display as the installation proceeds.

13.2.4 To produce debug output when using a bosinst_data resource

To enable debugging for the BOS install program, set the value BOSINST_DEBUG = yes in the control_flow stanza of the bosinst.data file that you are using for your bosinst_data resource.

A minimum bosinst.data file for debugging purposes would contain the following lines:

```
# cat /export/spot/spot1/bosinst.data | grep BOSINST_DEBUG
   #     BOSINST_DEBUG = no, yes
```

BOSINST_DEBUG = yes

- In addition to the processing you would normally do to install a client, include the modified bosinst_data resource as a resource for the operation. After the client boots over the network, it will use the bosinst_data resource to obtain settings for the installation. If the only data specified in your bosinst.data file is BOSINST_DEBUG = yes, you will be prompted for the remaining required information before the installation will continue. Debug output will be sent to the client's display as the installation continues.

13.3 Viewing NIM logs

Many NIM operations are writing log information in NIM logs during the execution of the operation. This information can be reviewed after the NIM operation has finished. Use the **showlog** operation to view the NIM logs. There are several log types; see Table 13-2 for the valid attributes you can use to specify which kind of log you want to see by using the showlog operation. To view the other kind of logs, you must specify a another value to the log_type attribute.

Table 13-2 NIM logs

Valid attribute for showing NIM logs	Description
devinst	Output from the installation of key system and device-driver software.
niminst	Output from the installation of user-specific software (including installation of NIM client software during a bos_inst operation).
bosinst	Output from the BOS installation program.
boot	The machine's boot log.
lppchk	A log of the output from the **lppchk** operation executed on a stand-alone NIM client (AIX Version 4.2 and later).
script	Output from any configuration script resources allocated for a bos_inst operation (AIX Version 4.2 and later).
nimerr	Errors encountered during execution of the **nim** command.
alt_disk_install	Output from the alternate disk installation command (AIX Version 4.3 and later).

See Example 13-4 for the boot log.

Example 13-4 nim showlog command

```
# nim -o showlog -a log_type=boot 43p150
....
Completed method for: gxme0, Elapsed time = 0
return code = 0
****************** no stdout ***********
****************** no stderr ***********
----------------
```

```
Time: 35        LEDS: 0x539
Number of running methods: 0
----------------
attempting to configure device 'rcm0'
Time: 35        LEDS: 0x594
invoking /etc/methods/cfgrcm -2 -1 rcm0
Number of running methods: 1
----------------
Completed method for: rcm0, Elapsed time = 0
return code = 0
****************** no stdout ***********
****************** no stderr ***********
----------------
Time: 35        LEDS: 0x539
Number of running methods: 0
----------------
Time: 35        LEDS: 0x538
invoking top level program -- "/etc/methods/startty" Time: 35        LEDS:
0x539
return code = 0
****************** no stdout ***********
****************** no stderr ***********
----------------
Time: 35        LEDS: 0x538
invoking top level program -- "/etc/methods/startsmt"
Time: 35        LEDS: 0x539
return code = 0
****************** no stdout ***********
****************** no stderr ***********
----------------
Time: 35        LEDS: 0x538
invoking top level program -- "/usr/lib/methods/defaio"
Time: 35        LEDS: 0x539
return code = 0
****************** no stdout ***********
****************** no stderr ***********
----------------
Time: 35        LEDS: 0x538
invoking top level program -- "/usr/lib/perf/cfg_perfstat load"
Time: 35        LEDS: 0x539
return code = 0
****************** no stdout ***********
****************** no stderr ***********
----------------
Time: 35        LEDS: 0x538
invoking top level program -- "/etc/methods/load_blockset_ext"
Time: 35        LEDS: 0x539
return code = 0
****************** no stdout ***********
```

```
****************** no stderr ***********
----------------
calling savebase
return code = 0
****************** no stdout ***********
****************** no stderr ***********
Configuration time: 36 seconds
Starting AIX Windows Desktop.....
Saving Base Customize Data to boot disk
Starting the sync daemon
Starting the error daemon
System initialization completed.
Starting Multi-user Initialization
 Performing auto-varyon of Volume Groups
 Activating all paging spaces
0517-075 swapon: Paging device /dev/hd6 is already active.
swapon: Paging device /dev/paging00 activated.
/dev/rhd1 (/home): ** Unmounted cleanly - Check suppressed
/dev/rhd10opt (/opt): ** Unmounted cleanly - Check suppressed  /dev/rhd10opt
(/opt): ** Unmounted cleanly - Check suppressed
 Performing all automatic mounts
Multi-user initialization completed
```

You can view the NIM logs in different ways. By default, the **showlog** operation, without specifying the log_type applied to a NIM client machine, shows the output of the niminst log from the last software which was installed.

From Web-based System Manager

Start the view from the Web-based System Manager as follows:

1. Start the Web-based System Manager.
2. Open the NIM container.
3. Select a machine or got to Resources and select a SPOT resource.
4. Go to **Selected** --> **Troubleshooting** --> **Show NIM logs**.
5. Select the logs you want to view.
6. If you want to see more than the last entry, you must uncheck the box. Only show the last entry in the log when applicable in the bottom of the menu.

From SMIT

Use the smitty as described in the following steps to view the NIM logs:

1. Start SMIT with the **nim_mac_op** fast path for viewing machines log data or with the **nim_res_op** fast path for viewing SPOT log data.
2. Select a target machine or SPOT.

3. Select the **showlog** operation.
4. Select a the log type.
5. If you want to see more than the last entry, change the Only Show The Last Entry in Log to no.

Related publications

The publications listed in this section are considered particularly suitable for a more detailed discussion of the topics covered in this redbook.

IBM Redbooks

For information on ordering these publications, see "How to get IBM Redbooks" on page 436.

- *AIX 5L Differences Guide*, SG24-5765
- *AIX 5L Porting Guide*, SG24-6034
- *AIX 5L Workload Manager (WLM)*, SG24-5977
- *AIX Version 4.3 Differences Guide*, SG24-2014
- *AIX Logical Volume Manager from A to Z: Troubleshooting and Commands*, SG24-5433
- *NIM: From A to Z in AIX 4.3*, SG24-5524
- *Printing for Fun and Profit under AIX 5L*, SG24-6018
- *Running Linux Applications on AIX*, SG24-6033

Other resources

These publications are also relevant as further information sources:

- *44P Series Model 170 Installation Guide*, SA38-0561
- *7006 Graphics Workstation Service Guide*, SA23-2719
- *7009 Compact Server Service Guide*, SA23-2716
- *7012 300 Series Service Guide*, SA38-0545
- *7012 G Series Service Guide*, SA23-2741
- *IBM RS/6000 7013 500 Series Installation and Service Guide*, SA38-0531
- *7013 J Series Service Guide*, SA23-2725
- *7014 Model S00 Rack Installation and Service Guide*, SA38-0550
- *7014 Series Model T00 and T42 Installation and Service Guide*, SA38-0577
- *7015 Model R00 Rack Installation and Service Guide*, SA23-2744

- *7015 R10/R20/R21 Service Guide*, SA23-2708
- *7015 Model R30, R40, & R50, CPU Enclosure Installation and Service Guide*, SA23-2743
- *7017 S Series Installation and Service Guide*, SA38-0548
- *7026 CPU Drawer Install and Service Guide*, SA38-0535
- *7043 260 Service Guide*, SA38-0554
- *7043 260 Setup Guide*, SA38-0555
- *7043 260 User's Guide*, SA38-0553
- *AIX Version 4.3 Kernel Extensions and Device Support Programming*, SC23-4125
- *Capacity Upgrade on Demand Installing and Upgrading Processors*, SA38-0583
- *Enterprise Server H Series CPU Drawer Installation and Service Guide*, SA38-0547
- *Enterprise Server H Series User's Guide*, SA38-0546
- *Enterprise Server Model F80 and pSeries 620 Model 6F1 Installation Guide*, SA38-0569
- *Enterprise Server Model F80 and pSeries 620 Model 6F1 Service Guide*, SA38-0568
- *Enterprise Server Model F80 and pSeries 620 Model 6F1 User's Guide*, SA38-0567
- *Enterprise Server Model H80 and pSeries 660 Model 6H1 Installation Guide*, SA38-0575
- *Enterprise Server Model H80 and pSeries 660 Model 6H1 Service Guide*, SA38-0566
- *Enterprise Server Model H80 and pSeries 660 Model 6H1 User's Guide*, SA38-0565
- *Enterprise Server S80, pSeries 680 Model S85 Service Guide*, SA38-0558
- *IBM 7024 E Series Service Guide*, SA38-0502
- *IBM 7025 F Series Service Guide*, SA38-0505
- *IBM RS/6000 7025 F40 Service Guide*, SA38-0515
- *IBM RS/6000 7043 Service Guide*, SA38-0512
- *IBM RS/6000 Adapters, Device, and Cables Information for Micro Channel Bus Systems*, SA38-0533
- *pSeries 640 Model B80 Service Guide*, SA38-0581

- *pSeries 640 Model B80 User's Guide*, SA38-0580
- *pSeries Customer Support Information*, SA38-0584
- *RS/6000 44P Series Model 170 Service Guide*, SA38-0560
- *RS/6000 44P Series Model 170 User's Guide*, SA38-0559
- *RS/6000 44P Series Model 270 Install Guide*, SA38-0574
- *RS/6000 44P Series Model 270 Service Guide*, SA38-0572
- *RS/6000 44P Series Model 270 User's Guide*, SA38-0573
- *RS/6000 7025 F50 Installation and Service Guide*, SA38-0541
- *RS/6000 7026 B80 Installation Guide*, SA38-0579
- *RS/6000 7046 B50 Service Guide*, SA38-0564
- *RS/6000 7046 B50 Setup Guide*, SA38-0562
- *RS/6000 7046 B50 User's Guide*, SA38-0563
- *RS/6000 Adapters, Devices, and Cable Information for Multiple Bus Systems*, SA38-0516
- *RS/6000 Diagnostics Information for Micro Channel Bus Systems*, SA38-0532
- *RS/6000 Enterprise Server Model M80 and eServer pSeries 680 Mod 6M1 Install Guide*, SA38-0576
- *RS/6000 Enterprise Server Model M80 and eServer pSeries 680 Model 6M1 Service Guide*, SA38-0571
- *RS/6000 Enterprise Server Model M80 and eServer pSeries 680 Model 6M1 User's Guide*, SA38-0570
- *RS/6000 Enterprise Server S80 Installation Guide*, SA38-0582
- *RS/6000 Enterprise Server S80 User's Guide*, SA38-0557
- *RS/6000 and pSeries Diagnostics Information for Multiple Bus Systems*, SA38-0509
- *RS/6000 and pSeries PCI Adapter Placement Reference*, SA38-0538
- *Site and Hardware Planning Information*, SA38-0508

The following resources can be found at:

`http://publibn.boulder.ibm.com/cgi-bin/ds_form?lang=en_US&viewset=AIX`

- *AIX 5L Version 5.1 Kernel Extensions and Device Support Programming Concepts*
- *AIX 5L Version 5.1 Performance Management Guide*

- *AIX 5L Version 5.1 System Management Guide: Operating System and Device*
- *AIX 5L Version 5.1 Commands Reference*
- *AIX 5L Version 5.1 General Programing Concepts and Debugging Programs*

Referenced Web sites

These Web sites are also relevant as further information sources:

- IBM RS/6000 Support Portal

  `http://techsupport.services.ibm.com/rs6000/support`
- IBM Server Support

  `http://techsupport.service.ibm.com/server/support`
- Fixes, drivers, updates, tools

  `http://techsupport.services.ibm.com/server/fixes`
- Unix Severs Library

  `http://www.rs6000.ibm.com/library`
- IBM @server pSeries and RS/6000 Microcode Updates

  `http://www.rs6000.ibm.com/support/micro`
- SSA support site

  `http://www.storage.ibm.com/hardsoft/products/ssa`
- AIX Toolbox for Linux Applications

  `http://www.ibm.com/servers/aix/products/aixos/linux/index.html`
- AIX Performance PMR Data Collection Tools

  `ftp://ftp.software.ibm.com/aix/tools/perftools/perfpmr`
- AIX 5L Version 5.1 references

  `http://publibn.boulder.ibm.com/cgi-bin/ds_form?lang=en_US&viewset=AIX`

How to get IBM Redbooks

Search for additional Redbooks or redpieces, view, download, or order hardcopy from the Redbooks Web site:

`ibm.com/redbooks`

Also download additional materials (code samples or diskette/CD-ROM images) from this Redbooks site.

Redpieces are Redbooks in progress; not all Redbooks become redpieces and sometimes just a few chapters will be published this way. The intent is to get the information out much quicker than the formal publishing process allows.

IBM Redbooks collections

Redbooks are also available on CD-ROMs. Click the CD-ROMs button on the Redbooks Web site for information about all the CD-ROMs offered, as well as updates and formats.

Special notices

References in this publication to IBM products, programs or services do not imply that IBM intends to make these available in all countries in which IBM operates. Any reference to an IBM product, program, or service is not intended to state or imply that only IBM's product, program, or service may be used. Any functionally equivalent program that does not infringe any of IBM's intellectual property rights may be used instead of the IBM product, program or service.

Information in this book was developed in conjunction with use of the equipment specified, and is limited in application to those specific hardware and software products and levels.

IBM may have patents or pending patent applications covering subject matter in this document. The furnishing of this document does not give you any license to these patents. You can send license inquiries, in writing, to the IBM Director of Licensing, IBM Corporation, North Castle Drive, Armonk, NY 10504-1785.

Licensees of this program who wish to have information about it for the purpose of enabling: (i) the exchange of information between independently created programs and other programs (including this one) and (ii) the mutual use of the information which has been exchanged, should contact IBM Corporation, Dept. 600A, Mail Drop 1329, Somers, NY 10589 USA.

Such information may be available, subject to appropriate terms and conditions, including in some cases, payment of a fee.

The information contained in this document has not been submitted to any formal IBM test and is distributed AS IS. The use of this information or the implementation of any of these techniques is a customer responsibility and depends on the customer's ability to evaluate and integrate them into the customer's operational environment. While each item may have been reviewed by IBM for accuracy in a specific situation, there is no guarantee that the same or similar results will be obtained elsewhere. Customers attempting to adapt these techniques to their own environments do so at their own risk.

Any pointers in this publication to external Web sites are provided for convenience only and do not in any manner serve as an endorsement of these Web sites.

The following terms are trademarks of other companies:

Tivoli, Manage. Anything. Anywhere.,The Power To Manage., Anything. Anywhere.,TME, NetView, Cross-Site, Tivoli Ready, Tivoli Certified, Planet Tivoli, and Tivoli Enterprise are trademarks or registered trademarks of Tivoli Systems Inc., an IBM company, in the United States, other countries, or both. In Denmark, Tivoli is a trademark licensed from Kjøbenhavns Sommer - Tivoli A/S.

C-bus is a trademark of Corollary, Inc. in the United States and/or other countries.

Java and all Java-based trademarks and logos are trademarks or registered trademarks of Sun Microsystems, Inc. in the United States and/or other countries.

Microsoft, Windows, Windows NT, and the Windows logo are trademarks of Microsoft Corporation in the United States and/or other countries.

PC Direct is a trademark of Ziff Communications Company in the United States and/or other countries and is used by IBM Corporation under license.

ActionMedia, LANDesk, MMX, Pentium and ProShare are trademarks of Intel Corporation in the United States and/or other countries.

UNIX is a registered trademark in the United States and other countries licensed exclusively through The Open Group.

SET, SET Secure Electronic Transaction, and the SET Logo are trademarks owned by SET Secure Electronic Transaction LLC.

Itanium is a trademark of Intel Corporation.

Other company, product, and service names may be trademarks or service marks of others.

Abbreviations and acronyms

AIX	Advanced Interactive Executive
ARP	Address Resolution Protocol
ASCII	American National Standards Code for Information Interchange
ATE	Asynchronous Terminal Emulator
ATM	Asynchronous Transfer Mode
ATMLE	ATM LAN Emulation
AVM	Active Virtual Memory
BIND	Berkeley Internet Name Daemon
BIST	Built-In Self-Test
BUMP	Bring-Up Multiprocessor
CD	Compact Disc
CD-ROM	Compact Disc Read Only Memory
CDE	Common Desktop Environment
CHRP	Common Hardware Reference Platform
CRC	Cyclic Redundancy Check
CSA	Current Save Area
DAR	Data Address Register
DAR2	Secondary Data Address Register
DBM	Database Manager
DHCP	Dynamic Host Configuration Protocol
DIMM	Dual Inline Memory Module
DLT	Digital Linear Tape
DNS	Domain Name Server
DSI	Data Storage Interrupt
DSIRR	Data Storage Interrupt Reason Register
DSISR	Data Storage Interrupt Status Register
ELAN	Emulated LAN
ESD	Electrostatic Discharge
EUID	Effective User ID
FRU	Field Replaceable Unit
IAR	Instruction Address Register
IBM	International Business Machines Corporation
ICMP	Internet Control Message Protocol
IGMP	Internet Group Management Protocol
IP	Internet Protocol
IPL	Initial Program Load
ISA	Industry Standard Architecture
ISI	Instruction Access Exception
ITSO	International Technical Support Organization
JFS	Journaled File System
JTAG	Joint Test Action Group
KDB	Kernel Debugger
LAN	Local Area Network
LCD	Liquid Crystal Display
LECS	LAN Emulation Configuration Server
LED	Light Emitting Diode
LLDB	Low Level Debugger
LP	Logical Partition
LR	Link Register

LES	LAN Emulation Server
LUM	Licence Use Management
LVCB	Logical Volume Control Block
LVID	Logical Volume Identifier
LVM	Logical Volume Manager
MAC	Medium Access Control
MAP	Maintenance Analysis Procedure
MCA	Micro Channel Architecture
MSR	Machine Status Register
MSS	Maximum Segment Size
MST	Machine State Save Area
MTU	Maximum Transfer Unit
NFS	Network File System
NIS	Network Information Service
NLS	National Language System
NUA	Network User Address
NVRAM	Non Volatile Random Access Memory
OCS	On-board Chip Sequencer
ODM	Object Data Manager
OEM	Original Equipment Manufacturer
PAP	Password Authentication Protocol
PCI	Peripheral Component Interface
PDT	Performance Diagnostics Tool
PID	Process ID
PMR	Problem Management Record
POST	Power-On Self-Test
PP	Physical Partition
PPID	Parent Process ID
PPP	Point-to-Point Protocol
PRI	Priority
PTF	Program Temporary Fix
PTX	Performance Toolbox
PVC	Permanent Virtual Circuit
PVID	Physical Volume Identifier
QIC	Quarter Inch Cartridge
RAID	Redundant Array of Independent Disks
RAM	Random Access Memory
RIO	Remote Input Output
RIP	Routing Information Protocol
ROS	Read Only Storage
RPC	Remote Procedure Call
SCSI	Small Computer System Interface
SIB	System Interface Board
SIMM	Single Inline Memory Module
SLIP	Serial Link Internet Protocol
SMIT	System Management Interface Tool
SMS	System Management Services
SNA	Systems Network Architecture
SPCN	Serial Power Control Network
SRN	Service Request Number
SRV	Segment Register Value
SSA	Serial Storage Architecture
SVC	Switched Virtual Circuit
TCP	Transmission Control Protocol
TID	Thread ID
UDP	UNIX Datagram Protocol
UID	User ID
UUCP	UNIX-to-UNIX Communication Protocol
VCI	Virtual Channel Indicator
VGDA	Volume Group Descriptor Area
VGID	Volume Group Identifier

VGSA	Volume Group Save Area
VMM	Virtual Memory Manager
VPD	Vital Product Data
VPI	Virtual Path Indicator
WAN	Wide Area Network
WLM	Workload Manager
XDM	X Display Manager

Index

Symbols

Numerics

A

D

E

M

P

Q

R

S

U

V

W

X

Y

Z